Micro Channel Architecture: Revolution in Personal Computing

Micro Channel Architecture: Revolution in Personal Computing

Pat A. Bowlds, Ph.D.
IBM Senior Engineer and Scientist

Illustrated by J. Marnell Bowlds

VNR VAN NOSTRAND REINHOLD
New York

Library of Congress Catalog Card Number 91-6342
ISBN 0-442-00433-8

Manufactured in the United States of America

Published by Van Nostrand Reinhold
115 Fifth Avenue
New York, New York 10003

Chapman and Hall
2–6 Boundary Row
London, SE 1 8HN

Thomas Nelson Australia
102 Dodds Street
South Melbourne 3205
Victoria, Australia

Nelson Canada
1120 Birchmount Road
Scarborough, Ontario M1K 5G4, Canada

16 15 14 13 12 11 10 9 8 7 6 5 4 3 2 1

Library of Congress Cataloging-in-Publication Data

Bowlds, Patsy A., 1942–
Micro channel architecture : revolution in personal computing / Patsy A. Bowlds
p. cm.
Includes index
ISBN 0-442-00433-8
1. Micro Channel (Computer bus) I. Title.
TK7895.B87B68 1991
621.39'16—dc20 91-6342
CIP

To my loving husband, Marnell, who gave me encouragement and inspiration, and to my children, Sarah, Grace, and Joe, who gave me love and understanding.

Contents

Foreword

In 1987, IBM announced the Personal System/2® family of computers, which was based on an innovative I/O bus called Micro Channel architecture. Since its introduction, this architecture has been incorporated into a broad range of sophisticated systems, including the IBM RISC System/6000™ family of technical workstations. Millions of systems have been shipped by IBM and other companies. Numerous independent developers have participated in the architecture by designing over 1000 Micro Channel expansion adapters, and many more are on the way. Micro Channel architecture has truly established itself as a new industry standard.

This new architecture has provided a quantum leap in function, ease-of-use, performance, and data integrity for today's users in a wide range of systems. It has also provided an architectural base to support the needs of the future as technology advances at a rapidly increasing rate.

This book provides an invaluable source of information about Micro Channel architecture for a wide range of readers. It will serve to broaden understanding of its current implementations and future directions. The approach to this very technical subject is pragmatic. It is filled with very useful information that addresses today's environment and today's problems. Readers will also appreciate the sections on applications of the architecture and transition planning from earlier bus architectures.

Readers will appreciate the clear and concise style of Dr. Bowlds and the logical organization of the book. The book not only contains a detailed description of Micro Channel architecture, but it provides a balanced view of computer architecture and design that further expands the scope of the book and its value to the reader.

Dr. Pat Bowlds was an engineering manager in the Storage Systems organization in IBM's Entry Systems Division during the development of the PS/2® systems. Since then, she has worked with Micro Channel developers, customers, consultants, and sales and marketing people to deliver technical information regarding Micro Channel architecture. She is internationally known in her role as Senior Technical Consultant from the Entry Systems Division Laboratory in Boca Raton, Florida, having delivered papers on Micro Channel architecture all over the world. She has been awarded several patents for her work and is the author of numerous technical publications.

This excellent book will deliver a better understanding of the power and depth of Micro Channel architecture as a platform for growth today and tomorrow. I trust you will find it as valuable as I did.

Robert L. Carberry, Ph.D.
ESD Vice President of Systems
IBM Entry Systems Division

Acknowledgments

Thanks to the IBM® corporation for giving me the knowledge and the opportunity to write this book. So many people have helped me that I almost feel that this is their book as well as mine.

My thanks to Mr. Robert L. Lohman and his department for their direct support and assistance. It is wonderful to have the opportunity to work with such a great group of people who are so very helpful. A special thanks to Mili Sanderson for her very helpful reviews and the use of several pages from the *Catalog of Micro Channel® Expansion Adapters,* and to Ralph Sorrentino for the in-depth technical reviews of the manuscript. Thanks to Rick Hughes for providing me with the most current information regarding Micro Channel systems.

Les McDermott, a very special friend of mine, is directly responsible for this book. Not only has he been an excellent teacher of Micro Channel architecture, but he has provided me with the confidence to write this book and has directly assisted in its publication. I can truly say that it would never have been written without him.

Thanks to all the other people who read the manuscript and provided helpful comments. Those unfortunate people who labored over the first drafts included Cmdr. George Anderson, Max Bouknecht, Louis Capps, Fred Strietelmeier, Dr. Dan Sucher, Bob Thorpe, Ed Tuggle, and Denny Wainright. Thanks also to Dr. Dave Bradley, Jerry Dixon, and Avery Lyford for their very helpful technical discussions.

To those final reviewers—Mary Forlenza, Chad Fentress, George Grosser, Rod Adkins, and Jan Winston—I owe a special acknowledgment for taking the time out of their busy schedules. Thanks to Jesse Kempter and Vynetta Ross for supplying photographs and copyright permissions.

Thanks to Jim Beesley of NCR™, Mike Jannery of Pixelworks™, Tim Santillian of Aox™, Steve Petracca of Reply™, John Symond of Core®, Armando Questa of Vidtech™, J. P. Woog of Advanced Logic Research®, and Vicki Yates of Olivetti®

for their product information and illustrations. My special thanks to the other developers of Micro Channel products who provided information.

Dick Conklin gets credit for much of the content and organization of this book. In his role as series editor, his helpful suggestions and patience during my numerous revisions contributed greatly to the final result. Many thanks to Dianne Littwin of VNR for her support in the publication of this book.

Thanks also to my daughter, Sarah Fuell, for her flying fingers on the keyboard in the final stages of the manuscript preparation.

The person I owe the most for this book is my partner in life and my illustrator, Marnell Bowlds. Without his exceptional illustrations, the quality of this book would have been greatly diminished. Without his support and encouragement, it would never have been written.

Trademark Acknowledgments

The author and publisher have made every attempt to supply trademarks about company names, products, and services mentioned in this book. Trademarks listed below were derived from various sources and are subject to change. The author and the publisher cannot attest to the accuracy of this information.

Advanced Logic Research is a registered trademark of Advanced Logic Research, Inc.
Academic System/6000 is a trademark of International Business Machines Corporation.
Actionmedia is a trademark of International Business Machines Corporation.
AIX is a registered trademark of International Business Machines Corporation.
ALR is a trademark of Advanced Logic Research, Inc.
AOX is a trademark of AOX, Inc.
Apple is a registered trademark of Apple Computer, Inc.
Apricot is a registered trademark of Apricot, Inc.
AS/400 is a registered trademark of International Business Machines Corporation.
AST is a registered trademark of AST Corporation.
AT is a registered trademark of International Business Machines Corporation.
Audiovisual Connection is a registered trademark of International Business Machines Corporation.
AutoCAD is a trademark of Autodesk, Inc.
AVC is a trademark of International Business Machines Corporation.
Chips and Technologies is a registered trademark of Chips and Technologies, Inc.
CNT-MCA is a trademark of Core International.
COMDEX is a registered trademark of Interface Group, Inc.
COMPAQ is a registered trademark of COMPAQ Computer Corporation.

CORE is a registered trademark of Core International.
Cumulus is a trademark of Cumulus Corporation.
Cypress/2 is a trademark of Lantana Technology, Inc.
Digital Equipment, PDP-11, and VAX are registered trademarks of Digital Equipment Corporation.
Digital Video Interactive is a trademark of RCA Corporation.
EasyWriter is a trademark of Information Unlimited Software, Inc.
Enterprise System/9731 is a trademark of International Business Machines Corporation.
Epson is a registered trademark of Epson America, Inc.
ES/9370 is a trademark of International Business Machines Corporation.
ES/9371 is trademark of International Business Machines Corporation.
Ethernet is trademark of Xerox Corporation.
Excel, Windows, and Word are trademarks of Microsoft Corporation.
Flexcache and Powercache are trademarks of ALR, Inc.
GEM is a trademark of Digital Research, Inc.
Grid is a trademark of Grid, Inc.
Hewlett-Packard is a registered trademark of Hewlett-Packard Company.
IBM is a registered trademark of International Business Machines Corporation.
ImagePlus is a registered trademark of International Business Machines Corporation.
Intel is a registered trademark of Intel Corporation.
International Business Machines is a registered trademark of International Business Machines Corporation.
i386, i486, i860, and 386SX are trademarks of Intel Corporation.
Isolan is a registered trademark of BICC Data Networks, Inc.
Linkway is a trademark of International Business Machines Corporation.
Lotus, Lotus 1-2-3, and Freelance are registered trademarks of Lotus Development Corporation.
Macintosh is a trademark of Apple Computer, Inc.
M–Control is a trademark of International Business Machines Corporation.
MediaLink/PM and RGB are trademarks of RGB, Inc.
MediaMaster and Vidtech are trademarks of Vidtech International, Inc.
Memorex-Telex is a registered trademark of Memorex-Telex Corporation.
METACOMP, PScomm2/4, and PSconnect are trademarks of Metacomp, Inc.
Micro Channel is a registered trademark of International Business Machines Corporation.
MicroCHIP is a trademark of Chips & Technologies, Inc.
MicroMASTER 386 and MicroMASTER 486 are trademarks of AOX, Inc.
Micro785+ is a trademark of YARC Systems Corporation.
Microsoft and XENIX are registered trademarks of Microsoft Corporation.
Mitac is a trademark of Mitac, Inc.
M–Motion is a trademark of International Business Machines Corporation.
Motorola is a registered trademark of Motorola, Inc.
MVS is a trademark of International Business Machines Corporation.
NCR is a trademark of National Cash Register Corporation.

NEC is a registered trademark of NEC Corporation.
Novell is a registered trademark of Novell, Inc.
NuBus and UNIBUS are trademarks of Texas Instruments, Inc.
Olivetti is a registered trademark of Ing. C. Olivetti.
OS/400 is a registered trademark of International Business Machines Corporation.
OS/2 is a registered trademark of International Business Machines Corporation.
Pagemaker is a registered trademark of Aldus Corporation.
PC386sx/MC, PC386/MC, PC486/MC, and S486/MC are trademarks of NCR Corporation.
Peachtext is a trademark of Peachtree Software, Inc.
Personal Computer AT is a registered trademark of International Business Machines Corporation.
Personal Computer XT is a registered trademark of International Business Machines Corporation.
Personal System/2 is a registered trademark of International Business Machines Corporation.
Pixelworks is a trademark of Pixelworks, Inc.
Portmaster is a trademark of International Business Machines Corporation.
Presentation Manager is a trademark of International Business Machines Corporation.
PS/1 is a registered trademark of International Business Machines Corporation.
PS/2 is a registered trademark of International Business Machines Corporation.
Radio Shack is a registered trademark of Tandy Corporation.
Reply is a trademark of Reply Corporation.
RISC System/6000 is a trademark of International Business Machines Corporation.
Siemens is a registered trademark of Siemens Corporation.
SPARC is a trademark of Sun Microsystems, Inc.
Storyboard Live! is a trademark of International Business Machines Corporation.
Subsystem Control Block Architecture is a trademark of International Business Corporation.
SuperFAX MC/ips is a trademark of Pacific Image Communications.
System/3 is a trademark of International Business Machines Corporation.
System/34 is a trademark of International Business Machines Corporation.
System/36 is a trademark of International Business Machines Corporation.
System/360 is a trademark of International Business Machines Corporation.
System/370 is a trademark of International Business Machines Corporation.
System/390 is a trademark of International Business Machines Corporation.
TARGA+ is a trademark of Truevision, Inc.
Texas Instruments is a registered trademark of Texas Instruments Corporation.
3270 Connection is a trademark of International Business Machines Corporation.
Truevision is a registered trademark of Truevision, Inc.
TurboProcessor is a trademark of Reply Corporation.
UltraClipper Graphics is a trademark of Pixelworks, Inc.
UNIX is a registered trademark of AT&T Bell Laboratories.

VersaCAD is a trademark of VersaCAD, Inc.
VM is a trademark of International Business Machines Corporation.
VM/370 is a trademark of International Business Machines Corporation.
VM/386 is a trademark of Intelligent Graphics Corporation.
WANG is a registered trademark of Wang Laboratories, Inc.
Western Digital is a registered trademark of Western Digital Corporation.
WordPerfect is a registered trademark of WordPerfect Corporation.
WYSE is a registered trademark of WYSE, Inc.
X-Windows is a trademark of MIT.
Xerox is a registered trademark of Xerox Corporation.
XT is a trademark of International Business Machines Corporationa.
Zenith is a registered trademark of Zenith Corporation.

Other brand and product names are trademarks or registered trademarks of their respective holders.

Introduction

In 1981 an astonishing bit of luck, coincidence, creativity, and astute business judgment launched the IBM Personal Computer, an event that changed the way people worked forever. This original design (Figure I-1) spawned a new industry and introduced standardization into a world that had none. The dominant manufacturers, Radio Shack® and Apple® Computer, along with a host of smaller companies, offered proprietary designs with neither hardware nor software compatibility.

In 1987 a purposeful decision based on technology and innovation launched the second generation of personal computing—the introduction of the IBM Personal System/2 (Figure I-2) computers and Micro Channel architecture. This event changed the future of personal computing forever by providing a platform capable of far more sophisticated applications than the original personal computers. On a broader scope, the entire structure of computing was altered—micros to mainframes. The once-simple role of a personal computer, how it is used, and who buys it will never be the same.

But what confusion this new architecture has created! Shopping for a personal computer used to be fairly simple. You either bought an IBM PC or a clone, or you bought an Apple computer. If the IBM design was your choice, you could select from many manufacturers of compatible expansion boards. But the introduction of systems based on Micro Channel architecture changed all that. Most of the software remained compatible, but none of the PC expansion boards could be used in IBM's new systems. Initially, the IBM brand was the only Micro Channel game in town—there was no second source if you wanted a computer based on this new design. More than that, it wasn't clear what benefits this new design offered that offset the disadvantages of board incompatibility in the first place.

To add to the confusion, in late 1988 a group of IBM-compatible PC manufacturers got together and proposed a design that extended IBM's original AT design to provide what appeared to be similar functions to those offered by Micro Channel

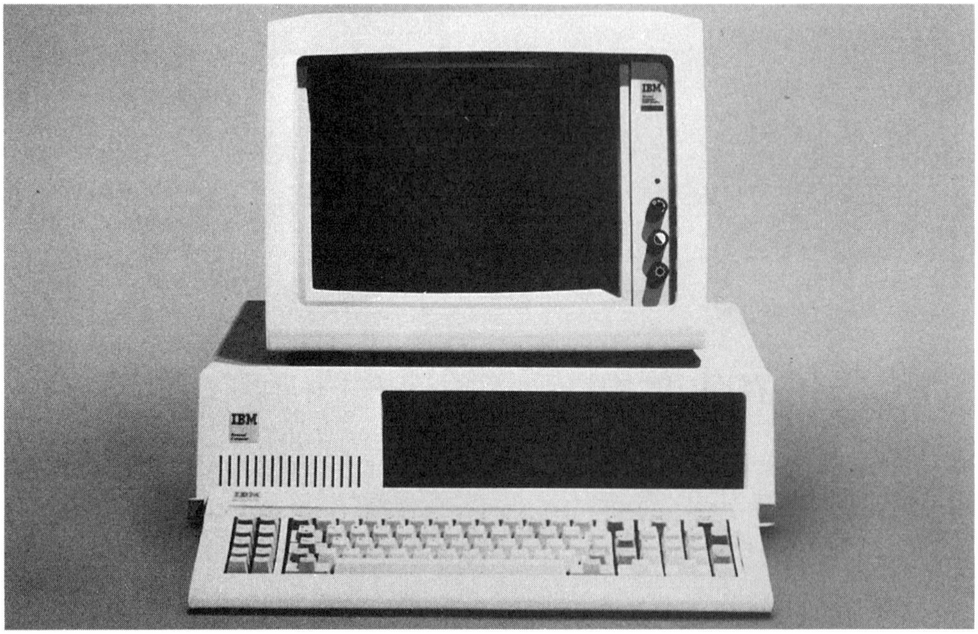

Figure I-1 The original IBM Personal Computer. (Courtesy of International Business Machines Corporation)

architecture, but retained compatibility on a hardware level with the old expansion boards (Figure I-3). "Why didn't IBM do that?" you wonder. This "gang of nine," the moniker given to the original group by the trade press[1], called their new architecture EISA, for Extended Industry Standard Architecture.

WHY THIS BOOK WAS WRITTEN

The primary objective of this book is to remove the confusion surrounding Micro Channel architecture. It is a comprehensive text that has been written for people who wish to understand how computer I/O bus architectures work and how the Micro Channel architecture meets the needs of modern computing environments. It is intended to be a user-friendly book for people who are involved in purchase decisions for personal computers, industry consultants, MIS managers, resellers, students, and interested end users as well as engineering and programming professionals. Because of its format and its extensive references, it is also suitable for textbook applications.

---

[1]The "Gang of Nine" consisted of AST® Research, Inc., Compaq® Computer Corporation, Epson® America, Inc., Hewlett–Packard® Company, NEC® Information Systems, Inc., Ing. C. Olivetti® & Co., Tandy® Corporation, Wyse® Technology, and Zenith® Data Systems

Figure I-2 The IBM PS/2 Model 50 Computer. (Courtesy of International Business Machines Corporation)

More has been written on this subject than perhaps any other PC-related topic (with the possible exception of the OS/2® operating system) in recent years. However, most has been limited to technical reference manuals and short trade press articles. This book attempts to provide the level of understanding and analysis that is greatly needed in today's computer-literate environment.

ABOUT THIS BOOK

This book ranges from a general description of computer architecture to highly specific topics relating to Micro Channel architecture and its implementations. Chapter 2, "The Basics," provides the necessary foundation and background information for the advanced topics that follow.

The beginning of each chapter states its purpose and a summary of the topics. Appropriate questions are provided at the end of the chapter. They are designed to emphasize important concepts and to add additional clarification of some generally misunderstood aspects of Micro Channel architecture. If the book is used as a text, these questions may also be useful in a classroom environment. Many of these questions have been posed to the author during numerous customer presentations, press and consultant briefings, user group meetings, and industry conferences.

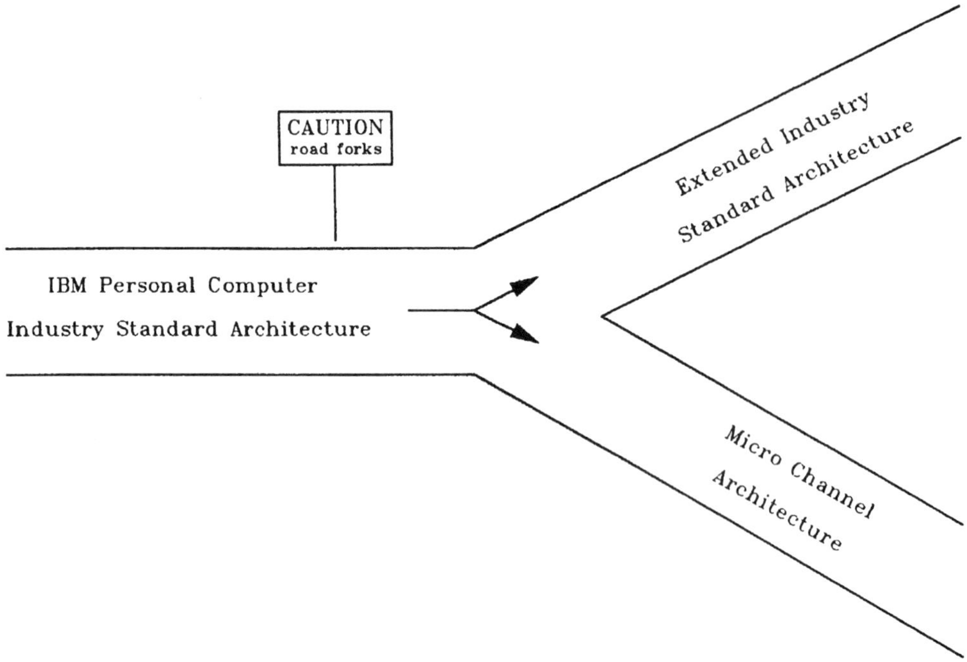

Figure I-3 Bus architectures based on the IBM Personal Computer.

SUMMARY OF CONTENTS

Chapter 1, "The Basics," provides an overview of basic computer structure. The elements of a computer architecture are described with special attention to the "information transfer structure" commonly referred to as I/O architecture. A description and short history of the IBM personal computer I/O architecture is included. Many of the terms used in the remainder of the book are defined. While parts of this chapter may be too basic for more knowledgeable readers, a review of current concepts and terminology may serve as a refresher and springboard for the rest of the book.

Chapter 2, "Overview of Micro Channel Architecture," provides an overview of Micro Channel architecture, its primary benefits and features, and its recent evolution.

Chapter 3, "Micro Channel Signals and Procedures," contains a technical description of Micro Channel signals and procedures and some general principles of its operation (in other words, how it works). While this chapter contains some relatively detailed technical information, it is not intended to be a complete treatise on the architecture nor to replace IBM's exhaustive technical reference manuals. The less technical reader may want to focus on the overview and bypass the specific signal and procedure descriptions contained in this chapter.

Chapter 4, "Advanced Micro Channel Features and Subsystems," describes some of the more advanced features of the architecture and their significance. The effect of Micro Channel architecture on various subsystems is also discussed. The use of Micro Channel architecture has broad implications on these subsystems in terms of both performance and functional benefits.

Chapter 5, "Micro Channel System Implementations and Applications," is devoted to a description of current system implementations and applications of the architecture. IBM's PS/2®, the RISC System/6000, and the ES/9371™ families are discussed. In addition, some non-IBM systems are described. Although some of the information in this chapter will become obsolete because of its dynamic nature, its inclusion still serves the purpose of illustrating the scope of the architecture and the range of designs it makes possible. The emphasis is on solutions that Micro Channel architecture provides for today's applications. These examples graphically illustrate the capabilities and benefits of the architecture.

Chapter 6, "Bus Wars: EISA and Other Warriors," includes a comparison of the technical features of Micro Channel architecture with the AT bus, EISA, and NuBus. It also provides a brief look at Futurebus.

Chapter 7, "Getting Down to Business," provides some guidelines for choosing a bus architecture and also addresses some transition problems in making changes from the AT bus to Micro Channel architecture. It also shows how the architecture addresses tomorrow's applications and coming advances in technology.

The appendices contain a quick-reference glossary of the main terms used in this book and some additional technical and nontechnical information that developers may find useful. This information is included for convenient reference and to provide additional understanding. A word of warning is in order, however. Because this material is frequently updated by IBM, it should not be relied on for hardware design or to replace or supplement the technical references published by IBM. Current sources should be consulted.

Let's turn the page and find out why Micro Channel architecture truly represents a new generation in personal computing!

Micro Channel Architecture: Revolution in Personal Computing

1

The Basics

In order to understand Micro Channel architecture, you are going to need a working knowledge of some fundamental concepts of computer structure and architecture. This chapter will provide you with this foundation.

We'll begin with an overview of the structure of computers and a description of some basic building blocks. Fundamental concepts such as time multiplexing, digital processing, and information transfer are introduced. The second part of the chapter is an introduction to computer system and subsystem architectures. "What makes a good architecture?" is also discussed.

The remainder of the chapter zeroes in on information transfer concepts and bus architectures. The evolution and history of the I/O bus architecture used in IBM's personal computers are described. Expansion board design concepts and their relationship to bus architecture form an important part of this chapter. The chapter concludes with a simple example of how information is actually transferred inside a computer.

If you feel that this is too basic for you, just zoom ahead. However, many important concepts and terms are introduced that will be required later in the book. You "zoomers" can refer back to this chapter when necessary.

THE HUMAN ANALOGY

The basic structure of a computer is relatively simple. Its elements are **microprocessors, memory, input devices, output devices,** a **bus** that serves as a communication path between the elements, and **software** to direct its activities.

A human analogy is often used to illustrate the structure of a computer. Let's take a simple example of a human task. Assume you are walking down the street and you meet a friend of yours and wish to say hello. You see the person, hear his voice, and recognize him as someone you know. You are able to recall his name and say, "Hello, Bill."

This sequence of activities is exactly analogous to what a computer does (Figure 1.1). Your eyes and ears represent input devices, your nervous system provides a communications pathway for the transfer of information and the control over its destination, your memory provides a method of temporarily storing information that you may need (for example, Bill's name, face, voice), and your cerebrum acts as a processor that allows you to compare the input parameters with the information that has been retrieved from memory (for instance, "Is it Bill?"). Your voice serves as an output device when you greet Bill.

(Pretty simple, huh? You just graduated from elementary school and are ready to examine these elements in greater detail.)

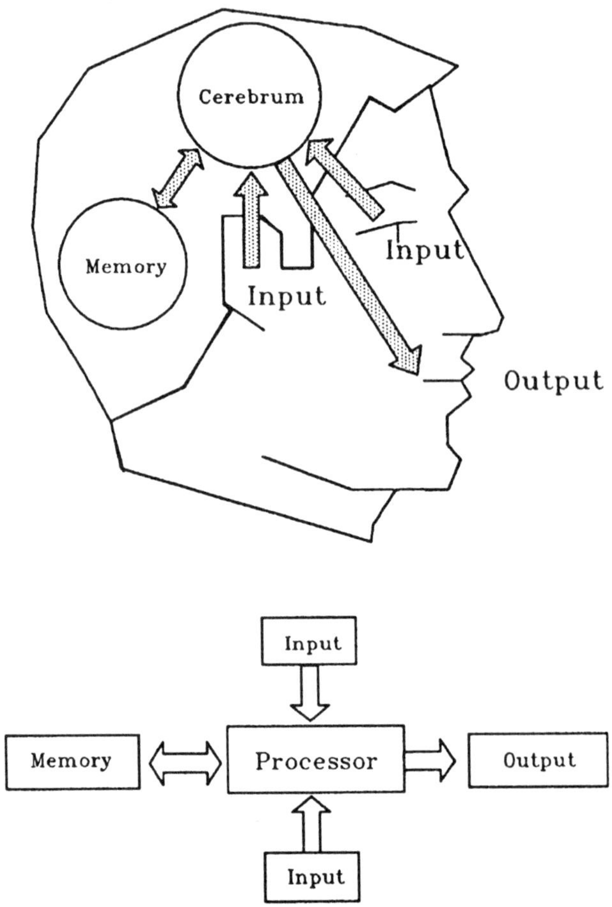

Figure 1.1 The human analogy.

Microprocessors

In the preceding analogy, the system **microprocessor,** or the **CPU** (Central Processing Unit)[1] corresponds to that part of the brain—the cerebrum—that is the seat of logical activities and its accompanying control circuitry. A microprocessor consists of a highly integrated collection of transistors that make up its digital logic circuits. It consists of several parts and executes control statements called **instructions.** Microprocessors also contain **registers** to hold information and instructions. Control circuitry and interface logic, which connect the microprocessor to other components of the system, are also required (Figure 1.2).

The collection of instructions **(instruction set)** supported by a microprocessor determines the specific operations it is capable of performing. The instruction set includes groups that transfer data, do arithmetic, perform logical operations, branch to another instruction (rather than take the next one in a sequence), provide high-level functions, and perform various control operations. However, the instructions making up each group are specific to the type of microprocessor. For example, some microprocessors can only add and subtract. They have no instructions for multiplications and divisions. Other microprocessors contain high-level command instructions that are more like a simple programming language.

Microprocessor registers provide a temporary storage place for data and "scratch pads," or working spaces, for intermediate results and status information. Data manipulations and calculations are performed in the registers. The number and type of registers are primary attributes of the microprocessor. For example, 32-bit microprocessors generally have registers that can hold 32 bits of data at a time.

[1]The terms **microprocessor, processor, and CPU** are often used interchangeably, although microprocessor is the preferred term today.

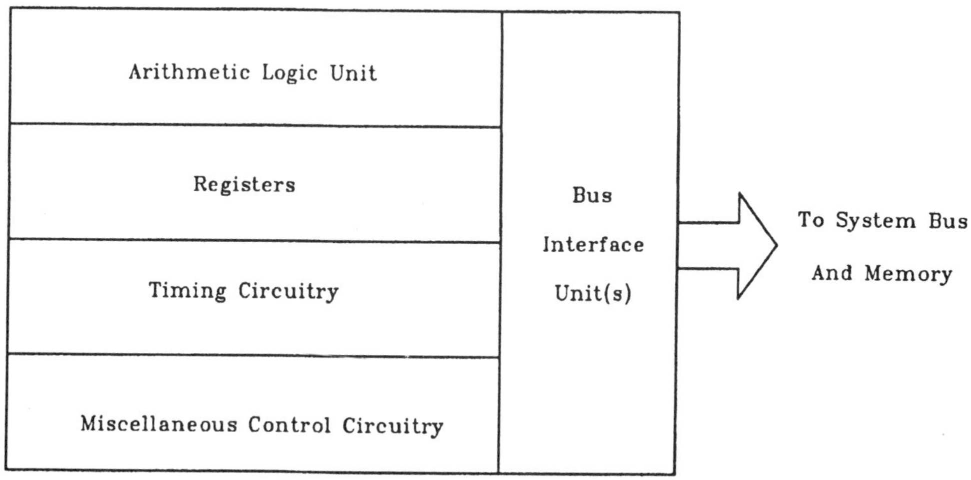

Figure 1.2 Basic microprocessor structure.

The control circuitry manages the information flow to, from, and within the chip. There is a data path used to move data in and out of the microprocessor, as well as an address path used to transfer information about the location of data in memory outside the chip.

Processor Speeds and Specs

Other important attributes of microprocessors are their **clock speeds** (generally expressed in megahertz, millions of cycles per second), their internal and external address and data path widths, their memory management capabilities, and their instruction sets. For example, the Intel® 8088 microprocessor used in the original IBM Personal Computer was a 4.77 MHz device capable of addressing up to 1 MB of internal memory with a 16-bit internal data path and an 8-bit external (I/O) data path. The Intel 80286 microprocessor, used in the 1984 version of the IBM Personal Computer AT®, was a 6 MHz device capable of addressing up to 16 MB of internal memory with a 16-bit internal and external data path. A summary of the characteristics of Intel microprocessors is shown in Table 1.1.

The amount of memory that a microprocessor can address is an important functional and performance consideration. The greater the amount of information that a microprocessor can access, the better, but it has to know where to find it. The memory address is a number that represents the location of the information in memory. The maximum number of memory addresses of a computer is a function of both the microprocessor design and the number of available address lines of a computer. The size of the microprocessor's address register determines the largest memory address it can hold. For example, the 8088 microprocessor has a 20-bit address register, allowing it to directly address one megabyte of memory. Mathematically, the number of addresses is 2^n where n is the size of the microprocessor's address register or the number of available address lines. For example, a 24-bit address path permits 16 million memory addresses.

TABLE 1.1 INTEL CISC MICROPROCESSOR CHARACTERISTICS

CPU	8088	8086	80286	80386SX	80386	80486
Clock Speed	4.77	8	6–12	16–20	16–33	25–33
Data Path Width (Internal)	16	16	16	32	32	32
Data Path (I/O)	8	16	16	16	32	32
Memory Addressability	1 MB	1 MB	16 MB	16 MB	4 GB	4 GB
Modes						
Real	X	X	X	X	X	X
Protect			X	X	X	X
Virtual 8086				X	X	X

Microprocessors may have different modes of addressing memory. For example, the 80286 microprocessor has two address modes associated with its memory management. The first mode is called the **Real Mode** and is the microprocessor's default condition. In this mode, the microprocessor uses the same instruction set that the 8088 and 8086 microprocessors use, making it fully compatible. In Real Mode, memory addressing is limited to 1 MB, and software that runs on 8088-based computers works exactly as it should. The second mode is called the **Protect Mode.** In order to use the memory above the first megabyte (sometimes called **extended memory**), the mode of the 80286 microprocessor must be changed to the Protect Mode. This mode is especially important in a multitasking environment because its internal memory management is designed to protect or isolate tasks from each other.

The Intel i386™ microprocessor is the third generation microprocessor used in IBM's personal computers and compatibles. Its key attributes are its 32-bit I/O data path and memory capabilities, enabling the addressing of up to 4 billion bytes (gigabytes) of memory and its high clock speeds (up to 33 MHz). The faster the clock speed, the faster the microprocessor can process instructions, if everything else is the same.

The i386 microprocessor has three modes of operation: the Real and Protect modes associated with the 80286 microprocessor, and a third mode, called the **Virtual 8086 Mode.** This mode simulates multiple 8086 microprocessors, making it possible to run several DOS applications simultaneously by dividing the available memory into 1 MB (or less) partitions. Another advantage of the i386 microprocessor is the ease in which it can be switched in and out of the Protect Mode. Mode switching in the 80286 from the Protect Mode to the Real Mode required a complete reset. The i386 microprocessor accomplishes mode switches using software commands, a much less radical operation.

Intel's i486™ microprocessor is an extension of the technology introduced in the i386 and is fully compatible with its predecessors. This microprocessor integrates several functions that were previously external discrete elements in systems based on the i386. These elements include a math coprocessor (a special device used for high-speed arithmetic operations), the memory management unit, miscellaneous support logic, and a type of high speed memory called static RAM that is used as a cache. A cache is a temporary memory storage area used to speed up the time it takes for a microprocessor to access instructions or data. It typically resides in a path between the microprocessor and system memory. The internal design and the integration of these elements with the i486 microprocessor enables additional parallel processing (simultaneous operations) and significantly increases the numbers of instructions processed in a given time. A diagram of the i486 microprocessor is shown in Figure 1.3.

CISC vs. RISC

Today, there are two widely divergent concepts used in microprocessors based upon their strategies for instruction sets. These are referred to as **CISC** (complex-instruction-set computers) and **RISC** (reduced-instruction-set computers). RISC

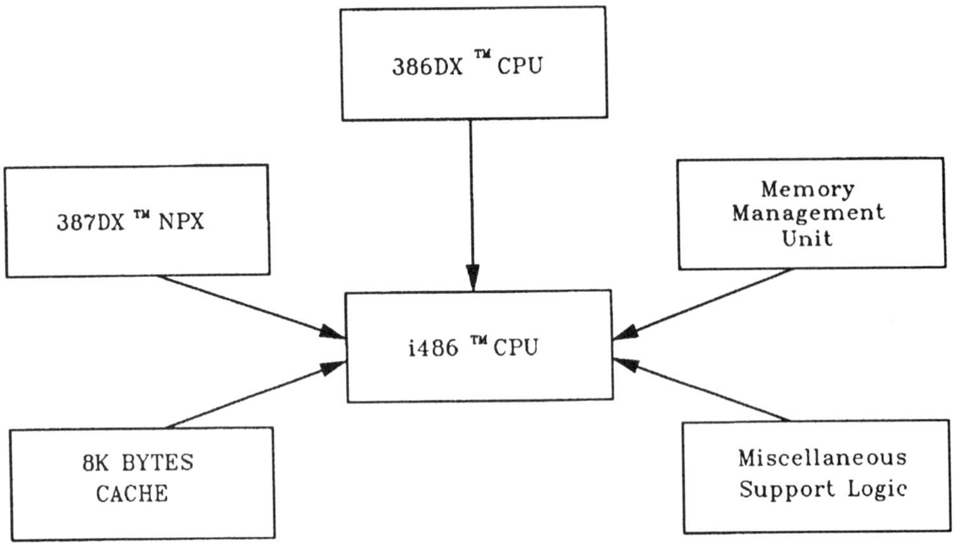

Figure 1.3 The Intel i486 microprocessor and its integrated components.(Courtesy of Intel Corporation.

architecture was originated by IBM in 1974 for a telephone-switching application and later used as the I/O processor in the IBM 3090, and as the microprocessor in the IBM 9370 and the IBM RT systems.

CISC processors use complex instructions that each require several microprocessor cycles to complete. RISC microprocessors use a small number of simple instructions that can be completed in one cycle. The RISC design also permits a greater degree of parallel processing inside the chip, which further boosts its processing power.

Microprocessors can generally execute instructions faster than the data can be retrieved or stored in memory. The RISC philosophy is designed to eliminate memory accesses whenever possible in both software and hardware. RISC microprocessors have many more registers than CISC chips. Internal registers function like a high speed cache. The effect is to greatly reduce the number of memory accesses.

The Intel microprocessors that have been used in IBM's personal computers have been of the CISC design. The Intel i486 microprocessor has some elements of RISC processing, which gives it significantly more power than the comparable i386 processor.

Many minicomputers and technical workstations use RISC processors today. IBM's RISC System/6000 family, Sun's SPARC™, Motorola's® 88000, and Intel's i860™ are current examples of RISC processors used in technical workstations and minicomputers today. Because of their power, RISC processors are expected to play a significant role in the future of personal computing. Unfortunately, programs written for a CISC computer (such as an IBM PS/2 system) won't run on a RISC computer since the basic instruction set is different.

The growth in computing power in the first decade of personal computers is simply incredible. For example, a 25 MHz 486 microprocessor is 33 times faster than the original 4.77 MHz 8088 used in the original IBM Personal Computer. This tremendous growth in the capabilities of microprocessors has effects on almost all elements of microcomputers. In order to utilize their enormous power, memory, I/O devices, and buses must be much faster. Operating systems must be developed to utilize their advanced functions like multitasking and 4 GB addressing. The amazing thing is that this exponential growth rate in potential microprocessor performance is expected to continue! This anticipated growth is one of the primary reasons for Micro Channel architecture.

Memory

Let's return to the earlier human analogy. Memory capabilities in computers are also similar to those of humans. People have both short-term and long-term memories. Sometimes, you may only need to remember something for a very short time. When you look up a telephone number and dial it, you may have no further use for it after the call is placed. This is similar to the volatile memory in computers. Its contents are lost when the computer is turned off. However, you may want to remember the phone number of your secretary. This is like **nonvolatile memory** in computers. Its contents are retained when the computer is turned off.

Another kind of long-term memory that computers and humans have in common is information that should not be altered or that we don't want to forget. In our human analogy, this is comparable to the permanent "memory" that regulates our respiratory and digestive processes. In computers, this type of memory is called Read Only Memory or **ROM.** An example is the nonvolatile memory used to store the **BIOS,** the basic input and output instructions for IBM personal computers. Another example is the BASIC programming language in IBM personal computers. The contents of ROM are always there, and don't have to be reloaded each time you power on.

RAM, or **Random Access Memory,** is a type of memory that can be read from or written to. Its name comes from the fact that any specific part of the memory can be randomly found and retrieved. This is the type of memory that is used to store your application program or data, for example. It is usually volatile memory but not always.

There are three types of RAM: dynamic **(DRAM),** static **(SRAM),** and nonvolatile random access memory **(NVRAM).** Computer memory (like the human brain) uses electrical charges to retain memory status. Memory that needs to be periodically recharged, or refreshed as it is generally called, is termed dynamic memory. Dynamic memory operates much like a capacitor that leaks its charge over time.

In contrast to dynamic RAM, static RAM does not require refresh cycles in order to maintain its memory. Current is constantly flowing through it on one path or the other. Static RAM functions as a switch to change the current flow from one direction to another. Static memory is usually faster and more expensive than dynamic RAM.

There is another type of memory that is used to store important information that can be changed, but also accessed very quickly. This type of memory is called NVRAM, or nonvolatile RAM. Through the use of a battery, this memory is retained after your computer is turned off. A good example of its use is for your computer's setup information, required during its POST (Power On Self Test) routine. Another example is your computer's time and date information. Some computers use NVRAM to set and store user passwords.

Some people confuse memory and storage. In the telephone number analogy, the phone book or your address book serve as storage devices. In a computer, examples of storage devices are fixed disk drives, back up tapes, and diskette drives. Unlike RAM, they require no electric power to keep their contents refreshed. Sometimes computer memory is referred to as primary or on-line storage.

Now that you understand the difference between various kinds of memory and storage, you are ready for the concept of **virtual memory**. Virtual memory is a memory-management scheme used by microprocessors such as the i386 and operating systems such as OS/2. It is used to support applications that are larger than the total RAM available. The role of the operating system is to load pages or segments from disk storage into memory as needed and unload segments that aren't being used as often. In the case of the i386, it can address up to 64 terabytes (trillion bytes) of virtual memory.

Two very important attributes of memory that affect system performance and overall computer design are its speed and its density. In order to keep up with the advances in microprocessor technology, memory components must be faster and denser. **Memory speed** is generally expressed as its **access** time in nanoseconds (one billionth of a second) or as its **cycle** time. **Memory access time** is not the same as memory cycle time. Its cycle time is dependent on the type of memory (DRAM vs. SRAM), as well as the memory access time. The minimum **memory cycle time** for DRAM chips is the sum of the time to recharge or **refresh** DRAM chips and the memory access time. For example, the minimum cycle time for a specific 100-ns DRAM chip is 187.5 ns.

The memory cycle time in a computer system is a function of the clock rate of its microprocessor. A minimum of two clock cycles are required—a cycle to read the data in the memory and a cycle to transfer the data to the microprocessor registers. In the case of a 10 MHz 286 microprocessor with a clock cycle of 62.5 ns, memory cycles cannot take place any faster than 125 ns. If memory cannot provide data fast enough to meet the microprocessor's demands, the processor must wait. Each "extra" cycle that it waits is called a wait state. Zero-wait-state memory does not require any additional processor cycles. In our example, a 100-ns DRAM chip is too slow for zero-wait-state access because of its 187.5 ns minimum cycle time.

The second important memory attribute, its density, also has significant effects on the design of a computer. The DRAM chips used in the original IBM Personal Computer were 16-KB chips. Today, 4-MB chips are readily available, 256 times the density of the original chips. If we were still using the 16-KB chips today, there would be room for little else. Just imagine the space required for the 4 gigabytes of memory that the i386 microprocessor can potentially address! This would require 1000 4-MB chips.

Memory characteristics influence many aspects of system design in addition to packaging. As we shall see later, it has a large effect on the characteristics of a computer's bus architecture.

Input/Output or I/O Devices

I/O devices are the means by which a computer communicates with the outside world. An example of an input device is a keyboard. The most used output device is a computer display. Some additional I/O devices are communication ports and adapters (for example, serial, parallel, and mouse ports, internal modems, network adapters), scanner adapters, printer adapters and printers, fixed disks and their controllers, and diskette drives and controllers. These devices may be built into the computer, reside on expansion boards, or be located outside the computer (in which case, they are called peripherals). This ability to accept a bewildering array of I/O devices is what gives computers their unique personality and flexibility for a wide variety of uses.

As is the case with microprocessors and memory, I/O devices are also becoming faster and faster. For example, the original 10-MB disk drive controller in the IBM Personal Computer XT® had a data rate of 0.05 MB/sec and a disk access time of over 100 ms. Today's high-speed storage interfaces can transfer data at 8 MB/sec, and access times in the 15 ms range are common. In terms of communication devices, in 1981 a 300-baud modem was the standard with a data transfer rate of 300 bits/sec. Today, 16 Mb/sec token ring adapters set the standard transferring data over 53,000 times faster and FDDI (Fiber Distributed Data Interchange) adapters transfer data at 100 MB/sec.

The story doesn't end with the enormous increase in the speeds of single devices, however. In a multitasking environment, I/O operations can occur concurrently. Through the intelligent use of caches and **buffers** (temporary holding places and staging areas prior to information transfers), data rates can be much higher than those of a single device in these environments.

There is also a much greater variety of I/O devices available today. For example, optical storage devices like CD ROM drives, voice input, high resolution displays, and network adapters were unknown just a few years ago. This increase in speed, variety, and numbers of devices attached to computers has important effects on a computer's bus architecture.

Information Transfer Buses

The brain and its memory, sensory devices, and motor systems require a vast number of neurons to connect them with the rest of the human nervous system. Many inputs can be received and processed simultaneously by the brain and many different activities can occur simultaneously because of the massive amount of circuitry. Some of us do this better than others, however!

In the human body, there are 12 cranial nerves that provide unique pathways for the transmission of information to and from input/output devices and the brain (Figure 1.4). Each device has a dedicated channel for its use. For example, the nose uses the olfactory nerve and the eyes use the optic nerve. This allows us to smell, see, walk, and talk simultaneously.

Microcomputers are far simpler in their design. In a computer, the pathway for information transfer is called a bus (Figure 1.5). In physical terms, a bus is a group of common conductors that connect the various elements of the system that is used for the transmission of electrical signals. Figure 1.6 is a physical representation of an 8-bit data bus.

Microcomputers allow for only one device at a time to transfer information on a bus. So the rules for bus ownership and the procedures for information transfers must be very well managed or the combined information from multiple devices will be garbled and unintelligible when it reaches its destination. If information transfer is very fast and the characteristics of the bus permit sharing or **multiplexing of the signals,** the effect allows several devices to utilize the bus in a short amount of time and a great deal of information to be transferred. The information transfer characteristics of the bus are, therefore, an extremely important performance parameter. The processing power of a computer, fast memory modules, and high-speed I/O devices cannot be effectively utilized without an efficient information transfer bus.

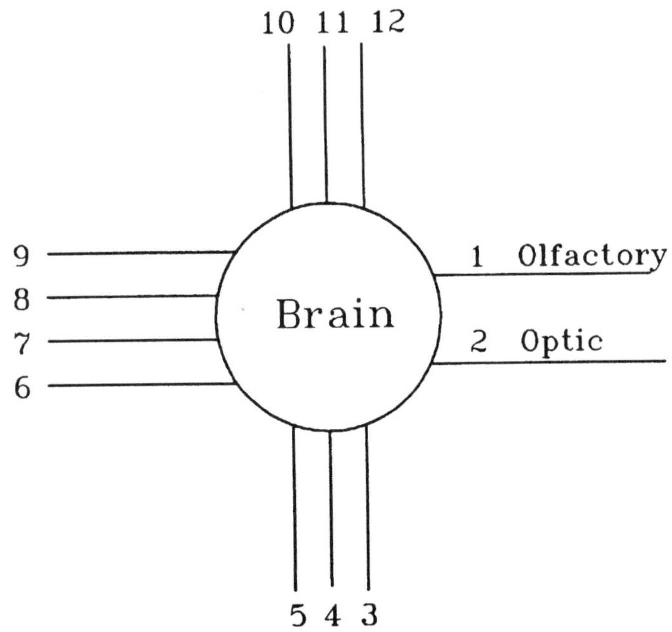

Figure 1.4 Human input and output organization. The cranial nerves provide for simultaneous operation.

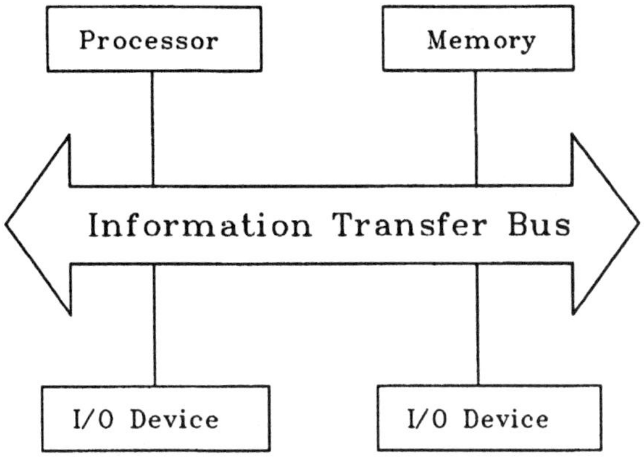

Figure 1.5 A simple information transfer bus. Devices use the bus sequentially for information transfers.

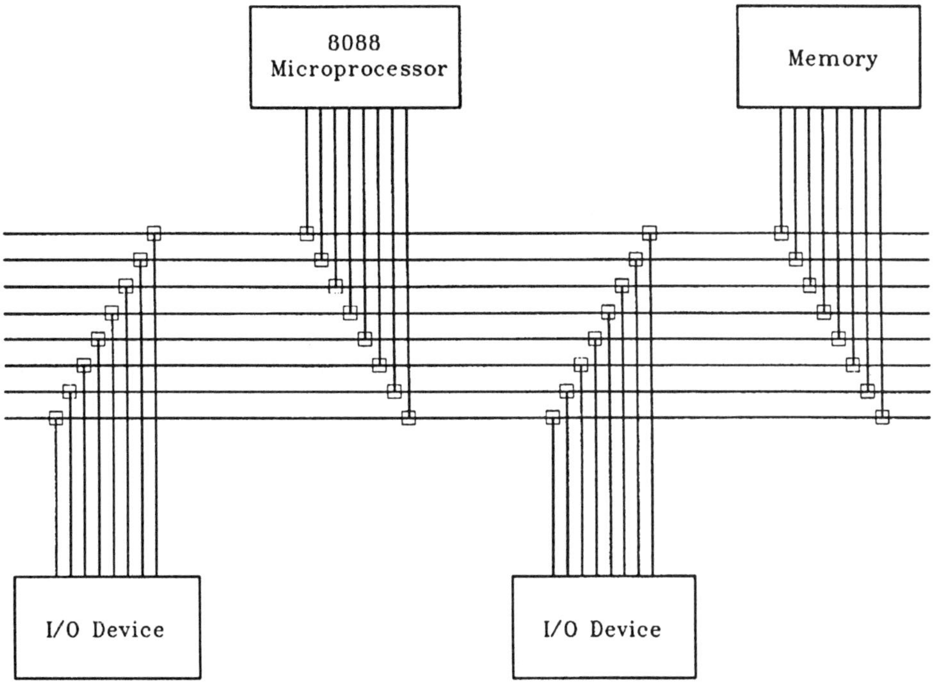

Figure 1.6 The 8-bit data bus of the original IBM Personal Computer.

A more realistic diagram of a typical microcomputer with common I/O devices is shown in Figure 1.7. The picture is not quite complete, however.

Software

Microprocessors, memory, input/output devices, and information transfer buses are useless collections of hardware without **software,** the last major element of basic computer structure. The definition of software gets a bit fuzzy at times. In this book it will broadly refer to a set of documentation, rules, procedures, and programs whose purpose is to direct the operation of a computer system. This generic definition includes application programs, operating systems, and microcode (sometimes called firmware because it is stored in ROM). A **program** is a sequence of related instructions organized for the implementation of a defined function by a processor.

In the human analogy, many levels of software are required. There are some logical routines that are deeply imbedded in our brains, such as the ability to reason and compare, that direct automatic functions such as digestion and blood circulation, and there are programs that enable us to perform routine tasks such as walking and running. There are also complex groups of instructions that enable us to coordinate several actions. These are applications like reading a book or

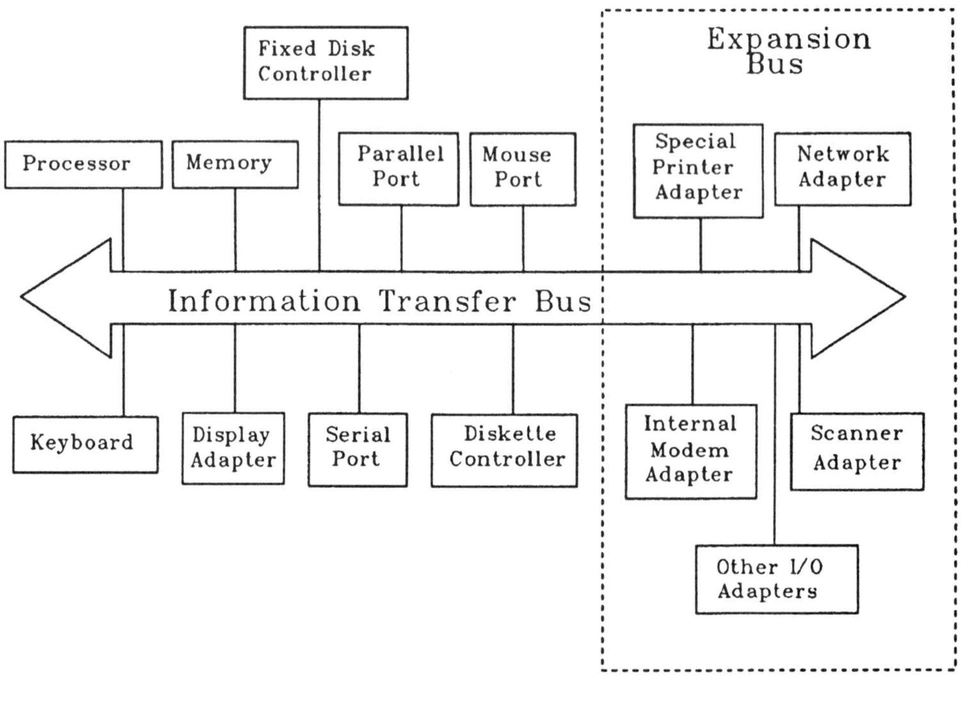

Figure 1.7 Typical system bus with common I/O devices.

playing soccer that use combinations of many basic routines and input/output functions. In computers, there are also many levels of software.

As is the case with human activities, software is required for computer functions. There are two general categories of software: **system software** and **application software.** System software is software that determines how application programs are executed, how system services are allocated and used, and how the interface between hardware and software is implemented. The system BIOS of IBM personal computers, the operating system of a computer are examples of system software. Basic computer programs that provide input and output instructions that are routinely in IBM personal computers are called the system **BIOS,** the Basic Input Output System. Specific programs for controlling or using various input and output devices are called **device drivers.** The **operating system** of a computer provides the functions required to make all the parts of the computer work together to perform useful work. For example, the operating system manages the system memory, the system microprocessor, the information transfer bus, the display, and the diskette drive to perform requested actions. Most of the time, a computer user is unaware of operating system activities.

Application software is what the user sees most of the time, the program that performs a service or part of your everyday job. Examples of application software are word processing, accounting, and drawing or graphics programs. These relationships are usually illustrated in a layered conceptual model as is shown in Figure 1.8.

ANALOG AND DIGITAL PROCESSING

In contrast to the human capability, logic and reasoning by computers is quite primitive. The brain accepts analog information that can have an infinite number of values. Digital computer information is **binary,** having only two values, 0 and 1, corresponding to the capabilities of microprocessors. Three states are required in computer design—two for the logic states and an inactive or isolation state.

Tristate Circuitry

1 and 0	Logic States
Z	Isolation or Inactive State

In digital computers, **transistors** provide a means for turning the flow of current on and off, forming the basis for digital logic devices. Used by themselves, in combinations, or in series or parallel, these "switches" are used to create the logic AND or OR gates used in modern digital devices.

The way computers communicate information using these logic states is through the use of high or low bus signal voltages. For example, the various combinations of high and low voltages on the different signal wires of the bus define a combination of 0s and 1s that represent the information being transferred. In the case of **ASCII** code, the letter A is represented by the following 8-bit

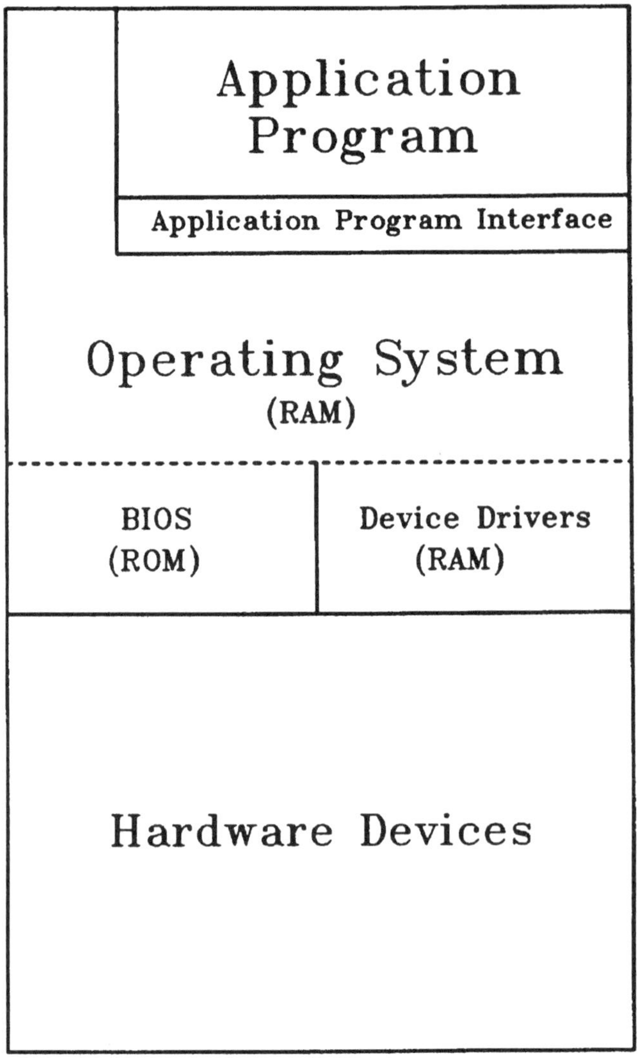

Figure 1.8 Software conceptual model, illustrating types of software and their relationships.

combination: 0 1 0 0 0 0 0 1. In a **parallel bus,** all eight bits are transferred simultaneously rather than serially, or one bit at a time.

The last decade has marked a sharp increase in the density of logic circuits. For example, Intel's i486 microprocessor contains 1,200,000 transistors in a package that is less than two inches square and two-tenths of an inch thick (Figure 1.9).

Figure 1.9 The Intel i486 is a highly integrated design containing 1,200,000 transistors. Courtesy of Intel Corporation)

This increase in density also has significant effects on computer designs, power, and packaging. As you shall see in the next chapter, Micro Channel architecture takes advantages of these advances in integrated circuitry.

COMPUTER ARCHITECTURE

The previous discussion centered around the basic structural components of a computer. These elements can be assembled in numerous ways and each has a large number of design possibilities. A specification describing one of these elements or the assembled system is not its architecture, however.

What Is Architecture?

The term **architecture** is a set of rules that provides commonality in structure and design and defines the limits of possible implementations. It includes a list of attributes that may be required or optional in order to conform to the architecture. Most of us are familiar with its use to describe building structures—gothic architecture, for example. Attributes of gothic architecture include pointed arches and flying buttresses. In computers, the attributes may include such things as signal specifications, timings, and procedures that are necessary to maintain hardware and software compatibility.

You are probably thinking, "Why should I care about architecture?" A good example is provided by the use of prehung doors and windows in the construction industry. Before their use became common, each door and window casing was unique and had to be done at the building site. By following a common architecture, doors and window casings could be constructed and prehung in a factory, saving a lot of money in labor and materials.

It is very easy to see the value of architecture. Application programs that follow the rules for standard programming interfaces will work across a number of operating system platforms, such as DOS and OS/2. Whenever you buy a new operating system, you don't have to buy new application software. Your application software investment is protected because of architecture.

Architecture is equally important for hardware. For example, if the i386 and i486 microprocessor did not have common architecture, an operating system that ran on a 386 system would not run on a 486 system. Another example of hardware incompatibility is the failure of some expansion boards built for the IBM PC and AT to function in some of the PC and AT clones that were built to be very close, but not exactly the same. The architecture was not very well specified for these systems and was interpreted differently by many manufacturers of systems and expansion boards.

Another value of architecture is that it allows the rapid integration of new technology, inventions, and, in our example, application programs. If every computer required unique software, an army of programmers would be required to develop software! Architecture enables the reuse of some of the more mundane elements of programs and allows programmers to concentrate on the really neat stuff.

So why should you care about architecture? **THE PRICE OF NOT HAVING AN ARCHITECTURE IS INCOMPATIBILITY, OBSOLESCENCE, HIGH COSTS, AND THE SLOW DEVELOPMENT OF NEW PRODUCTS.**

Architecture vs. Design

Computer and building architectures are used to define the limits within which the computer systems or building structures based on that architecture can be implemented. Architectures do not specify implementations, and implementations do not define architectures. The design characteristics of a building structure or a computer system only represent the limits to which the architecture has been implemented.

This distinction between design implementations and architecture is extremely important. Buildings may be designed using gothic architecture that range from a small chapel to a massive cathedral like Notre Dame. These structures have a common architecture but represent drastically different designs and architectural implementations (Figure 1.10). Like buildings, computers may also have a common architecture but differ greatly in design and system implementations. The architecture determines the functionality, flexibility, and usability of the systems

Figure 1.10 Implementations of gothic architecture range from the massive Notre Dame cathedral to this small chapel in Bimini in the Bahama Islands. (Photo: Marnell Bowlds)

or structures it governs. In computers, it is the degree of hardware and software compatibility among the different design alternatives and functional limits of the architecture that are of prime importance.

AN ARCHITECTURE IS A SUPERSET OF ITS IMPLEMENTATIONS. THE LIMITS OF AN ARCHITECTURE DEFINE THE LIMITS OF ITS IMPLEMENTATIONS.

Subsystem Architectures

Computer system architecture is a term used to define the data processing functions that are supported (but not necessarily included) in systems based upon that architecture. It is used to describe the boundaries or the limits within which the systems and structures can be implemented and the interfaces of their elements. These limits are determined by the four subsystem architectures that make up the system architecture and how they interact with each other. These four major subsystem architectures are the **microprocessor, memory, input/output,** and **software.**

In the vernacular, the architecture of a computer is expressed in terms of that subsystem which gives the system its most pronounced marketing advantage. Examples of this are references to the microprocessor type (a RISC or a 386 computer), the operating system type (a DOS or UNIX® computer), or the I/O bus structure (an AT computer or a Micro Channel system).

These delineations of architectural subsystems are not always discrete elements. In the original IBM Personal Computer and in the IBM Personal Computer AT, the interfaces between the system microprocessor, memory, input/output, and software architectures were not clearly specified. The bus architecture, the microprocessor, and the operating systems were tightly coupled. The I/O architecture of the original IBM Personal Computer was not much more than an extension of the connections going to and from the Intel 8088 microprocessor. The IBM PC bus was, in reality, a specification for a single design, not an architecture. Or, you could say, it was an architecture with a single implementation possibility. The system was, by definition, limited to the design characteristics of the "main processor" and its support logic. The key limitation of the IBM PC bus was that the "main processor" had to be involved in almost all I/O and memory operations.

In the next sections, we'll look at these four subsystem architectures in more detail.

CPU Architecture

A computing system must have one or more central processing units. The instructions that a CPU, or system microprocessor, can perform and the nature and organization of its parts determine its architecture. The instruction sets of microprocessors are analogous to the languages that people speak. Two people speaking different languages cannot understand each other unless they are conversant in both languages. CPUs are similar and cannot execute instructions of other CPUs based on different architectures unless they are bilingual or the instructions are translated for them.

In terms of the internal organization of a single system, it is possible for its structure to support more than one CPU in the same system. This opens up several architectural alternatives. For example, systems with more than one CPU may be based on a superior/subordinate (hierarchical) architectural concept. In this type of structure, one CPU is superior to the other CPU(s). Typically, the superior CPU commands the system, allocating and controlling the use of system resources (memory, I/O, and software execution schedules). All the subordinate CPUs must have interfaces that conform to the requirements of the superior CPU. In our human analogy, this organization is similar to several people working together on a project that is management-directed.

Another structural concept is one in which multiple CPUs are peers or equals. In this architecture, all of the CPUs have equal rights and privileges to the system resources. In this case, none of the CPU architectures are required to have a relationship. This type of computer system CPU structure is the most flexible and adaptable to change. Micro Channel architecture is an example of this type. This is similar to a committee, a team of people working together without management direction, or, alternately, several departments headed by peer managers working independently.

In both hierarchical and peer-to-peer structures, the CPUs may have the same architecture (homogenous) or different architectures (heterogeneous).

Memory Architecture

A computer system may have one or more memory architectures. A computer system's memory architecture is the sum of all of the memory architectures supported by the system. The memory architecture of a system determines the bounds of such characteristics as organization and address range, maximum and minimum size, access speed, and access method.

Memory architectures may be constructed to support both system and nonsystem memory. **System memory, like other system resources,** is managed by the primary operating system. **Nonsystem memory** is not allocated or controlled by the primary operating system. An example of nonsystem memory is that which is reserved for the BIOS, the self-test routines, and the video buffer in the IBM PC memory architecture.

A **memory map** is a useful tool to express memory organization. Figure 1.11 is a simple memory map showing these relationships for the IBM PC. Nonsystem memory is that region between 640 KB and 1 MB. System memory is the region below 640 KB (and in later systems, above 1 MB).

Memory can also be described as **public** or **private memory.** A memory architecture with a public structure (with respect to its organization and interface) exhibits the same characteristics and interfaces to all system resources and microprocessors that access it. System memory is an example of public memory. Private memory exhibits different characteristics and interfaces with respect to system resources and elements that access it. Because of this, it sometimes encourages interface incompatibility among the various components of the system and must be carefully implemented with respect to both hardware and software. However, it can provide significant performance benefits in many cases. Private memory can reside anywhere in the system and is often used as a cache that can be accessed only by certain elements of the system. Private memory is not counted as part of the system memory. Knowledge of its presence by other parts of the system is not required. An example of private memory is the memory cache that is on some fixed disk controllers. The rest of the system has no knowledge of its presence nor control over its access.

Software Architecture

The overall software architecture sets the bounds on how the computer system's hardware structures will be used. The software architecture determines the limits of such characteristics as system services, organizations supported, maximum and

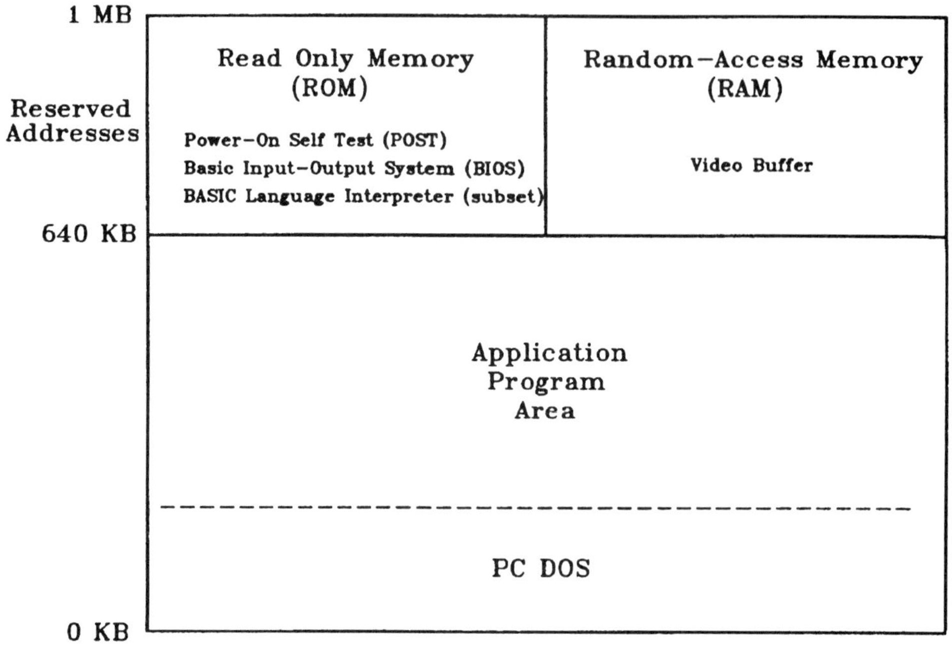

Figure 1.11 The memory map of the IBM Personal Computer. The area above 640 MB is referred to as nonsystem memory.

minimum sizes of system services (for example, memory and I/O addressability), and the nature of the interfaces between hardware and application software. The software architecture also affect how efficiently application programs run, that is, how many instructions are required to execute a system function.

A fundamental concern of software architecture is the hardware/software interface. This interface determines how the system's function is allocated between hardware and software.

A computer system may have one or more software sub-architectures. A system's overall software architecture is the sum of all the software architectures supported by the system. The native CPU instruction set may or may not be part of the software architecture by definition. That's because software can emulate, or pretend to be part of, a different architecture. For example, software running on a Motorola 68020 microprocessor can simulate the Digital Equipment Corporation VAX® CPU instruction set. To the application software, the software architecture of the computer system appears to be defined by the VAX CPU instruction set. In reality, it is defined by both the 68020 and VAX CPU instruction sets.[2]

[2]It should be noted, however, that these "tricks" result in system performance that is less than that of the native CPU instruction set.

Information Transfer and I/O Architecture

The **information transfer architecture** of a computer system is a documented set of signals, timing relationships, procedures for the use of these signals and timings, and the rules for its programming. It is sometimes called an **I/O channel.** Micro Channel architecture coupled with its software protocols, is a good example of a well-defined information transfer architecture and, therefore, defines a channel.

Information transfer architectures support the transfer of four different types of information: data, address, instructions, and control information. The source of the information and its destination can be to or from memory, the CPU(s), or the I/O devices.

An **I/O bus** is a type of information transfer bus. I/O buses are restricted to transferring input and output data, addresses, and control information to and from input and output devices. (Instructions are considered to be data when they are in a form where they cannot be executed.) A computer system may have one or more bus architectures. A computer's bus architecture is the sum of all the different bus architectures supported by the system.

Information transfer bus architectures range from simple, single bus structures to complex multiple bus structures designed for specialized purposes. The bus architecture defines the common elements of the various design alternatives. In general, the more complex the design, the fewer common elements that are possible. A general purpose bus architecture is based on a fairly simple structure that is extendable to more complex designs rather than a complex design that precludes simple structures and limits design alternatives. A general purpose bus architecture may have additional buses, referred to as subsystem buses, but does not require them. (More about subsystem buses later.)

The I/O architecture defines the rules for transferring data to and from I/O devices. It also provides a way to check the status of a data transfer. The I/O architecture determines the limits of such characteristics as the memory and I/O address ranges, data transfer widths, transfer speeds supported, and the access methods provided to hardware and application software.

In some computer systems, the transfer path between the CPU(s) and system memory is separate from the path to I/O devices. The method and form of data transfers between I/O devices and other system resources (for example, CPUs and memory) is determined (or limited) by the input/output architecture.

There are many important considerations in the design and architecture of information transfer buses. There are general purpose buses and special purpose buses. Some are faster, have greater capacity, or provide more functions than others. The alternatives and characteristics for information transfer architectures and designs are virtually unlimited! Each possibility has a set of unique advantages and disadvantages. For example, some designs may be more complex or expensive than others. Other implementations may offer additional performance in certain environments or increased expandability. An information transfer architecture may be flexible enough to encompass many designs, or may be so limited that design alternatives and new technologies cannot be accommodated. Information transfer architecture is an extremely complex subject with important implications on all aspects of hardware and software design and function. As you read this book, the full range of its significance will become apparent.

The Ideal Computer Architecture

Now that you know what architecture is and have a good idea of its value, you may wonder what makes an architecture good (or bad, for that matter). The first requirement for a computer architecture is to provide hardware and software **compatibility.** After compatibility, there are a myriad of attributes that are important.

One of these attributes is **affordability.** The very best architecture imaginable is of no use if it is not affordable for its intended applications. As is usually the case, features and functions add to the cost and limit the number of products that can use the architecture. Ideally, the higher cost elements of an architecture are optional features that can be added without affecting compatibility with other implementations.

Another important attribute of a computer architecture is its **data integrity** characteristics, or ability to handle information without error. For example, an extra or a missing bit of information could mean the difference between $100,000 or $1,000,000 in a banking transaction—a nontrivial sum! An erroneous instruction can cause an addition to be performed instead of a subtraction. An incorrect address could result in a confidential message sent to the wrong person on a local area network. At the very minimum, a computer system should have the ability to indicate that an error condition has occurred.

Some architectures focus on **ease of use** as a primary attribute. The software architecture of Apple's Macintosh™ focused on a graphical user interface with mouse support to promote ease of use. Another example is found in Micro Channel architecture's automatic configuration feature, which simplifies the setup of systems and the installation of expansion boards.

An architecture should provide for **expandability** of a computer system. The ability to add additional performance or functions to a system is extremely important. Some examples of expandability in computer architecture include the number of expansion slots, supported I/O devices, multiprocessor support, and maximum storage capacity.

Another good attribute is **extendibility.** The limits of an architecture should be extendible in order to accommodate improved design concepts that may not be invented yet. An example of this is the use of reserved pins in connector design. Reserving pins for future use provides the capability to add function that is not currently defined.

Flexibility is also a very important attribute. An architecture should provide a wide range of design and application alternatives. The original PC architecture lacked flexibility since it could be used only with the 4.77 MHz 8088, and its I/O bus could only handle 8-bit transfers. The consequence was that a major redesign was required for the IBM PC AT with its faster 16-bit 80286 microprocessor. In addition to promoting a broad range of implementation possibilities, flexibility and extendibility enhance the longevity of an architecture.

Another factor that enhances the value of an architecture is its acceptance by the industry and a critical mass of users. One reason for the success of the original IBM Personal Computer was its acceptance by the industry, as well as the standardization that it brought. The architecture became an industry standard. Another example lies in the industry acceptance of DOS. There are tens of thousands of DOS applications available from a huge number of industry developers. This greatly enhances its value as an operating system. **Industry acceptance** and user acceptance go hand in hand. The greater the number of potential users, the greater the financial opportunity for developers of add-on hardware and software applications. The availability of such products further increases a system's value to users.

A good computer architecture should provide a growth path and **investment protection** for the individual systems based on it.The ability to upgrade system performance or change its function enhances the value of a computer system and prevents its obsolescence.

Performance capabilities of an architecture are also extremely important. This is probably the attribute that is most affected by the limits of an architecture. The ability to add higher speed processors, more memory, or advanced operating systems are examples of how an architecture can affect performance.

Reliability, availability, and serviceability (IBM uses the acronym **RAS**) are also important attributes of computer architectures. Reduction of failure rates and fault-tolerant capabilities are also benefits of a good architecture. Problems should be easy to diagnose, and service should be quickly and easily performed.

Obviously, a truly perfect architecture incorporating all of these attributes can never be achieved. Les McDermott, one of IBM's lead architects, says "The ideal computer architecture supports an infinite number of functions, has unlimited performance capabilities, and costs absolutely nothing." Tradeoffs between cost and function must always be made. For example, an architecture that is suitable for supercomputers is totally unsuitable for personal computers. The challenge is to find the right balance.

An interesting academic exercise is the ranking of the characteristics of an ideal architecture. As you will discover, balancing the characteristics of the ideal computer architecture is a nontrivial task. But this is the same kind of exercise that IBM marketing, engineering, programming, product planning, manufacturing, and service engineers faced when they defined Micro Channel architecture.

Computer Architecture Characteristics *

Affordability	Flexibility
Compatibility	Industry Acceptance
Data Integrity	Investment Protection
Ease of Use	Performance
Expandability	RAS Characteristics
Extendibility	

* Not Prioritized

In ranking these elements, assume that some of the lower-ranking items may not be included in the architecture, or may have to be compromised. Which ones are absolutely essential? (We'll come back to this exercise later when you know more about Micro Channel architecture.)

Micro Channel architecture has almost all of the characteristics of an ideal architecture. Although Micro Channel expansion boards are not physically compatible with the original PC boards, they are compatible with the software that was developed for the IBM PC and AT. This compromise, while carrying its own cost, provides a number of benefits that are related to other characteristics of an ideal architecture.

Micro Channel architecture provides a flexible, high performance information transfer medium that can be implemented at low cost on personal systems. But it is also broad enough to be used by families of midrange and mainframe computer products. The architecture incorporates a highly flexible set of parameters that enhance its longevity by permitting a mixture of attachment devices that can operate at a wide variety of speeds. Its structure also minimizes the dependency on any single processor type or logic technology. The flexibility of the specifications also enables individual computer systems to be upgraded and enhanced. It is an open architecture that now has widespread acceptance by the computer industry (although a bit slower than IBM would have liked). Micro Channel architecture also provides better performance, reliability, and data integrity, which are extremely demanding in today's sophisticated multi-user and multitasking environments. These features will be discussed in depth in Chapter 2.

A CLOSER LOOK AT INFORMATION TRANSFER ARCHITECTURES

In the preceding sections of this chapter, the fundamentals of computer structure and architecture were described. Some of the considerations involved in information transfer architecture and design were examined at a "50,000 foot" level. Now it's time for a closer look at information transfer concepts.

(In other words, you just graduated from high school!)

Useful Terminology

One of the most confusing aspects that inhibit understanding of architectural concepts is the language that describes them. The terms function, board or card, adapter, and device all have specific meanings that are often used in very similar but confusing ways. A **function** is the purpose or role that a device serves. A **card** or **expansion board** is a collection of physical components, microcode, and "glue" to hold it together with a connector that plugs into a slot on an expansion bus. It is designed to accomplish a specific function(s). **Adapters** also provide a specific function(s), are used to connect a device(s) to a bus, and are required to make the device(s) operable. An adapter may reside on a card or may be integrated into the system board.

An example of an adapter that may reside on a card or be integrated into the system board is the video graphics adapter (VGA). It is used to connect a video display to the bus and consists of several components such as the video controller, the video processor, and the digital-to-analog converter that are required to drive the display. For example, the function of the VGA (with the display) is to provide the video display capabilities of the system. The video display is an output device that requires an adapter (the VGA) in order to be functional.

The direct memory access (DMA) controller and the CPU of a system are considered to be **devices.** They do not require an adapter in order to be functional. The junction where adapters or devices are connected to a bus is called the **bus interface.**

A **controller** is a unit that is used to regulate the function of another device or devices. An example is a memory controller on a memory card or a fixed disk controller. They may be located on expansion boards or integrated on system boards. In the original IBM Personal Computer, the diskette controller was on a card. In the IBM PC AT, it was combined with the fixed disk controller on a card. In most current systems, the diskette controller is integrated on the system board, or planar, as it is sometimes called.

These relationships are summarized in Figure 1.12. However, to further complicate matters, many people use all these terms interchangeably. But now that you know what they really mean, you have the right to use them interchangeably and incorrectly like the rest of the world! All clear?

Types of Buses

There are several terms that will be used in this book to describe bus types. The most important of these, **information transfer bus, I/O bus,** and **channel,** were described earlier in this chapter. This section contains a discussion of other types of buses.

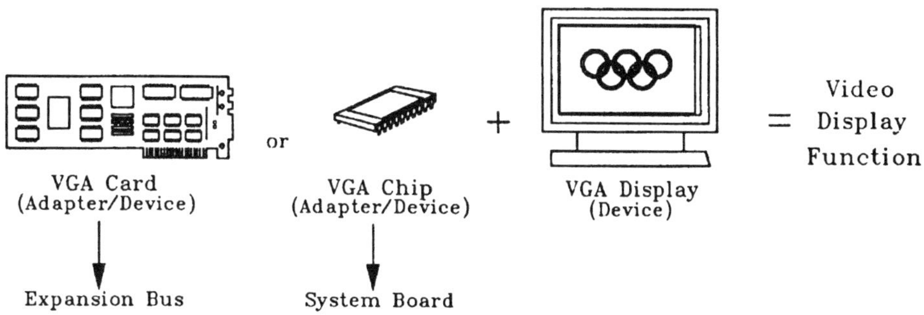

Figure 1.12 Useful I/O terminology. An adapter is a device used to connect another device to the bus in order to make it operable. An adapter may be located on an expansion board or on the system board.

Subsystem Buses

One convenient method for classifying buses is by what is attached to them. These are often called **subsystem buses.** One example of a subsystem bus commonly used in today's systems is a separate processor/memory bus. A special case of this design involves the use of a **memory cache** that allows a small amount of very fast memory to be accessed by the system's microprocessor. The cache is typically a small amount (32 KB–128 KB) of static RAM. This design requires a cache controller that is used to predict and retrieve the information likely to be needed next. The IBM Model 70-A21 is an example of a system with this type of cache (Figure 1.13). In this system, the cache controller is the Intel 82385, tuned to function with the system's i386 microprocessor. The IBM Model 90 and Model 95 have the structure illustrated in Figure 1.14, which includes both an external cache (in addition to the internal cache of the i486 microprocessor) and two banks

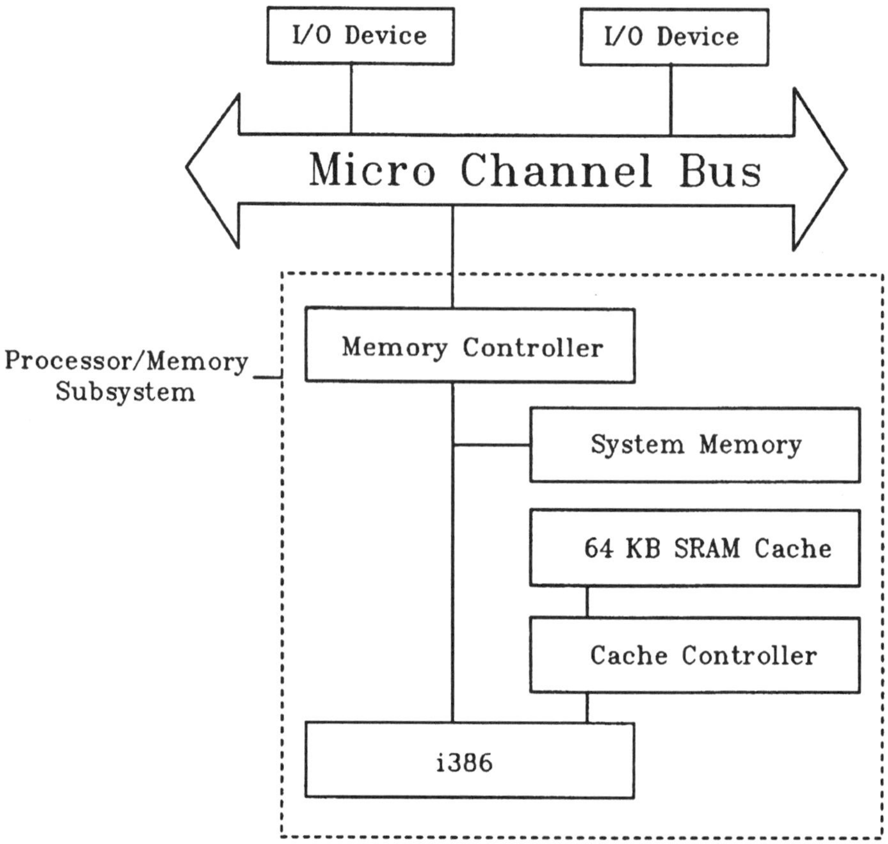

Figure 1.13 An example of a design with a memory cache, a special type of processor/memory subsystem bus used in the IBM Model 70-A21.

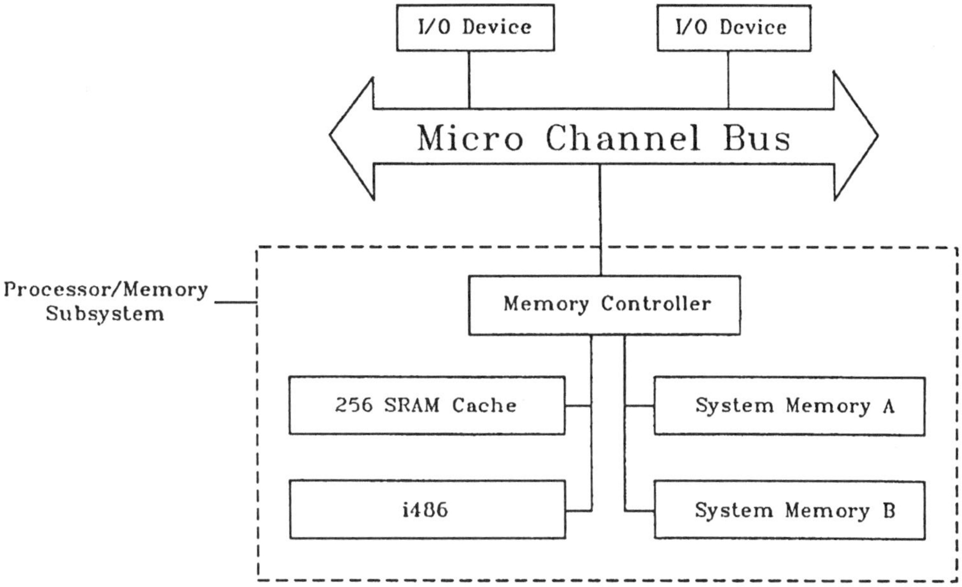

Figure 1.14 A design with a separate processor/memory bus and a memory cache. The IBM Model 90 and Model 95 are based on this design concept.

of memory. These implementations will be discussed in more detail in Chapter 5.

Another design alternative may allow for additional processors as a separate processor complex (Figure 1.15A) or on the common information transfer bus (Figure 1.15B). These additional processors may have their own private memory as well.

The **Small Computer Systems Interface (SCSI)** bus (pronounced "scuzzy" or "sexy," depending on the company culture) is a special case of an I/O subsystem bus used for the attachment of several devices with a common interface (Figure 1.16). This subsystem bus then attaches to the I/O bus or general information transfer bus via another interface. A detailed discussion of the interaction of the SCSI bus with Micro Channel architecture is in Chapter 5.

As you can see from Figure 1.17, it is possible to build extremely complex designs involving multiple subsystem buses that are part of a general information transfer architecture. The advantages of multiple bus designs are that they enable independent operation of the buses and may provide performance benefits under some conditions. The possible combinations of subsystem bus designs, controllers, caches, and system memory are endless, as the figures in this section indicate. As always, there are advantages and disadvantages to each.

A "junction" of two buses constitutes an interface. A method for transferring information from one bus to the other must be defined. This method of transfer may be simple or quite complex, depending on the characteristics of the two buses.

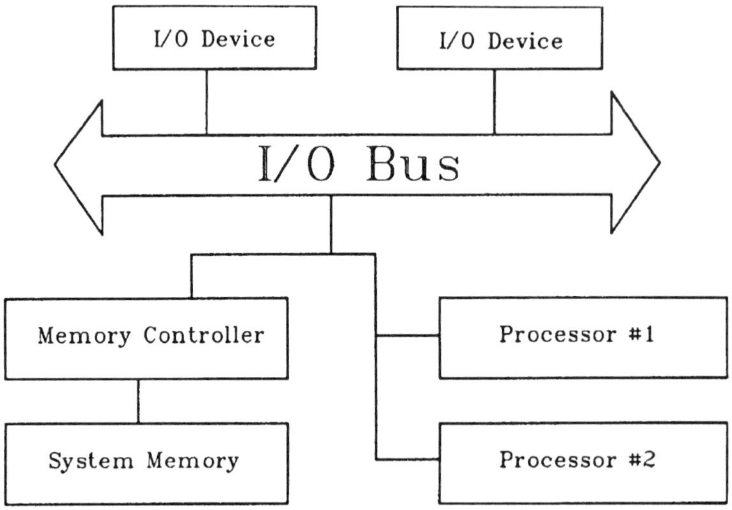

Figure 1.15A A multiprocessor design with a separate processor/memory bus and an I/O bus.

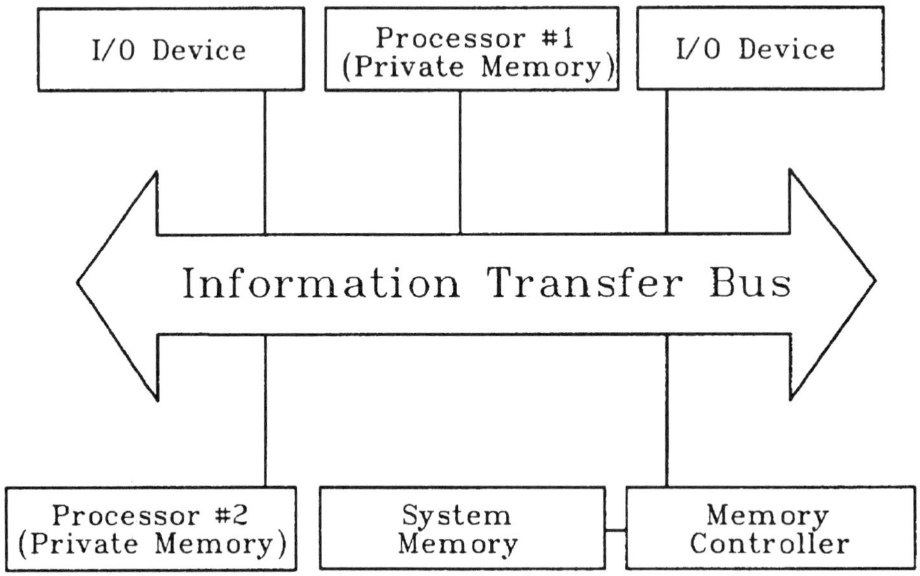

Figure 1.15B A multiprocessor design with a common information transfer bus and shared system memory.

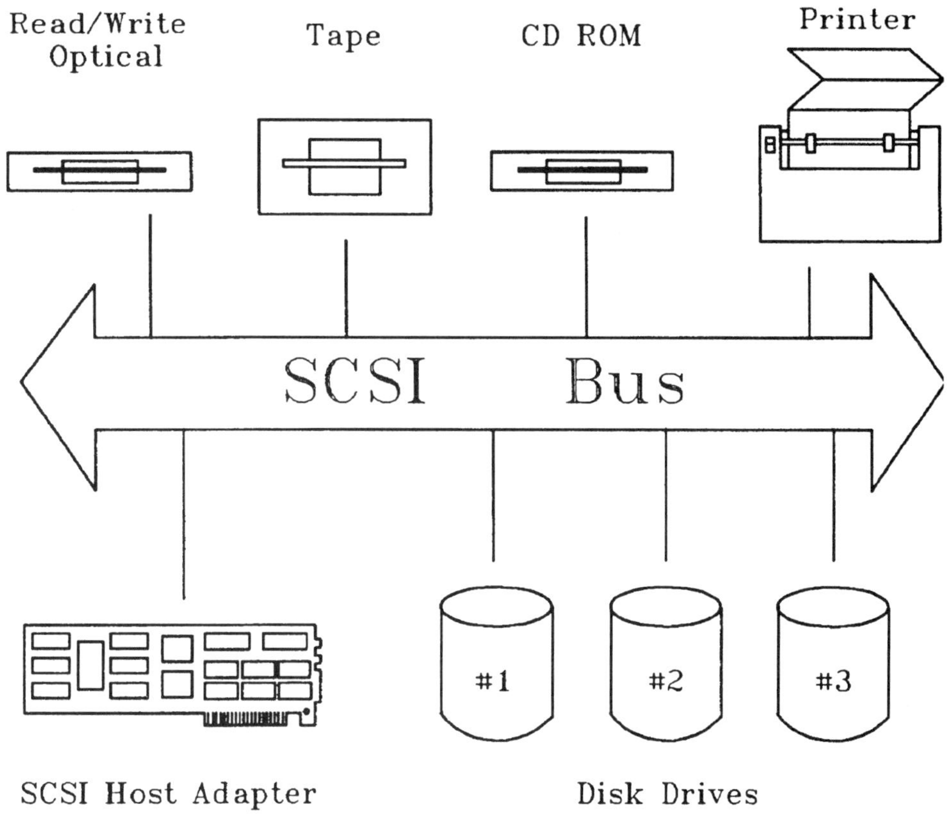

Figure 1.16 The SCSI bus is used to attach up to seven physical devices with a common interface.

If the two buses have similar characteristics (for instance, their timings and signal definitions are the same), the interface may be quite simple and comparable to those used by other devices on the bus.

If there are major differences between the two buses, a **bus controller,** or switch, is required between them in order to provide for the smooth transfer of information. This is analogous to the junction of two railroad tracks in which a switch is required to allow a train to move from one track to the other (Figure 1.18). Without an appropriate switching mechanism, it would be possible for a collision with another train to occur.

If one of the buses is busy when information transfer is required, there could be a delay, leading to **bus contention.** In the railroad analogy, this would occur if two trains needed to use the same track. One train would be forced to wait on a side track until the other train passed. This additional complexity is a disadvantage of multiple bus designs. Multiple bus architectures based on Micro Channel architecture will be discussed later in this book.

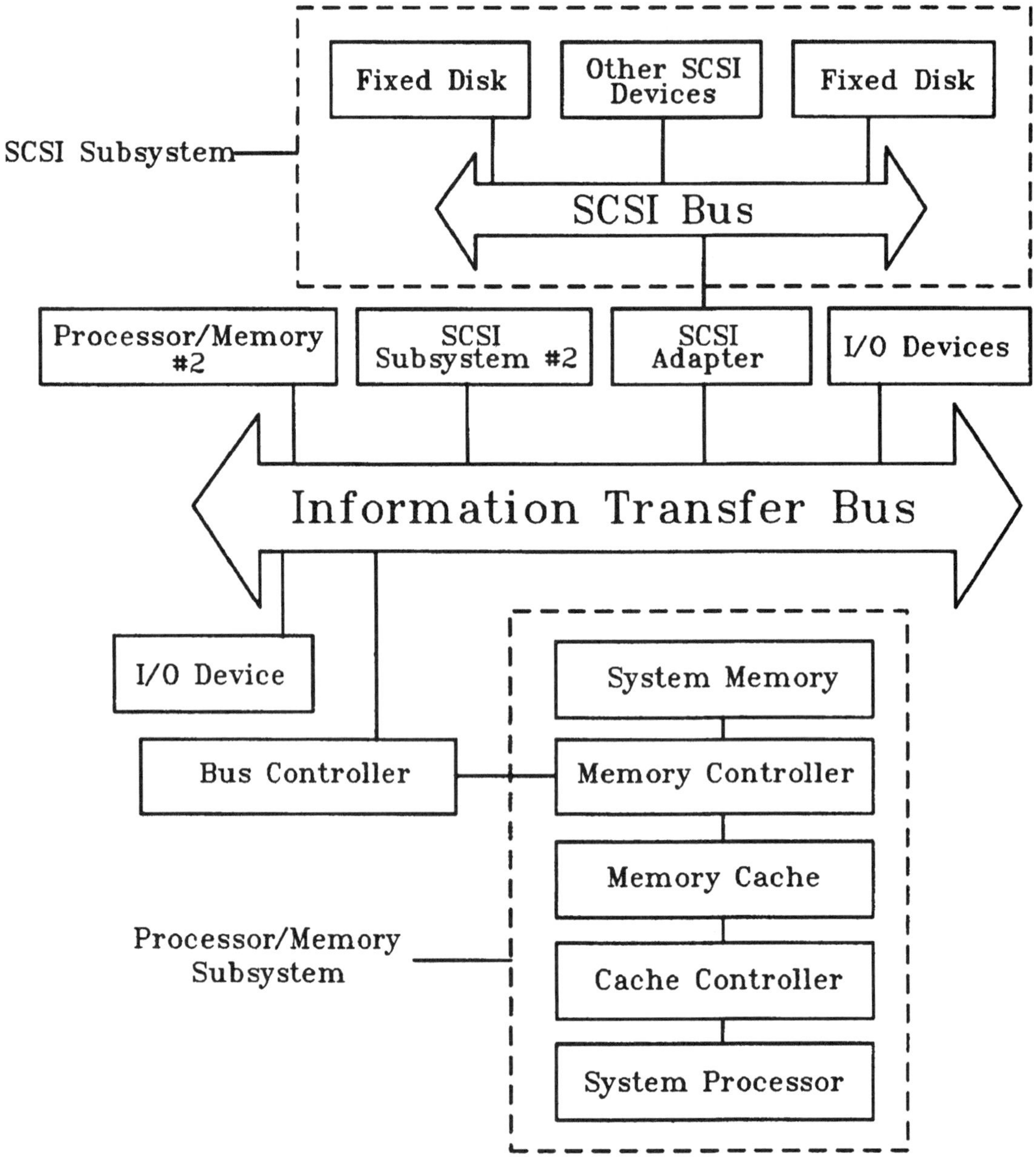

Figure 1.17 A design with multiple subsystem base.

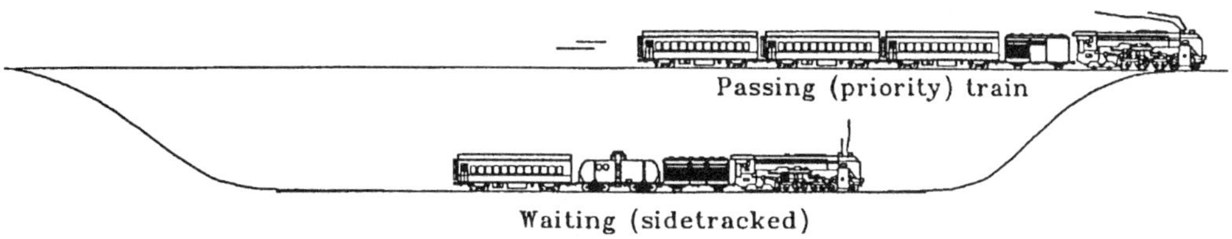

Figure 1.18 An appropriate switching method prevents collisions but imposes delays.

Expansion Buses

The I/O bus is a type of subsystem bus that is used to attach input and output devices to it. The **expansion bus** is a special type of I/O bus that supports the addition of adapter cards. It is this bus that allows you to customize the system for your uses or to add functionality. Some computers do not even have an expansion bus. The original Macintosh computer was unable to accept expansion boards, for example. There is a trend in low-priced and small desktop computers to "build in" all the basic I/O using integrated circuitry and offer very limited expansion. An example of this is the IBM PS/1® home computer system (Figure 1.19).

Figure 1.19 The IBM PS/1 home computer system. This system has numerous integrated features that reduce its expansion board requirements. (Courtesy of International Business Machines Corporation.

A primary attribute of any expansion bus design is the number of available slots that can accept add-in boards. Its significance is related to the number of built-in features, however. Some computers have almost no integrated functions, and add-in boards must supply basic requirements. The original personal computers had few built-in I/O functions, so add-in boards provided display, diskette, and printer support. Newer computers, such as the IBM PS/2 systems, may include devices such as the fixed disk controller, the diskette controller, serial and parallel ports, and graphics controllers, to name a few. This means that most users won't need to purchase as many add-in boards for missing functions.

The architecture generally defines the maximum and minimum number of devices that can be attached to the I/O bus. Some of these may occupy expansion slots and others may be integrated. Figure 1.20 is a photograph of the system board for the IBM Personal System/2 Model 80, which illustrates the integrated features and expansion slots. The photograph also shows some of the custom chips designed by IBM that are used for various support functions.

Expansion boards must include the connectors used to plug into the slots of the expansion bus. These connections provide the path upon which all information passes to and from the boards. There are physical, electrical, and logical considerations in connector design that define both function and compatibility. These attributes range from physical dimensions and electrical power requirements to the definition and arrangement of the signals that pass through them. The architecture may specify some or all of these attributes. Figure 1.21 illustrates

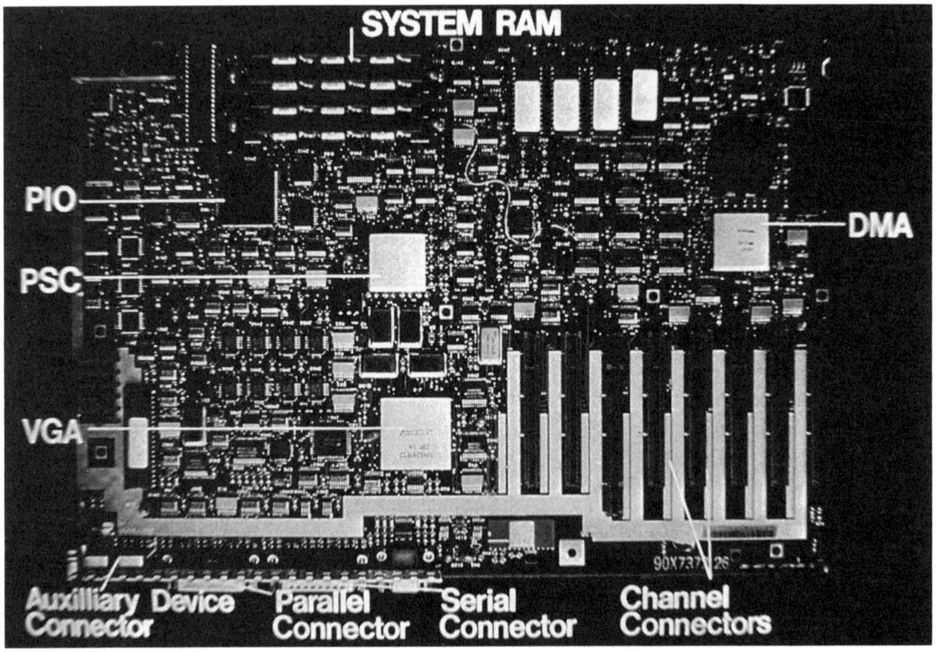

Figure 1.20 The IBM PS/2 Model 80 system board has eight expansion slots and numerous integrated features. (Courtesy of International Business Machines Corporation)

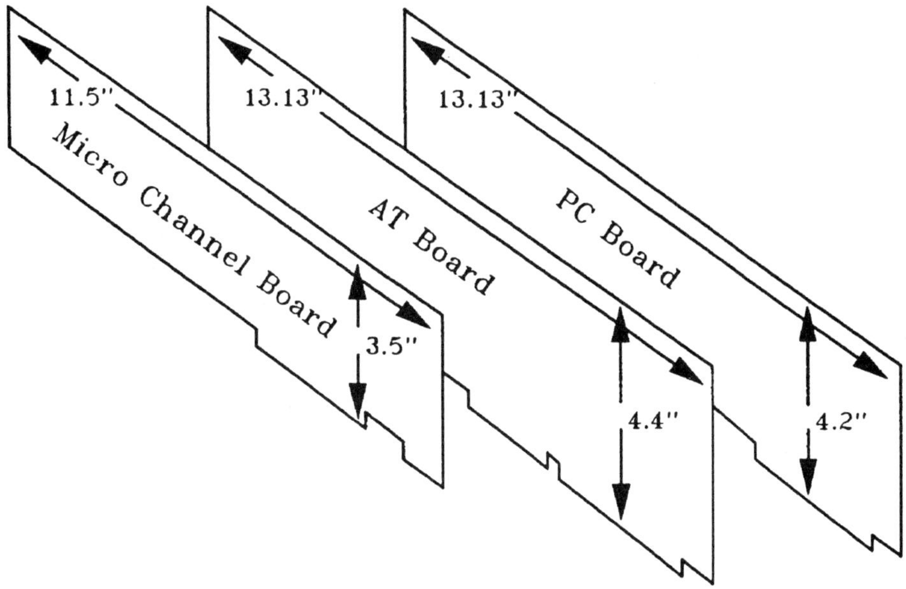

Figure 1.21 Expansion boards for IBM's personal computers.

some common board types for IBM's personal computers. It is apparent that just one of these parameters, such as the physical dimensions of a board, is critical to its compatibility across a variety of systems.

It is the incompatibility of Micro Channel expansion boards with the IBM Personal Computer and the IBM Personal Computer AT that was responsible for a great deal of the controversy surrounding IBM's new bus architecture. When IBM introduced the PC AT, the importance of expansion board compatibility with the original IBM Personal Computer and the Personal Computer XT was recognized. However, from the illustration (Figure 1.22), one can see that there are significant differences in the two board types. The compromise that was made by IBM involved upward compatibility. Most of the original boards would work in the AT (often called **upward** or **forward compatibility**), but the AT boards were not functional in the older systems (referred to as **downward** or **backward compatibility**).

This level of incompatibility was introduced to provide additional function and design improvements to the AT class machines. This is a classic dilemma faced by system designers: how can function be enhanced and designs be improved without sacrificing compatibility? What are the acceptable tradeoffs? In the case of Micro Channel cards, both upward and downward compatibility with the older boards were sacrificed for functional enhancements and design improvements. In Chapter 2 the benefits that were gained at the expense of compatibility will be described.

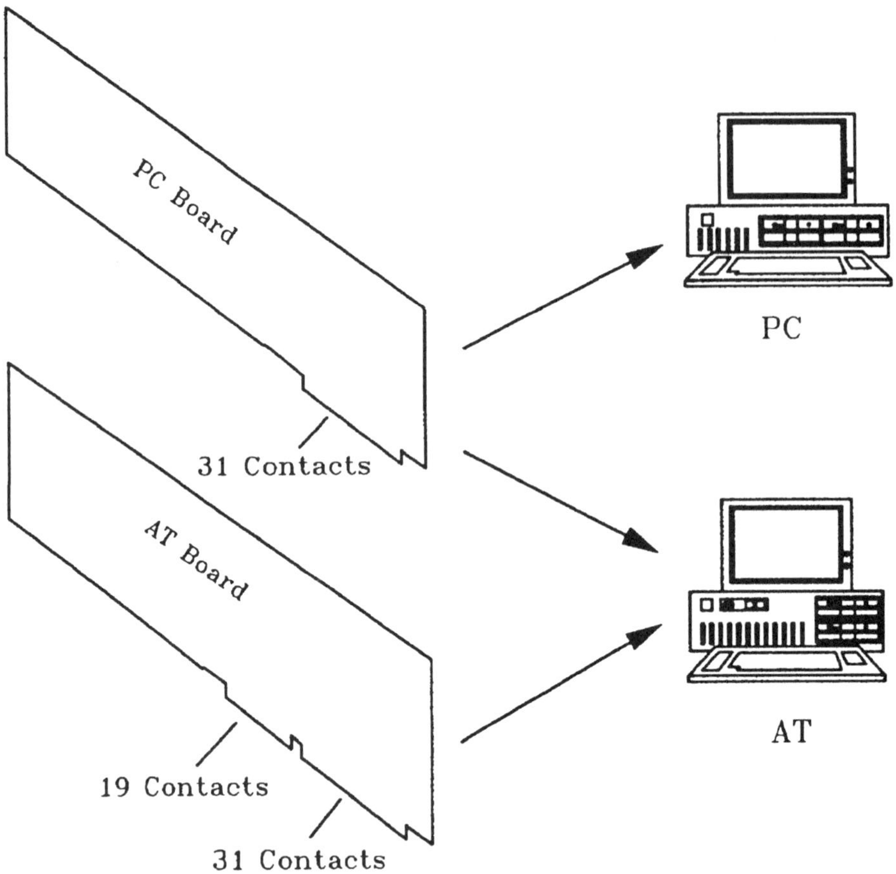

Figure 1.22 PC and AT board upward compatibiltiy.

Other Bus Types

Another method of classifying buses is by their function. Examples of these are **data** and **address buses.** These buses transport data and its corresponding destination. The arbitration bus is another bus type that is used to establish bus ownership. In Micro Channel architecture, the arbitration bus allows several devices to share the use and control of the bus (only one at a time, of course) instead of only one or two.

The control bus is concerned with control information and is the bus that actually causes data to flow. In the human analogy, this is similar to the control of the heart beat and the various valves in the circulatory system. The power bus does what you might suspect it to do—it supplies power and grounding for the bus and connectors. Most external devices (display, printer, and so on) have their own power supplies.

Elements of Bus Architecture and Design

There are several elements of bus architecture and design that we haven't considered. First of all, what are the signals that a bus uses and what do they mean? How are information transfers actually conducted? What are some of the considerations in bus timings? What types of devices are allowed to use the bus? What are some considerations in adapter design? The following is a brief discussion of these topics.

Signals

A bus's capability is largely determined by the number of signals and their definitions. A **signal** is a fluctuating electrical quantity such as current or voltage that represents coded information. Signals are used to define and control information transfers as well as to represent the actual information. In digital computers, signals are generally in one of three states: high, low, or inactive. It is through the use of these states that all information is communicated. The signals of the expansion bus are associated with discrete connections on the boards and card slots and reside on specific lines on the bus. These **pins** generally are given an alphanumeric designation and are defined in tables located in technical reference manuals.

The function of the various signals is to provide the framework for efficient information transfer. These signals are used to describe the origin and destination of the information to be transferred, when the transfer is to take place, and precisely how the data gets to its destination (Figure 1.23).

Table 1.2 lists the definition of the signals for the PC and XT expansion buses. As can be seen from a close examination of this table, the types of signals can be classified into five general types: data (D0–D7), address (A0–A19), timing and control (CLK, IO CH RDY, OSC, IOR, IOW, SMEMR, SMEMW, ALE, IRQ2–IRQ7, DRQ1–DRQ2, DACK1–DACK3, AEN,TC,), electrical (+5VDC, –5VDC, +12VDC, –12VDC, GND), and miscellaneous signals (RESET DRV, IO CH CHK) that provide additional function and other attributes about the transfer.

These signals, although relatively few in number, provided all the functions of the I/O bus of the PC.

When you examine the functions of the signals of the PC bus, they really aren't too complicated. There are:

- Data and address lines;
- A clock to synchronize bus cycles with the system CPU;
- A signal to insert wait states;
- Instructions to read or write to memory or I/O devices;
- A signal that indicates that it's okay to read the address;
- Several lines for interrupting the CPU;
- A signal that indicates that the DMA controller can take charge of the bus instead of the CPU;
- Several signals for DMA transfers and acknowledgement;

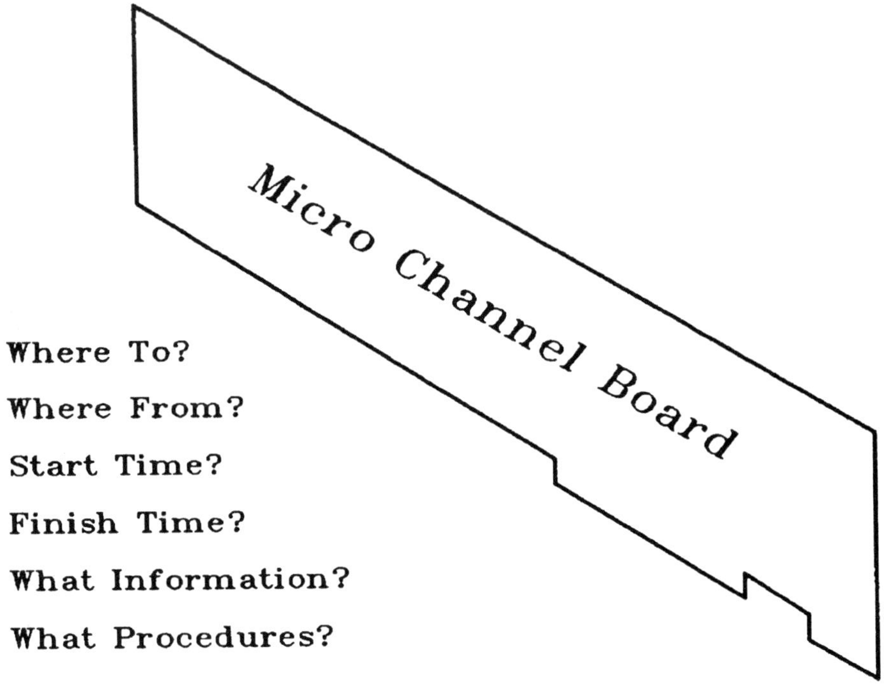

Figure 1.23 Information transfer requirements.

- A counter that signals the number of bytes transferred;
- Electrical and ground signals;
- A signal that indicates a parity error; and
- A reset signal.

Table 1.3 lists the signal definitions for the AT expansion bus. The first 62 signals are identical with those of the PC and XT (for compatibility purposes), with the exception of the zero-wait-state signal, which had previously been reserved. Thirty-six additional signals were added to accommodate the 16-bit characteristics of the 80286 microprocessor, to provide additional system resources, and to allow the bus to be shared by one additional entity—a very special type of device called a **bus master.** This last feature was rarely used, but was a forerunner of one of the most important features of Micro Channel architecture.

Data Lines and Data Path Width

The most important consideration for data signals is the number of parallel lines dedicated to carrying data, or the width of the data bus. The greater the number of data lines, the greater the amount of information that can be transferred in a

TABLE 1.2 PC AND XT BUS SIGNAL DEFINITIONS

Signal Type	Signal	Function
Data lines	D0–D7	8-bit data transfer.
Address lines	A0–A19	20 address lines for 1 MB addressability. (Only the first 10 are used during I/O cycles.)
Timing and control	CLK	Bus clock. Synchronizes bus and microprocessor operations.
	IO CH RDY	IO Channel Ready. Generates wait states.
	OSC	Oscillator. Runs clocks and timers. (Used by video boards, not synchronized with bus clock.)
	IOR IOW	Input/Output Read. Input/Output Write. Instructs I/O devices to read or write information to the data lines.
	SMEMR SMEMW	Memory Read. Memory Write. Instructs memory controller to read or write information to data lines.
	ALE	Address Latch Enable. Signals that memory address is valid.
	IRQ2–IRQ7	Interrupt request lines.
	DRQ1–DRQ2	DMA request lines.
	DACK1–DACK3	DMA acknowledge lines.
	AEN	Address Enable. Used for DMA transfers to signal the DMA controller to take control of the bus for a transfer.
	TC	Terminal count line. Used for DMA transfers to signal the number of bytes moved.

TABLE 1.2 PC AND XT BUS SIGNAL DEFINITIONS (continued)

Signal Type	Signal	Function
Electrical	+5VDC 5VDC +12VDC –12VDC	Power lines for various voltages.
	GND	Ground lines.
Miscellaneous	IO CH CHK	I/O Channel Check. Signals that a memory parity error has occurred.
	RESET DRV	Resets the system.

TABLE 1.3 AT BUS SIGNAL DEFINITIONS. The first group of 62 pins are identical to those of the PC and XT.

Signal Type	Signal	Function
Data lines	D0–D7	8-bit data transfer.
Address lines	A0–A19	20 address lines for 1 MB addressability. (Only the first 10 are used during I/O cycles.)
Timing and control	CLK	Bus clock Synchronizes bus and microprocessor operations.
	IO CH RDY	IO Channel Ready Generates wait states.
	0WS	Removes wait states.
	OSC	Oscillator Runs clocks and timers. (Used by video boards, not synchronized with bus clock.)
	IOR IOW	Input/Output Read Input/Output Write Instructs I/O devices to read or write information to the data lines.
	SMEMR SMEMW	Memory Read Memory Write

TABLE 1.3 AT BUS SIGNAL DEFINITIONS (continued)

Signal Type	Signal	Function
		Instructs memory controller to read or write information to data lines.
ALE		Address Latch Enable Signals that memory address is valid.
	IRQ2–IRQ7	Interrupt request lines.
	DRQ1–DRQ2	DMA request lines.
	DACK1–DACK3	DMA acknowledge lines.
	AEN	Address Enable Used for DMA transfers to signal the DMA controller to take control of the bus for a transfer.
	TC	Terminal count line Used for DMA transfers to signal the number of bytes moved.
Electrical	+5VDC 5VDC +12VDC –12VDC	Power lines for various voltages.
	GND	Ground lines.
Miscellaneous	IO CH CHK	I/O Channel Check Signals a memory parity that error has occurred.
	RESET DRV	Resets the system.
Data lines	D8–D15	Additional data lines for 16-bit transfers.
Address lines	LA20–LA23	Additional address lines for increased memory addressibility (16 MB).
	LA17–LA19	Unlatched address lines that duplicated latched address lines on the PC and XT bus.
Timing and Control	SBHE	Signals 16-bit data transfers.

TABLE 1.3 AT BUS SIGNAL DEFINITIONS (continued)

Signal Type	Signal	Function
	MEM CS16	Signals 16-bit transfer to/from memory .
	I/O CS16	Signals 16-bit transfer to/from I/O device.
	MEMR MEMW	Memory Read Memory Write SMEMR, SMEMW handle address ranges below 1MB.)
	IRQ10–IRQ12 IRQ14–IRQ15	Additional interrupt request lines. (IRQ 13 is reserved for the math coprocessor.)
	DRQ0 DRQ5–DRQ7	Additional DMA request lines.
	DACK0 DACK5–DACK7	Additional DMA acknowledge lines.
	MASTER	Allows bus master control.

given amount of time. Wider buses generally mean more capacity (amount of information transferred per unit time, usually expressed in megabytes per second). However, this potential also depends on the nature of the participants involved in the transfer (Figure 1.24). Let's take the case of a 32-bit device (source) transferring information to an 8-bit device (target) over a 32-bit bus. In this example, each 32-bit transfer of information must be divided into four 8-bit transfers. Similarly, the other examples illustrate that most of the allowed transfers do not use the 32-bit data path. Only in the case in which both devices are 32-bit participants is the information transfer 32 bits wide.

Address Lines

Information on **address lines** defines the exact location of the source or the destination of the data to be transferred. As with data lines, the most significant consideration for address lines is also their number. As mentioned earlier, the number of address lines determines the maximum amount of memory that can be addressed.

Did you ever wonder how a device knows that the information being transferred on a bus is intended for him? (Computer people have a personality quirk that makes them humanize all kinds of things about a computer!) Each device attached to the bus (for example, I/O or memory) has an address associated with it. The "sending" or "source" device puts the address information on the address bus, and

Data Path Width of Source Device	Data Path Width of Target Device 8-Bit	16-Bit	32-Bit
8-Bit	8-Bit	8-Bit	8-Bit
16-Bit	8-Bit	16-Bit	16-Bit
32-Bit	8-Bit	16-Bit	32-Bit

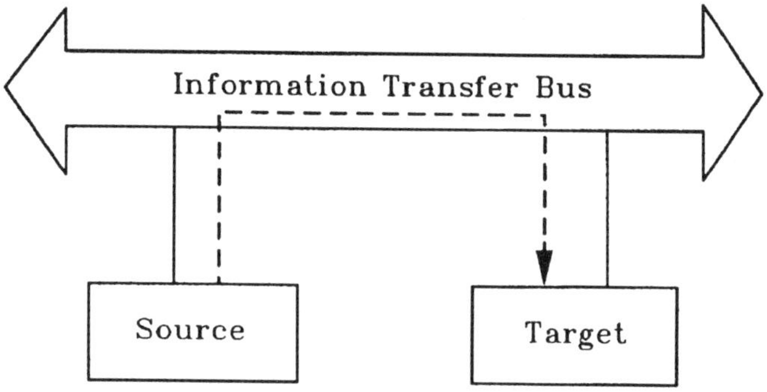

Figure 1.24 Data path widths for information transfers are based on the capabilities of the devices.

the "receiving" or "target" device interprets or "decodes" the address using its logic circuitry. Basically, he asks himself the question, "Does that combination of 0s and 1s match my address? (This is an oversimplified explanation of one type of addressing, but it will do for our purposes.) If the answer is "yes," the transfer of data can begin.

Timing Considerations

Buses are either **synchronous** or **asynchronous**. Synchronous designs utilize a clock that determines when information transfers can occur. The clock is analogous to a metronome for a musician. The timing of everything that happens in a synchronous bus system is related to the clock frequency. In asynchronous designs, clocks do not regulate bus activity. An information transfer may occur immediately after the last one is finished and need not wait until the next tick of the clock.

There are advantages and disadvantages for each type. The synchronous bus is generally considered to be a less complex design and may be somewhat faster than the asynchronous implementation, assuming that all the designs in the system are "tuned" for that frequency. In a synchronous design, every device in the system is designed to work with similar timing characteristics. However, all activities must occur at a fixed time interval. If the time interval is changed, some devices may no longer work or may require long delays. The PC, AT, and EISA buses are synchronous buses.

An asynchronous design permits a much wider latitude in timing characteristics and can be speeded up or slowed down as the requirements of devices change. This more flexible design allows us to speed up transfers without losing compatibility. The PC and the AT bus were synchronous buses, but the Micro Channel bus is asynchronous. In Chapter 3, there is a detailed discussion of how Micro Channel's asynchronous bus works.

Some architectures will allow for a wide range of cycle speeds for attached devices, whereas others allow only small variations without introducing hardware incompatibilities. This problem was experienced repeatedly as developers attempted to speed up the original AT bus to match faster processor speeds. Many adapters would not work in these systems because they were not designed to operate at the higher speeds.

Another important attribute for information transfers has to do with the speed of the transfers. Some designs offer faster cycle times than others. However, this does not necessarily mean that all transfers occur faster. The maximum data rate can only be achieved if both the source and target devices are capable of the higher data rates. Higher speed buffers (a small amount of memory that serves as a temporary storage location) may be used in slower devices, but the tradeoff is additional cost. Many I/O devices are inherently slower than the bus capabilities (for instance, optical storage devices), or some adapters may implement slower, less expensive components in their design. The conclusion is that faster bus designs may or may not enhance the speed of information transfers. Because of these differences in the timing characteristics of attached devices and the default cycle time of the bus, there is usually a bus signal that interjects wait cycles on a synchronous bus or signals for a slower cycle time on an asynchronous bus.

In dual bus architectures, including those with a memory cache, the speed of one bus may be independent of the other bus. This becomes advantageous when the system CPU is much faster than the I/O devices, which is almost always the case.

Another important consideration of bus timing characteristics has to do with the amount of overhead in setting up the actual data transfer. Several timing cycles may be required before the actual transfer can take place. Depending on the amount of information to be transferred, the efficiency of the software, and other overhead characteristics, these factors can be much more important than the actual data rates on the bus. In general, as the amount of information decreases, the setup time percentage becomes greater.

In today's environment, computer manufacturers often quote maximum continuous (burst) data rates of their I/O buses in their specifications. These are often used to draw erroneous performance conclusions, since burst data rates can only be used for a very short period of time. Allowance must be made for the requirements of other devices such as DRAM refresh and the use of the bus by other devices.

To summarize, the actual rate of data transfer is dependent on a complex set of factors that range from adapter design, software, and transaction overhead to the bus timing characteristics.

Controls

Control signals are used to define exactly when and how the information transfer is to take place, tell how much information is to be transferred, and to describe the type of transfer. There are also several ready or enable signals that are required to ensure the validity of the transfer. Acknowledge signals are used to ensure that all the "players," or participants, involved know what the rules are for that particular transfer. In some bus architectures, there are provisions to verify that all the information was transferred correctly and to the proper address. These features are referred to as **data** and **address parity,** respectively.

Participants

In some early computer systems, only the system CPU could move information from one location to another on the bus. In other systems, a device called a **direct memory access controller,** or **DMA controller,** could serve this function. In Micro Channel architecture, a specialized type of device called a **bus master** may access system memory or transfer the information from one device to another without the assistance of the system CPU or the DMA controller. This feature is one of the most important aspects of Micro Channel architecture. The benefits of bus masters will be described in detail later in this book. For the moment, they will be characterized as devices that can be used to enhance function or increase performance.

Devices other than the system CPU, the DMA controller, or the bus master are called **slave devices** or **slave adapters** if they are part of the expansion bus. If they utilize the DMA controller for information transfers, they are called **DMA slaves.** If they provide system memory, they are called **memory slaves.** If the slave device provides an I/O function, it is called an **I/O slave.**

The above terms are defined as they are generally used in the industry, but some companies may state them differently. These definitions are also used in a way that is related to the information transfer process. For example, an adapter that has a bus master function may also serve as an I/O slave. Confusing, huh? These definitions will become clearer as we get further into Micro Channel architecture.

Arbitration

In the PC bus design, there were very limited ways for any device other than the system CPU and the DMA controller to control the bus. Using the PC's 8088 microprocessor, passing the control of the bus from the CPU to the DMA controller was relatively simple. The 8088 had a CPU HOLD signal that was part of its instruction set. This signal was used to stop the CPU from accessing system memory and to allow the DMA controller to read or write information to memory over the DMA channels. Micro Channel architecture uses a separate bus called the

arbitration bus for this purpose. The function of the arbitration bus is to serve as a medium for allowing the "privileged" participants to use the bus. It provides a method for transfer of ownership from the system processor, the DMA controller, and bus masters.

One of the most important considerations in bus arbitration is the priority assigned to the different participants. The method of assigning priorities is extremely important because it determines the flexibility of the architecture. For instance, if the CPU always has the highest priority and the priority cannot be changed, your computer is forever subject to possible problems as the I/O demands for the bus increase. Micro Channel architecture has a very flexible method for assigning priorities, which will be described in detail in Chapter 3.

Types of I/O Operations

As described in the previous section, only certain participants (defined by the bus architecture) can control bus transactions. The types of I/O operations allowed by a bus are also defined by the bus architecture. The following section is a brief description of basic I/O operations.

Polling Operations. **Polling** operations are used when I/O devices do not have a method of signalling that they are ready to send or receive information. In most cases, the polling is under the control of the system microprocessor, which interrogates the device to see if it is ready for service. During this type of transaction, the system microprocessor is generally not available for other functions or has reduced availability, depending on the frequency of polling. In general, this kind of activity is reserved for asynchronous events or the unpredictable transfer of information (even though the actual transfer on the bus may be synchronous). An unbuffered printer or a game adapter/joystick are examples of devices that require constant polling.

This type of I/O can be quite rapid because it uses the power of the system microprocessor. Today, this can be very fast indeed! The disadvantage is that the system microprocessor has reduced availability for other activities and performance can be severely eroded. In the case in which there are multiple devices of this type, they may be polled in order of a software-established priority or "round-robin."

I/O adapters that require polling are not very common in today's environment, having been replaced by more efficient interrupt-driven devices.

Interrupt-Driven Operations. An **interrupt-driven** operation is an I/O technique in which a device signals another device when it is ready to send or receive information and is generally under the control of the system microprocessor. An **interrupt** is a request for service by an I/O device to another device capable of managing the required service. A good analogy is a telephone call. A telephone call is an unscheduled event that requires whoever answers to perform a certain routine and put other activities on hold until the call in handled. When completed, you return to whatever you were doing before the phone rang.

An **interrupt line** is assigned to each interrupting device.[3] The number of available lines and their management is an important factor in the configuration flexibility of a system and is determined by the bus architecture. In IBM personal computers, an interrupt causes a special kind of BIOS program, an **interrupt service routine,** to be executed. For example, pressing a single key on a keyboard generates an interrupt and a request for the system microprocessor to stop what it is doing and run the keyboard service routine.

Interrupt-driven processes are definitely an improvement over continuous polling because the system microprocessor can do other work until an interrupt occurs. These relationships are illustrated in Figure 1.25A and 1.25B.

The more devices a system has, the more interrupt processing acts like polling. The priority scheme is determined by the software and may be either prioritized or handled on a "round robin" basis.

Many instructions are required in order to service an interrupt, so reducing the number of interrupts is extremely important. Harry J. R. Dutton of IBM Australia has estimated that perhaps 200 instructions in DOS or 1000 instructions in OS/2 plus the instructions required for the actual interrupt service routine are required for each interrupt. Most well-designed I/O devices accumulate information and store it temporarily in buffers. When a reasonable amount of information is accumulated, the transfer occurs. This kind of buffering increases the performance in two ways: getting data from a memory cache or buffer is always faster than from the device itself, and transferring data in larger blocks requires less overhead.

Programmed I/O Operations. **Programmed I/O** operations are those in which the system microprocessor is used to transfer information to or from an adapter in two steps. In the case of transferring information from an adapter, the system microprocessor reads data into its registers and then moves it into system memory. Generally, only one byte is transferred at a time, making it a relatively inefficient operation. Some microprocessors are able to move several bytes at a time with little overhead, an operation called a **string move.**

This is probably the most common way of transferring I/O information and has the advantage of low cost. The disadvantage is that the technique uses a significant number of CPU cycles. If a number of programmed I/O devices are present in

[3]In some cases, more than one device can share interrupt lines. This important feature of Micro Channel architecture will be described later in this book.

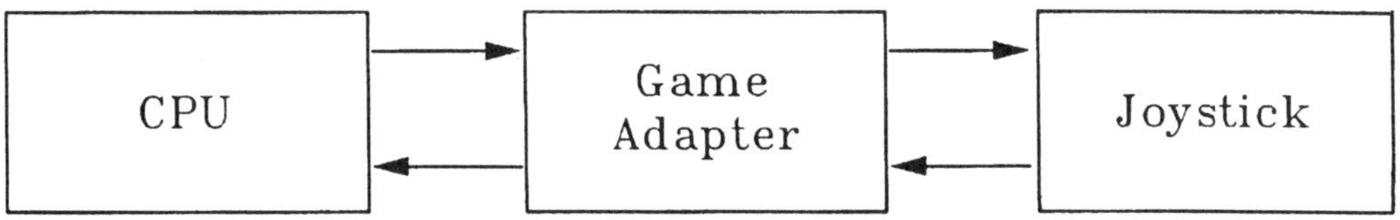

Figure 1.25A An example of a polling operation.

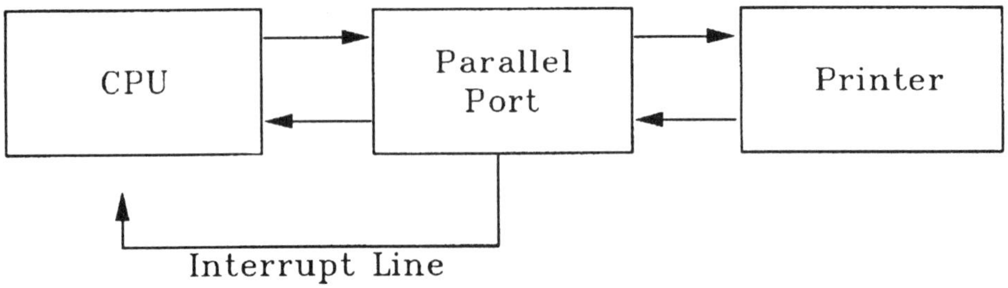

Figure 1.25B An example of an interrupt-driven I/O operation.

the system, significant degradation in performance can result. In addition, the system must be designed to accommodate devices that require timely service to prevent loss of data. Some older network adapters use programmed I/O in which every character created an interrupt. In the case of a buffered device, an interrupt is created whenever its buffer is full.

Direct Memory Access Operations. Another I/O technique, **DMA I/O,** barely uses the system CPU at all. Instead, it employs a third-party, the DMA controller, to manage data transfers between memory and I/O devices. An example of this type of I/O device is the diskette controller in IBM personal computers. The diskette controller, instead of tying up the system CPU, gets help from the DMA controller by sending a request over the DMA request line, which the DMA controller acknowledges. The DMA controller then gains control of the bus and manages the data transfer between system memory and the I/O device. The diskette controller uses a preassigned pathway, the **DMA channel,** to send its request to the DMA controller. After the transfer, control of the bus is relinquished. The advantages of this type of transfer are obvious. Fewer CPU cycles are needed for the data transfers.

Devices may be termed **memory-mapped** or **isolated I/O** (Figure 1.26). Memory-mapped devices reserve part of a system's address space for their exclusive use. The memory is physically located on the device and may be treated as system or nonsystem memory, depending on the purpose of the device and the system's memory architecture. It is most commonly part of nonsystem memory, however. Large amounts of information can be stored in this memory and then transferred to other addresses on the bus in large blocks. This generates fewer interruptions to the system processor or fewer DMA operations, and, in general, reduces the overhead involved in the transfers. As with almost any design, there are advantages and disadvantages, and memory-mapped I/O is no exception. In the memory-mapped case, all instructions that involve the I/O memory addresses operate on those located on the device. As a result, fewer instructions and less bus traffic are the results—definite advantages. A disadvantage is that part of the system's address space is used

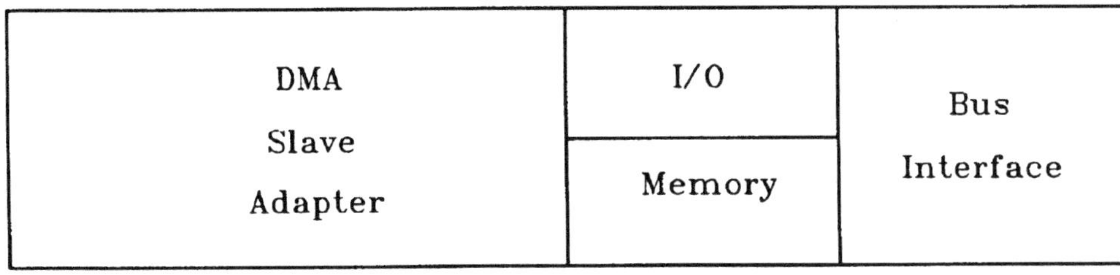

Figure 1.26 A memory-mapped DMA adapter and an isolated I/O slave adapter.

for this memory-mapping. A result is loss of flexibility in memory management or memory conflicts that can lead to configuration difficulties.

Bus Master Operations. The final type of transfer may involve a **bus master,** one of the most important features of Micro Channel architecture. A bus master is a function that a device or adapter card can have that allows it to move information to and from system memory or to and from another device. (Sometimes the device itself is called a bus master.) It does not require the services of the system CPU nor the DMA controller. It is capable of controlling the data, address, and control lines by itself. Bus masters are very smart indeed. They are even capable of executing programs on their own!

ADDITIONAL CONSIDERATIONS IN INFORMATION TRANSFER

It is important to appreciate bus architecture and related topics in light of how computers are used. Let's raise our heads a little and get out of the bits and bytes of information transfers. In this section, the relationship of computer hardware to the real world of software and user interaction will be considered.

Software

Computer hardware is of absolutely no value (boat anchors excluded) without the appropriate software that makes it do what we want it to do. Advanced bus features are of little benefit unless software can make use of them. For example, a 32-bit address path, no matter what its potential, depends on special 32-bit software to utilize it.

As we learned earlier, software falls into three general categories: application programs, operating systems, and device drivers. A very special type of software that is permanently imbedded in the hardware is the BIOS—The permanent programs that are "hard coded" into the hardware's read-only memory (ROM). These routines are used to service interrupts from standard devices such as diskettes, keyboards, printers, video, and asynchronous communications as well as for special utility programs such as print screen, real-time clock services, and so on. The BASIC language interpreter is also in ROM.

Each type of software isolates you from the hardware. The first class of software, application programs, are very familiar to all of us. Word processing, spreadsheet, or accounting programs are examples. They may include familiar commands like SAVE, PRINT, CALCULATE, or pull-down menus that you point to and click with a mouse. These high-level instructions are compiled into machine-executable instructions, and the operating system schedules the task. This starts the information transfer process.

In the early days of personal computing, application developers often used program commands that gave direct instructions to the hardware, bypassing the operating system and BIOS. This was done to speed up performance and was allowed by the Disk Operating System (DOS). Today, modern application programs are written to standard interfaces called **Application Program Interfaces** (**API** for short) that are part of the operating system and used in languages like C, COBOL, and Fortran. These standard interfaces are well defined in advanced operating systems like OS/2 and UNIX®, but are less so in older operating systems like DOS. Adherence to standard programming interfaces allows the program to be somewhat independent of the underlying hardware, device drivers, and BIOS. What this means is that a program can be "portable" between a large number of machines since specific hardware characteristics are isolated by the underlying operating system, device drivers, and BIOS.

Some hardware adapters and attached devices are not programmed by the BIOS operating system or the application program. They are so unique that they require the addition of special software written just for them. For example, a separate device driver is required to support the functions of most optical drives. These programs may be permanently embedded in the device as microcode (ROM) or may be loaded into memory as device drivers. Device drivers are generally shipped on a diskette with the hardware devices and installed during the setup routine.

The relationships between the various types of software and system BIOS were shown in Figure 1.8. This illustration of layered software and its relationship to the underlying hardware is an idealized one, at best. However, the value of layered software is significant. If strictly adhered to, application programs can be written that are independent of the hardware and the underlying software. What this means is that applications programs do not have to be revised in order to take advantage of new hardware features and that the benefits of new versions of the operating system (and new I/O devices) can be brought to applications with no change to the application program itself.

An example of how this works with OS/2 is shown in Figure 1.27. The application developer writes the application to the file system API. The file system is part of the base operating system for OS/2. Specific devices are managed by the device driver software or the BIOS routines. If the device changes, the device driver software is changed. If a more efficient file system is developed, it is replaced in the operating system. None of this should affect the application program. The key to this "magic" is the careful definition (and preservation) of the interfaces between the various layers of software.

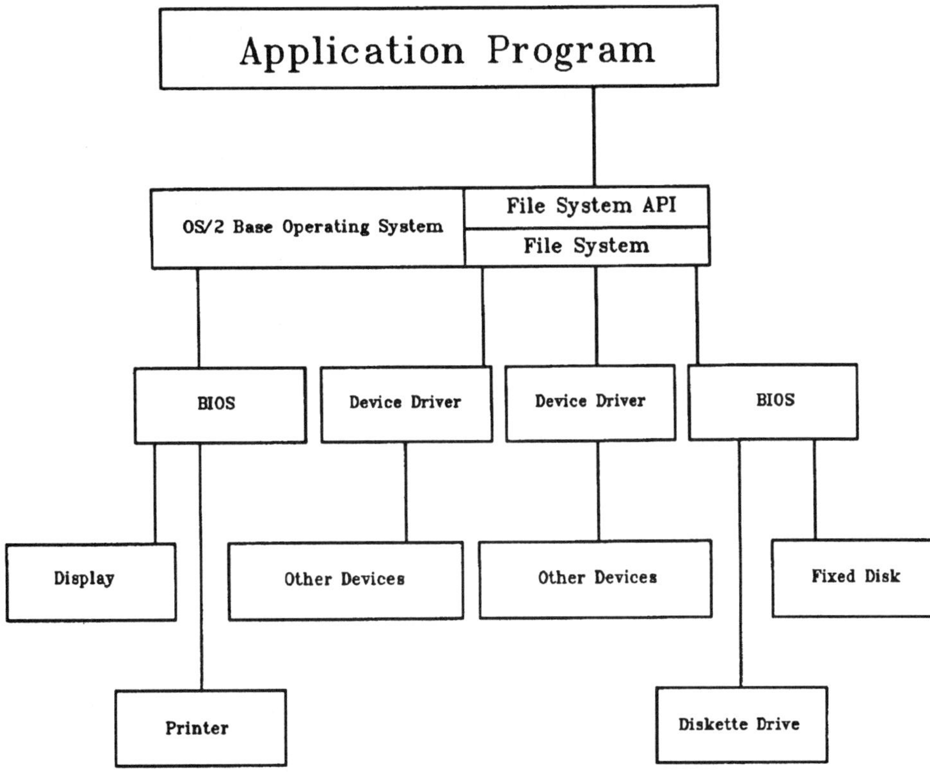

Figure 1.27 OS/2 software relationships.

It is the structure of this underlying software that is so significant in appropriately managing information transfers.

Information Transfer: An Example

Did you ever wonder what happens after you give a command from your application program? Suppose you want to print a letter stored on a diskette using your favorite word processing program? The program's menu offers an option for retrieving and printing a file from a diskette. This selection starts a series of events in motion.

In this example, the printer is a rather simple device such as the original IBM Personal Computer Graphics Printer. It can only accept a small amount of information at a time because it has very limited buffering capabilities. It is also comparatively slow and certainly can't print information as fast as the system can send it.

The information to be printed is stored on a diskette and must first be read into system memory. The application program gives a command to the operating system to read the information from the diskette and another command to print the file. The commands are broken down into very basic instructions that the BIOS, diskette controller, and printer recognize by using a compiler. The operating system schedules the task and gives the source and destination of the data transfers and the memory addresses in the system RAM that are used for temporary storage. The diskette controller, a device that uses the DMA controller for its transfers, finds the file containing the letter and signals the DMA controller. The first few characters are transferred over the bus by the DMA controller to a designated address in system memory.

Next, the operating system directs the CPU to move the information from its location in memory into the CPU registers. Then, the information is transferred to the system's parallel port (connector) to which the printer is attached. Next, the information is transferred to the printer's built-in memory buffer and printed. The parallel port is an interrupt-driven I/O device accepting streams of text (a line at a time). After each line, it interrupts the CPU and signals that it is ready for more information. The CPU then initiates the appropriate BIOS interrupt service routine. More information is then moved from the main memory to the CPU's internal registers and then to the I/O address of the printer port. This continues until the entire letter has been printed.

This summary of what happens during the simple movement of a text file from diskette to printer illustrates the many activities and other considerations involved in information transfers. Each of the elements affects the speed of the transfer. The application software, the operating system, the BIOS routines, the structure of the adapter, the data path of the bus, the speed of the bus, the diskette drive and controller characteristics, the speed of the memory, the speed of the system CPU, the number of instruction cycles involved in executing the print command, the rate of transfer of the printer port to the printer, and the speed of the printer all can affect how fast the letter gets printed! If any of these processes requires the output of a previous process in order to proceed, the overall performance is limited by the slowest operation. In some cases, the bus transfer speed is the fastest element in the information transfer and does not directly influence how fast a task is accomplished. In others, it may well be the most important factor.

Performance

As you have seen from the preceding discussion, many factors may influence how fast a given task is accomplished. This background is important in order to understand the performance benefits of advanced information transfer architectures. **Performance** is a measure of productivity. It is the amount of useful work that can be performed by a computer system in a given time. It is determined by a system's **throughput, response time,** and **availability.**

Throughput is the number of tasks that can be performed in a given interval of time. **Response time** is the duration of a task as seen by the user. Both the throughput and the response time are influenced by the application environment, the operating system, and the hardware and its device drivers. A system's **availability** is defined as the percentage of time it can be used when needed. Performance is definitely impacted if a system is not functional or if a system "hang" occurs, requiring a complete system reset!

Most personal computers are grossly underutilized today and do not approach either their potential throughput or their rated response times. This is due to a number of factors. The operating environment is probably the most important factor. In this book, four distinct environments are considered:

1. Single-tasking/single-user;
2. Multitasking/single-user;
3. Multi-user/shared logic; and
4. Multi-user/shared resource.

These relationships are illustrated below (Figure 1.28).

In the case of a single-tasking environment, the time to complete a task is usually the sum of the incremental times for each step. (This may be offset by some elementary forms of multi-tasking such as printer or adapter buffering.) This sequential processing is characteristic of the DOS environment.

In the case of multitasking, some activities may be concurrent, and the time required to complete an overall task is reduced as a result of parallel, rather than sequential, operations. OS/2 is a multitasking operating system.

If more than one user is allowed to share a system to do single or multiple tasks, the productivity of a single system is consequently enhanced as it would be in the AIX®, XENIX®, or other UNIX-derived environments.

Most of the history of personal computing has been in the single-tasking/single-

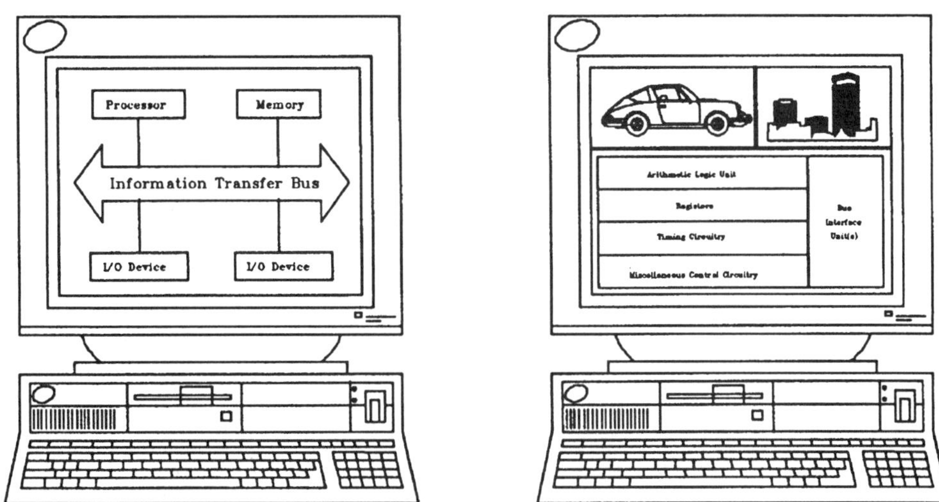

Figure 1.28 Usage environments.

(1) Single tasking/single user (2) Multitasking/single user

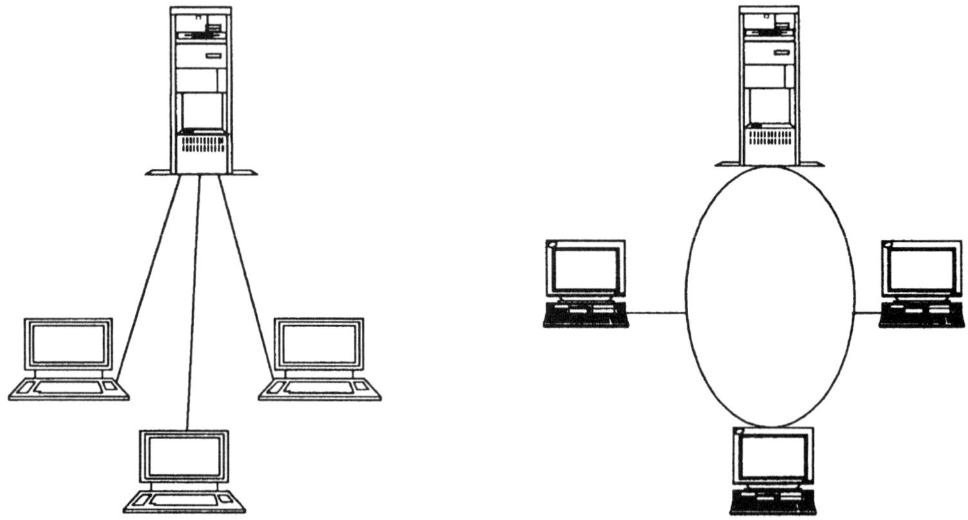

Figure 1.28 (continued) Usage environments.
(3) Multi-user/shared logic (4) Multi-user/shared resource

user environment. The operating system has been primarily DOS, and the goal of both hardware and software design has been for that environment. The introduction of advanced operating systems such as OS/2 and AIX provide the next three usage environments, and the real power of these systems will be evident.

Micro Channel architecture was designed to address **all** usage environments and can bring benefits to **all** users. The next chapter describes the primary features and benefits of the architecture.

(Congratulations! You just graduated from college and are ready for graduate school.)

QUESTIONS

1. How does architecture differ from design?
2. What is a channel? Distinguish between the terms information transfer architecture and I/O architecture. Which is Micro Channel architecture?
3. What is the function of a DMA controller? What are the benefits of DMA transfers?
4. What is a bus interface? What is a bus controller?
5. What is meant by parity checking?
6. What kind of parity checking did the IBM Personal Computer and the IBM Personal Computer AT have?
7. What is an interrupt? How are interrupt-driven processes different from programmed I/O operations.

8. What is an interrupt service routine? What software controls it?
9. How was bus ownership controlled in the IBM Personal Computer? What is an arbitration bus?
10. How does memory access time differ from memory cycle time? What is a wait state?
11. What is meant by memory refresh?
12. What is a memory cache and where is it generally located? What are some other possible locations?
13. What is meant by time multiplexing? What would be the effect on the design of a bus if there were no time multiplexing?
14. What are some factors that influence performance? Why is throughput not the same as performance?
15. What is the difference between system memory and nonsystem memory? What is meant by public and private memory?
16. What is a bus master?
17. What is a memory map? Why is it so important? What is meant by a memory-mapped device?
18. Why is architecture so important?
19. What are the attributes of the ideal computer architecture? Rank them in order of their priority.
20. What is meant by upward compatibility? Downward compatibility?

2

Overview of Micro Channel Architecture

The previous chapter was designed to provide a good technical foundation for the understanding of Micro Channel architecture. Basic computer structural and architectural concepts were introduced. With this background, you are now ready for the advanced topics presented in the remainder of this book.

This chapter gives an overview of Micro Channel architecture, its purpose, and key features and benefits. A more detailed technical description of the architecture and how it works is contained in Chapter 3.

WHY A NEW ARCHITECTURE?

Although the last chapter should have given you some ideas, you still may be wondering why IBM decided to change something as fundamental as the bus in its personal computers. The answer is that two trends combined to exceed the limits of the bus architecture. Computer technology advanced exponentially, and people placed far greater demands on their personal computers.

In Richard N. Foster's book, *Innovation,* the concept of limits and its effects on technology innovations is explored in depth. To illustrate the importance of limits, he relates the following story:[1]

In July 1985, Sergei Bubka of the Soviet Union broke the world pole vault record, clearing 6 meters during the Paris International Track and Field meet. Asked if he ever expected to reach 7 meters, he replied, "No, there will have to be another technical revolution before that height can be reached. There's just so high you can jump using a bending fiberglass pole."

[1]Foster, Richard W. 1986. *Innovation.* p. 32. New York: Summit Books.

The Changing Demands of Users

The AT bus was simply not designed to address the way most personal computers are used today. In order to understand the changing usage environment, a historical perspective is in order. In 1984 the IBM Personal Computer AT was introduced (Figure 2.1), and went on to become one of the most successful products in IBM's history. It seemed to have everything that a microcomputer would ever need: a 16-bit microprocessor capable of addressing a vast amount of memory, an internal architecture that enabled multitasking, a 16-bit I/O data path, software and expansion board compatibility with the original PC, and almost double the number of interrupt and DMA channels. The AT quickly became the industry standard and encouraged the development of an enormous number of peripherals and expansion boards as well as "clones" or copies of the system design by other manufacturers. The AT signalled the beginning of a new era in the role of personal computers.

Even more interesting than the technological achievement of the AT were the customers who purchased it and what they used it for. The original PC was used first by hobbyists and programmers and later by small businesses. It was marketed through computer stores as well as through IBM's traditional marketing channels, the "blue suiters." The dealer marketing channel was thought to be more appropriate for some of the potential purchasers— hobbyists and small businesses—of these systems than IBM's direct channels.

The PC was used as a single-tasking stand-alone machine, running basic

Figure 2.1 The AT signalled both the beginning and the end of an era in the role of personal computers. (Courtesy of International Business Machines Corporation)

applications such as word processing and simple spreadsheets. In other words, it was designed and used as a personal computer. By contrast, the AT was a much more powerful machine that found its way into much of IBM's traditional customer base through direct marketing channels. These systems were used differently than the earlier PC's: in highly connected environments with mainframes and local area networks (LANs), as controllers for manufacturing systems, communication gateways, file servers, engineering design systems, and uses that were previously unimagined for a "personal computer." People began to run their businesses on these systems. Large and small operations became dependent on them.

In large businesses, a trend known as **downsizing** was beginning. Some of the traditional functions of mainframe computers were moving to the desktop. Using a mainframe for centralized computing power in shared-logic applications with dumb terminals (IBM now calls them **nonintelligent workstations**) began to give way to the **intelligent workstation**, the personal computer.

However, in order to use the true power of these smaller systems, a micro-to-mainframe computing model that placed PCs at the heart of information systems rather than as peripherals was needed. Vast amounts of data were stored on these systems, and their total computing power exceeded that of some mainframes. The solution to getting at this power and storage was a distributed processing and data model in a highly connected environment with compatible software from micros to mainframes. This new architecture was called **SAA**, or **Systems Application Architecture** (Figure 2.2), announced in early 1987.

This new environment imposed reliability and data integrity requirements and performance demands that had been associated with much larger systems in the past. Configurations and option combinations that the designers of the AT never envisioned were routinely encountered. Computer graphics, desktop publishing, and file and data base servers with demands for high speed I/O became common. This rapidly changing application environment and the new micro-to-mainframe

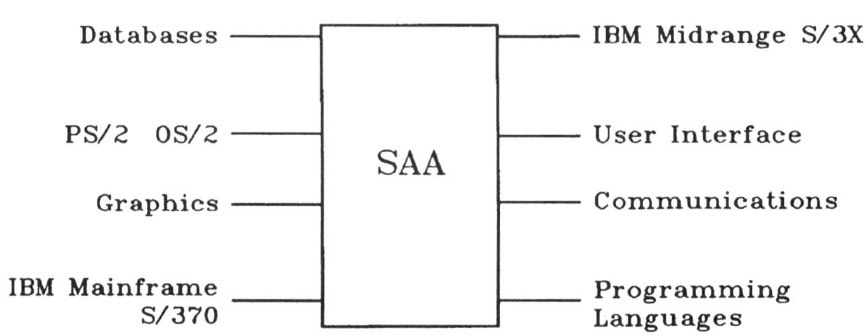

Figure 2.2 Systems Application Architecture defines commonality and compatibility in the user interface, communications protocols, data base languages, programming languages, and graphics primitives across IBM products and programs.

computing model were well beyond the design point of the AT bus. The AT signalled both the beginning and the end of an era in the role of personal computers.

Rate of Technology Change

In the last chapter, some of the dramatic changes in microprocessor, memory, I/O devices, and software were described. This climate of rapid technology change was highly instrumental in driving requirements for the new bus. However, it was the appearance of the Intel i386 microprocessor in 1986 that represented a "hard stop" for the AT bus. This high-speed processor with its 32-bit I/O capabilities could never be effectively utilized on the AT's 16-bit I/O bus. The i386 drove a firm requirement for a new bus architecture.

New storage devices with higher densities and higher data rates were already under development. It was impossible to transfer data from some fixed disk drives because their data rates exceeded the data transfer capabilities of the AT bus.[2] As a result, data was "interleaved" around the track on the drive, artificially spreading it out to slow it down. Some vendors solved the problem by using large memory buffers for temporary storage on the disk controllers until the AT bus could catch up with the drive, an expensive solution at best.

A bewildering number of expansion boards and other I/O devices were introduced that were difficult and sometimes impossible to configure in every system. That's because the PC, the XT, and the AT had different system resources provided by their architectures and different management schemes.

Memory and logic speeds were also increasing dramatically. No end was in sight for this ever-increasing rate of technology change. Table 2.1 illustrates the rate of change of technology in IBM's personal computers from 1981–1987.

The AT bus architecture was stretched to its limits to keep up with these technology advances. This was a period that spawned a lot of technical bandaids such as large buffers on devices and proprietary solutions for using the 32-bit capabilities of the i386.

Yet another problem fueled by rapid technology changes involved concerns about rapid obsolescence. Many purchasers reacted by buying only the cheapest equipment available. PCs were beginning to be perceived as a disposable asset that would need to be replaced about every two years. From IBM's perspective, this meant that part of its traditional customer base had begun to slip away.

An Industry in Chaos

The industry was speeding along an evolutionary path that attempted to accommodate these changes with a number of "fixes" that varied from manufacturer to

[2]The IBM PC AT disk controller was a programmed I/O adapter. Even though the burst data rate was adequate for most disk drives, the system microprocessor had to be shared with a number of other devices, some of which had critical service times associated with them. The DMA data rates were too slow for the drives with higher data rates and other devices.

TABLE 2.1 TECHNOLOGY CHANGES IN IBM'S PERSONAL COMPUTERS, 1981–1987

	1981	1987
CPU	8088	80386
Clock Speed (MHz)	4.77	20
Data Path Width	8	32
Memory Speed (ns)	250	85
Memory Density (MB)	0.016	1
Storage Data Rate (MB/s)	0.500	1.25
Display (Mb/screen)	0.128	6.291

manufacturer. Some attempted to speed up the AT bus in order to gain the performance advantage of the higher speed components. Others elected to separate the I/O bus from the processor-memory bus in order to accommodate the faster speeds. These designs differed dramatically, and a consequence was often hardware and software incompatibility. Some designs required unique versions of operating system software. Other systems could not use some expansion boards that were designed for the PC and the AT bus because of their unique timing characteristics.

A Controversial Decision

IBM's response to this chaotic environment was the development from ground zero of a whole new bus architecture, later called Micro Channel architecture. However, this solution was not chosen initially. IBM's engineers recognized the benefits of expansion board compatibility with the AT bus and attempted to extend it to a 32-bit bus with an 8-bit and 16-bit subset so that the PC and AT expansion boards could be used. This solution was very similar to the way the AT bus extended the old PC bus. As we saw in the previous chapter, this type of solution added additional signals to the original 8-bit design in order to accommodate the 16-bit capabilities of the processor. The bus was speeded up to increase the effective data rate.

IBM's initial attempt at 32-bit extensions produced some woeful shortcomings. First, the complexity of the design proposed was not amenable to microcomputers at that time because of the cost. In addition, the price of compatibility would prevent full utilization of the technology available at that time and would throttle future enhancements. There were also some significant engineering problems in dealing with higher-speed microprocessors and components that the grounding scheme of the AT connectors exacerbated. However, the greatest concerns were the shortcomings in the reliability and data integrity characteristics of the AT bus in demanding business and technical environments, especially in multitasking and multi-user applications.

These characteristics were part of the baggage that AT compatibility carried with it. The challenges of this new environment were not limited to that of the 32-bit bus, however. The rate of change of technology as well as the anticipated longevity of 16-bit I/O devices required a broader solution.

The possibility of a new bus architecture was very exciting (and controversial) inside IBM. The engineering crowd saw it as a chance to add substantial improvements to the original PC and AT bus. Starting from "scratch" would also provide the opportunity to have a real information transfer architecture with first-class documentation. The earlier systems had limited specifications on such critical parameters as timings and power. Other developers had approximated the requirements in their designs, but there were many timing errors that occasionally showed up in the form of system hangs, resulting in lost data.

The inventors loved the idea of a new bus and found the new architecture to be a fertile environment for their creative skills. IBM's marketing divisions also perceived its value. After seeing market share eroding rapidly due to the PC and AT "clones," systems that offered something unique were very intriguing. According to a *Wall Street Journal* report quoting Dataquest, a market research firm, IBM's participation in the IBM-compatible market had fallen from 70 percent in 1982 to about 45 percent in 1986. The engineers also believed that the new designs would be harder for competitors to copy.

The idea of a new bus was also very appealing to the developers of OS/2, a multitasking operating system that was under development at the same time by IBM and Microsoft®. As was discussed in the last chapter, the 80286 and i386 architecture made it possible to address a large amount of memory and partition it for multiple applications. However, its usefulness in AT class systems was limited, at best. A multitasking system increases the I/O activity substantially, and the proposed Micro Channel bus had many features that would exploit this environment.

Micro Channel architecture was thought to be so superior that IBM decided to bet their personal computer business on it. The plan was to announce all of the new models at one time for maximum marketing benefit. Older models would be replaced by the new ones and sold on an "as available" basis. The only products that would retain the original bus design were those based on the 8086 processor—the PS/2 Model 25 and Model 30 (Figure 2.3). This decision was made because the systems using the original bus were less expensive to build at that time. This market segment was also the most price-sensitive due to competition from numerous domestic and offshore clones. The decision to completely replace the old AT product line was so innovative that Dr. Fareena Sultan of the Harvard Business School, assisted by the author, has prepared a case study on the introduction and marketing of the PS/2 product line. (Case N9-590-026 is available by writing the Publishing Division, Harvard Business School, Boston, MA 02163.)

However, introducing a new bus architecture into a world in which many had standardized on the AT bus offered significant challenges. Customers had become accustomed to the old design, and the features of Micro Channel architecture were difficult to articulate. The systems were perceived by some as bringing no immedi-

Figure 2.3 The PS/2 Model 25 and Model 30 computers retained the original bus design. (Courtesy of International Business Machines Corporation)

ate benefits, costing a bit more, and being different. So the acceptance of Micro Channel systems by customers in the first months of introduction was mixed.

Worse, there were not many Micro Channel expansion boards available initially. The architecture was new and more complex than that of the earlier systems, making board development more difficult. In addition, the business opportunity for board developers was limited initially by the low number of systems sold, a classic "Catch-22" in the computer business. The AT-compatible world seemed to offer a safer opportunity for new product development at the time. Since so much of Micro Channel architecture's improved function and performance required add-in boards, the new architecture was slow in acceptance at first. The promise of enhanced functionality and performance benefits that relied on new board development got Micro Channel architecture off to a very slow beginning. It took additional development time with a concentrated focus by IBM on the external developer community with an eye on new customer requirements to deliver the advantages of the new architecture.

Another reason for the slow start was the delay in the development of OS/2. The original plan was that OS/2 would be available when the new systems were announced. However, the first release of OS/2 was actually shipped several months later. The initial offering included only the base operating system without the Presentation Manager™ (OS/2's graphical user interface) and the communications, data base, and LAN management capabilities that make up OS/2 Extended Edition. Many of the advantages of Micro Channel architecture awaited the multitasking operating system to show them off.

The slow start gave way to eventual acceptance. With the increase in PS/2 system sales, the slow but steady growing acceptance of OS/2, the availability of advanced function Micro Channel expansion boards, and the use of the architecture in other system families (for example, the IBM RISC System/6000 products), the promise envisioned by IBM for Micro Channel architecture is being fulfilled today. It has offered some of the most exciting opportunities for new product development in the history of microcomputers. Chapters 4 and 5 describe some of these products.

MICRO CHANNEL PERSPECTIVES

As we learned in the previous chapter, Micro Channel architecture is a true channel architecture, not just another I/O bus design. The name, **Micro Channel Architecture,** coined by Chet Heath, one of its developers, was chosen because of this.

The IBM Corporation has three strategic information transfer architectures to go with its three primary families of computers. The first is the System 360/370/390™ I/O channel architecture for host computers. This architecture was originally developed in the early 1960s. The second is that used by IBM's mid-range systems, such as the AS/400® and the ES/9370™ systems, whose roots lie in the IBM System/34™. The third is the Micro Channel architecture in IBM's

Personal System/2 computers, technical workstations, and low-end mainframe products.

There are a number of similarities among these three architectures. In 1964, the 1401 Series gave way to the IBM System/360. It was a transition from a single tasking to a multitasking operating environment. In 1974, the same transition occurred in the world of minicomputers from the IBM System/3™ to the multitasking System/34. In 1987, the transition to Micro Channel architecture began. All three are designed to perform work simultaneously and with a high degree of reliability, availability, and serviceability in multitasking and multi-user applications. They are highly extendible architectures that have been designed to take advantage of technology advances and new applications over a long period of time. Each architecture is uniquely suited to its application environment due to a number of factors ranging from software considerations to the number of users supported. However, there are a number of intersections that Micro Channel architecture provides. Later in this book, you will be introduced to a Micro Channel system that is capable of running VM/370™ applications, for example.

Several years of effort went into the development of Micro Channel architecture. All known bus and channel concepts were evaluated, and the best features and design elements of each were incorporated into the architecture. A fundamental goal was to provide a set of basic functions that would allow the easy addition of advanced functions as user requirements change. Maximum flexibility, system longevity, and architectural endurance were key objectives used by the architects.

IBM gambled a multibillion dollar business on the value of Micro Channel architecture. The entire future of microcomputers and larger systems has been altered as a result of its introduction. Let's find out why.

WHAT IS MICRO CHANNEL ARCHITECTURE?

Micro Channel architecture consists of three distinct buses, their associated signals, and additional control signals. The three buses are the address bus, the data bus, and the arbitration bus. The basic architecture provides address and data path widths from 8 to 32 bits. The address bus provides a method of addressing up to 4 GB of memory. Three types of "bus owners," or masters, are supported, including the system microprocessor (or **system master**, as it is called in Micro Channel parlance), a DMA controller, and a bus master. Both synchronous and asynchronous data transfer procedures between a controlling master and memory or I/O devices are supported. Improved methods of interrupt handling and DMA procedures are provided. A programmable procedure for system configuration, called **Programmable Option Select**, is also included. The architecture includes an expansion bus with improved electromagnetic compatibility characteristics with optional video and matched-memory extensions. A programmable procedure for system configuration is provided. An optional procedure provides for 64-bit data transfers. Also included are procedures for reporting exception conditions and optional address and data parity support. Audio signal transfer support is also provided.

The primary features of the architecture are summarized below:

- An arbitration procedure that provides for bus ownership for up to 16 masters, one of which must be the system master.
- Memory and I/O data transfers of 8, 16, 24, or 32 bits.
- Synchronous and asynchronous procedures for information transfers between masters and slaves.
- Memory addressability of up to 16 MB in 24-bit address width implementations and up to 4 GB in 32-bit address width implementations. I/O addresses up to 64 KB are supported.
- A direct memory access (DMA) procedure with multiple channels, channel flexibility, and burst data transfers.
- A flexible system configuration procedure called Programmable Option Select that uses programmable registers on devices.
- Level-sensitive interrupt handling and interrupt sharing at all levels.
- An expansion bus interface with provisions for 16- and 32-bit connectors. The 16-bit connector supports a 24- bit address bus and a 16-bit data bus. The 32-bit connector supports a 32-bit address bus and 32-bit data bus.
- Optional extensions to the 16-bit and 32-bit connector for video and matched-memory.
- Improved electromagnetic compatibility characteristics.
- An optional procedure that enables 64-bit data transfers and faster 16-bit and 32-bit transfer rates.
- Optional address and data parity support.
- A procedure for reporting exception conditions.
- Audio signal transfer support used to drive signals to the system audio output and between devices.

Got all that? If you looked in the Micro Channel architecture document, you would find a similar list. (About this time, you're probably thinking this book is for the "technoweenies" and you shouldn't have bought it!) It probably raises more questions than it answers. For example, what's new? How does it differ from the AT bus? What do these features mean to you and to your application? What's the big deal about Micro Channel architecture? What good is it? The remainder of this chapter focuses on these questions. Let's return to a more down- to-earth discussion and examine these features in terms of their benefits. (Technoweenies, stand by. You'll get your chance in the next chapter.)

FEATURES AND BENEFITS OF MICRO CHANNEL ARCHITECTURE

Remember the list of characteristics of the ideal architecture described in Chapter 1? How Micro Channel architecture measures up to these criteria offers a good way to describe its features and benefits. For convenience, the list is recreated below:

Computer Architecture Characteristics *

Affordability	Flexibility
Compatibility	Industry Acceptance
Data Integrity	Investment Protection
Ease of Use	Performance
Expandability	RAS Characteristics
Extendibility	

* Not Prioritized

We'll save the important prioritizing of this list for later. Right now, let's just look at Micro Channel's features that apply to each item. We may as well begin with affordability since it is at the top of the list.

Affordability

One of the most significant aspects of Micro Channel architecture is that its advantages are not limited to 32-bit systems and 32-bit devices. Micro Channel architecture defines an 8- and a 16-bit subset for the data path and a 24-bit subset for the address path. What this means is that lower-cost systems and boards can be built that conform to the architecture. Low-cost 286 and 386SX™ systems are available that share in the advantages of this advanced bus architecture. The large number of systems and their available expansion slots drives systems and expansion board prices lower because of the economies of scale in manufacturing. In addition, those users who do not need 32-bit functionality don't have to pay for it.

There are additional factors that make Micro Channel systems more affordable, however. The real cost of a system is related to the number of years of useful life for your system and is best expressed by the following formula:

REAL COST PER YEAR = (PP+ME+SE+OE-RV)/YR
Where PP = Purchase Price
ME = Total Maintenance Expenses
SE = Total Support and Training Expenses
OE = Total Operating Expenses
RV = Resale Value
YR = Years of useful life for your application

Of course, there are a number of other factors that are not included, such as the return on your investment, the productivity increases provided by the system, the tax treatment of the asset, the interest on the money if you hadn't bought it, and so on. But this formula is adequate for our purposes. This is similar to the logic that you would use if you were buying an automobile or almost any major purchase.

As you will learn later in this chapter, Micro Channel systems have a longer system life because they are upgradeable and flexible. The effect is to increase the number of years of useful life for a given system and to enhance its resale value. There are also certain features that reduce service costs, increase reliability, and decrease operating costs. Micro Channel systems also have some ease-of-use features such as automatic setup that reduce support requirements. These characteristics are described later in this chapter.

Compatibility

The short-term and long-term compatibility over a range of system designs and software is one of the most important characteristics of a computer architecture. Architecture provides the foundation for compatibility and commonality in structure and design. There are several aspects that are important in defining the compatibility to an architecture. Let's begin with software compatibility.

Software Compatibility

Compatibility considerations can be divided into hardware and software factors. Of the two, software compatibility is far more important, since the development of application software usually requires considerably more time and resource than does hardware. Far more important, however, is the effect of software incompatibility on the end user. If existing programs don't run on new systems, neither they nor the new hardware have any value. A good place to begin a discussion on Micro Channel's software compatibility is with its implementation in PS/2s.

The PS/2 implementation of Micro Channel architecture is compatible with PC and AT software. The old BIOS (referred to as the **compatibility BIOS or CBIOS**[3]) is present even though the underlying hardware is substantially different. PS/2s incorporate the AT BIOS (which was already compatible with earlier PC and XT BIOSs). CBIOS provides upward compatibility from the PC, XT, and AT. Strictly speaking, the system BIOS is not part of Micro Channel architecture, however. Non-PS/2 Micro Channel systems must have a completely different BIOS and hardware device drivers to compensate for their differences.

What is important is that the software architecture is independent of the bus architecture in Micro Channel systems. This leads into a discussion about DMA channel assignments and other more technical topics. Let's reserve this until we get to Chapter 4.

Micro Channel architecture is a processor-independent architecture. This means that applications that were designed to run on microprocessors other than the Intel series can also run in Micro Channel systems if they have the appropriate microprocessor installed. As a consequence, Micro Channel systems make it possible to run a broader range of software applications than earlier systems. For

[3]IBM PS/2 Micro Channel systems also have an advanced BIOS (ABIOS) designed for the OS/2 operating system.

example, it is possible to run applications requiring a Motorola 68020 processor on a PS/2 by installing one along with the appropriate software.

Another important aspect of software compatibility is future compatibility. In the past, in order to take advantage of advances in software, the underlying hardware had to be changed. In most cases, this required replacing the system. There are several features of Micro Channel systems that will allow them to take advantage of software advances. An example of one of these features is the ability to use the capabilities of a 32-bit operating system like OS/2 Version 2.0 when it becomes available. Additional elements providing future software compatibility are procedures that are supported by Micro Channel architecture. These will be discussed in depth in Chapter 3.

AT Board Compatibility

In terms of hardware compatibility, Micro Channel systems cannot use older PC/XT/AT expansion boards. Engineers found that there was absolutely no way to maintain this compatibility without sacrificing many of the other attributes of the ideal computer architecture. IBM considered the importance of this backward compatibility in deciding to make this compromise. One study conducted by DataQuest indicated that very few boards are transferred from an older system to a newer one (Figure 2.4). Approximately 98 percent of the time, the boards remain with the system they were purchased for. In most businesses, PCs and ATs are moved, with their cards intact, to other users whose needs can be met by those systems.

Many of the add-in boards for PC/XT/AT systems provided functions such as video, printer and serial ports, and diskette and fixed disk controllers that are built into today's systems. In addition, most newer systems accommodate adequate memory on the system board and do not require memory expansion cards. Many older cards are 8-bit devices or use obsolete memory and logic technology, making them exact a performance penalty in newer systems.

When Micro Channel systems were first introduced, the lack of availability of new boards called attention to the problem. This was especially the case with third-party boards that provided specialty functions and communications adapters. As a glaring example of this problem, the absence of Ethernet™ boards for the new systems prevented their acceptance by many businesses. Admittedly, if the new systems could have used the older boards, this problem would not have surfaced. Fortunately, the eventual industry acceptance of Micro Channel architecture rectified the lack of board availability. Almost every conceivable function is now available for Micro Channel systems, as well as many cards that offer unique bus master capabilities that the earlier systems could not provide.

Another problem that exacerbated the lack of board compatibility was the prices for the new cards. Immediately after the introduction of the first systems, there was a limited, captive market for those few developers that provided boards. In addition, the low initial demand did not provide any significant "economy of scale" for large-scale manufacturing. Micro Channel adapters, having additional functions and signals, were also more expensive to make. Because of the lower board

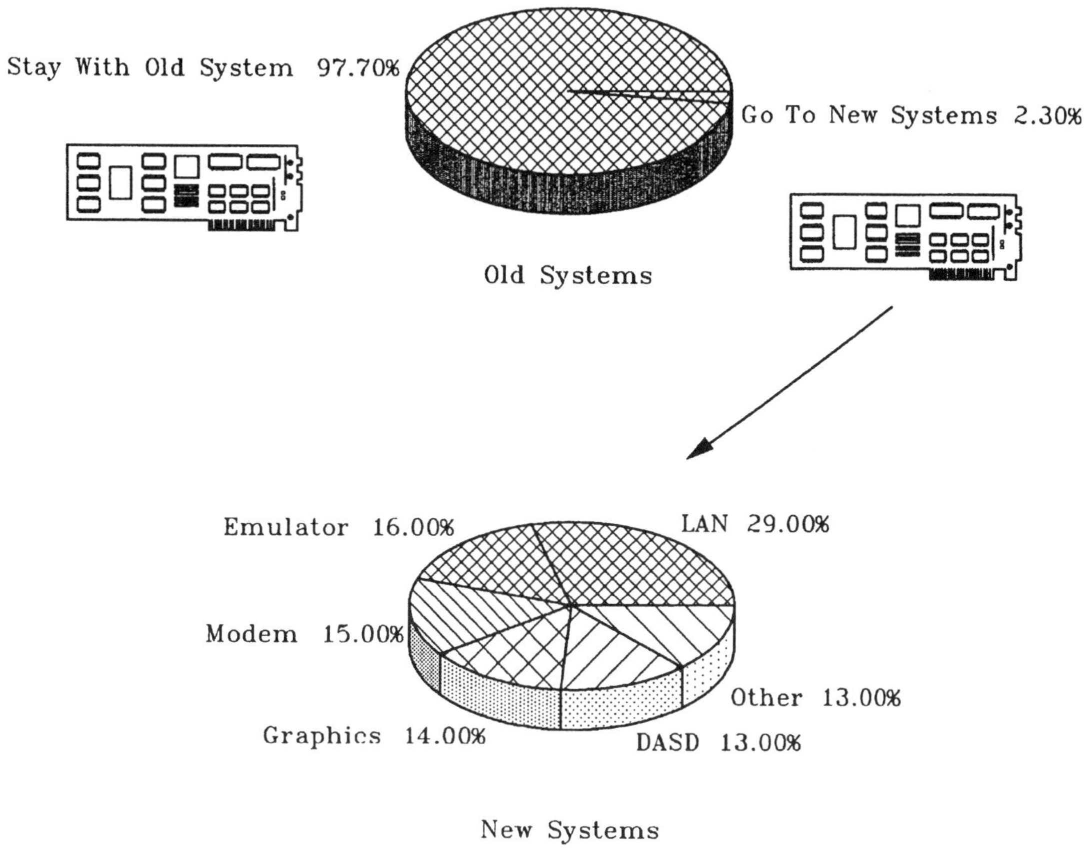

Figure 2.4 Only a small fraction of expansion boards are transferred from older systems to newer systems, according to this Dataquest study.

real estate, manufacturers were forced to squeeze function using large scale integration. However, the price differential between AT and Micro Channel boards has essentially disappeared.

Micro Channel Board Compatibility

Now that we've discussed AT board compatibility, let's move on to Micro Channel compatibility. The very first requirement for compatibility is that all new Micro Channel systems in a family must be able to use previous expansion boards. This degree of compatibility was possible for AT systems as long as the differences were small, but prevented any substantial enhancements, such as higher speed buses.

As was described in Chapter 1, the Micro Channel bus is asynchronous. This characteristic provides flexibility and maximizes the life of the architecture and the systems based upon it. For example, the architecture is not dependent on a given processor speed or logic technology. Micro Channel systems may have some internal dependencies related to the components used in their particular design. However, these dependencies are not extended to expansion boards that share the bus.

Micro Channel's asynchronous structure permits a wide latitude in the timing characteristics of adapters. Older, slower Micro Channel adapters can be accommodated on future buses with much faster cycle times. A mixture of attachment devices running at a wide range of speeds can be accommodated in a single system.

Another important feature associated with compatibility is the fact that the architecture provides an expansion board connector design that can be used in both 16-bit and 32-bit slots. What this means is that a developer has the flexibility to build a 32-bit adapter that is functional in 16-bit systems (as a 16-bit device). In terms of the 8-bit capability, it also allows for 8-bit devices to reside on the buses that are compatible with 16-bit and 32-bit transfers. This widens the range of Micro Channel systems from the most advanced down to very low-priced systems.

A 16-bit expansion board can be inserted into either a 16- or 32-bit Micro Channel slot. Any adapter can be inserted into a 32-bit slot, even those that include special features such as the streaming data or matched-memory capabilities. (These special slots will be discussed later.)

Another interesting compatibility feature lies in the architecture's extension to IBM's larger and more powerful systems beyond the desktop. Here, upward physical compatibility is the rule, but many higher function adapter cards will be built that can also be used in the Personal System/2 environment. In some advanced systems, there are some system-specific boards that exceed the power and physical dimensions of the PS/2. These boards are limited to those special systems. Their functions are not appropriate for the general microcomputer environment. For example, some of these boards are built for manufacturing control equipment by IBM's Manufacturing Systems Products organization.

There is only one Micro Channel architecture that is defined by the IBM Corporation, although there are a range of implementation possibilities. There is no "Micro Channel II," a term that is sometimes used by the trade press and consultants. However, it is possible to implement subsets of its features and functions. There are some advanced features that future systems and boards may have that older systems and boards may not have. Some examples of these optional features are higher speed data transfers and data and address parity support. In this case, future systems and expansion boards will communicate with older boards at the level of the older boards. For older systems with newer expansion boards, the capability will be at the level of the older systems. In the case of two newer boards in older systems, advanced functions are possible between the two newer boards if their design permits. These relationships are summarized in Table 2.2.

It is important for an architecture to first provide new function and then grow as technology and applications change. The anticipated capability for future

TABLE 2.2 COMPATIBILITY RELATIONSHIPS IN MICRO CHANNEL SYSTEMS AND EXPANSION BOARDS

	Current Boards	**Future Boards**
Current Systems	Yes (Current Function)	Yes (Current Function)
Future Systems	Yes (Current Function)	Yes (Advanced Function)
Current Boards	Yes (Current Function)	Yes (Current Function)
Future Boards	Yes (Current Function)	Yes (Advanced Function)

implementations that are able to take advantage of such changes is the most important compatibility provision that an architecture can provide. Micro Channel architecture does this. In contrast, all other extensions of the AT architecture have either introduced a degree of incompatibility for existing cards or have sacrificed future growth for AT compatibility.

Data Integrity Features

A lot of people would place data integrity at the top of their list of requirements for a computer architecture. If your data is not secure, if information can be lost in transfer on the bus, or if your system hangs frequently, a fundamental requirement of computer architecture is not being met. This is the one area that Micro Channel architects singled out for particular focus. In terms of architectural priorities, data integrity was at the top of IBM's list.

There are three things that can go wrong in transferring data across a bus. The information could be sent to the wrong address, you could end up with missing or extra bits of data, or you could get a failure in the execution of an instruction. The data integrity features of Micro Channel architecture are designed to prevent the corruption of data and ensure that the information goes to the proper address and that instructions get executed correctly. The architecture has the capability to signal that a data integrity problem has occurred—called **exception condition reporting** procedures.

An indirect measure of the data integrity characteristics of computer systems is their **error rates.** An error has occurred when a system reset must be performed, when the system must be powered down and restarted, or is otherwise irrecoverable by any other measure. Most of us refer to this condition as a **system hang.** A system hang is one of the possible responses to an exception condition.

A recoverable error occurs when the system retries an operation and is successful. An example of a recoverable error is reading a diskette drive several times. In most cases, you are unaware of these retries unless you get a failure. (Sometimes the sound of a drive's multiple retries can get your attention, however.)

Errors can result from a variety of causes in either a system's hardware or software. A **failure** occurs when an error is irrecoverable, and a repair action may be required. An example of a failure condition is the familiar "General Failure Reading Drive A" message that your diskette drive may give you. The number of failures is a measure of the hardware reliability of systems.

There are five general provisions for data integrity in Micro Channel architecture: improved interrupt handling, improved electromagnetic compatibility, timing specifications, data and address parity, and exception condition reporting.

Improved Interrupt Handling

As you may recall from Chapter 1, an interrupt is a request for service by an I/O device. It initiates what is called an interrupt service routine, which is a BIOS program that the microprocessor executes to provide the requested service. Micro Channel systems provide a new method of handling interrupts that prevents the old problem of the loss of real interrupts and misinterpretation of false interrupts. The new method uses a signal level rather than a signal edge (as did the PC the XT, and the AT) on the device's assigned interrupt-request line to send an interrupt to the processor. The newer level-sensitive interrupt handling is a method of detecting interrupts that requires a bit on the device to remain active until it is serviced. In the older edge-triggered interrupt method, the interrupt request is a transient or momentary event that must be detected on the edge of the signal and can easily be lost.

The benefit of Micro Channel's level-sensitive method is that the signal from the I/O device stays active until it is serviced, thus preventing lost interrupts or false interrupts that generally appear as transient events or noise. Level-sensitive interrupt handling is used in IBM's larger systems and other advanced computers. The relationship between edge-triggered and level-sensitive interrupt handling is shown in Figure 2.5. The consequence of lost interrupts can be loss of data. The consequence of false interrupts may be a system hang in extreme case.

A good analogy comes from Tikiri Wanduragala of IBM Europe. Think of a situation where a person has two telephones at his desk (representing two interrupting devices). If the telephones operated like edge-triggered interrupts, they would only ring once. That would be okay if one phone rang after the other because the person could answer one at a time. However, if both phones were ringing at the same time, one of the calls could be lost if no one answered. If the phones operated like level-sensitive interrupts, they would keep ringing constantly until they were answered. There would be no chance of missing a call (or an interrupt in our analogy).

Level-sensitive interrupt handling is a much more reliable method because of the reduced electrical noise susceptibility. In addition, it reduces hardware re-

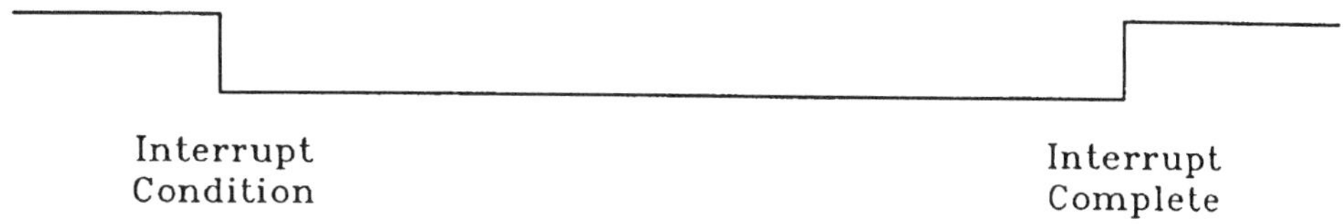

- ☐ Interrupt request signal active until completion.
- ☐ More than one device may share the same interrupt request line.
- ☐ Hardware/Software Interlock.

Figure 2.5 Level-sensitive interrupt handling.

quirements because it required less logic to implement. A detailed discussion of the Micro Channel's interrupt-handling procedure is contained in the next chapter.

Improved Electromagnetic Compatibility

Improved **electromagnetic compatibility (EMC)** is the second provision for superior data integrity. The air in an office or home is filled with a great deal of electrical noise that can interfere with the operation of computers. Computers can also generate noise that can interfere with the operation of devices such as television sets and other computers (Figure 2.6). In addition, devices within a computer can interfere with each other due to the generation of electrical noise and cross-talk.

Electromagnetic compatibility is tested and regulated rigidly by the Federal Communications Commission (FCC) in the United States and by comparable agencies in other countries. The degree of electromagnetic compatibility is rated in classes relating to the usage environment in which systems may be operated. FCC Class A covers office use. IBM's PS/2s, as well as IBM's earlier personal computers, were rated for home use, the more sensitive FCC Class B, since so many systems are used in home offices or are brought home on occasion. This is an extremely sensitive test that provides one of the greatest engineering challenges in the development of systems.

Susceptibility to electrical noise increases error rates. This means there is a

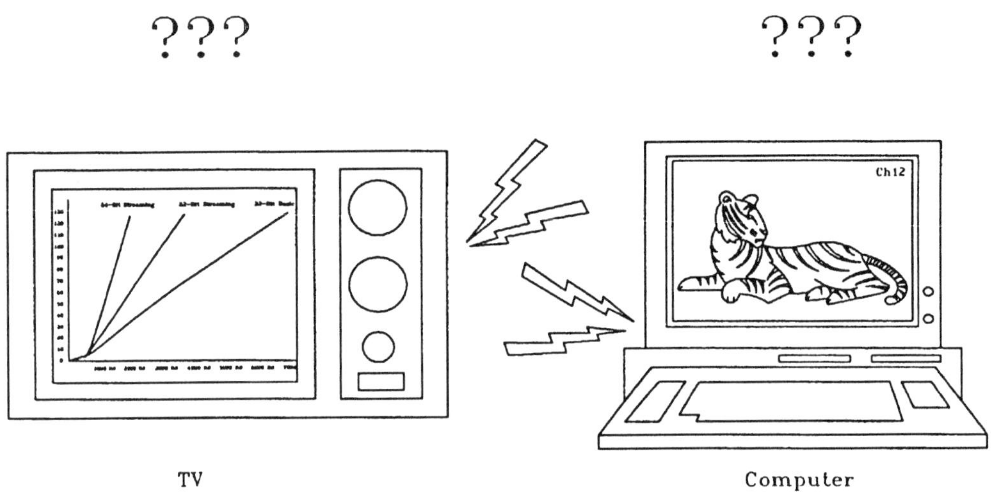

Figure 2.6 Electromagnetic compatibility includes emissions as well as susceptibility to RF radiation.

possibility of lost data (system hangs) in the case of irrecoverable errors or a reduction in throughput in the case of recoverable errors. Internal or external electromagnetic interference can conceivably result in data corruption in the form of missing or extra bits.

One of IBM's customers related a story that he had several ATs located near a bank of elevators that were experiencing numerous system hangs. When he replaced these systems with PS/2s, the problem went away. Admittedly, this was an extreme case that exceeded normal electromagnetic conditions, but the improvement was evident.

This improvement in electromagnetic compatibility is due to the superior design of the Micro Channel connectors. The way the connectors are designed and grounded is one of the most significant factors in reducing electromagnetic interference. Every fourth pin in Micro Channel connectors is a grounding pin, as shown in Figure 2.7. Grounding draws electromagnetic radiation away from other wires that can act like little antennae. In addition, the Micro Channel connectors are smaller than those of the AT, which reduces the radiating area. The PC, the XT, and the AT used the card bracket as a grounding conduit for stray electromagnetic radiation to the metal frames and covers. Its effectiveness depended on how well the card bracket screw was tightened, a chancy arrangement at best. Micro Channel connectors are isolated from the rear bracket, which limits their electromagnetic susceptibility as well as reducing stray radiation. The card bracket is not part of the grounding scheme. A plastic handle insulates the card from any contact with the cover, further preventing a current loop that could create increased emissions.

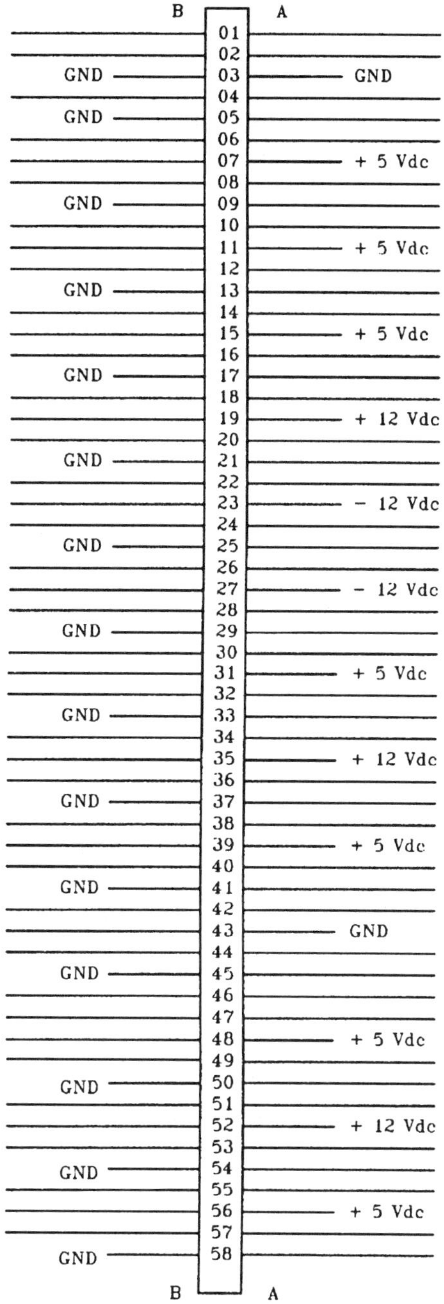

Figure 2.7 Power and ground pin distribution in Micro Channel connectors. The numerous power and ground pins improve the EMC characteristics.

Micro Channel systems have a higher speed bus and support much higher speed microprocessors than the earlier systems. The superior EMC design provides for this increased activity as well as for future enhancements and even higher frequencies. This is important because electromagnetic activity is proportional to the square of the frequency and to the current flowing in the system. These relationships of design follow the relationship:

$$E = KAIF^2$$

where

E is the radiation,

K is a constant,

A is the cross-sectional area of the conducting surface,

I is current, and

F is the frequency.

The superior EMC characteristics of the Micro Channel bus are becoming more and more important as the speed of components and microprocessors increase. Today, the norm for 386 and 486 technology is 25–33 MHz. Microprocessor frequencies of over 200 MHz by the end of the decade are predicted, which will make electromagnetic compatibility one of the greatest challenges (and expense) of developing computers.

Timing Specifications

The third feature of Micro Channel architecture that adds to its data integrity is its well-specified timings. These timings, along with detailed diagrams, are contained in IBM's technical reference manuals. Some of these are also included in the appendix of this book. These detailed specifications are designed to prevent timing errors. When information does not reach its destination in a specified amount of time, a timing error can occur that generates what is called a **nonmaskable interrupt,** or **NMI.** You guessed it. The outward manifestation of this is a system hang. Timings were not documented very well for the PC, the XT, and the AT systems. Developers basically determined what worked and then implemented it. However, because a combination of components may exhibit significant variations in their timing characteristics, timing errors due to their combined tolerances frequently resulted. The superior documentation of Micro Channel architecture greatly reduces the probability of timing errors and reduces the number of nonmaskable interrupts from timing errors.

Parity Features

With so much activity going on in today's systems and millions of bytes being transferred per second, did you ever wonder how a computer knows whether the right information was sent to the correct address? One method by which computers verify information transfers is called parity checking. Parity checking is common in larger systems, because the consequences of errors can affect large numbers of users and critical information (like your bank balance). Parity may be checked by examining the eight bits in a byte transferred, counting the number of ones, and sending a ninth bit (called the parity bit), which is a one if there is an even number of ones in the byte transferred. If the count of ones is an odd number, the ninth bit is a zero (Figure 2.8). If this convention is used, this is called odd parity. Even parity is just the opposite.

Micro Channel architecture has an optional feature that provides for address and data parity checking. Parity checking between the memory controller and memory is included in PS/2, of course, as it was on the PC, the XT and the AT systems. However, neither the PC nor the AT architecture had defined methods for address and data parity checking on the bus. Less sophisticated methods of data parity checking were sometimes used in the PC and the AT when they were required, such as doing two reads or writes, an obviously inefficient design that is software rather than hardware controlled.

In Micro Channel systems, address and data parity may be implemented on some devices and systems and not on others, depending on the usage requirements. For example, some devices do not require parity checking because a missing or extra bit may be inconsequential, such as a missing pixel on your display. Other devices may have extremely critical requirements such as encryption devices. The IBM RISC System/6000 systems, for example, have both address and data parity checking capabilities at the system level. In almost all modern computers, memory parity checking is implemented in order to ensure that the data and address in memory are valid.

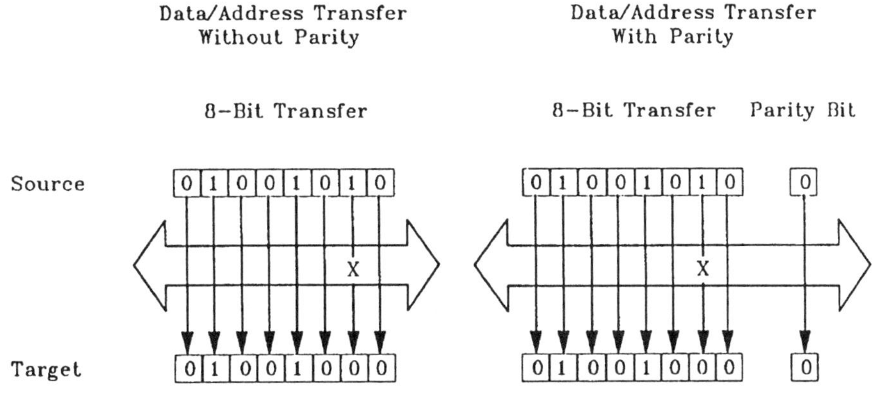

Figure 2.8 Micro Channel provides for address and data parity, using the odd parity convention. The target device counts the total number of '1' bits and determines that sum of the 9 bits is an even number—in orther words, a parity error has occurred.

Exception Condition Reporting

An exception condition is defined as an event that alters the normal flow of processing and procedures in a computer. Micro Channel architecture has a number of procedures for reporting the various kinds of exception conditions. One of these methods, called synchronous exception condition reporting, is able to detect the exact cycle and the participants involved in which the problem occurred. Because of this, it is possible to simply repeat that cycle and recover the information that would have otherwise been lost because a system reset would have been required.

A feature called **Programmable Option Select,** or **POS,** is a key part of the exception condition reporting procedures. Each device attached to the bus is identified and controlled by its POS number. In addition, each device attached to the bus has an exception condition indicator, which allows the source of parity errors to be identified. The failing device can be disabled and another enabled through the use of POS, a capability important for fault-tolerant applications. A complete discussion of Micro Channel's data and address parity features and exception condition reporting is included in Chapter 4.

Ease-of-Use and Ergonomic Features

POS is also used to set up systems automatically, an important ease-of-use feature. In the PC, the XT, and the AT systems, the user had to manually set a collection of switches located on the expansion boards and the system board in order to install feature cards (Figure 2.9). These switches controlled the use of system resources. For example, the interrupt request lines, the DMA channels, or the memory address range are selected by setting these switches. The number of switches required and their possible combinations became unmanageable as configurations became more and more complex.

In Micro Channel systems, a simple software program, resident on the system's reference diskette, replaces the switches. This is a far simpler procedure, and one that avoids erroneous combinations that could conceivably result in system or card damage. Each type of Micro Channel device is assigned a unique identification number by IBM. This identification number and other required information is included on the setup diskette shipped with the device. During installation, this information is copied to the reference diskette, which is where the software program for automatic configuration resides.

Potentially, one of the most important ease-of-use features for Micro Channel systems is their audio capabilities. The use of voice in personal computers is still in its infancy. Micro Channel systems have a complete audio subsystem that provides for the transfer of near-FM sound quality. This is a separate bus that allows the simultaneous transfer of audio with other data. Potentially, this is part of a solution for a new set of multimedia applications that will make computers much easier to use. For example, voice-driven training tools will be of enormous benefit in the educational environment. Other possibilities are application programs that replace error messages with audible warnings or provide vocal help features. Text-to-speech conversion is an example of an application using this capability today.

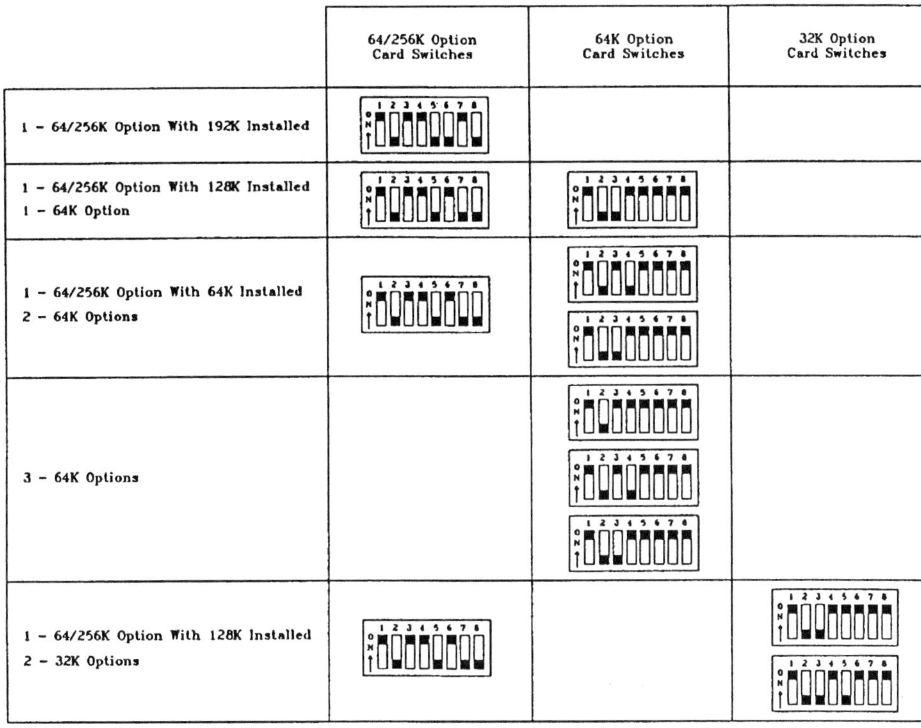

Figure 2.9 The PC and AT boards required DIP switches set in various combinations to assign system resources.

The ergonomic benefits of Micro Channel systems are due to their smaller size and reduced noise. Smaller desktop systems facilitate the convenient positioning of systems and displays, helping reduce back and eye strain. Another ergonomic feature of Micro Channel systems indirectly related to the architecture is their lower internal temperature and reduced system noise. Since Micro Channel systems generally require less power (due to their increased use of VLSI and lower power of expansion boards), a smaller cooling fan (the biggest noise source) can be used. Even though the power specifications are system dependent and may be higher for larger Micro Channel systems, the design implemented in IBM's PS/2 systems have low power requirements and generate much less noise than did the Personal Computer AT. While not technically part of the architecture, their huge numbers effectively drive a de facto standard.

Expandability

When you think of expandability, the first thing you think of is the number of expansion slots in your system. Expansion slots have been used to add functionality since the introduction of the very first PC. The number of slots is one measure of the expandability of a system. However, it is more of an implementation characteristic rather than an architectural limitation. The number of slots is usually chosen to match the application environment of the system. For example, single-user applications do not generally have the same requirements as multi-user applications. Some applications place a premium on small system size, which limits the number of possible slots.

In the context of an architectural characteristic, the term expandability is used in two ways. First of all, the maximum number of devices that an architecture can support is a measure of its expandability. The available system resources and their flexibility defines the number of the various types of devices and the combinations that are allowed. The second measure of expandability is the functionality per device that is supported by the architecture. Devices that are capable of several functions or the management of extensive I/O subsystems certainly add to a system's expansion characteristics.

Micro Channel architecture makes it possible to support a much larger number of devices of various types and combinations than did the AT architecture by increasing the available system resources. The system resources include the number of interrupt levels, the memory address and I/O address space, the number of DMA channels, and the number of available arbitration levels available for potential "bus owners."

In the AT, there were 11 interrupt levels available for devices. In most cases, this meant that there could only be 11 interrupting devices. Micro Channel systems also have 11 interrupt levels available for use, but the number of interrupting devices supported is much greater than 11. This is due to the ability to have more than one interrupting adapter per interrupt request line, a capability provided by level-sensitive interrupt handling. In this method, each interrupting device posts an interrupt-pending bit that does not go away until it is serviced as described earlier. In the PC and AT, each interrupting adapter required a dedicated interrupt request line to prevent lost interrupts because of their edge-triggered interrupt handling.

The number of interrupt levels and how they can be used is a real limitation to expandability. The problem occurs when a program recognizes only one interrupt level but needs to control two devices requiring the same interrupt line. This occurs frequently when more than one device of the same type is installed in a system as in multiple serial or parallel devices or multifunction cards.

The amount of addressable memory allowed by Micro Channel architecture is up to four gigabytes in a 32-bit system, surely enough for most of us! Up to 65,536 I/O ports, each of which is one byte, is available. Each of these I/O ports are uniquely assigned to devices in a given system so that they do not require the same I/O address space. That should be enough to handle almost any conceivable number and combination of I/O devices!

Micro Channel systems generally have eight DMA channels available. However, there are also seven virtual channels available for use. The effect is to be able to support more DMA devices. Even more important than the number of DMA channels is the flexibility in their assignment. The bottom line is that DMA devices can pretty much use any channel. In the PC and AT, the assignments were fixed by either hardware or software requirements. In Chapter 4, there is a detailed discussion of the DMA procedures and channel assignments.

In terms of the number of arbitration levels, Micro Channel architecture allows for up to 16 different bus owners or masters. The multimaster capability provides the basis for the second dimension of expandability—the amount of function per device. It is in this context that Micro Channel architecture truly excels. Bus masters add functionality by enabling the efficient operation of extensive subsystems. An example is a storage subsystem in which multiple I/O devices can be attached to a single adapter card. Another example of this type of expansion is the use of a single slot to provide multiple RS-232 or RS-422 ports, such as is used in IBM's ARTIC card.

The subject of bus masters is so important that a large part of Chapter 4 is devoted to the subject. Numerous examples of large I/O subsystems are also described in Chapter 5.

Extendibility

One of the most powerful features of Micro Channel architecture is its extendibility. The ability to enhance the architecture by defining new procedures to increase performance or add function and retain compatibility with existing systems and adapters is extremely important for its longevity. In the original Micro Channel implementations, there were signals that were reserved for future functions. Most of these signals have since been defined.

In 1989, IBM announced the streaming-data procedures and other extensions to the architecture that provide additional capabilities. The streaming-data procedures double and redouble the data transfer rate of the Micro Channel bus. The architecture was also extended to include additional parity checking features and diagnostics capabilities. Detailed descriptions of these extensions are in Chapter 4.

In terms of future extensions, there are a number of signal combinations that remain undefined that can be used for future functions. IBM has not announced any plans for further extensions, however.

Flexibility

One of the most significant areas in which Micro Channel architecture has advantages over other advanced bus architectures is in its flexibility. Micro Channel architecture is a general information transfer bus that allows for the attachment of numerous devices and combinations of devices. It is an architecture that enables extensive subsystems for processors and I/O devices, but does not require them. It is not limited to one processor family, but may be utilized for generically unrelated processors or processors with variable frequencies. Because of its asynchronous design, it enables adapters to run faster or slower than the default cycle time of systems.

A closer look at this processor independence is of value here. Because of its capability to accept multiple bus masters and the latitude provided in assigning priority to these devices, Micro Channel architecture can be used with almost any processor type. One of the first examples of this processor independence utilizing bus masters was provided by the IBM 6152 Academic System (Figure 2.10). In this system, compatible applications could be run on the 80286 Intel microprocessor or on the RISC processor that resided on an expansion board. In the RISC mode, the system used IBM/4.3, a derivative of the Berkeley 4.3BSD operating system. In the PS/2 mode, the system was capable of running DOS or OS/2 applications.

This same processor independence also allows for higher speed processors to be installed. A system is not locked into the timing characteristics of the original CPU/Memory complex. For example, processor cards may range from 16-, 20-, 25-, and 33-MHz 386 implementations with their own memory and memory controllers. The application of Micro Channel architecture to the RISC System/6000 and the Enterprise System/9371 are also examples of the processor-independent nature of Micro Channel architecture. These implementations will be described in Chapter 5.

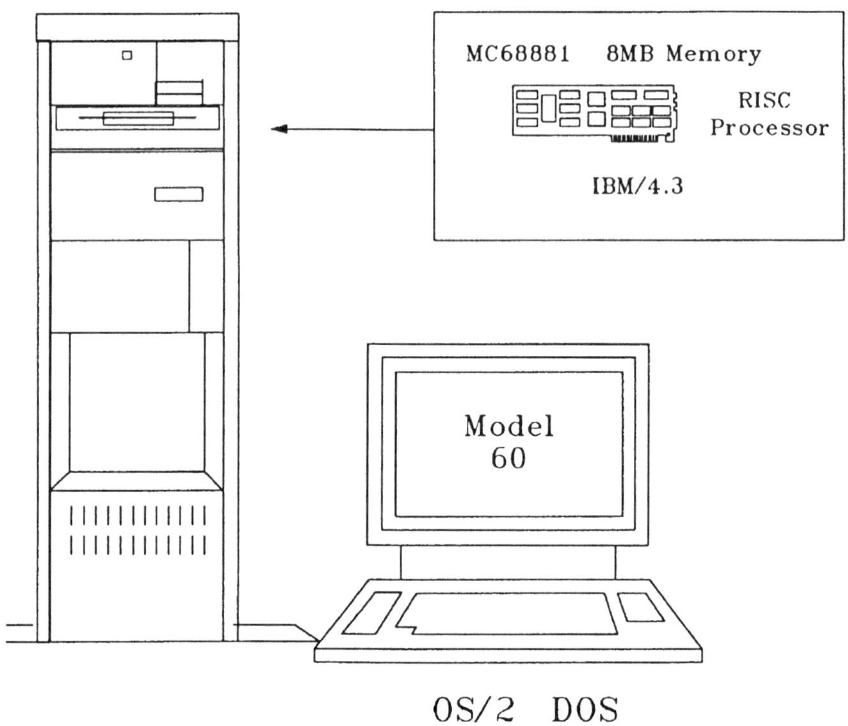

Figure 2.10 The IBM 6152 Academic System was one of the first applications of the bus master feature of Micro Channel architecture. The RISC processor on an expansion board and the system's 80286 made a broad range of applications available.

In terms of Micro Channel's asynchronous characteristics, timing flexibility for devices and bus cycle times is the chief recipient. Both slower and faster adapters can be accommodated without losing compatibility. This is important because the characteristics of the bus are not forever locked into the slowest card ever built.

Micro Channel architecture also provides increased flexibility in system configurations. In addition to ease-of-use, Programmable Option Select allows system resources to be assigned in such a way as to avoid conflicts between installed devices. What this accomplishes is the ability to put together combinations of devices that could not be coresident in the past. In the PC, the XT, and the AT systems, multiple devices of the same type were difficult, if not impossible, to configure in the same system. There were also numerous conflicts between communications adapters of different types and between communications and graphics adapters. In today's Micro Channel systems, these conflicts are resolved automatically using a convenient setup program and the Programmable Option Select feature.

Industry Acceptance

One of the most important requirements for any computer architecture in today's microcomputer environment is the degree of acceptance by third- party developers. This is the one area in which Micro Channel architecture got off to a rocky start. There are several explanations for this lack of early acceptance. Some of the reasons were based on the economic realities of the limited revenue and profit opportunities for board developers in the initial period of the PS/2 release. Other reasons for the slow start were related to some engineering and design difficulties experienced by the board developers that were due to the increased functionality and complexity of the new architecture and the smaller board size.

Perhaps the most important reason for the slow start was the industry momentum and inertia behind the AT board industry. The earlier systems spawned a huge industry that had grown steadily for several years. Hundreds of developers, large and small, offered products at affordable prices.

The "heads-down" developers inside IBM, however, had not focused a great deal of their attention to this industry during the development of the first Micro Channel systems in the 1985–1987 timeframe. As had been the case with earlier systems, IBM did not have an aggressive support program for these developers prior to the announcement of the new systems. There was no prototype board available as there had been for the PC and AT. There were no Micro Channel chip sets for the bus interface that developers could use. They were forced to develop their own if they wanted to participate. Some of the developers were also suspicious of IBM's motives in requiring an identification number for each expansion board. There was also a great deal of media confusion about IBM's licensing of the new architecture, such as whether the board developers would have to pay royalties to use the architecture.

A possible explanation for IBM's attitude lies in the environment inside IBM during the development of the Personal System/2 family. This was a period of extreme schedule pressure and constrained development resources. Prior to the

1987 introduction of the Micro Channel systems, several enhancements to the PC, the XT, and the AT were also under development. In addition, the development of an entire line of systems based on a new bus architecture with new graphics, keyboard, and BIOS, new storage devices and controllers, new frames and covers, and many other innovations was extremely challenging, even to IBM. This continued evolution of the earlier systems and development of the revolutionary new systems and the accompanying resource strains caused the IBM developers not to focus on the third-party hardware development community and their products.

The initial slow acceptance of the architecture by the industry and IBM's increasing awareness of the importance of the added value of third-party hardware developers' products spurred IBM to action. A new emphasis on marketing and technical support to encourage industry participation was launched in early 1988 and has been very successful. Micro Channel interface chips and bus master chips sets are now available to assist developers. The National Software Testing Laboratory (NSTL) has developed a certification procedure for compatibility testing of Micro Channel expansion boards and systems.

One of IBM's most innovative activities has been its informal "business partner" relations with developers, which have provided an opportunity for merchandising assistance ranging from listing products in a catalog published and distributed worldwide by IBM to joint sales activities.[4] Mr. Robert D. Lohman and members of his department in Boca Raton, Florida have been very successful in managing and encouraging these relationships. The result is that over 1,000 Micro Channel expansion boards with almost every imaginable function are available at competitive prices (Figure 2.11). The number of developers, both large and small, is large and growing and currently numbers almost 400. In addition, a substantial number of these developers are located outside the United States.

The economic opportunity for these companies is probably the largest driving force for the increased activity. The number of Micro Channel systems available from IBM and other manufacturers is now in the millions. Micro Channel architecture has opened up a new market for these developers by providing an opportunity for innovation in a high-tech, high-visibility, and high-demand market.

Another testimony to the industry acceptance of Micro Channel architecture is the number of "clones" available. Several of these are made by "first tier" companies known for building high-quality systems. Some of these systems have proprietary features that provide for product differentiation and marketing advantage. A partial list of the companies that have announced their intention to manufacture or are currently making Micro Channel systems is shown in Table 2.3. The range of companies, small to large, is quite broad. Some of these companies are also part of the EISA consortium which will be discussed later.

---

[4]This is an informal noncontractual association that is to the mutual benefit of IBM and other companies and is distinguished from the formal contractual relationship that IBM has with its dealers and other resellers.

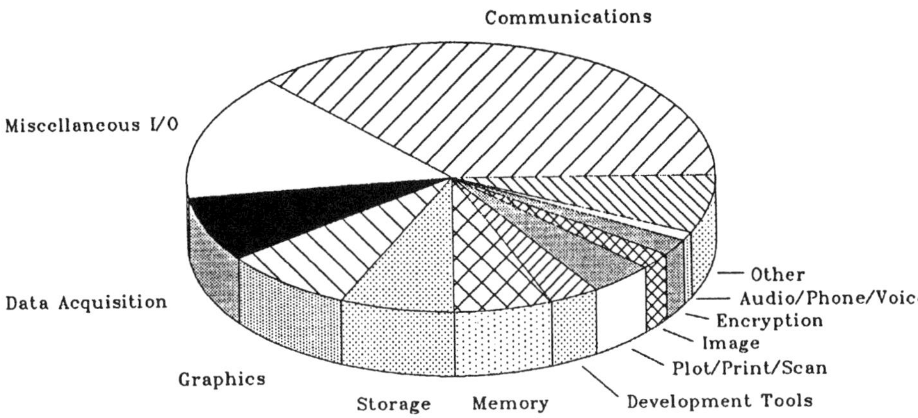

Figure 2.11 Micro Channel expansion board function distribution.

The degree of industry acceptance is related to how open an architecture is perceived to be. When IBM announced Micro Channel architecture, it was clear from the degree of documentation provided that it was intended to be an open architecture. There was no attempt by IBM to limit its use by IBM alone, which would have made it a proprietary architecture. The BIOS listings were not included in the reference manuals as had been the case with the earlier systems, but this was done not out of secrecy, but to encourage developers to use the "official" software interface instead of writing to the hardware directly.[5]

Perhaps the area of greatest misunderstanding about Micro Channel architecture has been in IBM's licensing policies. IBM has historically worn a "white hat" in its licensing practices with its competitors and other companies for many years and has had an open licensing practice for its inventions. Other companies in the industry, notably Apple Computer, have been exclusionary in terms of their licensing practices.

It is obvious that IBM's licensing practices have been open when you look at the number of PC, XT, and AT clones and Micro Channel manufacturers. The companies making these systems range from very small to some of the largest companies in the industry.

However, it was also clear that IBM did not intend to allow the use of its inventions without some consideration of its development expenses. IBM's licensing fees that related to personal computer inventions were raised from a maximum of 1 percent to 3 percent in 1987. The increase was designed to offset increased research and development expenses as a result of PS/2 development. Bill Lowe,

[5]As stated previously, the PS/2 BIOS is not considered part of Micro Channel architecture.

TABLE 2.3 MICRO CHANNEL SYSTEMS ANNOUNCEMENTS[1]

Acer
ALR
Apricot
Arche
Daewoo
Darius/Mission
First Class
Ferrante PLC
Grid
Handok
Memorex-Telex
Microdirect
Mitac
NCR
Normerel
Olivetti
Panasonic
Reply
Research Machines
Tandy
Wang
Wells American

All of the above are trademarks and/or registered trademarks of their respective companies.
[1]A partial list.

former president of the Entry Systems Division of IBM, explained that the increase was to "level the playing field" with other manufacturers using IBM's inventions in their products.

IBM's current licensing practices are the same for all of its inventions, regardless of the bus architecture involved. It is important to realize that IBM licenses inventions, not architectures. Many of the inventions apply equally to PC systems, AT systems, Micro Channel systems, and EISA systems.

IBM divides its patent portfolio into Category I and II patents. Currently, IBM charges a royalty of 1 percent of the selling price of systems for the use of the first Category I patent. Another 1 percent is charged for the use of all the remaining Category I patents that are used in the licensee's product. An additional 1 percent is charged for the use of each Category II patent. At this time, the only Category II that can be reasonably applied to Micro Channel systems is the Christiansen patent (U.S. Patent 3,812,475), which covers direct memory access. This patent conceivably affects any system that utilizes a DMA controller or any bus master. (A summary of IBM's patent licensing policy is included in Appendix I.)

An alternate method is based on the royalty portion selling price, defined as the selling price multiplied by the ratio of the sum of the manufacturing cost of its patented portions to the total manufacturing cost. The royalty in this method is 8 percent of the royalty selling price. The licensee has the choice of the two methods.

In practice, IBM has entered into cross-license agreements with some system manufacturers to produce Micro Channel machines. As has been the case in the past, IBM has exchanged intellectual property with other companies for the freedom to use their inventions and designs if a need has existed. There is generally a negotiated payment between the companies that relates to the relative value of the inventions to be cross-licensed. The beneficiaries of such licensing procedures are both the manufacturers and all of us that purchase these systems. An examination of the companies shown in Table 2.3 would indicate that IBM's approach has not been exclusionary to either small or large companies.

Further information on IBM's licensing practices may be obtained from the following source:

IBM Commercial Relations
2000 Purchase St.
Purchase, N.Y. 10577

Sometimes the protection of intellectual assets by large companies is perceived as being unfair and usurious. However, without the ability to protect intellectual property, it would be possible for other companies to utilize inventions without the research and development expenses associated with them. A company investing heavily in R & D would be at a serious disadvantage with those companies that used inventions without the appropriate royalty payments. If this were the case, a company would have no incentive to invest in R & D.

In 1989, in order to further encourage third-party development activity and to provide future directions, IBM announced enhancements to the architecture prior to their incorporation into products. This was done to provide developers with a road map for future development activities. Hardware specifications for these enhancements were also made available including the definition of reserved signals that will be used in future products.

Investment Protection

The rate of change in the computer industry is accelerating and technology is diversifying. Several of these changes were described in Chapter 1. The rate of change of microprocessor technology and the introduction of RISC technology into microcomputers are key factors in the "change equation." RISC technology generally increases the processing power of an order of magnitude compared to the traditional CISC technology. Memory density has been increasing dramatically as well, approximately doubling every three years. IBM has recently demonstrated 16-Mb memory chips. You can almost foresee the advent of gigabyte memory modules! As a result of these rapid changes, one of our greatest concerns today is the obsolescence of equipment.

In the past, in order to take advantage of technology changes, systems had to be replaced. Most of the replaced systems found new homes in the companies who owned them, serving users whose needs were less demanding. Some could still access newer systems over the company local area network. This philosophy is changing, however. Most white collar workers in the United States already have a personal computer today, so that the opportunity for shifting older systems to new users is not as great as before.

Another reason for the changing attitudes is that there are a lot more interactions and interrelationships among systems and applications than in the past. This drives a requirement for common functions and common capabilities. A coming example of this requirement will be in the conversion from 16-bit operating systems to 32-bit operating systems. Because of the added capabilities of the i386 microprocessor, such as the ability to run multiple concurrent DOS applications and 32-bit applications under OS/2 Version 2.0, an organization may wish for all users to have that capability. A CPU upgrade path would be highly desirable in this environment.

There is also a psychological aspect to the downgrade philosophy. Some people feel like second-class citizens in accepting an older system. Other people feel an attachment based on familiarity with their systems and really don't want to change.

There are four general areas in the architecture that are associated with prolonging the useful lives of these systems:

1. System master and other bus master upgrades;
2. Graphics upgrades;
3. Memory upgrades; and
4. Expansion board uniprocessor upgrades.

The first of these is the ability to upgrade the system master or provide enhanced processing capabilities by adding of a bus master. For example, a 10-MHz 286-based system may be upgraded to a 33-MHZ 386 system by adding the appropriate expansion board. This capability is quite different from that provided by the "turbo" cards for the previous systems that augmented, but could not functionally replace, the system master. Micro Channel architecture enables the bus master to have control of the system resources after the system has been initialized. The original microprocessor may be used for other purposes, such as supporting I/O functions, or it can be deactivated. The operating system can be run on any bus master installed in the system. Multiple bus masters may also be used to provide multiprocessor capability that can operate concurrently with the appropriate operating system and software support.

The second feature of the architecture that provides investment protection is the ease of graphics upgrades. The video extension is an optional feature that has been incorporated in PS/2 Micro Channel systems. This is an auxiliary connector attached to a special slot that is used to attach higher function graphics boards. This connector is used to access the graphics functionality that generally resides on the system board. This enables lower cost upgrades since the graphics circuitry on the system board does not have to be duplicated on the upgrade board. In prior designs, all the graphics functionality had to reside on the upgrade board. Its presence was required to maintain compatibility with the prior graphics standards such as CGA, EGA, and VGA.

The third investment-protection feature is associated with memory upgrades. Memory that resides on expansion boards in Micro Channel systems can be treated as part of the system memory. It is addressable by the system microprocessor in the same way as memory installed on the system board. This allows memory upgrades or memory expansion beyond the capabilities of the original system design, although there is a trend to have adequate system memory on the system board rather than have it installed on the Micro Channel bus. In the case of nonsystem memory additions, performance gains can be achieved through the use of memory cards that act as high-speed caches. This capability also permits bus masters attached to the Micro Channel bus to share part of this memory for increased functionality and performance.

The final investment-protection feature is that associated with expansion board design. Faster devices utilizing higher-speed logic will be available in the future as well as those using the streaming-data procedures described earlier. Expansion boards working with others of similar capabilities will be able to provide extremely high rates of data transfer to 32-bit systems whose cycle times are considerably higher than those of the older cards. In addition, almost all existing cards can be used in future systems, so their investment is also protected.

Performance

Micro Channel architecture provides many features designed for performance. As discussed in Chapter 2, the performance of a system is related to many factors ranging from the system processor, the information transfer bus, and the adapter and device driver implementation to the operating system. In this section, factors that affect performance related to Micro Channel architecture will be discussed. Micro Channel's wider data path, faster cycle times, bus master support, and asynchronous characteristics are the key features that contribute to Micro Channel's performance capabilities.

The most obvious performance feature of Micro Channel architecture is that of the 32-bit data bus width. This feature enables 32-bit data operations to take place between all 32-bit participants on the bus. This is important since it does not limit 32-bit transfers to those involving the system microprocessor as do some other architectures. (Examples of this are systems with 32-bit microprocessors on the 16-bit AT bus.) Any 32-bit device transferring information to any other 32-bit device is capable of taking full advantage of this feature on 32-bit Micro Channel systems. All IBM models with i386 and i486 microprocessors have 32-bit data path capabilities.

In addition to the 32-bit data bus implementation, there is an extension to Micro Channel architecture, called the streaming-data procedure, that effectively provides for a 64-bit data transfer capability. This is done by using both the data and address buses for data transfers. This procedure will be described in detail in Chapter 4.

The data transfer rate is also related to the timing characteristics of the bus. In Micro Channel transfers, the default cycle time is a minimum of 200 ns. Therefore, the maximum data rate that is achievable in 32-bit transfers is 20 MB/sec, a rate that is almost four times faster than the maximum rate on the AT bus. For 16-bit transfers, the maximum rate is 10 MB/sec on PS/2 Micro Channel systems.

It's important to understand that the architecture allows for much faster cycle times than that of the default time implemented in these systems. IBM has announced two difference procedures in which the cycle time has been reduced. The **matched-memory procedure** is an optional system-dependent extension to the architecture that allows for a faster cycle time between the system processor and a device, usually a memory card. This procedure was used in the Model 80-041 to reduce the cycle time from 250 ns (the 16-MHz default) to 187.5 ns. The procedure could be used in any future system implementation to balance memory and processor speeds or could be used to permit specialized devices to be tuned to the transfer characteristics of specific systems for maximum performance benefits.

However, there is another feature, called the **streaming-data transfer procedure,** that is superior to the matched-memory procedure, rendering it less desirable in future implementations. One aspect of the streaming-data procedure provides for 100 ns cycle times, half that of the current minimum default time in PS/2s. The potential to reduce the time even further, to 50 ns, has been announced by IBM. These relationships of timings and data transfer rates are summarized in Table 2.4. These procedures are described in Chapter 4. Assuming that all the announced procedures were implemented in future systems, the maximum data transfer rate could be as high as 160 MB/sec, over 20 times faster than that of the AT!

Another performance feature of Micro Channel architecture is its **burst transfer capabilities.** This is a feature that allows multiple bytes of information to be transferred by a device in one operation, or in a burst. In the AT architecture, most information transfers were conducted one or two bytes at a time, with a significant amount of overhead associated with each transfer. Micro Channel systems can transfer multiple bytes of information with much less overhead per transaction. For example, up to 128 bytes of information can be transferred on a 32-bit system with the same overhead as a one-byte transfer.

TABLE 2.4 MICRO CHANNEL DATA TRANSFER RATES

Transfer Type		Cycle Times (ns)	Data Rate (MB/sec)
Basic Transfer	16-bit	200	10
Basic Transfer	32-bit	200	20
Streaming Data Transfer	16-bit	100	20
Streaming Data Transfer	32-bit	100	40
Streaming Data Transfer	64-bit	100	80
Streaming Data Transfer	64-bit	50	160

Perhaps the most significant performance benefit is that provided by the bus master feature of Micro Channel architecture. Bus masters enhance performance in three ways:

1. They can be used to increase the overall processing power of a system.
2. They increase the degree of concurrency possible.
3. They reduce the number of processor interrupts.

Bus masters may be used to increase the overall processing power by upgrading the system master, as was described earlier. Bus masters may also serve as associated processors that augment the original microprocessor or that provide true parallel processing capabilities. Because of the flexibility of the architecture, almost every conceivable configuration of processors is possible. The bus master feature and the protocols associated with it, Subsystem Control Block Architecture™, provide a well-documented interface that facilitates the development of device driver and software support.

Another way that bus masters increase performance is by offloading functions from the system master. An excellent example of this capability is that provided by the bus master implementation of a LAN adapter. Traditional LAN adapters are under direct control of the system master. A bus master token ring adapter has the ability to access memory directly and also to transfer information to and from other adapters such as disk controllers—functions that are done by the system master in the traditional design. In this example, the system master is free to do other processing. The result is an increase in concurrency, or the number of operations that can be executed at the same time. In sequential operations, there is generally a great deal of waiting since one operation cannot begin until another has been completed. The multimaster capabilities of Micro Channel architecture used in a multitasking operating environment like OS/2 help to reduce this waiting.

The third way that bus masters increase performance is by reducing the number of interrupts to the system master. An interrupt can generate a large number of instructions, especially in a multitasking environment, since the system master must put all of its activities on hold in order to service an interrupt. The interrupt overhead of an information transfer may require an order of magnitude more time than the actual data transfer on the bus! Bus masters do not use the system master in transferring information to and from memory or to and from other adapters.

Another way that bus masters reduce interrupts is through their use of some new software protocols called **command chaining.** Command chaining, a feature of Subsystem Control Block Architecture, will be discussed in detail in Chapter 4, but a brief explanation is provided here. Command chaining is a software technique that bus masters use that allows a number of similar commands to be grouped together and executed. An example would be grouping commands for accessing a file stored on a disk drive and transferring it to another system on a LAN. In a normal case, there are a large number of discrete actions involving small blocks of information being read from the disk and transferred to the LAN adapter and then to the system on the LAN. Each of these actions would normally constitute an interrupt. With command chaining, all of these actions would be grouped together and executed in the proper sequence by the storage system bus master. Upon completion of all the commands, the bus master interrupts the system master, advising that the task has been completed.

One more factor that enhances Micro Channel throughput is its self-pacing capabilities. Because it is an asynchronous bus, one transfer can begin as soon as the previous one has been completed, instead of waiting for the beginning of the next clock period (as would be the case with a synchronous bus), thus increasing the efficiency of the use of the bus.

Reliability, Availability, and Serviceability

Reliability does not have the same meaning as data integrity, although the terms are sometimes used interchangeably. Reliability is related to the hardware failure rate of a system. As previously stated, a failure is defined as a condition that generates a hardware repair action. Reliability is measured in terms of a quantity called the Mean Time Between Failure (MTBF).

Micro Channel architecture improves the reliability of systems by encouraging integration of the circuitry used and by lowering the overall power requirements. The smaller size of the PS/2 Micro Channel card encourages VLSI (Very Large Scale Integration). VLSI is an electronics packaging technique that incorporates tens of thousand of circuits inside a single chip, but has very few connections going to and from the chip. The fewer the connections, the higher the reliability. In addition, VLSI components are cooler and require less power than conventional electronics. Components that run cooler last longer.

In addition to the increase in the use of VLSI circuitry, Micro Channel systems generally require less power than those based on the PC and AT bus. Increased integration is one factor in the power equation, but the power specification for PS/2 Micro Channel expansion boards is also reduced. The smaller the power supply, the cooler the system, and the lower the failure rate for comparable systems.

It is important to note that power specifications are an expression of design, not architecture. However, Micro Channel architecture does enable a decrease in power for comparable function. As was discussed previously in this chapter, some Micro Channel systems may increase the specification on adapter power as is appropriate for its usage.

Micro Channel systems are loaded with diagnostics features that enhance serviceability. Several of these are related to the POS function mentioned earlier. One of these features is called the presence test. This convenient feature identifies the devices that are installed in the system without the cumbersome necessity of removing the covers and examining them. POS also allows for adapters to be enabled or disabled without their physical removal from the system in order to aid in diagnostics or to let a system continue its operation. The presence test and the enable/disable feature assist both on site and remote diagnostic capabilities.

Another POS feature is channel check reporting. This feature is used to identify the source of exception conditions—in other words, which device was responsible for failures or intermittent soft errors in the system. In the original PS/2 implementation, channel check reporting was implemented in a manner that allowed errors to be logged that were associated with an adapter card. This error logging made it possible to replace a board that was beginning to fail, but, perhaps, had not caused a hard failure, bringing the system down. In the Micro Channel enhancements announced in 1989, this capability, called synchronous channel check reporting, was extended to allow channel check reporting to coincide with the time of the error to further assist in the diagnostics.

These advanced features enabled by POS are extremely important in a fault-tolerant environment, where availability of the system is a prime consideration, and will allow dynamic reconfiguration and redundant cards to be activated if necessary. This is clearly a much better alternative than powering down the system!

SUMMARY

Micro Channel architecture is a general information transfer bus that provides numerous benefits for today and tomorrow. Its characteristics arguably approach the ideal architecture for microcomputers. The most serious area that was compromised was that of upward expansion board compatibility from the PC, the XT, and the AT. The tradeoffs involved in this compromise more than compensate for its loss. This is becoming more and more apparent as new functions that were not possible with the prior architecture are introduced.

QUESTIONS

1. Name some examples of the limits of the AT bus architecture. What are some ways that the industry has coped with these limits?
2. What features of Micro Channel architecture apply to 16-bit systems?
3. What is meant by downsizing? How will downsizing affect microcomputers in the future?
4. Contrast the personal computers today with those of the early 1980s.
5. Why did IBM decide not to extend the AT architecture to 32-bit?
6. What is a common problem that causes loss of data in AT bus systems? What are some of the causes? How did Micro Channel architecture alleviate this problem?
7. What are IBM's three strategic information transfer architectures? How are they similar? How does their usage environment differ?
8. What are some of the benefits of Programmable Option Select?
9. Discuss upward and downward compatibility in the PC, the XT, and the AT expansion bus. How does that compare with Micro Channel architecture?
10. How do the PS/2 Micro Channel systems retain software compatibility with the AT?
11. What are some of the optional features of Micro Channel architecture? How do they affect compatibility?

12. Describe the processor-independent nature of Micro Channel architecture. What are some of its implications?
13. What is meant by data integrity? What are some features of Micro Channel architecture that are associated with data integrity?
14. How does level-sensitive interrupt handling enable interrupt sharing?
15. What are some possible consequences of poor EMC design? How does the Micro Channel connector improve electromagnetic compatibility?
16. What is the effect of higher frequency operation on electromagnetic compatibility?
17. Contrast the expansion capabilities of the AT bus and the Micro Channel bus.
18. Is Micro Channel an open architecture? Why or why not?
19. What are some benefits of open licensing of inventions?
20. What are some design parameters of Micro Channel expansion boards that influence performance?
21. What are some features of Micro Channel architecture that would be useful in a fault-tolerant environment?

3

Micro Channel Signals and Procedures

In the previous chapter, you got an appreciation of the features and some of the benefits of Micro Channel architecture. But, up to this point, very little of the technical aspects of the architecture has been described. This chapter is dedicated to the "technoweenies" that want to delve a bit deeper into the architecture. But you really don't have to be one to understand and appreciate its contents. While parts of the chapter may be a bit challenging, the foundation of Chapter 1 should provide an adequate base for most readers.

This chapter contains a detailed description of the architecture, its structure, signals, procedures, and physical requirements. Development engineers and programmers may find this information useful as a technical introduction to the architecture. It is not intended to replace or supplement any formal architecture document, however. While it does review most of the important elements of the architecture, it is not intended to give a level of detail that includes every procedure and timing diagram. (Some of these are included in Appendix B, however.) For the "official" information, you need to consult the Micro Channel architecture document that is included as part of IBM's technical reference manuals. If you prefer, you can skip this chapter all together if you aren't interested in this level of detail. It is not a "prerequisite" for the remaining chapters.

Computer buses, broken down into their elements, are fairly simple. Because of their simplicity, individual activities must be described in meticulous detail, however. Let's return to an earlier diagram (Figure 3.1) in order to appreciate this. In order for information transfer processes to occur, all of these questions must be answered: Who? What? When? Where? and How? This chapter focuses on these interrogatives in order to further describe Micro Channel architecture.

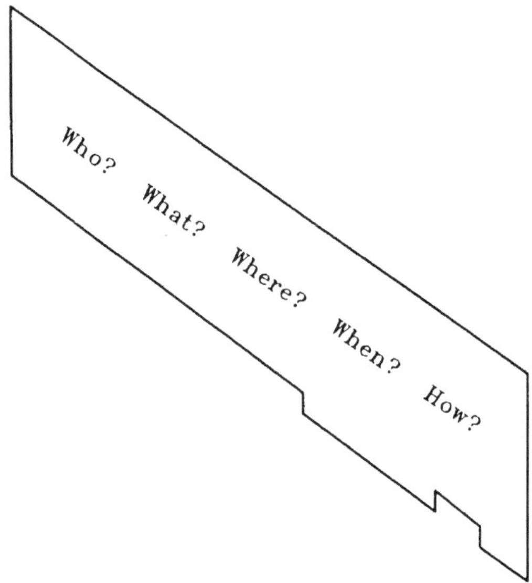

Figure 3.1 Information transfers must be specified in meticulous detail.

THE PARTICIPANTS—THE WHO?

In Chapter 1, the participants associated with information transfers were introduced. Let's return to "The Who?" and look at them in more detail.

Micro Channel architecture has only two types of devices that participate in transfer processes. These are masters and slaves. All data transfers are controlled by masters. Slaves send and receive data under control of a master. Masters know the origin and destination of the information to be transferred and manage its transfers. Slaves require the help of a master. Only one master and one slave combination participate in a single transfer cycle. Micro Channel architecture derives much of its value from its ability to define a variety of simple, high performance procedures between masters and slaves.

Masters

A master controls data transfers to or from a slave. It is a function that a device or an expansion board can have that enables it to drive the address and data bus transfer control signals. In simple terms, a master owns the bus. Micro Channel architecture supports up to 16 masters. Bus ownership is established using the central arbitration control point, the arbitration bus, and the arbitration procedures. While the highest priority master gets control of the bus, a procedure ensures that other masters still get their fair share. The three types of masters are described below:

System Master. The system master is responsible for controlling the allocation of system resources, managing the system configuration, and executing the commands of the primary operating system. It may also be the master that owns the bus whenever no other bus has it (default master). The system master supports the transfer of data between I/O slaves or memory slaves. An example is the transfer of data from system memory to the system master, a **memory read** operation.

Bus Master. A bus master can serve most of the functions of the system master, with the exception of managing the system configuration. By definition, a bus master has direct memory access. It arbitrates for the use of the bus, but it may also be the default master in some implementations. A bus master supports the transfer of data with I/O slaves or memory slaves. An example of a bus master is the SCSI adapter used in some of the IBM PS/2 systems. Bus masters are described in detail in Chapter 4.

DMA Controller. The DMA controller is responsible for assisting information transfers between DMA slaves and memory slaves. This type of transfer is sometimes called a third-party DMA operation in order to distinguish it from those transfers that occur directly between a device and memory (Figure 3.2). In contrast to a bus master, the DMA controller does not initiate arbitration. DMA slaves are responsible for the initiation and completion of the procedure. The arbitration procedure is monitored by the DMA controller for the DMA slave requests. The DMA controller is usually, but not necessarily, part of the system board logic.

Slaves

A slave needs a master to transfer information since it can't initiate bus transfer cycles itself.[1] However, a slave can initiate a service request, as is the case with interrupts. In event-driven systems, most of the activity is driven by slaves requesting services. The keyboard is an example of a slave of this type. One way to express the function of slaves is to say that they "respond" to the Micro Channel bus cycles.

[1]However, DMA slaves can initiate arbitration cycles.

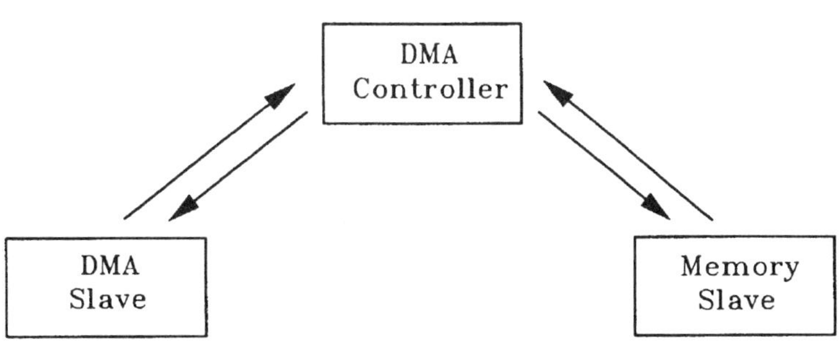

Figure 3.2 A third-party DMA operation involves a "middle man," the DMA controller.

Micro Channel architecture supports 8-, 16-, and 32-bit transfers. The data port determines the maximum data transfer width, but lower widths are supported. For example, in an 8-bit transfer to a 16-bit slave, the 16-bit slave acts like an 8-bit slave.

The three types of slaves are described below:

Memory Slaves. A memory slave is a device whose principle function is to provide a block of system memory. Memory that is used for other purposes is not considered to be a memory slave. (As you may recall from Chapter 1, system memory is that whose allocation is dynamically controlled by operating system software.) The selection of memory slaves in a transfer is done by the memory addresses. Memory slaves respond to read and write cycles by placing the requested data on the bus or writing data from the bus to RAM. Memory-mapped I/O devices are also selected by memory addresses and respond to memory read and write cycles. However, the allocation is not controlled by operating system software, but by the initial setup routine.

I/O Slaves. An I/O slave is a device (or adapter) that performs an input/output function. It usually communicates with or controls another piece of equipment, such as a printer. I/O slaves may respond to memory or I/O addresses, depending on their design. They may also contain private memory—blocks of onboard memory that the system can't access or control. Their designs may range from very simple devices like a serial port to extremely complex subsystems.

DMA Slaves. DMA slaves are the only slaves that can initiate control of the bus. The request is made for the DMA controller to assist with the transfer of information to another participant, that is, a third-party DMA operation. A DMA slave has an assigned arbitration level and arbitrates for the use of the bus, along with masters and other DMA slaves. Information is transferred to a DMA slave from memory during a DMA read operation and from a DMA slave to memory during a DMA write operation. A DMA slave may also function as an I/O slave. Memory and I/O slaves can also be DMA slaves. It is also possible for DMA slaves to be involved in transfers managed by bus masters instead of the DMA controller. The requirement is that the instructions or data must pass through a third-party master. In the cases where blocks of information are to be transferred, DMA slaves can provide significant performance advantages using the burst transfer capability of Micro Channel architecture. This important feature is explained in detail in Chapter 4. For now, the burst capability allows the DMA controller to control the bus for more than one cycle. Several bytes of information can then be transferred without losing control of the bus.

To summarize, the relationships between Micro Channel participants are shown in Table 3.1. The table illustrates that both bus masters and DMA controllers can be used to perform similar tasks and to offload work from the system master.

TABLE 3.1 MICRO CHANNEL PARTICIPANTS AND THEIR RELATIONSHIPS

Masters	I/O Slave	Memory Slave	DMA Slave
System Master	yes	yes	
Bus Master	yes	yes	
DMA Controller	yes		yes

The Business Analogy

The way a business is organized and operated is a good analogy for explaining the roles of Micro Channel participants. Most businesses have several managers with various supervisory responsibilities and employees with specific roles. In this analogy, managers are similar to the various masters in our computer. Imagine that there is one administrative manager who is responsible for unlocking the doors, turning on the lights, checking to see who is present, and so forth. This manager may be the "boss," but not necessarily. Our default master is somewhat like this manager and usually winds up doing jobs no one else is assigned to do. The system master, or "boss," in our analogy, works on more important things, such as allocating tasks and controlling resources.

A business may have a number of other managers, analogous to Micro Channel bus masters, who are generalists or specialists, with jobs ranging from supervising very simple functions to managing extremely complex activities. The value of this type of organization is that the "boss," or system master, does not have to do all the work, nor contend with numerous interruptions from subordinates. In addition, some of these managers, because of their special skills, can do a better job than the "boss," just as highly specialized bus masters adapters are designed to do a particular function very efficiently. For example, an entire communications subsystem may be managed by a bus master device far more efficiently than the system master could do the job. The DMA controller is analogous to a highly specialized type of manager who doesn't actually do very much, but acts as a liaison between other employees to help them get their work done.

The various types of slaves will also fit into our company analogy. Suppose our company is in the service business. When someone has a problem, they call the service hot line to report it. There is a data base of service problems and solutions that is stored in a filing cabinet (fixed disk drive). Files that contain frequently encountered problems are removed from the filing cabinets and placed within easy reach of the people that need them (memory). When a call comes in, the data base is searched for the problem resolution and someone makes an outgoing call to the customer, indicating the action to be taken to correct the problem.

In our analogy, the I/O slaves are like the employees who take the incoming calls and make outgoing calls. Memory slaves contain the frequently used information or data. The I/O slaves do not have access to this data directly, but must rely on masters to access it for them. It would be far more efficient if the people making the incoming and outgoing calls had access to the data base directly. This is exactly how the multimaster capability of Micro Channel architecture adds to the efficiency of data transfers: a bus master has the ability to access memory and storage directly and does not rely on the help of a "middleman."

A good way to think of the role of the DMA slave is that he knows what he wants out of memory but needs the help of a supervisor, the DMA controller, to get it for him and to keep him from interfering with others who also need the same information.

Employing versatile people who can serve more than one function and can access the data base directly is desirable in this business. Those who don't interrupt others or rely on their help add to the overall efficiency of the business. This is just as true in computer architecture as it is in a business operation!

An earlier discussion of Micro Channel participants is somewhat of an oversimplification. The terminology refers to how participants are used in a particular type of transfer as well as the functions that devices and adapter cards may have. A Micro Channel expansion board can also contain more than one type of device. It is identified by the device type representing its principle function. For example, a bus master adapter often may serve as an I/O slave. However, it would be referred to as a bus master adapter, not an I/O slave. Figure 3.3 illustrates these relationships.

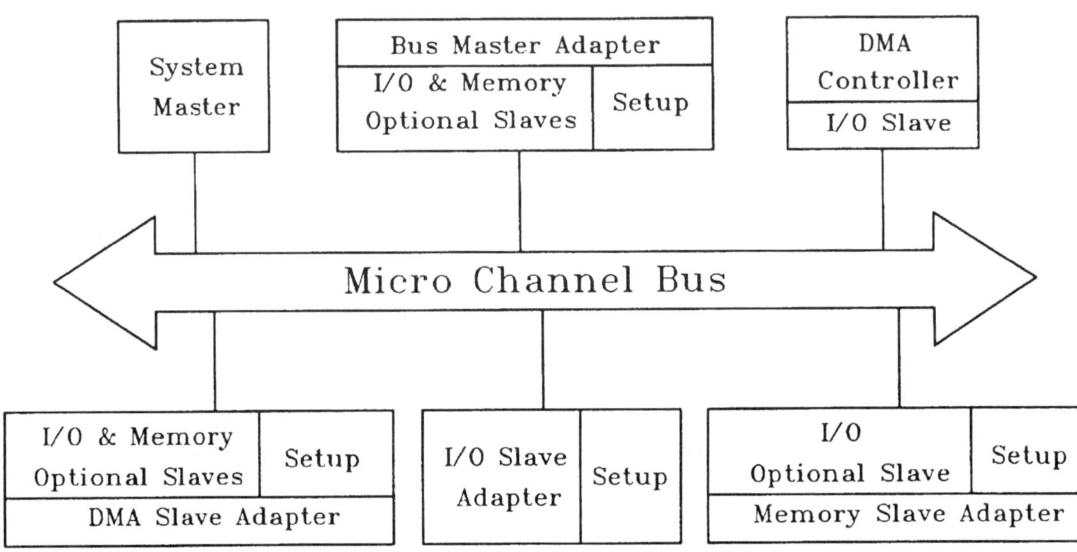

Figure 3.3 Micro Channel participants may serve several functions.

MICRO CHANNEL STRUCTURAL OVERVIEW

Micro Channel architecture consists of three buses and their associated signals: an address bus, a data bus, and an arbitration bus. Interrupt signals and additional Micro Channel signals are also included along with optional video and matched-memory extensions. The **Central Arbitration Control Point (CACP)** is attached to the system master via a private bus and is responsible for controlling the arbitration process. The central steering and translator logic used to manage the different combinations of signals associated with data steering are also packaged within the system logic. In addition, the system logic includes circuitry for channel reset, memory refresh, and the clock.

Figure 3.4 illustrates the basic structure and signals and their relationships to the various Micro Channel participants.

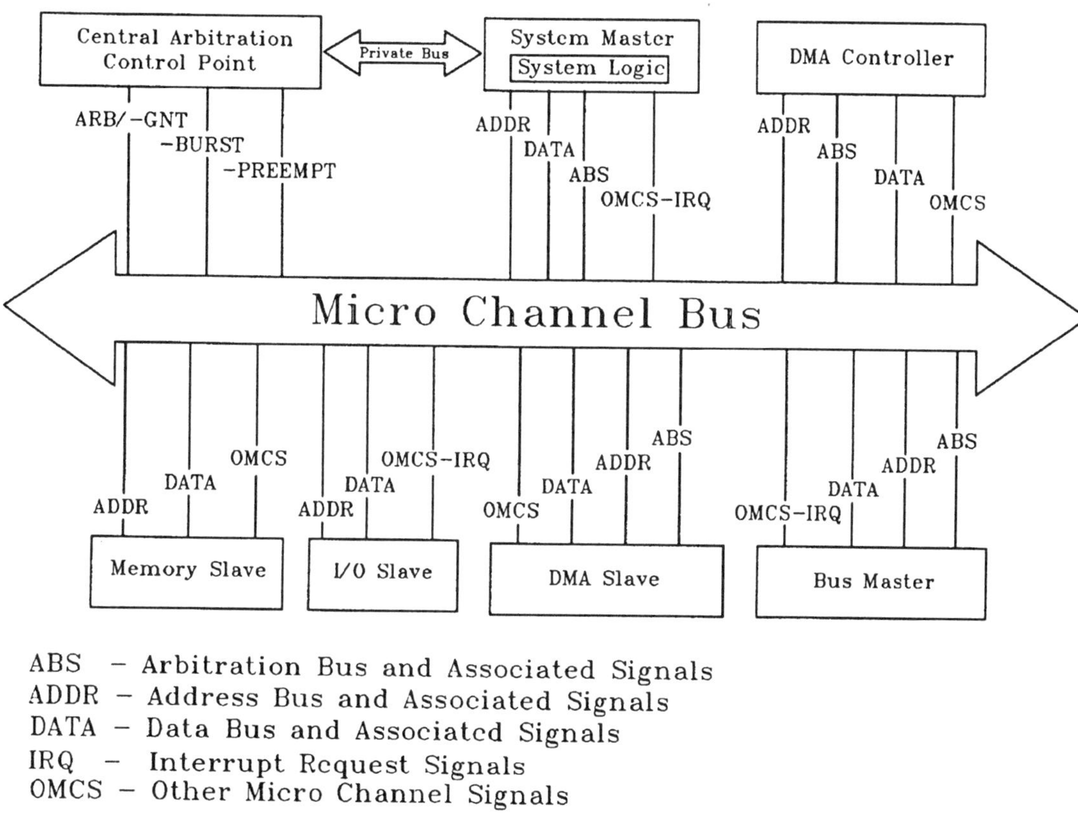

Figure 3.4 Basic Micro Channel structure.

Signal Definitions

The signal definitions for Micro Channel architecture are summarized in the following sections. Some of the functional similarities with the PC and AT signals listed in Chapter 1 are obvious. What is also obvious is that Micro Channel architecture has many more signals. The base architecture defines 116 signals for 16-bit implementations and 62 additional signals for 32-bit functionality for a total of 178 signals. The video extension adds 20 signals to either a 16-bit or 32-bit slot, and the matched-memory extension adds eight additional signals to a 32-bit slot. These relationships are summarized in Figures 3.5 and 3.6.

These signals and the appropriate procedures combine to provide the answers to the fundamental questions associated with information transfers. The "Who?" is determined by the arbitration signal group. The "Where?" is supplied by the address signal group. The "What?" is provided by the data transfer group. The "When?" is provided by the control group. And, finally, "The How?" is determined by the Micro Channel procedures.

Address Group A (0–23) –ADL –CD SFDBK MADE 24 M/–10 (24–bit address width)	**Data Group** –CMD D (0–7) D (8–15) –TC –SO, –S1 CD CHRDY –CD DS 16 –SBHE CHRDYRTN –DS 16 RTN (8/16–bit data width)
Arbitration Group ARB (0–3) ARB/–GNT –BURST –PREEMPT	**Other Signals** AUDIO AUDIO GND –CD SETUO –CHCK CHRESET OSC –REFRESH
Interrupt Signals –IQR(9–12,14,15) –IQR(3–7)	**Optional Data Parity** DPAR (0–1) –DPAREN **Optional Streaming Data** –SD STROBE –SDR (0)
16–Bit Connector (116 Pins)	
Matched–Memory Signals (8 additional pins)	Optional Video Signals (20 additional pins)

Figure 3.5 The 16-bit Micro Channel architecture signals.

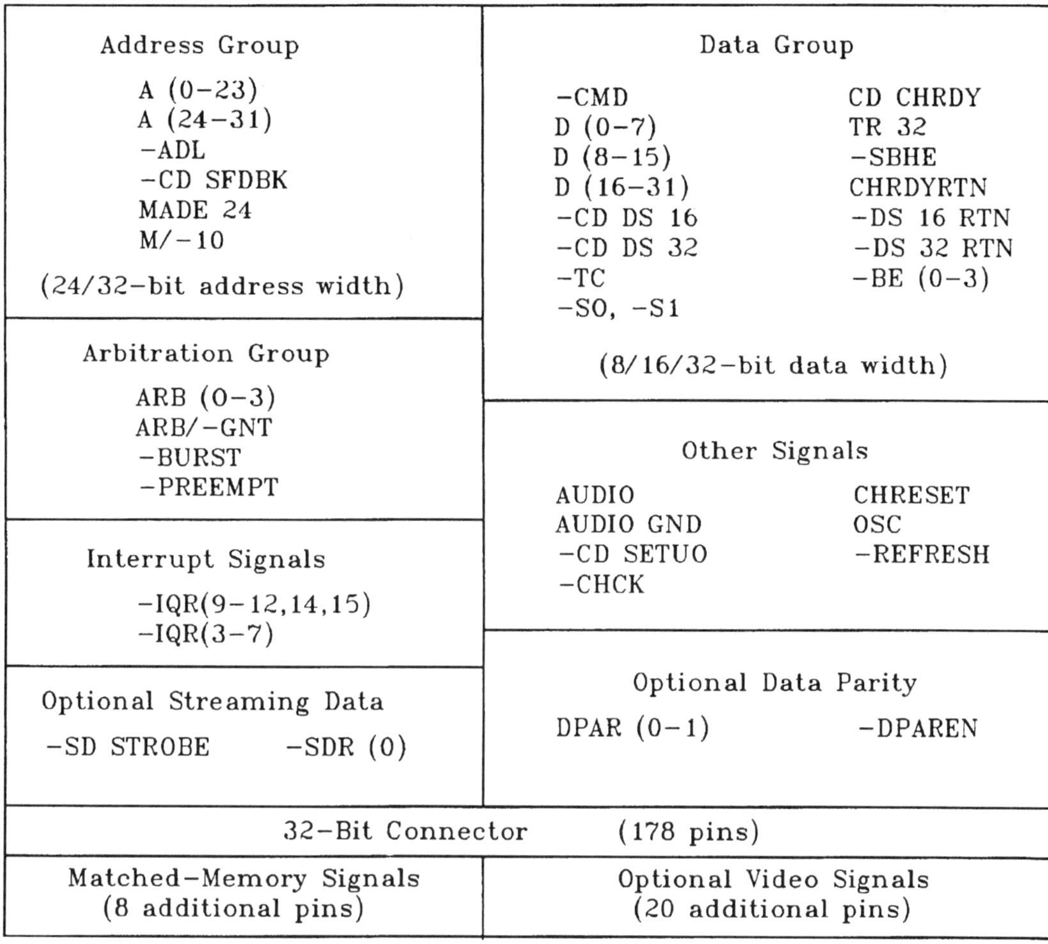

Figure 3.6 The 32-bit Micro Channel architecture signals.

By convention, a minus sign (-) is used to indicate that the signal is active when at the low-voltage level. When there is no minus sign before the signal, it is active at the high-voltage level. For convenience, the signals are grouped according to the following: the arbitration, address, and data groups; interrupt signals; other Micro Channel signals; and the optional matched-memory and video extension signals.

The Arbitration Signal Group

The signals in this group comprise the 4-bit arbitration bus and its control signals. They are used to establish and transfer ownership to the eligible participants. The system master, bus masters, and DMA slaves are the participants involved in the arbitration process. The arbitration process is controlled by a required logic unit, the CACP. Arbitrating devices are granted control of the bus by a procedure specified by the architecture, described later in this chapter. The default master has the lowest priority and is given control of the bus when no other bus master owns it or during exception conditions.

ARB0–ARB3: Arbitration Bus Priority Levels. These signals are used by arbitrating devices to indicate their arbitration levels. All arbitrating devices monitor the arbitration bus, and those with lower priority temporarily withdraw their signals while there is a higher priority arbitrating device on the bus.

-PREEMPT: -Preempt. A signal on this line indicates that a device wants control of the bus. This causes an arbitration cycle to occur, with the requesting device referred to as the **local arbiter.** When the bus ownership is granted to one of multiple requesting devices, the winner turns off its own -PREEMPT request signal until each arbitrating device has been satisfied.

ARB/-GNT: Arbitrate/-Grant. Indicates that an arbitration cycle is in process or that a device has been granted control of the bus. The CACP activates or deactivates this line. When in the arbitration state, the ARB signal is active. When ownership is granted, the -GNT state is used to acknowledge the grant to the participants. At the end of a transfer, the signal is again driven to the ARB state to signal completion by the CACP.

-BURST: -Burst. A signal that is used to indicate to the CACP that a master is executing multiple bus cycles (a burst cycle) without relinquishing control of the bus. It is driven by the winner of the arbitration process.

The Address Signal Group

The Micro Channel address model consists of a range of I/O addresses and memory addresses, or space. The signals in the address group are used by the controlling master to identify the specific address, to indicate whether it is a memory or I/O address, enable a slave to latch (capture) the address and status signals, and to indicate that an address is greater than 16 MB. An address width of 24 bits supports up to 16 MB of address space. An extended width of 32 bits is used to address a 4 GB address space. The first 16 address lines are used for I/O addresses and must be decoded, or interpreted, by the I/O slave. The address lines are driven by the controlling master and are used to address memory, I/O slaves, and, optionally, DMA slaves.

A0–A31: Address Lines (unlatched). Unlatched address lines require that a device retain or capture the address if needed after the memory read or write command is given. The effect is to free up the bus for other activities. All address lines on the PC bus were latched. The AT also had unlatched address lines.

A0–A23: Address Bits 0 through 23. Used as part of the 16-bit and 24-bit memory bus subset and the 16-bit I/O address bus. These are the first 24 address lines, which define up to 16 MB of memory address space.

A24–A31: Address Bits 24 through 32. Used with A0–A23 as part of the 32-bit address bus to define up to 4 GB of memory address space.

MADE 24: Memory Address Enable 24. This signal is used to indicate whether or not a memory address exceeds 16 MB. In other words, when this signal is active, it indicates that the 24-bit addressing range is being used instead of the 32-bit range. The signal is driven by the controlling master. Memory slaves receive the signal.

M/-IO: Memory/-Input Output. Used to signal whether an address is a memory or an I/O address. Distinguishes a memory cycle from an I/O cycle. It is driven by the controlling master and must be received by all slaves.

It is through combinations of these signals that memory and I/O cycle addresses are determined. For example, a 32-bit connector transferring information to a memory slave in an address range equal to or greater than 16 MB would have the following signal combinations:

M/-IO	1
MADE 24	0
A0–A23	Valid
A24–A31	Valid

The valid address signal combinations for I/O and memory cycles are shown in Tables 3.2 and 3.3.

-ADL: -Address Decode Latch. Provides a convenient way for a slave to latch valid addresses and status bits. Driven by the controlling master.

-CD SFDBK (n): -Card Selected Feedback. A signal driven by I/O and memory slaves to indicate that they have been selected by a master. It is used as a positive acknowledgement of the presence of the I/O or memory slave at the specified address. The signal is unique to each channel connector. This is just one of a number of "checks and balances" in Micro Channel architecture.

TABLE 3.2 VALID ADDRESS SIGNAL COMBINATIONS FOR I/O CYCLES

Signals	16-Bit Connectors	32-Bit Connectors
M/-IO	0	0
A0–A15	Valid	Valid
APAR0–APAR1 (Optional)	Not Applicable	Valid
MADE 24	Not Significant	Not Significant

TABLE 3.3 VALID ADDRESS SIGNAL COMBINATIONS FOR MEMORY CYCLES

Signals	16-Bit Connector	32-Bit Connector	
	<16 MB	<16 MB	=>16 MB
M/-IO	1	1	1
MADE 24	1	1	0
A0–A23	Valid	Valid	Valid
A24–A31	Not Applicable	Not Significant	Valid
APAR0–APAR2 (Optional)	Not Applicable	Valid	Valid
APAR3	Not Applicable	Not Significant	Valid

-SFDBKRTN: -Selected Feedback Return (32-bit extension). An optional signal from the slave to the master that the slave is at the address specified. In order for address parity to be supported, masters must receive this signal. The -CD SFDBK and the -SFDBKRTN signals are used to communicate to the master that the slave "knows" that it has been selected and is at the specified address.

-APAREN: -Address Parity Enable (32-bit extension). Optional signal driven by a master that indicates to a slave that the address parity signals are valid. Driven by a master when it places an address on the bus.

APAR0–APAR3: Address Parity Bits 0 through 3 (32-bit extension). Used to indicate the odd parity of the address bits on the address bus during read and write cycles. Driven by the controlling master. Each one of these four bits are used to represent the odd parity of the four bytes of A(0–31). In the case of the 64-bit streaming-data procedure described later in this chapter, these signals are also used to represent data parity.

The Data Signal Group

Micro Channel architecture supports data transfers of either 8, 16, 24, or 32 bits of data. The signals in this group are used to transfer the data and to characterize the transfer. As described earlier, the width of the data transfer is controlled by the capabilities of the device with the lesser data path width.

D0–D15: Data Bits 0–15. The 16 signal lines used for 16-bit data transfers. Also used as half the signal lines in 32-bit data transfers. D0–D7 are used for 8-bit transfers. It should be noted that transfers from a 16-bit master to an 8-bit slave are achieved in two 8-bit transfers on D0–D7. Signals in this group are driven by any device, master or slave, transferring data.

D16–D31: Data Bits 16–31. Used with D0–D15 for 32-bit data transfers. In this case, transfers from a 32-bit master to an 8-bit slave are achieved in four 8-bit transfers on D0–D7. Transfers from a 32-bit master to a 16-bit slave are accomplished in two 16-bit transfers, using D0–D15. Signals in this group are driven by any device transferring the data.

-BE0—BE3: -Byte Enable 0 through 3. Used to signal which of the four data bytes contains valid data on the 32-bit data bus. For example, when only one byte of data is to be transferred using D0–D7, -BE0 is active.

-SBHE: -System Byte High Enable. Used to signal transfer of data on D8–D15. Used by 16-bit slaves but not 8-bit slaves. Driven by the controlling master.

-CD DS 16 (n): -Card Data Size 16. Driven by either I/O or memory slaves to indicate that their data port size is at least 16-bit. The signal is not active for an 8-bit data port and is not driven by 8-bit slaves. The (n) is used to indicate that the signal is unique to each channel connector.

-CD DS 32 (n): -Card Data Size 32. Driven by either I/O or memory slaves to indicate that their data port size is 32-bit. The (n) is used to indicate that the signal is unique to each channel connector position. This signal is inactive for an 8-bit or 16-bit data port.

-DS 16 RTN: -Data Size 16 Return. Used by a master to determine the size of the data ports of I/O and memory slaves.

-DS 32 RTN: -Data Size 32 Return. Used by a master to determine the size of the data ports of I/O and memory slaves.These signals, -DS 16 RTN and -DS 32 RTN, are used in combination to allow the controlling master to monitor information about the slave's data port size.

-S0, -S1: -Status Bits 0 and 1. Driven by the controlling master to indicate the start of a data transfer cycle and to indicate whether the cycle is a read (S0) or write (S1) operation. When used with M/-IO, memory read/write operations can be distinguished from I/O read/write operations. For example, the following signal combinations are used to describe an I/O Write Command:

M/-IO	0
-S0	0
-S1	1

-CD CHRDY (n): -Channel Ready. Normally active (ready). Used by I/O and memory slaves to indicate that they can execute the default cycle time. If the signal is inactive, it indicates that the I/O or memory slave requires additional time. This signal is unique to each device and is independent of others on the bus.

CHRDYRTN: Channel Ready Return. A signal used by masters to determine that the slave selected is ready for the transfer. Used with the CD CHRDY signal. If both signals are active, the transfer is allowed to proceed.

-CMD: -Command. Driven by the controlling master. Indicates when data is valid on the data bus. Signals when to execute the transfer. The trailing edge or end of the signal marks the end of the bus cycle. Beginning with the leading edge of the -CMD signal, slaves can latch address and status information.

-TC: -Terminal Count. Used to indicate that the count has been reached for the transfer. It indicates to the DMA slave the last cycle of a DMA transfer to be performed. Available only during DMA operations. It is driven by the DMA controller.

TR 32: Translate 32. Used to indicate that a 32-bit master is in control of the bus.

-SDR0, -SDR1: Streaming Data Request. Optional signals that are used by a slave to indicate to a master that it is capable of streaming data. They also indicate the maximum clocking rate that the slave can support. For example, the following signal combinations are used for a 100 ns minimum cycle time:

-SDR(0)	0
-SDR(1)	1

-SD STB: -Streaming Data Strobe. A signal used by the controlling master and slave to clock data on/off the data bus. Driven by the controlling master. Also used to signal that the controlling master supports streaming data.

-MSDR: -Multiplexed Streaming-Data Request. Driven by a slave. Used to indicate to the controlling master that the slave supports 64-bit streaming-data transfers.

-DPAREN: -Data Parity Enable. Optional signal driven by a participant that indicates that the data parity signals are valid. (APAR0–APAR3 are used for data parity during 64-bit cycles.)

DPAR0–DPAR1: Data Parity Bits 0 and 1. Optional signals used to represent odd parity on the data bus during read and write operations. Odd parity is defined as the condition in which the total number of 1s in a byte of data (including the parity bit) is odd. Driven by the participant.

DPAR2–DPAR3: Data Parity Bits 2 and 3 (32-bit extension). Optional signals driven by the participant and used to indicate when data is placed on the data bus. These signals are used to represent the odd parity of the data bits during read and write operations. DPAR0, DPAR1, DPAR2, and DPAR3 are used to represent odd parity on D(0–7), D(8–15), D(16–23), and D(24–31), respectively.

Interrupt Signals

-IRQ 3–7, -IRQ 9–12, -IRQ 14–15: -Interrupt Request. Driven low by an I/O slave when it is requesting an interrupt. Used by a device to signal that it needs attention. More than one slave can share the same interrupt level concurrently due to the polarity of these signals.

The Audio Signal Group

The audio signal group consists of an analog audio voltage sum node and the audio ground. Separate audio circuitry on devices on the bus is not required because of this feature, which provides a medium fidelity audio signal. The audio line connects to the built-in speaker and can be used by any device in the system. Audio signals may be transmitted independently and simultaneously with data on the bus. IBM describes the quality as telephone-grade, but it is closer to FM quality. For higher quality sound, external amplification can be used from a device output.

AUDIO: Audio Sum Node. Used for communication of audio signals between devices on the bus or to the system speaker. The response of the audio line is 50 Hz to 10 kHz +/- 3 dB. The analog signal amplitude is 2.5 V peak-to-peak with a dc offset of 0 +/- 50 millivolts.

AUDIO GND: Audio Ground. Used as the audio ground return signal.

The Power and Ground Signals

Micro Channel architecture has 20 power and 26 ground lines in the base architecture. There are 28 with the matched-memory extension. These power and ground pins are numerous and are arranged in such a way as to minimize cross-talk and electromagnetic interference. Extra ground lines help draw stray radio frequency signals away before they can be radiated. Data integrity, system reliability, and transfer capabilities are increased as a result.

The Matched-Memory Signal Group

The matched-memory signal group supplies the signals for an optional procedure supported by the architecture but not implemented on all systems. It provides the capability for decreasing the cycle time to less than the default value of a system.

Data can be transferred to system memory or system memory-mapped I/O devices that are using the matched-memory signals and the matched-memory procedure. It has been used to provide a method of utilizing higher-speed memory devices attached to the bus. Its use is limited to specialized devices, with the capabilities tuned to the transfer characteristics of specific systems. However, this procedure requires that devices designed for the procedure also function with all other devices designed to the Micro Channel architecture specification.

-MMC: -Matched-Memory Cycle. Used by bus masters or the system master to indicate that they can execute a matched-memory cycle.

-MMCR: -Matched-Memory Cycle Request. Used by memory or memory mapped I/O slaves to request a matched-memory cycle.

-MMC CMD: -Matched-Memory Cycle Command. Used by bus masters or the system master in place of -CMD during a matched-memory cycle. Indicates when the data is valid on the data bus.

Video Extension Signals

These signals are used for a video subsystem on an adapter. Their purpose is to provide a method of sharing video resources with the video function on the system board (or another adapter). Since these signals are system dependent, the technical reference manuals provided for specific systems should be consulted for additional information.

This optional feature has been used to provide access to the VGA and XGA function on the system board in IBM's Personal System/2 systems. Advanced function graphics adapters do not have to provide their own VGA or XGA logic because of this feature. This capability is not limited to just accessing VGA or XGA. When additional graphics function is incorporated into future systems, new video extension signals may be used. The signals that have been used in PS/2s with VGA are listed below.

VSYNC: Vertical Synchronization. This is the signal used for vertical synchronization of the display.

HSYNC: Horizontal Synchronization. This is the signal used for horizontal synchronization of the display.

BLANK: Blanking Signal. Analog display technology is used in the IBM PS/2s. The blanking signal is connected to the blanking input digital-to-analog converter (DAC). When this signal is active, it causes the DAC to drive its analog color output to 0 VDC.

P0–P7: Palette Bits. This group of eight signals is used for the picture element (PEL) address inputs to the DAC.

DCLK: Dot Clock. This signal is used by the DAC to latch the palette bit signals and serves as the PEL clock.

ESYNC: External Synchronization. The buffer that drives BLANK, VSYNC, and HSYNC is enabled by this signal. When ESYNC is low, the adapter drives BLANK, VSYNC, and HSYNC. When ESYNC is high, the system board function drives these signals.

EVIDEO: External Video. The buffer that drives the palette bit signals is enabled by this signal. When EVIDEO is low, the adapter drives P0–P7. When the signal is high, the system board function drives the signals.

EDCLK: External Dot Clock. The buffer that drives the dot clock is enabled by this signal. When EDCLK is low, the adapter drives DCLK. When EDCLK is high, the system board function drives the signals.

Other Micro Channel Signals

-CD SETUP(n): -Card Setup. Used to indicate a setup cycle. Unique to each device. Used to select a specific device and to allow access to its configuration data. The device's ID and configuration data is read during an I/O read operation and stored by an I/O write operation. These signals are fundamental elements of the POS feature. Driven by the system logic.

-CHCK: -Channel Check. This signal is used to indicate an exception condition such as a parity error. It is driven by a slave or, optionally, by a master.

OSC: Oscillator. This line is for an oscillator with a frequency of 14.31818 MHz. Driven by the system logic.

CHRESET: Channel Reset. Used to reset or initialize devices during power on or during a low voltage condition, such as would occur during a power interruption.

-REFRESH: -Refresh. Used to indicate the execution of memory refresh cycles. Driven by the system logic.

MICRO CHANNEL PROCEDURES

Now that the signal definitions are complete, it's time to dig into how they work together to define the various Micro Channel procedures. In order to completely define the procedures, detailed timing diagrams are required. It is not the purpose of this section to make you a design engineer, however. For the dedicated "tech-noweenie," the procedures are described with some pertinent timing diagrams in Appendix B.

The Micro Channel procedures are divided into five major groups: bus ownership, data transfers, special-purpose operations, Programmable Option Select, and exception condition reporting.

Bus Ownership

The hardware-mediated procedure for sharing and transferring bus ownership is an important attribute that distinguishes Micro Channel architecture from less sophisticated buses, like that of the PC and AT. Understanding this procedure is key to appreciating the value of bus masters and the master-slave structure of the architecture. This section focuses on the arbitration procedures used in Micro Channel architecture.

The arbitration procedure uses the arbitration signal group described earlier in this chapter and the arbitration bus. Up to 16 arbitration levels are possible using the four lines ARB0–ARB3. Only those participants that are assigned an "arbitration level" (during system configuration) can own the bus. With the ability to support 16 masters, Micro Channel architecture supports very flexible system structures.

The arbitrating devices may be the system master, bus masters, or DMA slaves. The DMA controller becomes the owner of the bus if a DMA slave "wins" an arbitration. The third-party DMA controller is programmed to recognize the arbitration levels assigned to the DMA slaves it supports. (The DMA slave and third-party DMA controller must also be programmed to use the same DMA channel.) Arbitration levels range from hex 0 to hex F, with hex F assigned the lowest priority. The default master, assigned hex F, owns the bus when no other master has it. As mentioned earlier, the default master is the system master in many cases, but it is not a requirement. Ownership is transferred when the arbitration bus contains the owner's arbitration level and the ARB/-GNT signal is in the -GNT (Grant) state.

It should be noted that the number of DMA slaves arbitrating for the channel plus the number of bus masters and the system master cannot exceed 16. Each of the DMA slaves has a DMA channel associated with it and is assigned an arbitration level. The DMA controller is not included in the count of the sixteen devices. The number of DMA channels is fixed by the design of the system. For example, in the IBM Personal System/2 Model 80, the number is eight. Therefore, the number of additional arbitrating devices is eight, so the maximum number of bus masters allowed in the Model 80 is seven. (The sixteenth master must be the system master.)

Bus ownership is controlled by the central arbitration control point. Which bus participant owns the bus is determined by the arbitration cycle procedure. The CACP detects requests for ownership (-PREEMPT active) and the end of transfer condition (-CMD, and -S0,-S1 inactive) and initiates an arbitration cycle. The arbitration cycle starts when the CACP changes the state of the ARB/-GNT signal to ARB. During the arbitration cycle, all devices vying for the bus drive their arbitration levels onto the arbitration bus. All potential bus owners monitor the arbitration bus and remove their own signal if it is not the highest arbitration level on the bus. Once the highest priority level is stable on the bus, the CACP grants ownership by changing the state of the ARB/-GNT signal to -GNT. The following steps summarize the arbitration process:

1. Local arbiters request the bus by driving -PREEMPT active.
2. The CACP initiates the arbitration cycle by driving ARB/-GNT to the ARB state.
3. Local arbiters drive their arbitration levels onto the bus using ARB0–ARB3.
4. Lower priority arbiters stop driving their levels onto the bus. The highest priority device is declared the "winner," and the CACP drives the ARB/-GNT signal to the -GNT state.
5. After the bus ownership is granted, a master or DMA slave may indicate that the transfer involves multiple data transfers. In this case, the arbitrating participant drives the -BURST signal active and holds it active until all transfers have been completed or until there is another request for the bus. In that case, the bus owner must release

the channel and signal that the transfer is completed within 7.8 microseconds. (It should be noted that the cycles associated with refreshing system memory are typically executed by the default master's support logic and may occur while ARB/-GNT is in the ARB state.)

6. The completion of the transfer is signalled by the trailing edge of -S0, -S1, -BURST, or -CMD, depending upon which occurs last.

There is a provision, called the **fairness feature,** associated with arbitration that ensures that the participants equitably share the use of the bus with all the requesters. All participants that utilize the Burst capability must support this feature. As mentioned above, the bus must be released within 7.8 microseconds when -PREEMPT is active. This is done to give lower priority requesters an opportunity to use the bus. If the device has the fairness feature enabled, it must enter into an inactive state until there are no requests for the bus by other devices (in other words, until -PREEMPT is inactive). In the event that the fairness feature is disabled, the bus still must be released within a specified period of time in order for memory refresh cycles to occur.

The arbitration process is conducted much like showdown poker. Those that want to play begin by putting up their ante. The cards are dealt face up and each player examines them to see if his cards are better. The player with the best hand wins and the others fold up their cards. In this analogy, each contender for the bus is like a poker player. The -PREEMPT signal is used by the device to indicate that it wants to get in the arbitration game. When a contending master sees others with higher priorities, it stops driving its level onto the arbitration bus. The function of the CACP is simply to open up the arbitration game and also to declare the winner.

The priority of a potential master is included in a software file known as the **adapter description file** or **ADF.** It is usually recorded on the diskette shipped with an option or is on the system's reference diskette for devices included with the system. In the case of conflicts, the setup program included on the reference diskette is used to resolve them. This is part of the POS feature described later in this chapter.

MICRO CHANNEL TRANSFER PROCEDURES—"THE HOW"

Perhaps the most elegant aspect of Micro Channel architecture is the simplicity of the procedures used to transfer instructions and data between masters and slaves. Masters are responsible for beginning, executing, and completing all Micro Channel bus cycles. All Micro Channel transfer cycle procedures are defined to be flexible, compatible, and to utilize every opportunity to enhance performance.

Transfer cycles begin when the device address is placed on the bus by the controlling master. Slaves continually use raw address decodes to check for their address ranges to see if they have been selected for a transfer. The slave realizes that a transfer cycle has begun when it detects its address and a read or write status signal. This efficient procedure minimizes the address and device selection time. Transfer cycles are terminated at the trailing edge of the Command signal

(-CMD). A cycle is defined as one or more data transfers and occurs between the leading and trailing edges of the Command signal.

There are really only four commands involved in data transfer:

1. Memory READ;
2. Memory WRITE;
3. I/O READ; and
4. I/O WRITE.

The type of transfer is indicated by the proper combinations of the M, -IO, -S1, and -S0 signals.

There are four types of data transfer procedures that are specified at this time:

1. Basic Transfer Procedures;
2. DMA Transfers;
3. Streaming-Data Transfers; and
4. Matched-Memory Transfers.

The following section describes the Micro Channel transfer cycle procedures, the signals used, and their effects.

Basic Transfer Procedures

There are three types of basic transfer procedures: the default cycle, the synchronous extended cycle, and the asynchronous extended cycle. These procedures are the "rules and regulations" for conducting Micro Channel information transfers between masters and I/O or memory slaves. A special procedure is used for third-party DMA transfers, described in a later section.

Default Transfer Cycle (200 Nanoseconds)

The default transfer cycle time is 200 nanoseconds. Unless there are signals that are used to request slower or faster transfer cycles, masters assume that 200 nanoseconds is the *minimum* bus cycle time that can be executed.

The basic transfer cycle begins when the master drives a stable memory or I/O address onto the bus. At the same time, the M/-IO signal is driven to indicate whether the address is memory or I/O. The MADE 24 signal is given if the memory address exceeds 16 megabytes. The TR 32 signal is driven if the controlling master is 32-bit. If the slave is designed to use raw address decode logic to determine if the address on the bus is within its range, the device selection time is minimized.

In our business analogy, imagine that there is only one telephone line used for interoffice communications and it works like a party line. All of the employees have telephones, but they must listen to determine if the call is for them, in other words, whether or not it is their "ring." Just as soon as the employee recognizes his ring, he answers the telephone. In our analogy, this is like decoding the raw address after the signal is valid.

After the address is driven (within ten nanoseconds), the read (-S0) or the write (-S1) STATUS signal is driven to indicate the type of cycle and direction of the transfer. The slave indicates its data port size by driving -CD DS 16 and/or -CD

DS 32 within 55 nanoseconds. The slave must then drive -CD SFDBK to indicate that it has been selected within 60 nanoseconds. The data port size of the slave is determined by the master using -DS 16 RTN and -DS 32 RTN.

It is important to remember that the master that controls the bus also controls the number of bytes to be transferred during the cycle. When multiple cycles are to be used to transfer a block of bytes, the master has the capability of altering the number of bytes transferred on a cycle by cycle basis. The size of the master's data port, its transfer efficiency, the size of the slave's data port, the byte address alignment, and, potentially, a CPU instruction determine the number of bytes transferred. Once the number of bytes to be transferred has been determined, the master drives the -SBHE appropriately. This is used to indicate to the slave if the high byte (D8–D15) of each 2-byte transfer is valid. If the master is 32-bit, it also drives the Byte Enable (-BE(0-3)) signals appropriately. These signals provide an efficient way for 32-bit slaves to manage transfers. The various combinations of address signal lines, -BE, and -SBHE are used by masters and slaves to indicate valid data bytes and to determine their location.

This is the point at which the master must make an important decision. If the master wishes to terminate the cycle before it is completed, it must be done before the leading edge of the Address Decode Latch (-ADL) is driven. Driving the -ADL signal provides two gating signals early in the cycle. The two edges of the -ADL signal can be used to transparently latch the address, status, and internal device selected signals. It can also be used for the activation or deactivation of other logic functions.

A minimum of 40 nanoseconds must elapse after the leading edge on the -ADL signal before the master can drive -CMD signal active. In a write cycle, the master must drive the data bus signal at the same time or before driving -CMD active. It is the leading edge of the -CMD signal that is the indicator for the slave to execute the read or the write command. The minimum pulse width of the -CMD signal is 90 nanoseconds. Typically, the leading edge of the -CMD pulse is used to latch the write data from the master. (The leading or trailing edge of the -CMD can be used). In the case of read data from the slave, it must be valid on the bus a maximum of 60 nanoseconds after the leading edge of -CMD.

The trailing edge of the -CMD ends the bus cycle. After the trailing edge of -CMD, write data must be held on the data bus for a minimum of 30 nanoseconds. Prior to the leading edge of the next -CMD signal or when the current master loses control of the bus, write data must be off the data bus. Read data must be held on the bus at least until the trailing edge of -CMD signal, and must be off the bus no more than 40 nanoseconds after the trailing edge of the -CMD signal. After the leading edge of -CMD and at or before the trailing edge of the -CMD signal, all address and control signals are removed from the bus. The cycle is ended by the trailing edge of the -CMD signal.

A special consideration and advantage is that the address and STATUS signals for the next cycle can be driven on the bus before the current cycle is completed. It is the responsibility of the controlling master executing these overlapped cycles to ensure that they appropriately manage slaves with fast response times. Proper termination of the current cycle is the responsibility of the master executing overlapped cycles. This consideration is especially important when executing transfer cycles other than default transfer cycles. Figure 3.7 is a timing diagram that illustrates the basic transfer cycle procedure.

Synchronous Extended Cycles

The synchronous extended transfer cycle is a minimum of 300 nanoseconds long. The primary difference between the default transfer cycle and the synchronous extended cycle is that the pulse width of the -CMD signal is a minimum of 190 nanoseconds instead of the 90 nanoseconds of the default cycle. This procedure is used to optimize the performance of slaves that require between 60 and 160 nanoseconds of data setup and hold time.

A synchronous extended cycle is requested by a slave by pulsing the Channel Ready signal (CD CHRDY). The synchronous extended cycle is identical to the default transfer cycle with the exception of the pulsing of the CD CHRDY signal and the extending of the -CMD pulse. To request a synchronous extended transfer

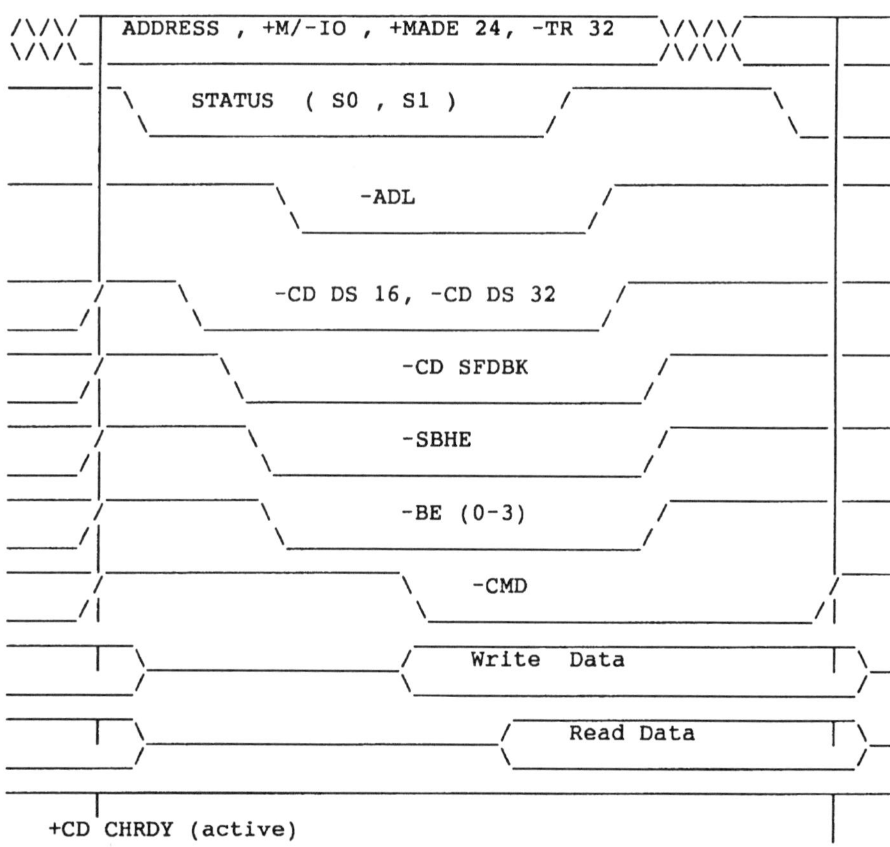

Figure 3.7 Basic Micro Channel data transfer procedure.

cycle, the slave drives the CD CHRDY low a maximum of 30 nanoseconds after the STATUS signal (-S0 or -S1) becomes active. Within a maximum of 30 nanoseconds after the leading edge of the -CMD signal, the CD CHRDY signal must be released.

Asynchronous Extended Cycles

The asynchronous extended transfer cycle is also a minimum of 300 nanoseconds long. The primary difference between the basic transfer cycle and the asynchronous extended cycle is that the pulse width of the -CMD signal is greater than 190 nanoseconds at a minimum. As is the case with the synchronous extended cycle, the purpose of this procedure is to help slaves that require more data setup and hold time.

The asynchronous extended transfer cycle is identical to the default transfer cycle with the exception of the use of the CD CHRDY signal and the extending of the -CMD pulse. To request an asynchronous extended transfer cycle, the slave must drive CD CHRDY low a maximum of 30 nanoseconds after the S0 or -S1 signal becomes active. The slave must drive +CD CHRDY active to permit the master to end the cycle. The CD CHRDY signal must not be held inactive by the slave longer than 3.0 microseconds.

These extended cycles are important because they allow slower devices to be built for Micro Channel architecture. At this time, there are many devices that do not meet the default cycle time. One reason for this is that slower devices can be built and sold for a lower cost. Over time, it is anticipated that most devices will meet the default cycle time as logic speeds increase and costs decrease.

Direct Memory Access Procedure

This feature allows the transfer of data to and from an I/O device into a memory address under the control of a third-party device, the DMA controller. This feature provides full software compatibility with the programs written for earlier IBM personal computers (and compatibles). Functional and performance enhancements are also included. This procedure allows higher system throughput than possible with transfers controlled by the system master.

Micro Channel architecture permits the DMA controller to execute either single or multiple transfers (BURST). The serial DMA procedure enables DMA controllers to be designed that can implement read and write cycles independently. Data widths may also be optimized to the target device. The Serial DMA procedure is a significant improvement over the older parallel DMA procedure used in the PC, the XT, and the AT. This procedure required a read followed by a write operation that occurred at the data rate and the data width of the slowest device. Today, hardware designers have more options for optimizing their cost/performance objectives.

The third-party DMA transfer cycle procedure is a specification for implementing instruction or block data transfers under the control of a third-party bus master. This bus master is usually, but not necessarily, the DMA controller. These third-party DMA transfers may use the basic data transfer procedures (default, synchronous extended, or asynchronous extended transfer cycles) or, optionally, the streaming-data procedures and are controlled by the third-party bus master.

A full-function master is required to initialize the DMA controller. The master provides transfer direction, starting address of the target area, and other control information specific to the DMA controller design. The initiation of this process may be due to an interrupt from a DMA slave or an application program. By activating the -PREEMPT signal, the DMA slave initiates the request for control of the bus for the third-party master. The arbitration procedure will eventually grant bus ownership to the DMA slave. The third-party DMA master is responsible for identifying that a DMA slave that it controls has ownership of the bus. Then the DMA controller executes the single or multiple cycles necessary for the transfer.

This procedure requires the use of a special signal called Terminal Count (-TC). The Terminal Count signal is driven by the third-party master and is used to indicate the last transfer of data to the DMA slave. The -TC signal is driven during the last bus cycle for a DMA read operation. This operation consists of reading from a memory address and writing to the DMA slave. In the case of DMA write operations, the -TC signal is driven during the next to last bus cycle. This operation consists of reading from the DMA slave and writing to memory addresses. The Micro Channel DMA feature is described further in the next chapter.

Streaming-Data Procedures

This optional procedure is used to provide significant performance benefits for transferring blocks of data, up to 80 MB per second. A single address is used for the transfering the block of data, in multiple 16-, 32-, or 64-bit transfers, using what is called a streaming-data cycle.

Those devices that support streaming-data procedures must also support basic transfer procedures between those devices that are not capable of the procedure. A device that is capable of the streaming-data procedure must have a bit in the appropriate POS space that indicates this capability.

The description below is not intended to be complete, but, rather, to provide a summary of the features of typical 16-, 32-, and 64-bit procedures. The Micro Channel streaming-data procedures are discussed further in the next chapter.

16- or 32-Bit Streaming-Data Procedure The 16- and 32-bit streaming-data transfers are initiated using the appropriate basic transfer cycle procedures. An example of a 16- or 32-bit write cycle follows.

A 16- or 32-bit write cycle begins with the controlling master driving the address bus, M/-IO, MADE 24, -APAREN, and APAR(0-3) valid. The slave selected for the transfer responds with the -CD SFDBK as an acknowledgement of its selection. It indicates its data port size using -CD DS 16 (for 16-bit) or -CD DS 16 and -CD DS 32 (for 32-bit). The master indicates a write cycle by driving -S0 active (-S1 inactive). If the cycle is to be extended, the slave drives CD CHRDY inactive. A 32-bit master drives the appropriate Byte Enable signals to indicate valid data bytes. The master drives -ADL valid. The slave indicates that it is capable of a streaming-data transfer by driving -SDR(0,1) active. The combination of the states of these two signals also indicates the minimum cycle time that the slave supports (100 ns, for example).

The master then drives the write data onto the bus. If data parity is supported,

-DPAREN is also driven active and DPAR(0-3) valid. Next, the master drives -CMD active and the -ADL signal inactive. The cycle is extended if CD CHRDY has been driven inactive. The master uses the -SD STROBE signal to indicate its streaming-data capability. The master then drives the status signal inactive, followed by the slave driving -SDR(0,1) inactive.

In preparation for the next cycle, the -CD SFDBK, -CD DS 16, and -CD DS 32 signals are updated by the slave. The M/-IO and S(0,1) can become valid for the next cycle. The -SD STROBE is driven inactive by the master. The transfer cycle is completed when the master drives -CMD inactive and the slave receives the data from the data bus.

64-Bit Streaming-Data Procedure The 64-bit streaming-data transfer cycles are performed using the basic transfer cycle procedures for 32-bit transfers. An example of a 64-bit streaming-data write cycle follows.

The initial sequence is identical to that described above for 16- and 32-bit streaming-data transfers. The Byte Enable signals are driven to binary 0000 by a 32-bit master. (16-bit masters do not support 64-bit streaming-data transfers.) The master then drives the -ADL signal valid. The slave indicates that it is capable of a streaming-data transfer by driving the -SDR(0,1) active. The combination of the states of these two signals indicates the minimum cycle time that the slave supports.

The master then writes the data onto the bus. If data parity is supported, -DPAREN is also driven active and DPAR(0–3) valid. Next, the master drives -CMD active and the -ADL signal inactive. The cycle is extended if CD CHRDY has been driven inactive. The master uses the -SD STROBE signal to indicate its streaming-data capability. The method used to indicate 64-bit transfer capability is by driving the Byte Enable signals inactive, driving the four most significant bytes of the 8-byte transfer on the address bus. If data parity is enabled, the master drives APAR(0–3) valid and -APAREN inactive. For the remainder of the cycle, both the data bus and the address bus are used for the transfer of data yielding the 64-bit data transfer procedure. Both the controlling master and the slave use the -SD STROBE signal to transfer the data with new data being placed on the two buses each time there is a high-to-low transition.

The master then drives the status signals inactive on the final high-to-low transition of the -SD STROBE signal followed by the slave driving -SDR(0,1) inactive. Other slaves can then drive the -CD SFDBK, -CD DS 16, and -CD DS 32 signals in response to data on the address bus. The state of these signals is not monitored by the master during the data transfer. The transfer cycle is completed when the master drives -CMD inactive and the slave receives the data from the data bus.

Matched-Memory Transfer Cycles

Micro Channel architecture has a procedure that allows data to be transferred in cycles less than the default 200 nanoseconds. The matched-memory procedure is the only procedure that is system specific. The matched-memory signals and procedure may be used to transfer data between system memory or memory-mapped I/O devices and masters. This procedure can be used to permit specialized devices to be tuned to take advantage of the transfer characteristics of specific hardware. Devices designed to use the matched-memory procedure must still function with all other devices designed to the Micro Channel architecture specification.

Matched-memory transfer cycles are very similar to asynchronous extended cycles. The principal differences are that -ADL and -CMD signals are not activated, and -MMC, -MMCR, and -MMC CMD are used. The Matched-Memory Cycle (-MMC) signal is driven during all bus cycles. The -MMC signal is driven with the address signals. It tells a slave capable of participating in matched-memory cycles that the master can drive such cycles. The slave replies to the master that the current cycle can be a matched-memory cycle by driving the Matched-Memory Cycle Request (-MMCR) signal active. The -ADL and -CMD signals are held inactive. The Matched-Memory Cycle Command (-MMC CMD), driven by the master, is used to instruct the slave to execute the read (-S0) or write (-S1) transfer cycle.

During matched-memory transfer cycles, the CD CHRDY signal can be used by the slave to extend the cycle. If CD CHRDY is driven inactive (low), the -MMC CMD pulse width is extended. Slaves can be used to extend the -MMC CMD period to enable them to drive or latch data and instructions.

Memory Refresh Cycles

Micro Channel Architecture includes a procedure that provides for refresh of dynamic-memory. As was mentioned in Chapter 1, dynamic-memory must be periodically recharged to prevent memory loss. The timing for this procedure is under the control of the system logic. Dynamic-memory refresh is provided by executing Read (-S0) bus cycles with the REFRESH (-REFRESH) signal active. The dynamic-memory controller refreshes a row of dynamic-memory locations by executing Read cycles with the -REFRESH signal active. Micro Channel architecture supports single or multiple row refresh cycles in a single operation. In the Personal System/2, refresh cycles are performed during arbitration cycles as previously discussed.

Interrupt Procedures

Micro Channel architecture uses a procedure for interrupt handling that is detected by the level of the interrupt request signal. This method allows for sharing of the interrupt request lines by several devices. The procedure used is a combination of hardware and the software that is part of the interrupt-service routine.

A device signals an interrupt condition by driving the -IRQ(N) signal active by using the interrupt level (N) assigned to it. It also sets an interrupt-pending bit that the software can read. The master begins executing the interrupt-handling code. The interrupt handler reads the interrupt-pending bit for each device until it detects the device requesting the interrupt. The interrupt-service routine then operates the device hardware, which, in turn, resets the interrupt-pending bit. The interrupt service routine completes the interrupt handling. If another device has set an interrupt-pending bit, the process is repeated. Figure 3.8 illustrates a typical implementation of interrupt sharing.

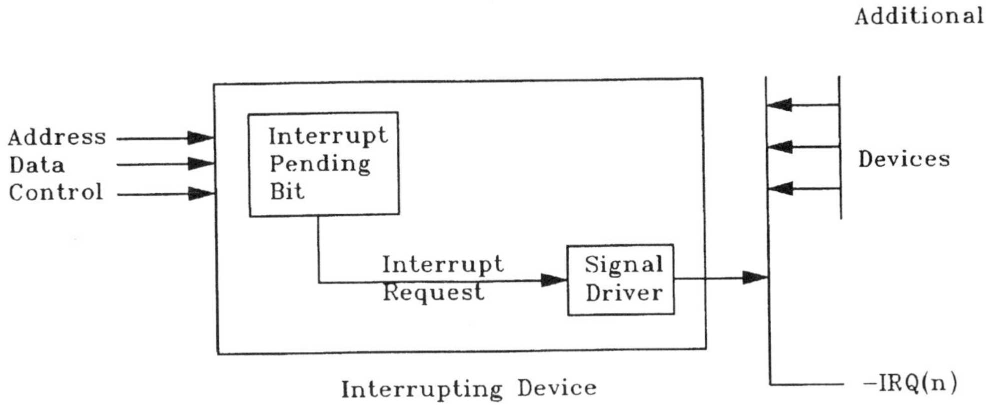

Figure 3.8 An example of Micro Channel interrupt sharing. (Courtesy of International Business Machines Corporation.

Configuration with Programmable Option Select

The POS feature of Micro Channel architecture has done a lot to make these systems easy to set up and install. This includes automatic system configuration and eliminating hardware switches, configuration flexibility, dynamic system configurability, and exception condition support (parity errors and fault identification, for example).

Required for this procedure are the device identification number (obtained from IBM and included in ROM on each device), the device configuration data (on diskette), the POS registers, and the NV RAM (generally located on the system board and used to store the configuration data and the timing specifications). The system master is responsible for controlling the setup cycles. The system accesses configuration data from the POS registers.

An additional discussion of the POS feature is contained in Chapter 4.

POS Configuration Fields

The device identification and configuration data are contained in eight 1-byte registers. The POS registers contain ten fields of information. Figure 3.9 illustrates the structure of the POS registers. There are three types of information fields: required, conditionally required, and optional. All devices must implement the required fields. The conditionally required fields must be included when a device supports a specific function. The use of the optional fields depends on the implementation of specific functions in the devices, but these are not required.

Required Fields

Device ID Field (Required). The Device ID field is a read-only field contained in POS bytes 0 and 1. The device ID is a unique number provided upon request by the IBM Corporation. It identifies the type of bus/channel participant.

Bit Assignments

	7	6	5	4	3	2	1	0
xxx0 READ ONLY	DEVICE FUNCTION				DEVICE ID			
xxx1 READ ONLY	DEVICE ID							
xxx2 READ/WRITE	DEVICE UNIQUE							CEN
xxx3 READ/WRITE	DEVICE UNIQUE							
xxx4 READ/WRITE	DEVICE UNIQUE							
xxx5 READ/WRITE	CHK	CHK STAT	DEVICE UNIQUE					
xxx6 READ/WRITE	CHCK STATUS or SUBADDRESS EXTENSION							
xxx7 READ/WRITE	CHCK STATUS or SUBADDRESS EXTENSION							

Card Function is defined as follows:

x = 0 for non IBM Devices
x = 1 for IBM Devices
x100= Reserved
x101 =DMA Slave
x110 = I/O Slave
x111 = Memory Slave or System Memory-Mapped Card

x000 = Master
x001 = Reserved
x010 = Reserved
x011 = Reserved

Figure 3.9 Programmable Option Select registers.

Device Enable Field (Required). The Device Enable field is located in POS register 2 and bit 0. It is used to enable and disable the Micro Channel interface of a device, and is, therefore, a read/write field. The default state of this field is 0, or disabled, and is enabled by the setup cycle.

Channel Check Field (Required). This is a bit that is used to indicate if the device has driven -CHCK active. The device sets this field to 0 to indicate that an exception condition has occurred. It is reset to 1 by the system master after the condition has been handled. It is bit 7 of POS register 5.

Conditionally Required Fields

Arbitration Level Field (Conditionally Required). The Arbitration Level field is used if the device is an arbitrating participant and is located in a position determined by the designer. It is a 4-bit read/write field used to hold the arbitration level assignment and is required for arbitrating devices.

Auto-Incrementing Enable Field (Conditionally Required). The Auto-Incrementing Enable field is required if the POS Subaddress Extension field is used. It is a read/write 1-bit field that enables or disables automatic incrementing.

Channel Check Status Indicator Field (Conditionally Required). The Channel Check Status Indicator is used if the device supports -CHCK. It is a 1-bit read-only field whose default condition is 1, indicating that status for the channel-check condition is not available.

Data and Address Parity Enable Field (Conditionally Required). The Data and Address Parity Enable fields are used if the adapter supports data or address parity. It is a 1-bit read/write field that is required if the device supports data or address parity, but it can also be a 2-bit field to individually enable data and address parity.

Device I/O Address Assignment Field (Conditionally Required). The Device I/O Address Assignment field is a 6-bit field used to hold the Device I/O Address field provided by the system. All devices that require a total I/O address space greater than 32 bytes are required to support this field. This total is defined as the number of bytes required by one device multiplied by the maximum number of devices of that type supported in a system.

Device I/O Address Select Field (Conditionally Required). The Device I/O Address Select field is used if two or more of the same type of devices can be installed in a system. It is a 1- to 3-bit field that can be used to allow up to eight devices of one type in the system by providing programmable I/O addresses.

Device ROM/RAM Address Select Field (Conditionally Required). The ROM/RAM address select field is used to determine the starting address of the ROM/RAM address space for the device. This is used by memory-mapped devices that map into the nonsystem memory address space above 640 KB. It is a read/write 4-bit field that represents 16 consecutive 8-KB blocks. If more than one device is to be supported in the system, it must provide a programmable capability for setting the memory address.

Fairness Enable Field (Conditionally Required). The Fairness Enable field is a read/write field used to enable and disable the fairness option if the device drives -BURST. When the fairness option is disabled, a master can gain greater access to the bus. It is a one-bit field whose location is determined by the designer.

Matched-Memory Enable Field (Conditionally Required). The Matched-Memory Enable field is used if the device supports the matched-memory capability. This is a 1-bit read/write field that enables or disables support for the matched-memory signals. Its default state is disabled.

Selected Feedback Return Exception Enable Field (Conditionally Required). The Selected Feedback Return Exception Enable field is used if the bus master receives –SFDBKRTN. This is a 1-bit read/write field that is used if a master reports select-feedback-return exceptions. Its default state is disabled.

Streaming-Data Enable Field (Conditionally Required). The Streaming-Data Enable field is used if the device supports streaming-data procedures. This is a 1-bit read/write field used to enable support for streaming-data procedures. Its default state is disabled, which causes the basic transfer procedures to be used.

Optional Configuration Fields

Option Select Data (Optional). This field is used to hold four bytes of device-unique information that can be used for customizing configuration data.

POS Subaddress Extension Field (Optional). The POS Subaddress Extension field may be used to extend the POS register space. This field provides up to 128 KB of additional information for each device. Devices that support this feature must use the auto-incrementing field to enable it.

Status Information Field (Optional). This optional field is used to indicate channel-check status or point to channel-check status. Its location is in POS registers 6 and 7.

System Configuration Procedure

The system configuration procedure uses setup cycles to transfer information to and from devices and the system master. The information transferred consists of the device identification and its configuration data. Setup cycles are used to read or write data from/into the POS registers. These cycles are almost identical to asynchronous cycles. The principal difference is that each card slot (or device on the system board that is a bus participant) has a unique "setup signal." The purpose of this signal is to notify the device that its POS registers are being accessed. The other difference is that only the three low order address bits are used to address the POS registers.

Exception Condition Reporting and Handling

An exception condition is defined as an event that alters the normal processing and procedures of a master. Micro Channel architecture has several procedures for reporting and handling exception conditions. Of all the features of Micro Channel architecture, these may well be the least appreciated. Micro Channel architects paid very close attention to their most important responsibility, that of ensuring that errors are not propagated. For computer architects, this is analogous to the Hippocratic Oath, "First, do no harm."

There are several types of exception conditions that Micro Channel procedures support. These include the following:

- Channel data and address parity exception conditions;
- Non-parity exception conditions;
- Exceptions that are master- and slave-dependent;
- Exceptions that are catastrophic in nature; and
- Channel time-out exceptions.

These features are described in the following section.

Channel Data and Address Parity Exceptions

Data and Address parity checking is used to determine whether all the information (no extra or missing bits) in a transfer was sent to the correct address. Micro Channel architecture has an optional procedure defined for data and address parity checking on the Micro Channel bus. The procedure is optional because it may be more important in some applications than in others. For example, financial applications that may involve multiple uses of information that affect large sums of money generally require parity checking because the consequences of errors is much greater than in other applications. This kind of parity checking has been common in larger system implementations for many years. Micro Channel architecture brings this level of data integrity to smaller systems, enabling them for applications that have previously been reserved for minicomputers and mainframes.

Some conditions that may affect data and address integrity of systems are power fluctuations, electromagnetic interference problems, or cards that are improperly seated. Intermittent failures of devices due to failing components may also generate data integrity problems.

As described in Chapter 2, data and address parity checking are implemented by adding an additional bit of information following the transfer of a byte of information. This ninth bit is "0" or "1," depending on whether the number of ones in the preceding byte is odd or even, respectively. By comparing what the parity bit should be with what it is, the validity of the information transferred can be determined. Micro Channel architecture supports odd parity.

In terms of implementation, data and address parity is optional, and both parity and non-parity devices may exist on the Micro Channel bus. However, in order for parity exceptions to be reported, both the target and the source of the information for the transfer must support parity.

If the parity check is incorrect, the Channel Check (CHCK) signal is activated. This signal is used to indicate that an exception condition has occurred. The response to the exception condition is that the master involved in the transfer suspends operation and interrupts the system.

System masters, bus masters, DMA controllers, and slaves may implement data and address parity in Micro Channel architecture. However, parity checking only occurs between the devices that have the capability. In Personal System/2 systems built to date, none are capable of address and data parity at the system level. The RISC System/6000 systems include data and address parity checking. However, expansion boards that are capable of address and data parity checking can be used in either system family.

Non-Parity Exception Conditions

These are exception conditions other than data and address parity exception conditions. These conditions can be signalled by the system master, bus masters, DMA controllers, or the current slave. It is detected by an invalid combination of the -DS 16 RTN and -DS 32 RTN signals.

Another non-parity exception condition can occur when the Selected Feedback Return Exception Enable field is enabled with -SFDBKRTN inactive. Bus masters monitor this field. In this case, the bus master suspends the transfer and interrupts the system master.

Master- and Slave-Dependent Exceptions

The previous exception conditions were related to the Micro Channel bus and not to the participants. Master- and slave-dependent exceptions are, conversely, related to the participants and their unique characteristics. These are reported using an interrupt or -CHCK, preferably synchronous if it is supported. (The synchronous and asynchronous procedures are described later in this chapter.) Some examples of exceptions of this type are an internal parity error, a command queue overflow, or total failure of the device, a catastrophic exception condition.

Channel Timeout Exception. A channel timeout exception occurs if a controlling master or DMA slave does not release the bus within the 7.8 microseconds of -PREEMPT going active. In this case, the central arbitration control point can drive the arbitration bus to its arbitration state.

Exception Condition Reporting. There are three methods of reporting exception conditions that are defined by Micro Channel architecture: **synchronous exception condition reporting, asynchronous exception condition reporting,** and **interrupts.**

Synchronous exception condition reporting uses the synchronous channel check procedure. This reporting method is normally used by slaves. Masters report exception conditions using interrupts and termination of bus ownership.

Synchronous exception condition reporting utilizes the synchronous -CHCK signal. If the channel check signal is activated by the slave, the master suspends the operation and signals an interrupt. This interrupt generates a routine that handles the exception condition. The conditions that are reported using synchronous exception condition reporting are data and address parity errors, non-parity exceptions, and slave- dependent exceptions.

Asynchronous exception condition reporting is achieved by driving the channel check signal active asynchronously to a data transfer. In this case, the -CHCK signal remains active until reset by the system master. Asynchronous exception reporting can identify the source of the error using the POS ID number, but not at the time the error occurred. Synchronous exception reporting identifies the source of the error at the time of its occurrence, in other words, in the same bus cycle. If an error occurs using synchronous exception reporting, the only information that is lost is that which is associated with that bus cycle, which can then be repeated. All the other information transferred previously is not affected. Asynchronous channel check can cause channel activity to be suspended for participants and could require a system reset.

All IBM Personal System/2 Micro Channel systems built to date have implemented asynchronous channel check reporting. The RISC System/6000 family has implemented synchronous channel check reporting.

Another method of reporting an exception condition occurrence is by using an interrupt. This type of reporting is used by masters. If an interrupt is posted, an indication of the type of exception condition that occurred must be supplied (for example, a data parity error). If an interrupt is posted, the recovery procedure involves the interrupt service routine and is system-dependent.

Exception Handling

In the previous sections we have learned about the different types of exceptions that can occur and how they are reported. This section describes the methods of handling exception conditions. These include handling channel check conditions and select feedback exceptions.

If a -CHCK condition occurs and a bus master owns the bus, it either suspends the data transfer and posts an interrupt, or completes the data transfer and posts an interrupt. Obviously the first action is preferred. If the system master is the controlling master, it handles the exception condition. The action taken is system-dependent. The method for handling exceptions is also software-dependent. The application determines the appropriate action, whether it be a repeat of the data transfer activity or a termination of all activity on the system.

If the DMA controller is the controlling master, the system master reads the exception status of the DMA controller and DMA slave at the end of the DMA operation. During the operation, the DMA controller records the exception information, which is read by the system master.

A select feedback exception occurs when the controlling master does not detect the proper select feedback return signals. These are handled differently depending on the type of participant involved in the exception. If a bus master encounters this exception condition, the data transfer is suspended and an interrupt is posted, or the data transfer is completed and an interrupt is posted. If the system master encounters this exception condition, its handling is system dependent.

If the DMA controller encounters a select feedback exception condition, the terminal count signal is driven active. At the end of the operation, the system master reads the status of the DMA controller and DMA slave to determine if the operation was successfully completed.

PHYSICAL CHARACTERISTICS

IBM considers the physical dimensions of Micro Channel expansion boards and the power supplied to them to be system specifications, as opposed to architectural attributes. Larger Micro Channel boards are used in system-specific implementations, such as IBM RISC System/6000 systems. It is possible that some of the larger Personal System/2 systems may also allow larger boards and greater power in the future, although this would probably be limited to standard devices rather than options for mainstream products. What follows are the physical specifications for the standard Micro Channel expansion boards.

Micro Channel Expansion Board Specifications

The maximum dimensions of the standard raw card are 3.475 in. x 11.51 in. with a thickness of 0.062 in. +/- 0.005 in. The maximum spacing from center to center is 0.085 in. These dimensions are system-dependent.

The maximum load current for +5.0 Vdc is 1.6 A for the 16-bit connector and 2.0 A for the 16/32-bit connector. For both 16-bit and 16/32-bit connectors, the maximum load current is 0.175 for +12.0 Vdc and 0.040 A for -12Vdc. These specifications are also system-dependent.

An example of a system-dependent implementation is that of the RISC System/6000 expansion boards. While most expansion boards used in these systems meet the standard specifications described above, the RISC System/6000 specification permits a larger board and greater power to accommodate some advanced functions expansion boards. The raw card physical size is 4.825 in. x 13.1 in.

The larger power supplies used in the RISC System/6000 systems enable current capabilities to exceed those defined for the standard boards. The maximum load current is 6.5 A for +5.0 VDC, 1.0 A for + 12.0 VDC, and 0.4–0.5 A for -12.0 VDC (model dependent). However, the recommended current ratings are considerably lower than these maximum currents, but higher than those of the standard card. These specifications and others are provided in the six-part RISC System/6000 hardware technical reference manual:[2]

[2]IBM publications can be ordered through your local IBM branch office librarian. In some cases, certain publications may be ordered through special toll-free numbers or fulfillment centers.

IBM RISC System/6000 POWERstation and POWERserver Hardware Technical Reference—General Information Manual (SA23-2643)
IBM RISC System/6000 POWERstation and POWERserver Hardware Technical Reference—Options and Devices (SA23-2646)

IBM RISC System/6000 POWERstation and POWERserver Hardware Technical Reference—7012 POWERstation and POWERserver (SA23-2660)

IBM RISC System/6000 POWERstation and POWERserver Hardware Technical Reference—7013 and 7016 POWERstation and POWERserver (SA23-2644)

IBM RISC System/6000 POWERstation and POWERserver Hardware Technical Reference—7015 POWERserver (SA23-2645)

IBM RISC System/6000 POWERstation and POWERserver Hardware Technical Reference—Micro Channel Architecture (SA23-2647)

Types of Micro Channel Connectors and Slots

There are six distinctly different types of Micro Channel connectors: 16-bit, 32-bit, 16/32-bit, 16-bit with video extension, 32-bit with video extension, and 32-bit with matched-memory extension.

The 16/32-bit connector allows a 32-bit adapter card to function in a 16-bit expansion slot. What this means is that a single design can be used for both 16-bit and 32-bit systems. However, its function is limited to 16-bit in 16-bit systems or in 16-bit slots.

There are also five different types of slots on the system board: 16-bit, 32-bit, 16-bit with video extension, 32-bit with video extension, and 32-bit with matched-

TABLE 3.4 COMPATIBILITY OF MICRO CHANNEL ADAPTER TYPES WITH PS/2 MICRO CHANNEL SYSTEM BOARD CONNECTORS

Board Type	System Board Connector Type: 16-bit	32-bit	16-bit Video	32-bit Video	32-bit MMemory
16-bit	yes	yes	yes	yes	yes
32-bit	no	yes	no	yes	yes
16/32-bit	yes*	yes	yes*	yes	yes
16-bit Video	no	no	yes	yes	no
32-bit Video	no	no	no	yes	no
32-bit MMemory	no	no	no	no	yes

*16-bit Functionality

memory extension. Table 3.4 shows the relationships that are possible between the different adapter connector types and the slot types.

Figure 3.10 shows the types of channel connectors with their optional extensions. The connectors have two sides. The A side refers to the row of pins that are farther away from the system board connector. The pin assignments for the various connector types are illustrated in Figures 3.11, 3.12, 3.13, 3.14, and 3.15. Pins 01 through 45 are used for 8-bit operations. Pins 46 and 47 are physical notches (key) that are used for board alignment. Pins 48 through 58 are used for 16-bit operations along with pins 01 through 45. Additional power and ground pins are also included in this group. Pins 59 and 60 are used for those 32-bit boards that function in 16-bit connectors. Pins 61 through 89 are used for 32-bit operations along with pins 01 through 58.

SUMMARY

This chapter was designed to contain a fairly formal description of the signals and procedures of Micro Channel architecture. While not complete, it should give you a good idea of how the architecture works and the range of its implementation

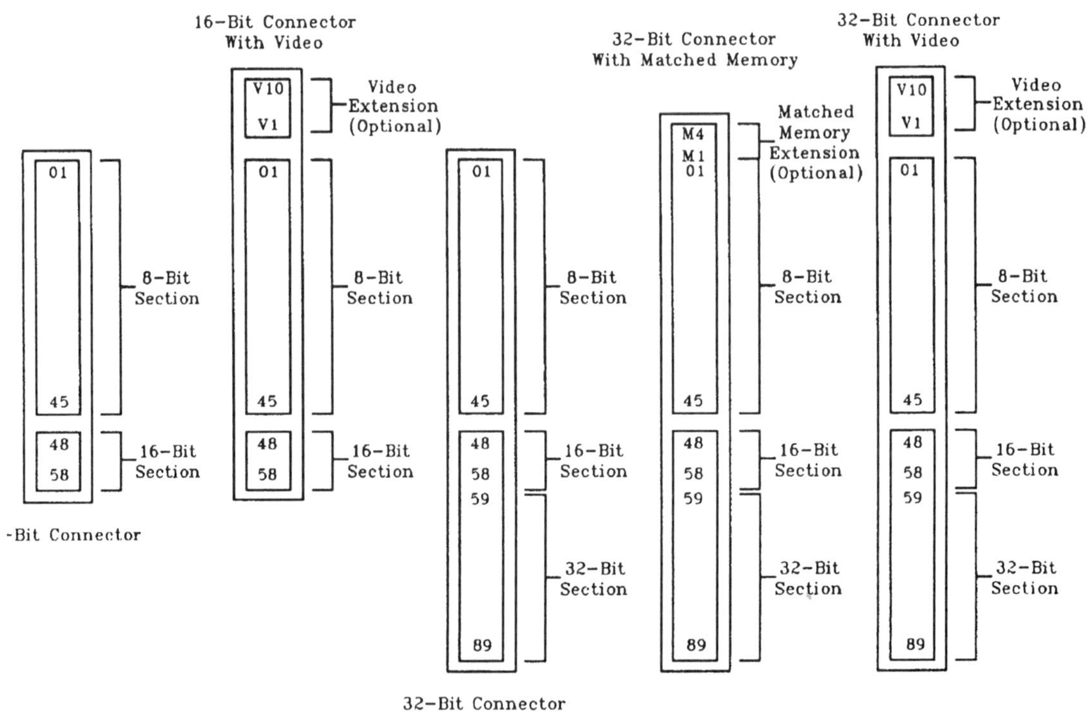

Figure 3.10 Micro Channel connectors and their optional extensions.

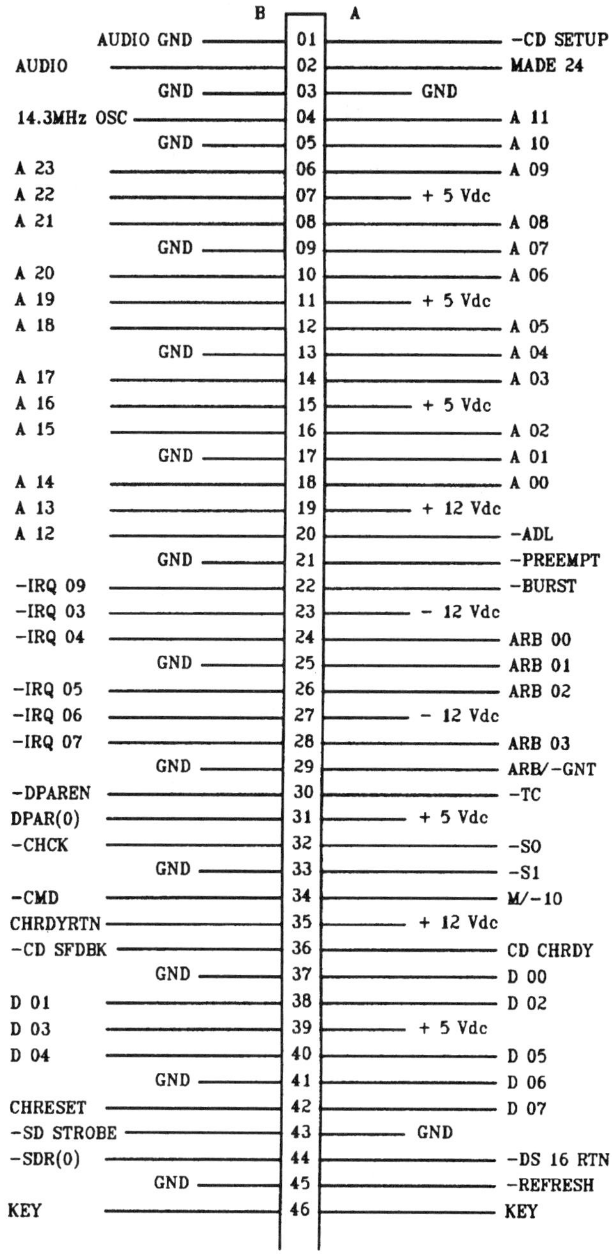

Figure 3.11 Micro Channel connector pin assignments (8-bit portion).

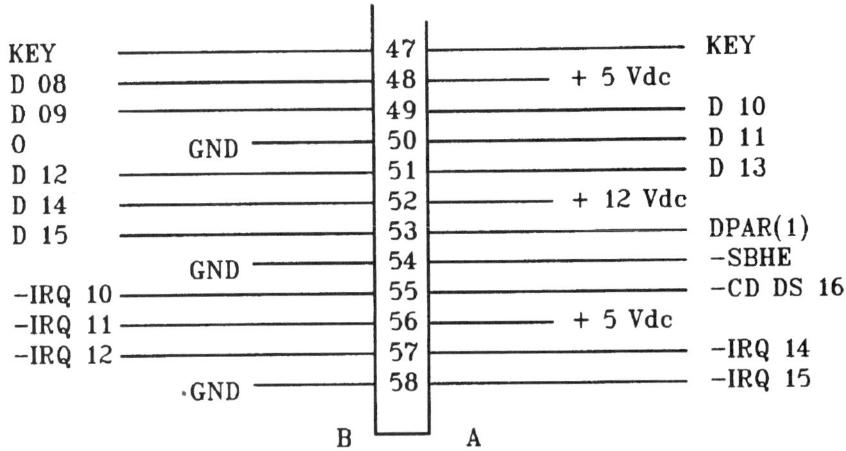

Figure 3.12 Micro Channel connector pin assignments (16-bit portion).

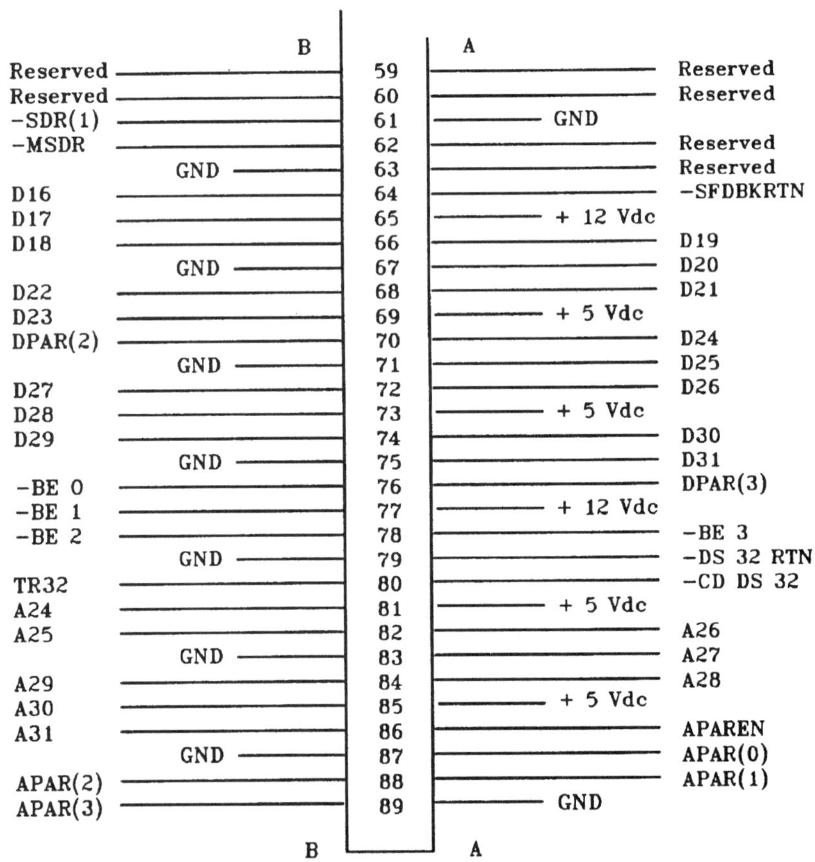

Figure 3.13 Micro Channel connector pin assignments (32-bit portion).

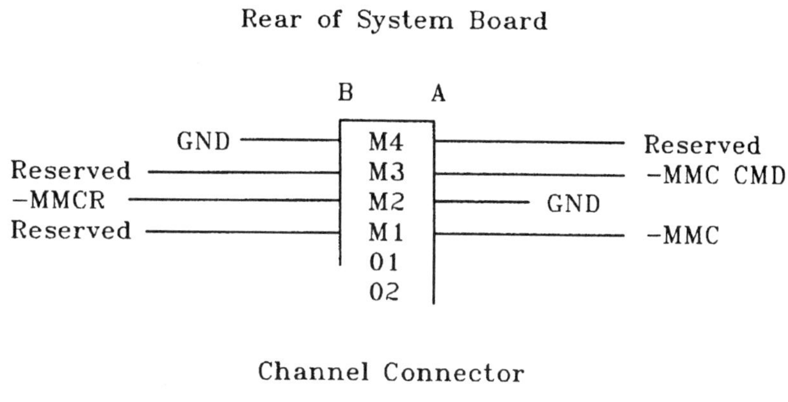

Figure 3.14 Micro Channel connector pin assignments (matched-memory extension).

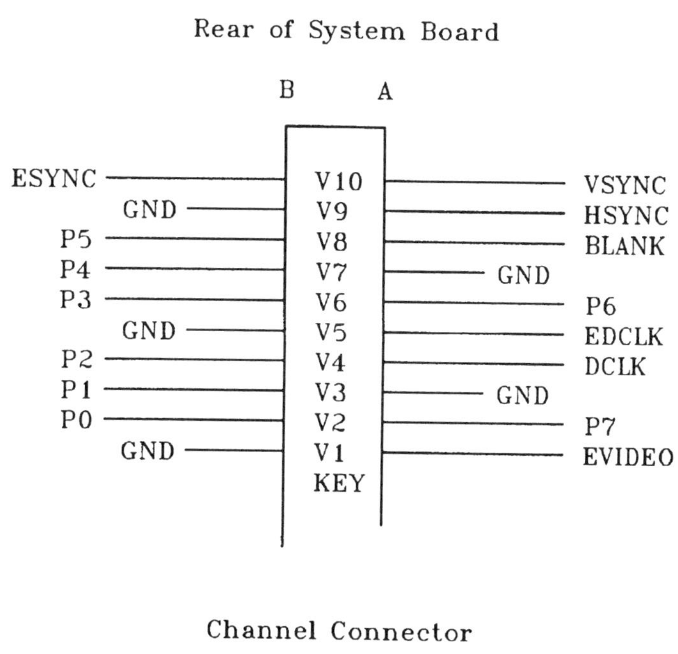

Figure 3.15 Micro Channel connector pin assignments (video extension).

possibilities. If you would like to know more about the technical details of Micro Channel architecture, the following is a list of recommended publications:

IBM PS/2 Hardware Technical Reference Manual (S68X-2330)[3] and Supplements.

IBM Micro Channel Architecture Technical Reference Supplement (S15F2160).

IBM PS/2 BIOS Interface Technical Reference Manual (S68X-2341) and Supplement (S15F2161).

Dutton, Harry J.R. 1990. *A Plain Man's View of the IBM Micro Channel*. Boca Raton, FL. IBM (GG24-3584-00).

For current information on part numbers and pricing for technical publications, call:

1-800-426-7282 in the U.S.

1-414-631-1429 in Canada

1-407-443-3358 in Latin America

44-256-475050, Ext. 8106, in Europe

03-808-4912 in Japan

61-2-481-1205 in Asia

61-2-634-9360 in Australia and New Zealand

(Part numbers and titles of publications may differ from country to country.)

In the next chapter, some of the advanced features of the architecture will be described. In Chapter 5, specific system implementations and application solutions will illustrate how the architecture is being used.

QUESTIONS

1. Who are the participants of Micro Channel architecture? What are their relationships?
2. What are the special duties of the system master?
3. Make a list of all the different types of data transfers that are possible in Micro Channel architecture. (Hint: Don't forget the optional features.)
4. What procedures are used if a device is too slow for the default cycle time (200 ns)? What procedures are available for faster devices?

[3]It is anticipated that IBM will release a new version of the PS/2 technical reference manual soon.

5. Describe the arbitration process. How would Micro Channel architecture be affected if the arbitration priorities for devices were fixed?
6. How does Micro Channel architecture ensure that all requesting devices get their turn to use the bus? How much time is available to a device if another device is not requesting the bus. How much if another device is requesting the bus?
7. Describe the three Micro Channel buses and their signals. What participants can use -BURST?
8. How does Micro Channel ensure compatibility between devices that implement optional features?
9. What are some of the functions of POS?
10. What is the purpose of the audio signal group? The matched-memory signal group? The video extension?
11. Describe what happens in the basic-transfer cycle.
12. Why does Micro Channel architecture use a serial DMA procedure? Compare serial and parallel DMA operations. Under what conditions is serial more efficient? Under what conditions is parallel more efficient?
13. What are the required POS fields?
14. What are some "exception" conditions that you have personally encountered? What was the system response?
15. What are the benefits of synchronous channel check reporting?
16. What are the types of Micro Channel connectors?
17. Why are power and connector dimensions not part of Micro Channel architecture? Should they be?
18. Make a list of the "checks and balances" included in Micro Channel architecture.

4

Advanced Micro Channel Features and Subsystems

In the last chapter, you were introduced to the "nuts and bolts" of Micro Channel architecture. As a result, you have a pretty good idea of what it does and how it does it. Hopefully, your interest is "tweaked" enough to want to know more about some of the advanced features of the architecture that were not explained in detail in the preceding chapters. If you skipped the last chapter because it was too technical, you can pick up where we left off in Chapter 2.

This first part of this chapter focuses on four of the most advanced features of Micro Channel architecture: multimaster support, direct memory access, streaming-data procedures, and Programmable Option Select. It is these advanced features and their implementation that distinguishes Micro Channel architecture from other bus architectures.

The second part of the chapter discusses some of the implications of Micro Channel architecture on the primary subsystems: processor, memory, I/O, and software. A brief description of Subsystem Control Block Architecture, which defines the communications structure and interfaces between the system and a subsystem and between subsystems, is also included.

It is the purpose of this chapter to add additional depth to the advanced features of Micro Channel architecture and to provide a perspective on their use.

MICRO CHANNEL BUS MASTERS

One of the most powerful features of Micro Channel architecture is its support of multiple masters. A Micro Channel master is a microprocessor or any circuit designed to gain control of the bus and drive the address, data, and control signals.

This capability enables a device to transfer information between system memory or between devices.

In case you skipped Chapter 3, a few definitions will be given. There are three types of masters: the system master, the DMA controller, and the bus master. The system master allocates the system resources and runs the primary operating system. In previous personal computers, this was synonymous with the system microprocessor. It is usually the default master in the system, but it is not a requirement (more about this later in the chapter). The default master owns the bus when no other master requires it.

The DMA controller is a specialized type of master that transfers data between DMA slaves and memory slaves. A DMA controller does not arbitrate for control of the bus, but services the DMA slave that is the arbitrator. A bus master arbitrates for use of the bus and supports information transfers with an I/O slave or memory slave.

Since all three types of masters can gain control of the bus and drive the address, data, and control signals, the distinctions between them are sometimes blurred. For example, some people use the term master and bus master interchangeably. A DMA controller is sometimes referred to as a bus master. The definitions used in this book are consistent with those used by IBM in the *IBM Micro Channel Architecture Supplement for the PS/2 Hardware Interface Technical Reference* (IBM Form Number S15F2160).

It is also possible for a bus master to functionally replace the system master, a very powerful capability that allows systems to be upgraded, from a 386 to a 486 machine, for example. It is also not a requirement that the bus master function physically reside on an expansion board since it can be integrated into a VLSI chip and reside on the system board.

The following sections provide a brief history of the bus master function, a description of the various types of bus masters, and some of their applications.

History

The concept of bus ownership shared by more than one master is relatively new to personal computers, but has been around elsewhere for some time. It is an evolved concept that has origins in earlier IBM systems and in other bus architectures. Many of the historical applications have been in systems that were I/O intensive, such as manufacturing floor applications. The VME bus, the MultiBus, and the IBM Series/1 buses all have various implementations of the concept.

To really appreciate the Micro Channel bus master feature, you need to look at the evolution of earlier IBM I/O architectures. There has been a steady progression from complete I/O control by the CPU of the system to distribution of this control among other devices. Figure 4.1 illustrates this progression in IBM's computers.

All I/O operations were controlled directly by the CPU in early systems such as the IBM 1401. The CPU was fully responsible for information transfers to and from memory or I/O devices. Many of its processing cycles were consumed by I/O management. And, as in today's PC, throughput was often limited by the speed of an I/O device. The CPU was forced to wait until an I/O operation was completed

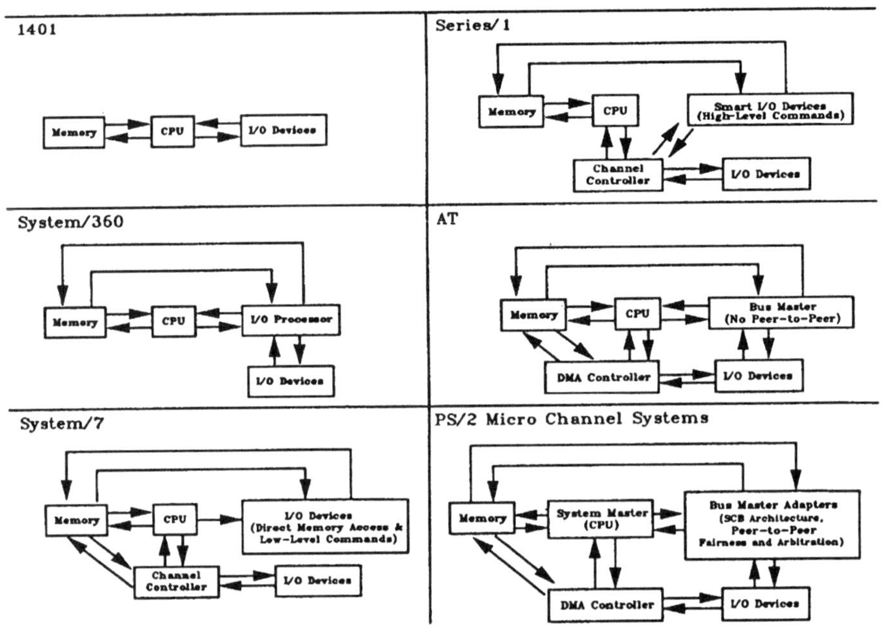

Figure 4.1 Evolution of bus masters in IBM's computers.

before any other activity could begin. Such an architecture denied any possibility of concurrency.

In the System/360, I/O management was transferred to a device called the I/O processor. This 1964 architecture offered significant benefits in performance and concurrency over the 1401 design. The CPU delegated the responsibility of I/O management to the I/O processor using high-level commands. The I/O processor subsequently managed all the data transfers between I/O and memory. This evolved over the years to the channel architecture used in today's IBM mainframes. It consists of an I/O processor and multiple I/O channels and their controllers and is appropriate for today's mainframe computing environment with its centralized storage and processing. In addition, the channels can be cabled across the floor to meet a variety of peripheral requirements.

The System/7 introduction in the early 1970s first permitted I/O devices to have direct memory access (DMA).[1] IBM's early use of DMA by devices other than the CPU laid the foundation for today's bus masters. In the System/7, I/O devices were

[1]Interestingly, IBM never called it "DMA"—that was a term coined later by the industry. IBM referred to it as "cycle stealing" because the I/O device was able to "steal" memory cycles from the CPU.

able to execute low-level commands from the CPU. The System/7 also had a channel controller that was similar in function to that of the I/O processor. As Figure 4.1 shows, data transfers from one I/O device to another required many steps and the participation of several parties. However, as cumbersome as this design may seem today, it offloaded a significant amount of work from the CPU to I/O devices.

The Series/1 system introduced the concept of intelligent adapters, or "smart I/O." As Figure 4.1 shows, these smart I/O devices interpreted and executed their own commands, which gave them additional independence from the CPU. The Series/1 used new software protocols called **control blocks**. They permitted Series/1 adapters to access memory directly (referred to as a first-party DMA operation) as well as communicate with the channel controller.

The AT architecture took two steps forward and one step backward on this evolutionary path. The channel controller was replaced by the DMA controller. The DMA controller could take control of the I/O bus and act as a third-party in the transfer of information between devices and memory over multiple DMA channels. The AT, with its MASTER signal, also introduced the capability of bus ownership by one additional device, a "bus master." This device was given direct memory access, using a single dedicated DMA channel. However, there was no provision in the architecture for the transfer of information between masters themselves (peer-to-peer information transfer). There were also no provisions in the hardware for arbitration by multiple devices or preemption capabilities. Since there was no defined method for equitable bus ownership, it would have been possible for a "bus master" to gain control of the bus and to prevent its use by other devices. This could have caused the loss of data from the loss of memory refresh cycles. Even though it was possible for a device and its device driver to be designed in such a way as to prevent these problems, developers rarely used the AT's MASTER signal.

With the introduction of Micro Channel architecture in 1987 in IBM's PS/2 product line, true bus master capabilities were implemented. The hardware-mediated arbitration process, the method of preemption, and a fairness algorithm for equitable sharing of the bus are the primary differences between the Micro Channel master capability and that of the AT.

There is also a defined protocol, Subsystem Control Block Architecture, which provides the procedures for peer-to-peer communications and data exchange between masters. While not technically part of Micro Channel architecture, this powerful architecture provides the road map for the high-level command capabilities associated with the bus master function. Subsystem Control Block Architecture will be described later in this chapter.

This historical perspective on the evolution of the master capabilities in IBM's personal computers is only part of the story, however. IBM's invention of DMA is probably the most significant event leading to the capability, but there are buses other than those in IBM systems that have multimaster and peer-to-peer capabilities. Actually, the first system that had true multimaster capability with peer-to-peer transfers was the PDP-11®, developed by Digital Equipment Corporation® in the early 1970s. The bus was called the UNIBUS™.

NuBus, introduced in Apple's Macintosh II in 1987, also supports multiple masters. NuBus is based on a bus that was conceived at the Massachusetts Institute of Technology (MIT) in the late 1970s. This 32-bit standard has many similarities with the Micro Channel bus and some significant differences, which will be described in Chapter 6.

The EISA bus, first introduced in systems in late 1989, also has multimaster capabilities. EISA is an extension of IBM's AT architecture that evolved from a consortium of IBM-compatible system manufacturers led by Compaq. The objective of the Extended Industry Standard Architecture (EISA) is to retain compatibility with the AT bus while providing a 32-bit I/O bus with advanced architectural features. There are other bus architectures with multimaster functions. These are special-purpose architectures that are beyond the scope of this book. Chapter 6 is devoted to the comparison of the Micro Channel bus with other significant microcomputer bus architectures, focusing on the specific attributes of their multimaster features.

Bus Master Requirements and Types

The requirements for "bus mastership" can be somewhat confusing at times. It is important to note that a bus master *does not* require a microprocessor. Also, bus masters must respond as slaves when accessed by another master or during the setup procedure (Figure 4.2). This diagram illustrates a bus master that also serves as an I/O or a memory slave. The only specified requirement of a bus master is the ability to gain control of the bus through its internal arbitration logic and then to control the execution of a defined bus cycle. By not utilizing a processor, the bus master developer can lower the price/performance ratio and reduce the cost of production. The ability to reduce system overhead, increase performance, and be manufacturable at a cost equivalent to DMA slaves makes the bus master one of the most attractive features of Micro Channel architecture.

There are three basic types of bus masters: full-function bus masters, special-function controllers, and programmable special-function controllers. The fundamental differences between them are their degrees of flexibility, function, and cost. The full-function bus master is the most flexible and generally has the most function and the highest production cost. The special-function controller has the

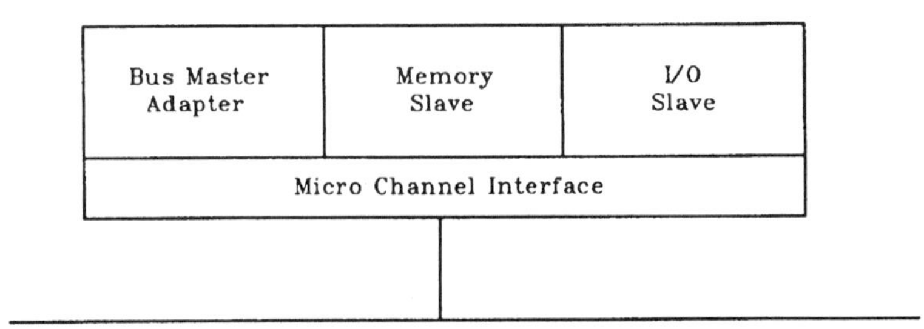

Figure 4.2 A Micro Channel bus master may also serve as an I/O or memory slave.

least flexibility and generally has the least function and cost. The programmable special-function controller can span the range between the full-function bus master and the special function controller.

A full-function bus master has its own CPU and is *capable* of controlling the system resources with appropriate operating system software, which, in turn, controls and allocates system resources. Micro Channel architecture makes it possible for more than one operating system or multiple copies of the same operating system to run concurrently on a system with multiple bus masters. It also means that each application program can run on its own "CPU" card for maximum performance with appropriate software support. This provides a broad range of software flexibility and compatibility while significantly increasing system performance.

Special function controller bus masters are devices that use on-board logic circuits (but have no CPU) to perform a specific function with little or no assistance from other masters. Examples of special function bus masters are communication adapters and storage controllers. These devices can move blocks of data and perform other functions with little or no support from the CPU or other masters and use few (if any) interrupts. Special function controllers can maximize system performance by minimizing system overhead and freeing up CPU cycles.

Programmable special-function controller masters are devices that span the range between full-function bus masters and special-function bus masters. The fundamental difference between a special-function controller and a programmable special-function controller is the ability to modify the function and/or execution characteristics of the bus master. They can contain processing units, or their programmability can be as simple as setting a control register(s). Examples of programmable special-function controllers are storage controllers and page printer controllers. (The third-party DMA controller is a programmable special-function controller that is a type of master, but it is not referred to as a bus master in this book.) With the possible exception of cost and performance, these bus masters have the same advantages as special function controllers. However, they have the ability to be attached to a variety of I/O devices.

Bus Master Benefits

Many of the benefits of bus masters were described in Chapter 2. This section contains a brief summary of those benefits from a different perspective. Bus master benefits can be divided into roughly three categories: performance, design flexibility, and functional enhancements. Let's look at performance first.

The performance benefits of bus masters are heavily dependent on the application and operating system. Most of their benefits are not realized in a single-tasking environment, but rely on multi-tasking software support. Another way of looking at this is that bus masters contribute to performance because they enable multiple simultaneous operations. However, this is of no benefit if there is no software support for these operations. For PS/2 systems, this translates to an OS/2 or UNIX environment.

Bus masters provide performance benefits in a number of ways:

1. By offloading functions from the system master;
2. By minimizing interrupts;
3. Through their own processing power; and
4. Through elimination of third-party DMA transfers.

Figure 4.3 illustrates how bus masters eliminate steps in information transfers and free up the system master. As the illustration shows, a bus master may use one-half to one-quarter the steps required by the system master or the DMA controller to transfer identical information. As significant as this is, the reduction in interrupt servicing and transfer overhead is even more important. These efficiency gains can be so dramatic that the difference between 16-bit and 32-bit bus masters may be relatively small for some operations.

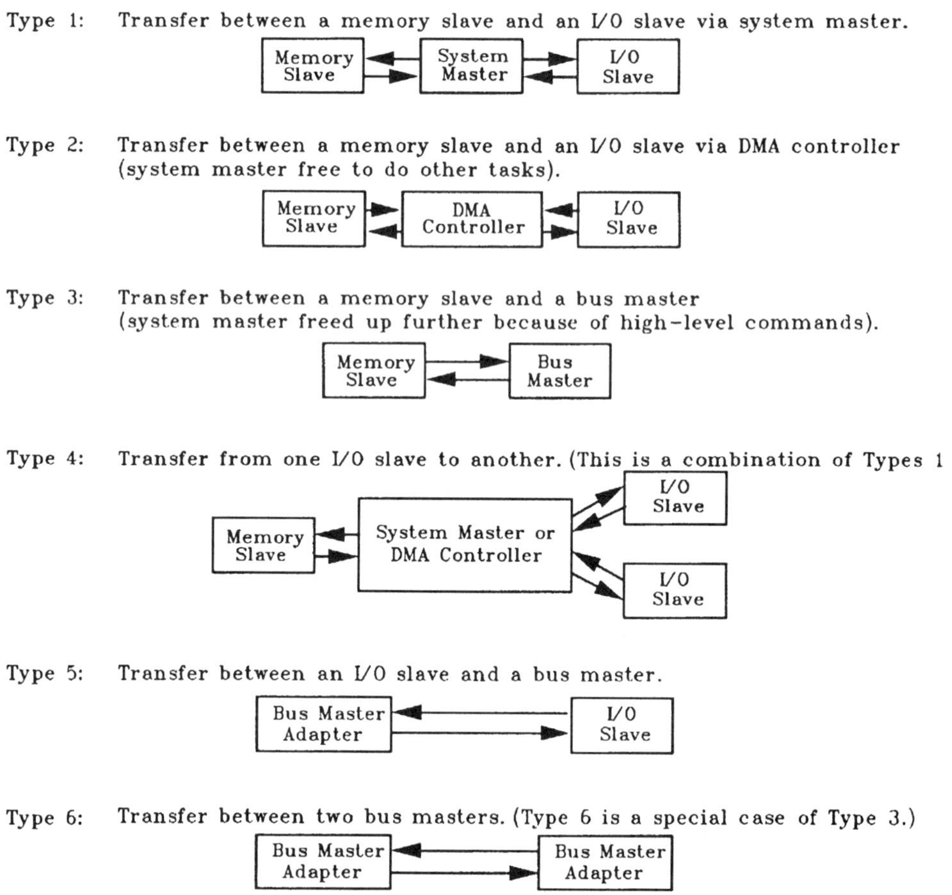

Figure 4.3 Micro Channel information transfers. Bus masters reduce the number of steps required to move information.

Bus masters enhance system performance with their own on-board processing power. Many bus masters have powerful microprocessors that are used to execute complex commands. This contributes to the overall processing power of a system by freeing up the system master, or in many cases, by the fact that the bus master microprocessor has been designed with a particular task in mind, such as floating-point arithmetic, and can perform the task faster than the system microprocessor.

It is important to realize that bus masters do not necessarily increase system performance. If the system microprocessor is not busy doing other tasks, and is very powerful, an I/O slave implementation may be faster than a bus master implementation with a less powerful processor. Another way of saying this is that the bus master performance benefits are observed in systems in which the system microprocessor (or the I/O bus) is busy and near saturation. IBM's performance labs have estimated that a 30-percent CPU savings of a bus master over a non-bus master is reasonable.[2]

Bus masters can be used to upgrade the processing capability of systems by adding a new CPU subsystem that serves as a replacement for the system master. The new CPU subsystem can be given control of the system resources after the default master has initialized the system. The default master can be made quiescent, relegated to supporting I/O functions, or operate concurrently with the new CPU subsystem. Because multiple bus masters are supported by Micro Channel Architecture, multiple CPU subsystems can (with the appropriate operating system and software support) operate concurrently. This concurrent processing can provide significant system processing capabilities without wasting any existing system logic.

The added CPU(s) can have a completely different software architectures from that of their host system. For example, it is possible to add a RISC bus master to a non-RISC system. Because Micro Channel architecture is separate from the CPU architecture of the system, maximum design flexibility is achieved.

Bus masters may provide functional enhancements to systems by using intelligent controllers to manage complex functions. Some examples of these are graphics, image, communications, and storage applications. The use of bus masters to manage I/O subsystems is described later in this chapter.

Bus Master Applications

The appearance of Micro Channel bus master applications was relatively slow initially. This was due to a number of factors ranging from business considerations of developers, design complexity, manufacturing considerations, and the lack of software that exploited the capabilities of bus masters. Initially there was a limited market for Micro Channel expansion boards of any type. With the growing number of installed Micro Channel systems, the largest business opportunity was in developing slave adapters. With the exception of the built-in devices, all of the functions that were available in AT type systems needed to be "ported" over to

[2]*IBM Personal System/2 Performance Guide*, (G326-0041), p. 71.

Micro Channel systems. As a consequence, developers concentrated on the most obvious needs in the market such as serial boards and memory expansion boards.

The design of bus masters seemed more complicated to developers. Most of the developers for previous IBM-compatibles had no experience in developing bus masters and faced a new learning curve. In addition, IBM had no bus masters that were available as examples. There were also many implementation possibilities that represented significant technical risks for product developers. The technical documentation available from IBM for bus master functionality was also subject to varying interpretations.

Development of IBM's internal bus masters was retarded by some of the same factors that limited external development. Supplying expansion boards for critical gaps in product options was the first priority. In addition, IBM was faced with a resource shortage in development personnel as a result of cutbacks in hiring and head count reductions. During 1988 and 1989, the IBM Corporation faced a period of lower earnings that drove these resource reductions. In terms of development priorities, expansion board development generally was lower on IBM's list than were system development activities. As a consequence, no bus master was offered by IBM until 1988.

The third challenge that bus master applications offered to developers was limited board space for the more complex designs. In order to physically fit all the required function on the boards, a significant amount of integration was required. Even though VLSI circuitry provides many technical advantages over conventional packaging technology, the development tools and techniques required are more sophisticated. In addition, VLSI packaging can be more expensive for low manufacturing volumes.

Bus Master Chip Sets

IBM's response to the slow bus master development was to work with two major chip vendors to develop some common building blocks for bus master functions, a set of general purpose VLSI chips. In late 1989, IBM announced a joint development activity with Intel and Chips and Technologies for these chip sets. In addition, a series of design seminars were held during 1990 to assist developers in utilizing these tools.

These common building blocks for bus master development reduce developer learning curves, reduce development expense and time, ensure compatibility and consistency, use less board space, and set implementation examples. From a business perspective, the chip sets reduce board costs and business risks associated with bus master development.

These chips provide common Micro Channel functions such as loadable registers for the device identification numbers, programmable I/O and memory ranges, programmable arbitration and interrupt levels, the ability to enable/disable optional features (for instance, parity and data streaming), and other features used in the POS function.

As many common functions as possible are integrated in the chips to minimize board space. Required latches, buffers, drivers, address decoders, POS functions, arbitration, bus master controls, burst and preempt management, address generation, data buffering, and control are some of the functions included in the chips.

The design point for these chips was one of maximum flexibility to provide for their use in a broad range of applications. Variable data path widths, broad interface ranges for subsystem functions, variable speeds for memory and subsystems, and the ability to support different methods for attachment are included. The chips support direct memory access of local and system memory, provide a memory and I/O slave interface for the subsystem, and support address and data parity and variable levels of data transfer modes.

In order to satisfy all the requirements in a cost-effective manner, two different chip sets were developed: Intel's 82325 and Chips and Technologies' 82C614. These chip sets are intended for use in IBM's products as well as those of external developers.

Intel's 82325 bus master interface controller chip set is a general purpose bus master interface for intelligent adapters. This design provides the basis for a full function bus master, one of the three types of bus masters described previously. The chip set provides three different logical interfaces to the Micro Channel bus: a memory slave interface, an I/O slave interface, and the bus master interface.

The chip set consists of two members: the Intel 32825MD chip, which is designed primarily for data transfers, and the Intel 32325MC chip, which is responsible for most of the control signals. Combined with the appropriate support logic and interfaces to the Micro Channel bus, these two chips provide support for an intelligent bus controller.

Key features of the 82325 chip set are:

- A 16/32-bit Micro Channel data bus;
- A 24/32-bit address bus;
- Address and data parity support;
- Micro Channel and local interrupt lines;
- Full POS registers;
- 32-bit DMA channel and port;
- A 64 byte data buffer;
- BURST control;
- An interface for a 386SX or 80186 local microprocessor interface; and
- Support for 100 ns streaming-data transfers.

The 82C614 BUS MASTER Micro CHIP™, the Chips and Technologies® product, is intended to provide the basis for a programmable special-function bus master type as described previously. It also provides three logical interfaces to the Micro Channel bus: a Micro Channel I/O slave interface, a memory slave interface, and a bus master interface.

The 82C614 chip features an 8/16-bit data path and supports a full 32-bit address path. Data transfer rates of up to 20 MB/sec can be achieved using the streaming-data procedure. The 82C614 also supports parity generation and checking and synchronous channel check, and has an local bus interface with an AT-like structure for ease of interfacing. It also contains a total of eight multifunction pins that can support eight input and eight output functions, which further eliminates additional components and lowers adapter cost. A 16-bit data bus and up to 24 address lines are supported on the local bus. The 82C614 allows DMA operations on the local bus to run concurrently with DMA operations on the Micro Channel bus. This concurrency can effectively double the data transfer throughput of DMA operations. Using the streaming-data procedure, the data rate can be quadrupled.

The 82C614 chip is intended for cost-effective applications that do not require a local CPU, as well as for applications that would otherwise use a DMA controller. Potential applications include graphics adapters, disk controllers, high speed printer controllers, high performance LAN adapters, SCSI host adapters, high speed serial adapters, and other high speed DMA intensive applications.

The Intel and Chips and Technologies products have greatly accelerated the development of Micro Channel bus master products. A list of Micro Channel chip sets, including the Intel and Chips and Technologies products, is included in Appendix C.

Bus Master Products

A summary of bus master products and other Micro Channel products currently available and a brief description of each may be found in the *Catalog of Micro Channel Expansion Adapters*, available through the nearest IBM branch office or IBM authorized dealer. Ask for G360-2824. This information is also posted on the IBM National Support Center Bulletin Board System at (404) 835-6600 in Atlanta, Georgia and is updated monthly. The bulletin board operates 24 hours a day and is available worldwide on a toll-call basis with no access charge. (Requirements include a 300 to 9600 baud modem set for 8 data bits, 1 stop bit, no parity.)

Appendix D of this book contains descriptions of some of the bus masters that are available for Micro Channel systems and their sources. It is included to illustrate the types of functions that bus masters can provide and is not intended as a comprehensive and current source. Because of the rate of change of this information, current catalogs, bulletin board listings, and manufacturers represent the best sources.

The following section contains a brief description of several types of bus masters that illustrate the range of functions available. Chapter 5 also contains several application solutions that utilize bus masters.

Processor Cards

Aox MicroMaster™. A series of processor upgrade bus masters are available from Aox, Inc. The MicroMASTER 386™ product is an example of an 80386-based processor upgrade for the IBM PS/2 Model 50, 50Z, and 60, or compatible computers, and is used to increase the performance up to six times for certain applications (Figure 4.4). It holds the distinction of being the first processor upgrade board to take advantage of the bus master capabilities of the Micro Channel architecture to become the system master. These cards are available in a full range of processor frequencies and are designed to accept 80387 math coprocessors and up to 8 MB of 32-bit memory on the card. Zero wait state cache memory provides an additional performance boost and can access on-board 32-bit memory or the system's 16-bit

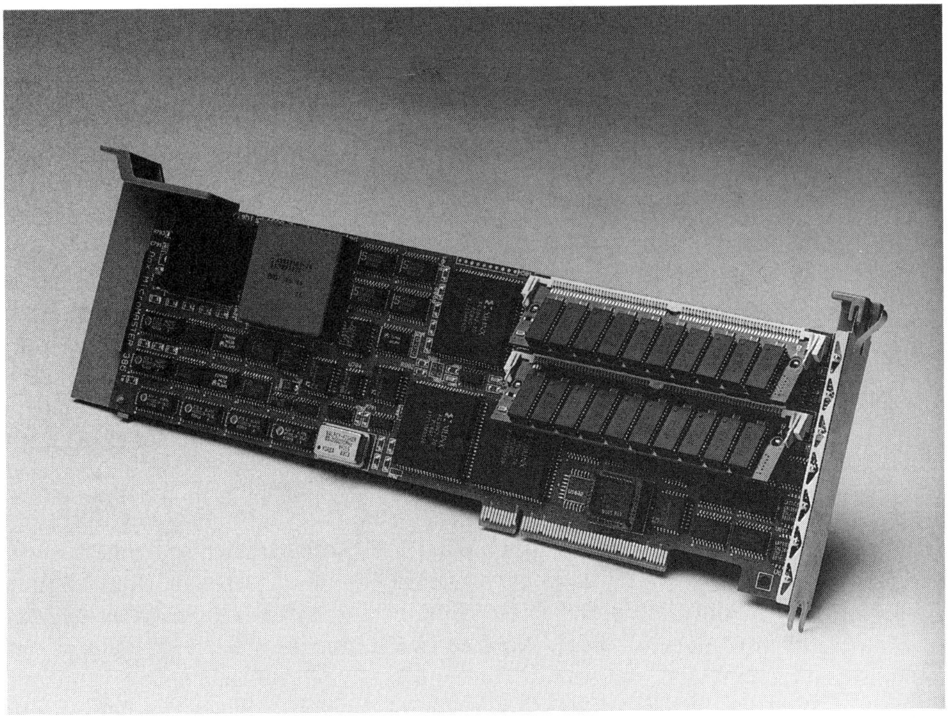

Figure 4.4 AOX MicroMaster 386.

memory. The upgraded processor can access existing peripherals and memory as though it were the system master. A 486 version is also available that increases the overall speed of standard systems by up to ten times. The Aox cards are also used to bring multiprocessing capabilities to Micro Channel systems. A server solution utilizing an Aox card in this manner is described in Chapter 5.

Prometa BusMaster WS/88K. The WS/88K BusMaster is a product from PROMETA AB that is based on the Motorola 88000 RISC architecture. This bus master and its software provide a complete UNIX System V workstation and enables Micro Channel systems to run all 88Open BCS UNIX applications. The product is available with one to four processors offering 17 MIPS (million instructions per second) per processor or 7 MFLOPS (million floating point operations per second) per processor. The system is capable of running UNIX and OS/2 or DOS simultaneously and is designed to function in either a 32- or 16-bit Micro Channel slot.

YARC Micro 785+™. The Micro 785 +, available from YARC Systems Corporation, features a Motorola MC68020 microprocessor running at 40 MHz that provides 5 VAX MIPS of processing power. The system supports FORTRAN, C, and Pascal compilers and applications. An application example support by the product is MIRA from Oklahoma Seismic.

IBM PS/2 Wizard Adapter. IBM's PS/2 Wizard Adapter, a bus master adapter with a 33 MHz i860 RISC microprocessor, is an application accelerator for general purpose PS/2 systems. It is used for numeric intensive applications such as financial modeling and statistical analysis and graphics such as CAD (computer aided design) and image analysis. In terms of operating system support, the Wizard device driver is used to execute the transfer of information across the Micro Channel bus. The primary application runs on the system master and transfers secondary pieces of the application to the Wizard adapter as a subroutine. This code segment is executed and returned to the primary application running on the system master. The Wizard product is a good example of asymmetric multiprocessing using Micro Channel architecture (discussed later in this chapter).

Storage Controllers

IBM PS/2 SCSI Adapters. IBM's 16-bit and 32-bit SCSI bus masters provide support for up to 7 SCSI devices and provide both synchronous and asynchronous SCSI data transfers. Both internal and external connectivity is provided. These products are further described in Chapter 5.

Core CNT-MCA. The CNT-MCA, a bus master available from CORE International is a 20MHz ESDI hard disk controller that supports two drives. The CNT-MCA works independently of the CPU and also features an on-board DMA controller. Two controllers support duplexing under Novell 2.15 or NetWare 386 software. Disk-intensive applications, including communications, graphics, and facsimile benefit most from the Core bus master design. This device can coexist with IBM controllers and has been used effectively to upgrade older Micro Channel systems.

Graphics and Image

Pixelworks Ultra Clipper Graphics™ Adapter. The Ultra Clipper Graphics product is a high performance, high resolution graphics subsystem with mainframe graphics features available from Pixelworks, Inc. The product supports bus master and DMA slave operations. It features programmable interrupts, I/O ports, and DMA channels. AutoCAD™, VersaCAD™, GEM™, and other popular drivers are available. Full 2D, 3D integer, and optional floating point transformations are supported.

IBM PS/2 Image Adapter/A. IBM's Image Adapter/A is a bus master adapter that includes a 32-bit 8.5 MIP display processor. The product also has a 16-bit subset that allows attachment to 16-bit systems such as IBM PS/2 Models 50, 50Z, 55SX, and 60. This high resolution device also provides high-speed compression and decompression. There is a provision for attaching auxiliary function cards such as printer and scanner daughter cards. Chapter 5 contains an additional discussion of this product.

SuperFax MC/iPS. The SuperFax MC/iPS, available from Pacific Image Communications, Inc. is a 16-bit bus master solution that runs under Windows and OS/2. Up to seven FAX boards can run concurrently in the background with no degradation to the foreground task.

Communications

Lantana Cypress/2™ . The Cypress/2 is a bus master controller that is available from Lantana Technology, Inc. It is a 16-bit Token Ring LAN adapter rated at 4 Mb/sec transfer rate.

BICC 4110-3 ISOLAN® MCA. The 4110-3 ISOLAN MCA controller, available from BICC DATA NETWORKS, is a 16-bit Ethernet bus master that is unique because it does not include a CPU.

METACOMP PScomm4™. The PScomm4, a 16-bit bus master available from METACOMP™, provides programmable intelligence for high-level data communications processing. The adapter hosts a 16-bit 80C186 CPU running at 16 MHz for processing complex data communications protocols. Some applications include network gateways, protocol servers, and communications concentrators.

Multiport adapters are particularly suitable for bus master implementations. These adapters are used to communicate with multiple devices that may have different characteristics and communication protocols. Some examples of these devices include point-of-sale terminals, ASCII terminals, scientific instrumentation, manufacturing equipment, and other systems ranging from PCs to mainframes. Advanced multiport adapters generally are capable of managing complex communications subsystems with a multitude of concurrence tasks. Most contain one or more microprocessors such as Intel's 80C186. Bus master implementations of multiport adapters greatly increase the efficiency of these applications by their direct memory access capabilities and through peer to peer communications on the Micro Channel bus.

IBM Portmaster™ Adapter/A. The ARTIC bus master card, the IBM Realtime Interface Coprocessor Portmaster Adapter/A, supports up to 8 RS-232 or RS-422 ports. The expansion board has an onboard Intel 80C186 microprocessor running at 12.5 MHz. Two DMA channels are provided per serial port. The adapter card can accommodate up to 2 MB of memory. Up to four adapters per system are supported, providing support for up to 32 devices in a single system. The Portmaster Adapter is capable of peer-to-peer transfers. Solutions using this product are described in Chapter 5.

METACOMP pSconnect™. PSconnect™, available from METACOMP, Inc. is a bus master adapter that allows users to connect from 8 to 256 asynchronous devices to Micro Channel systems. These async devices are connected to a remote concentrator unit. Each of these concentrators can support 8 or 16 asynchronous devices. Its expandability is further increased by using a hub controller that supports up to 127 remote async concentrators. The hub controller acts as a repeater for communications between the bus master adapter and remote async concentrators by receiving data from the bus master adapter and retransmitting it over several other ports.

The bus master adapter offloads processing from the system master by managing the serial I/O processing. The adapter is built around an Intel 80C186 microprocessor and an 80C188 microprocessor operating at 16 MHz. In this very powerful communications subsystem, the capabilities of the bus master adapter to manage this enormous workload are extremely impressive.

MICRO CHANNEL DIRECT MEMORY ACCESS

The term direct memory access is used to refer to the capability that masters have that enables them to read information from and write information to system memory. The following section describes DMA channel utilization, performance factors, and DMA controller attributes. The focus is on operations performed by the DMA controller, but it's important to remember that bus masters can also perform DMA operations more efficiently than the DMA controller.

DMA Channel Utilization

DMA channels provide the pathways that are used for transfers to and from system memory. The number of DMA channels and the flexibility for their use is a fundamental architectural attribute that affects almost every aspect of information transfers.

In order to appreciate the DMA capabilities of Micro Channel architecture, it is necessary to examine the DMA utilization in earlier systems. The IBM Personal Computer had three DMA channels that were permanently assigned for specific functions. Channel 0 was designated as the channel for refreshing the dynamic RAM of the system memory. DMA Channel 1 was assigned the function of supporting communications, specifically, SDLC (synchronous data link control). Channel 2 was assigned to the diskette controller. With the introduction of the IBM Personal Computer XT, a fourth DMA channel was provided for the fixed disk drive controller. In addition to the channels described above, the CPU of each system had a dedicated DMA channel for its use.

These DMA channels could not be used for any other purpose other than these specific assignments. The bus connections went from that specific device to the system memory only. There was no physical pathway for other devices to utilize the same DMA channel. The system software, BIOS and DOS, and applications that addressed the hardware directly also depended on these fixed assignments. There was no capability of reassigning these DMA channels even if they were unused.

With the introduction of the AT, three additional 16-bit DMA channels were added in order to utilize the advanced features and 16-bit I/O capabilities of its 80286 microprocessor. The original assignments for the PC were kept for compatibility purposes. In addition, the channel that had been dedicated to the fixed disk controller was now shared by PC Network. When there was network activity, the fixed disk controller could not use its DMA channel. In this event, the AT's 80286 processor assumed these operations.

However, the AT's new channels could not be used by DOS because of the way that DOS required the data to be aligned. Other operating systems were able to make efficient use of these channels, but it was primarily a DOS world at that time. Even though the AT had additional DMA channels, the design was relatively inflexible, with limited channel availability.

Micro Channel architecture has very flexible DMA procedures and DMA channel management. There are no fixed assignments for the channels and up to 15 DMA slaves can be supported. All the channels are selectable and are under software control. For compatibility purposes, Channels 1, 2, and 3 were preassigned the functions that they served on the earlier buses as their default assignments. However, even these assignments can be dynamically changed if necessary. Any device can use any channel, and there is no fixed data path width associated with a given channel as there was in the PC and AT assignments.

In terms of system implementations, current Micro Channel systems have eight DMA channels that can support up to 15 DMA slaves or bus master devices. There are eight physical channels and seven additional virtual channels that are supported.

DMA Transfer Rates

There are four factors that influence data rates associated with DMA transfers: the cycle times, the data path width, the number of steps, and the overhead (Figure 4.5). Again it is helpful to look at Micro Channel's DMA capabilities compared to those of PC, XT, and AT bus architecture.

The cycle time of the original PC and XT was 1,050 nanoseconds. The data path width was 8 bits. This translates to a DMA data transfer rate of 1.05 MB/sec. The cycle times for the 6 and 8 MHz AT systems were 1,670 and 1,250 nanoseconds,

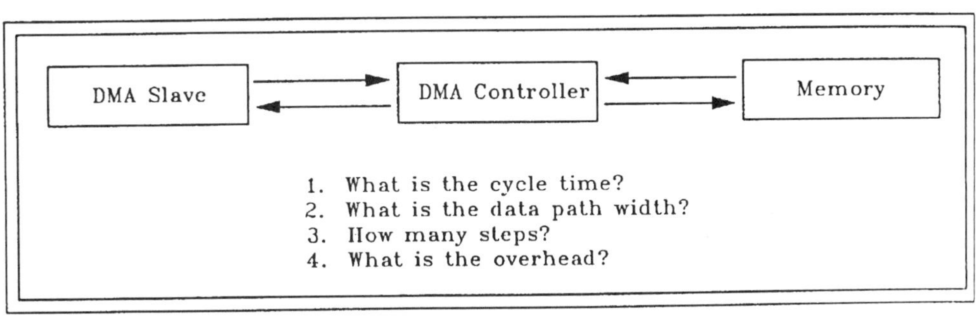

Figure 4.5 Factors that influence DMA data rates.

respectively. The AT had two DMA controllers: an 8-bit controller for DOS compatibility and a 16-bit controller. Assuming 16-bit transfers, this corresponds to data rates of 1.2 MB/sec and 1.6 MB/sec for the 6 and 8 MHz AT. However, as was explained in the previous section, little use was made of the AT's 16-bit DMA channels.

For Micro Channel transfers, the current 10 MHz bus speed corresponds to a 200 nanosecond default cycle time. This translates to an instantaneous data rate of 10 MB/sec for 16-bit DMA transfers and 20 MB/sec for 32-bit DMA transfers. However, if the DMA transfer utilizes the DMA controller instead of a bus master, two steps are required as illustrated in Figure 4.6. In the case of a DMA read operation, one cycle is required for memory read and another is required to complete the transfer to the DMA slave. This serial DMA procedure, as it is called, leads to an instantaneous data rate of 5 MB/sec for a 16-bit DMA controller considering both operations. For 32-bit DMA transfers, this instantaneous data rate would increase to 10 MB/sec. The first Micro Channel systems available from IBM did not implement a 32-bit DMA controller, and so the instantaneous data rate was 5 MB/sec. However, DMA transfers involving 32-bit bus masters could achieve 20 MB/sec using the basic transfer rates or higher if the streaming-data procedure was utilized. These DMA transfer rates are summarized in Table 4.1.

There are two very important factors that have been omitted from this discussion to this point, however. These factors are the overhead and the software support for the various DMA transfers.

Let's look at the overhead factor first. In Micro Channel DMA transfers, a burst capability for moving large blocks of data is included. This greatly reduces the overhead associated with transfers. It is possible to conduct up to 312 transfers with a single bus arbitration in Micro Channel systems. DMA transfers on the PC and AT bus are conducted one or two bytes at a time, with overhead associated with each transfer. For Micro Channel systems, the percent of overhead decreases as the block size increases.

The second factor that is important in this discussion of DMA data rates is the software support. The system software must support the data transfer widths associated with DMA transfers (or any transfers for that matter). DOS only

TABLE 4.1 DATA TRANSFER RATES

Bus	Participant	Cycle Time	Cycles	Data Rate[a]	Data Path
PC	DMA Controller	1050 ns	1	1.0 MB/sec	8-bit
AT (8 MHz)	DMA Controller	1250	1	0.8	8-bit
AT (8 MHz)	DMA Controller	1250	1	1.6	16-bit
Micro Channel	DMA Controller	200	2	5.0	16-bit
Micro Channel	DMA Controller	200	2	10.0	32-bit
Micro Channel	Bus Master	200	1	10.0	16-bit
Micro Channel	Bus Master	200	1	20.0	32-bit

a. Higher data transfer rates are possible for Micro Channel systems using streaming data procedures.

supports 8-bit DMA operations. OS/2 versions 1.2 and lower support 8-bit and 16-bit DMA operations. The 32-bit version of OS/2 (Version 2.0) will support 32-bit DMA operations when it becomes available.

DMA Controller Operations

The DMA controller supports information transfers between I/O devices (DMA slaves) and memory, acting as a third-party device that couples DMA slaves and memory slaves during data transfers. The DMA controller manages the information transfer instead of the system master making the system master available for other tasks and reducing interrupts.

There are two types of DMA operations that are conducted by the DMA controller: DMA read operations and DMA write operations. A DMA read operation consists of reading the information from the memory slave and transferring it to the DMA slave. A DMA write operation is just the opposite: the DMA slave provides the information, which is then stored by the memory slave.

As was mentioned in the previous section, Micro Channel architecture specifies a serial DMA procedure. As Figure 4.6 illustrates, there are two sequential steps involved in these operations. In the PC and AT architecture, the procedure was conducted in a single step and was termed a parallel DMA procedure (Figure 4.7). Because the Micro Channel serial procedure requires two separate steps, one might assume that it is a less efficient process than the parallel procedure used in the PC and AT systems. This is not necessarily the case, however.

In the case of parallel DMA transfers, the width of the data transfer must be that of the lesser participant. For example, a DMA read operation from a 16-bit memory slave to an 8-bit DMA slave occurs as two 8-bit transfers. If the transfer involved a 32-bit memory slave to an 8-bit device, four 8-bit transfers would have

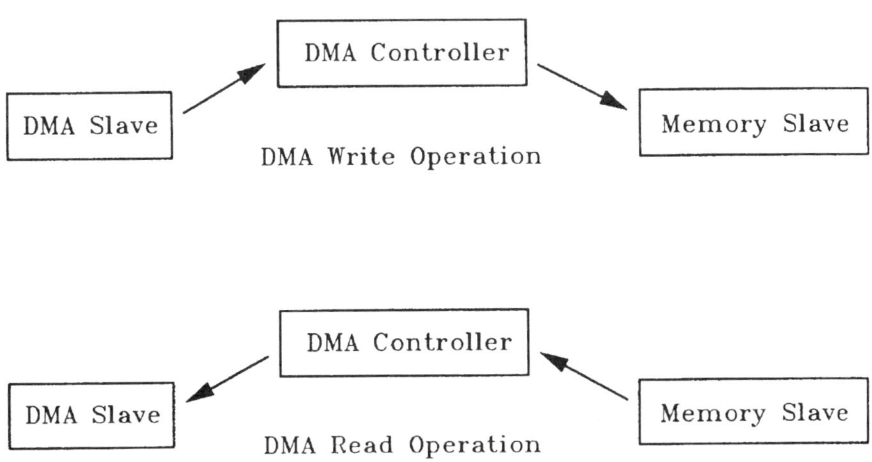

Figure 4.6 Micro Channel's serial DMA capability allows DMA controllers to execute read and write cycles independently.

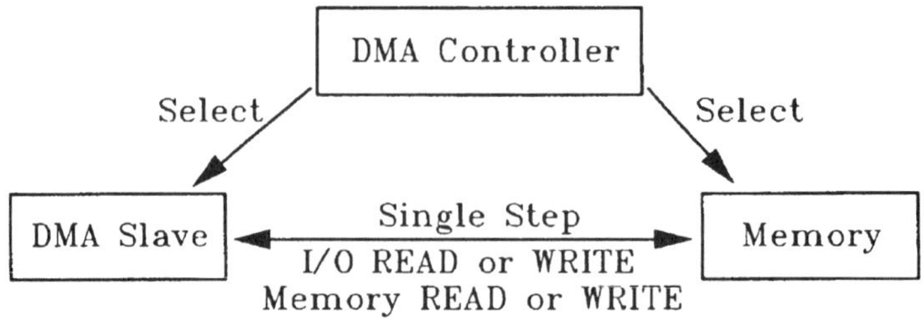

Figure 4.7 The PC, PC XT, and PC AT implemented parallel DMA transfers.

been required using a parallel DMA procedure. Another effect of parallel DMA operations is that transfer times are matched to the timing characteristics of the slowest device. In the 32-bit example given, the time required will be four times that of the slowest device to complete the four 8-bit transfers.

In the case of serial DMA transfers, the two separate operations are conducted at the maximum data transfer rates and widths of the participants. Using the same 32-bit example above and a 16-bit DMA controller, two 16-bit transfers are required for the transfer from the memory slave to the DMA controller. Four 8-bit transfers are required for the transfer from the DMA controller to the DMA slave. Assuming that the transfers are conducted at the default cycle time of 200 ns, the total time for the six transfers is 1200 ns. Using the 1250 ns cycle time for the AT shown in Table 4.1, four 8-bit transfers would require 5000 ns, over four times what the Micro Channel system would require with a 16-bit DMA controller.

Micro Channel's serial DMA procedure also provides the flexibility for other transfers that would be far more cumbersome with the parallel DMA procedure. The separate read and write operations potentially allow memory to memory transfers and DMA slave to DMA slave operations, although these operations are not currently supported by system software.

STREAMING-DATA PROCEDURES

In September 1989, IBM announced new procedures for data transfers that significantly increase the maximum data rates possible for Micro Channel systems. The timing of this announcement was somewhat controversial. Because the first systems based on EISA architecture were anticipated later in the year, it was speculated that the streaming-data announcement was aimed at reducing some of the impact of the EISA systems. IBM has maintained that the announcement timing was unrelated and was directed toward the developer community. IBM views the early announcement of the streaming-data procedures as an open road map for future development activities for the industry and strong evidence for an open architecture.

In the previous section, the data rates associated with basic Micro Channel transfers were described. For 32-bit data transfers using the 200 ns basic cycle time, this rate translated to an instantaneous data rate of 20.0 MB/sec. Using the matched- memory procedure with a 125 ns cycle time, an instantaneous data rate of 32.0 MB/sec can be achieved between a memory slave and the system CPU. The streaming-data procedures describe a method of increasing the data transfer rates to 40 MB/sec and 80 MB/sec. One of these procedures defines a 64-bit Micro Channel data transfer.

Participants

The participants in the procedure include Micro Channel masters and slaves.

Streaming-Data Transfers

There are actually three different procedures that comprise streaming-data transfers. These procedures increase the data transfer rates of Micro Channel systems to 40 MB/sec, 80 MB/sec, and, potentially, to 160 MB/sec. (The 1989 extensions to the architecture did not completely define the procedure for 160 MB/sec, however.)

From Chapter 3, the basic transfer cycle consists of several steps that can be grouped into two basic categories: the address portion and the data transfer portion. These two portions require 200 ns for each cycle. Each data transfer is preceded by its address. If the address is sequential, it is possible to designate the address in the beginning of the transfer and to increment the address based on the number of bytes of information transferred. This is exactly how the first streaming-data procedure is conducted.

In this procedure, the address portion is only given once at the beginning of the transfer of a block of information. The effect is to reduce the cycle time to 100 ns, a 50 percent reduction. This achieves an instantaneous data rate of 40 MB/sec for 32-bit transfers and 20 MB/sec for 16-bit transfers.

A second streaming-data procedure is defined by using the address bus to transfer data in addition to the data bus. This effectively provides a 64-bit data transfer path. The address is designated initially, leaving the address bus free to be used for data transfers. Using this procedure, data transfers rates of 80 MB/sec may be achieved for sequentially ordered data. Another streaming-data procedure is possible that enables data transfer rates up to 160 MB/sec potentially. This a combination of the 64-bit streaming-data procedure and a further reduction in the cycle time to 50 ns. The 16-bit, 32-bit, and 64-bit streaming-data procedures are shown in Figure 4.8.

Relationship to Existing Systems and Expansion Boards

Streaming-data procedures may be used between two expansion boards, between system masters and expansion boards, and between system memory and expansion boards. Both participants in the transfer must have the capability for streaming data. If only one participant is capable of the streaming-data procedure, the transfer will not utilize the streaming-data procedure. It is a fundamental requirement that streaming-data participants must support the basic transfer procedure

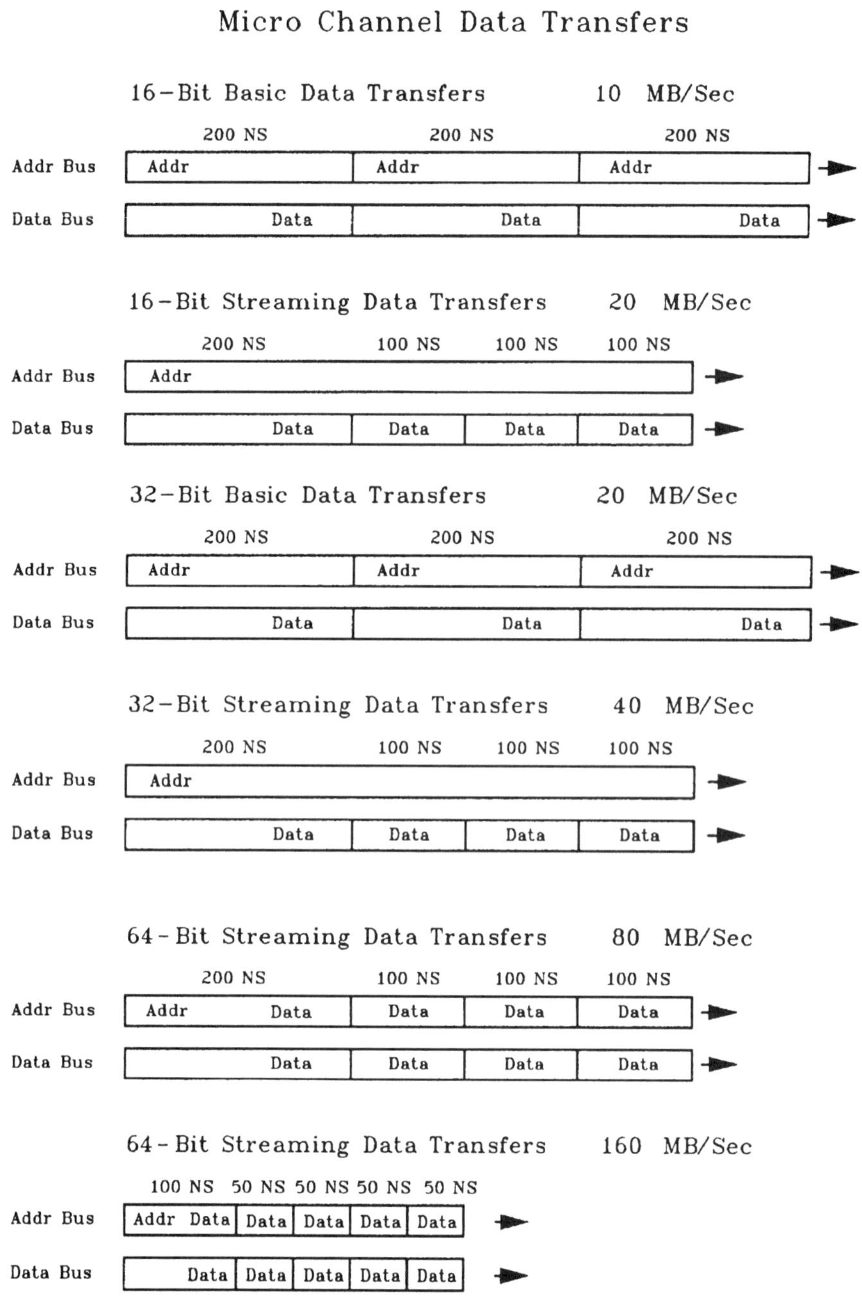

Figure 4.8 Micro Channel data transfer rates.

in order to be fully compatible with nonstreaming-data participants. In addition, the transfers incorporate automatic speed matching between the participants. Transfers will occur at the maximum capability that is supported by both the source and the target of the data transfer. These powerful procedures allow the architecture to move forward with technology improvements in memory, logic, and I/O devices and retain full compatibility with earlier systems.

In terms of current system implementations, the RISC System/6000 family can support up to 40 MB/sec data transfers between the system board (specifically, the I/O channel controller that will be described in Chapter 5) and expansion boards and between expansion boards designed to support the higher data rates. Many of IBM's PS/2 Micro Channel systems also support 40 MB/sec data streaming between expansion boards, and it is anticipated that future 32-bit PS/2 systems will also support the 40 MB/sec rate at the system board level. Widespread usage of the streaming-data procedures is expected in the near future, with the introduction of Intel and Chips and Technologies chip sets that support the procedure (described earlier in this chapter).

The streaming-data procedures up to 80 MB/sec can be achieved without changes in hardware technology. However, it is possible that new signal drivers and receivers may be required in order to achieve data transfer rates of 160 MB/sec.

The implementation of these very high data rates in Micro Channel systems is feasible today, but may not be used in some systems because of component costs and characteristics. Since the data rates of most I/O devices are significantly slower, these high data rates may not translate into direct performance benefits. (Remember, all things wait at exactly the same rate.) However, over time, these capabilities will contribute to the longevity of the architecture.

Streaming-Data Applications

The applications that benefit most from streaming-data procedures are those that transfer significant amounts of data in one burst. The actual data transfer rate achieved is a function of the total burst (packet) length. This is because the overhead associated with the transfer (the arbitration procedure and the address designation of the burst) is effectively "amortized" over a greater amount of data. The relationship between the number of bytes transferred in a given time for various data transfer procedures is shown in Figure 4.9.

As discussed above, the procedure can only be used for sequential data transfers. The most probable applications for streaming-data transfers are those involving high speed devices that transfer large blocks of data. Examples of such applications are high speed LAN adapters and storage devices. FDDI (fiber distributed data interchange) adapters and SCSI adapters are definite possibilities in the near future. It is also likely to be implemented for channel-attached memory that can be accessed at a very high data rate by other devices. (For example, utilization of the procedure between a memory card used as a high speed DASD cache and other bus masters is a probable application because of the sequential address requirement of the procedure.)

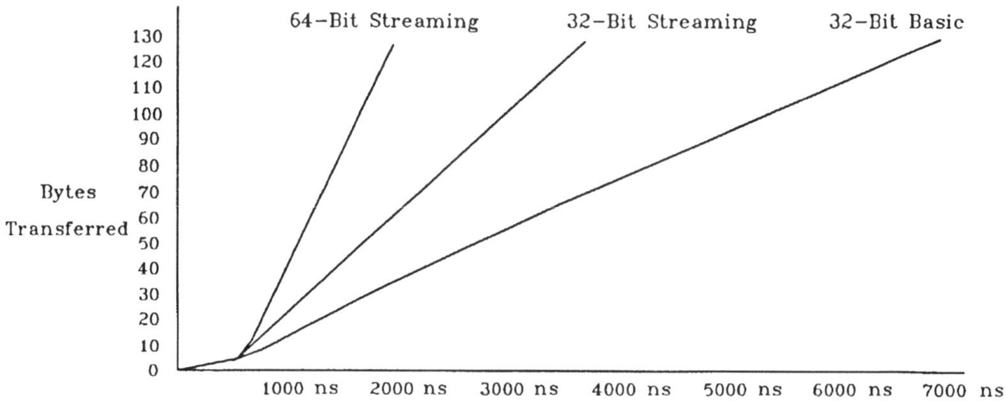

Bytes Transferred

Transfer Type	4	8	16	32	64	128
32-Bit Basic	500ns	700ns	1100ns	1900ns	3500ns	6700ns
32-Bit Streaming	500	600	800	1200	2000	3600
64-Bit Streaming	500	500	600	800	1200	2000

Figure 4.9 Streaming data procedures increase throughput and reduce device selection overhead.

PROGRAMMABLE OPTION SELECT

Programmable Option Select provides several basic functions:

- Eliminates the need for setting hardware configuration switches;
- Identifies the device installed;
- Identifies the location of the device;
- Resolves conflicts in the assignment of system resources;
- Enables the installation of multiple identical devices;
- Allows devices to be enabled/disabled;
- Identifies the device causing an exception condition; and
- Enables dynamic system configuration (when supported by the appropriate software).

An introduction to some of the benefits of this extremely powerful feature of Micro Channel architecture was given in Chapter 2. A technical description of the technical implementation of POS was given in Chapter 3. This section is intended to expand on that knowledge base and to further describe the function and importance of POS.

Automatic Configuration and Configuration Flexibility

Automatic configuration is accomplished through using information that is either already on the reference diskette supplied with the system for standard devices or that is supplied on an option diskette in the form of the adapter description file. This information includes all the resources required by the device, such as memory addresses and interrupt requirements. If a conflict occurs, the configuration program assists the user in resolving it.

Each device attached to the bus is identified and controlled by its POS number, which indicates its type. The various types of devices include bus masters, DMA slaves, I/O slaves, and memory slaves. It is through the control bit in a device's POS register that a device may be identified, enabled, or disabled.

Whenever an expansion board is installed or removed from a system, some method of allocating (or reallocating) system resources is required. Each device that is attached to a bus must have assigned the system resources that it is permitted to use, including memory addresses, I/O addresses, arbitration levels, and interrupt request lines. In the PC and AT architecture, this was accomplished by physically setting switches that were located on the system board and on attached devices in the proper combinations. A typical installation of an AT expansion board requires locating the required documentation, examining the switch setting diagrams, and changing the switch settings to the correct combination.

Manual switch settings can require significant time and may also introduce errors since there are many possible combinations for the settings. If the settings are in error, the device simply will not work in the best case. In the worse case, damage to the device or to the system can conceivably occur. As the number of device types proliferate and the number of possible combinations increase, manual switch settings have become increasingly complex. The documentation required may be located in several different places, as well. The POS feature of Micro Channel architecture has virtually eliminated manual settings of hardware switches by using a programmable procedure.

Each Micro Channel expansion board must be fully programmable. (The ten fields of information contained in the programmable POS registers were described in the previous chapter.) In addition, each Micro Channel system utilizes NVRAM (nonvolatile random access memory) to save the configuration information whenever the system is turned off or loses power. When the system is turned on, the configuration information is read as part of the startup routine of the system so that the user does not have to repeat the configuration routine each time.

POST Routine

When a system is first turned on, there are a series of tests that are executed as part of the POST (power on self test) routine. POST checks the system memory, CPU, other devices on the system board (for instance, the interrupt controller), and the nonvolatile RAM containing the POS information. After the POST routine is completed, the POS routine is executed. First, the IDs of all the devices that are stored in the system's NVRAM are compared with the identification numbers of all the devices installed in the system, beginning with the first slot. If there is a difference in the stored values and what is installed, an error code is displayed on the screen indicating a configuration error (Figure 4.10). If this is the case, the system reference diskette is required to boot the system. The user is then given the opportunity to run the configuration program.

If there is no configuration error during POST, the POS information is then transferred from the NVRAM to the POS ports on the devices, enabling them for proper operation.

Adapter Description Files and Configuration Utility

The configuration information is already on the reference diskette supplied with the system for many devices or is supplied on an option diskette in the form of a file called the adapter description file. The ADF file contains information needed for configuration, such as the I/O addresses, memory addresses, interrupt levels, and arbitration levels. It may also contain text for help and prompts. The appendix contains a summary of PS/2 Micro Channel features and configuration information.

When an expansion board is to be installed in a system, the adapter description file is copied from the diskette supplied by the option vendor to the reference diskette. These ADF files can be identified by their .ADF extension in their file name. An example of an ADF file is shown in Figure 4.11. This is the adapter description file for the IBM Internal Modem used in the IBM Personal System/2 Model P70 386 and other systems.

Adapter description files are named according to the adapter ID's four hexadecimal digits. For the file listed in Figure 4.11, the adapter ID is 0EDFFH and the file name is @EDFF.ADF. In this example, the first two lines of the adapter description file contain the adapter ID and the name of the adapter. The third line contains the number of bytes of POS information that will be used during the POS operation. Up to four bytes of information are supported directly, but the architecture has a provision for extending this if more should be required in the future.

Figure 4.10 The PS/2 POST routine advises the user of a configuration error if the device IDs stored in the NVRAM do not match those installed in the system.

```
AdapterId 0EDFFH

AdapterName  "IBM Internal Modem"

NumBytes 1

NamedItem
     Prompt "Serial Configuration"
      choice "SERIAL_1"  pos[0]=XXXX000Xb  io 03f8h-03ffh  int 4
      choice "SERIAL_2"  pos[0]=XXXX001Xb  io 02f8h-02ffh  int 3
      choice "SERIAL_3"  pos[0]=XXXX010Xb  io 3220h-3227h  int 3
      choice "SERIAL_4"  pos[0]=XXXX011Xb  io 3228h-322fh  int 3
      choice "SERIAL_5"  pos[0]=XXXX100Xb  io 4220h-4227h  int 3
      choice "SERIAL_6"  pos[0]=XXXX101Xb  io 4228h-422fh  int 3
      choice "SERIAL_7"  pos[0]=XXXX110Xb  io 5220h-5227h  int 3
      choice "SERIAL_8"  pos[0]=XXXX111Xb  io 5228h-522fh  int 3
   Help
"The IBM Internal Modem can be assigned to use Serial 1
through Serial 8.  Use the F5=Previous and the F6=Next
keys to change serial port assignments.  Conflicting
assignments are marked with an asterisk and must be
changed."
```

Figure 4.11 Adapter description file for the IBM internal modem, illustrating multiple choices for serial port selection.

The NamedItem section names the option and the choices that are available. In this case, the choices available to the user are to assign the IBM Internal Modem to serial port assignments one through eight. The F5 (previous) and F6 (next) keys are used to change the serial port assignments. The pattern of switches that implement that choice is shown. A value of "X" means that the setting is unchanged. Values of 0 and 1 correspond to turning the software switch "off" or "on," respectively. The I/O port address used by the adapter in each setting is also shown along with the interrupt level corresponding to each setting.

ADF files contain a series of key words used to identify information needed in the configuration process. The following is a list of some of the ADF key words:

ADAPTERID	POS ID of the device
ADAPTERNAME	Name of the device
NUMBYTES	Number of POS bytes used
FIXEDRESOURCES	Indicates that device requires specific system resources
NAMEDITEM	Indicates that device requires the use of system resources but provides choices
ARB	Indicates that device is an arbitrator

INT	Interrupt level
IO	I/O address
HELP	Used for assistance at a prompt

A configuration program that resides on the reference diskette supplied with the system serves to sort out all the various options and combinations that are possible and set the appropriate "software switches." The program gives a choice of automatic configuration or manual configuration (Figure 4.12). The program is called the system configuration utility (SC.EXE) and is used to set the POS registers appropriately. During the setup procedure, the program compares the resources used by the various adapters in the system. If there is a conflict, an asterisk (*) is displayed and the selection must be changed. In the example shown in Figure 4.11, the ability to configure multiple serial devices is obvious because of the flexibility provided by the device.

In PC and AT architecture, this was difficult if not impossible. The system configuration utility program is a user-friendly program that is very simple to execute. If a user selects the automatic mode, the configuration choices are selected with no user interaction required. The program works by selecting the first configuration choice available for each device. If there is a conflict with other devices, the second choice is selected. If there are no choices available without conflicts, automatic configuration cannot be successfully completed.

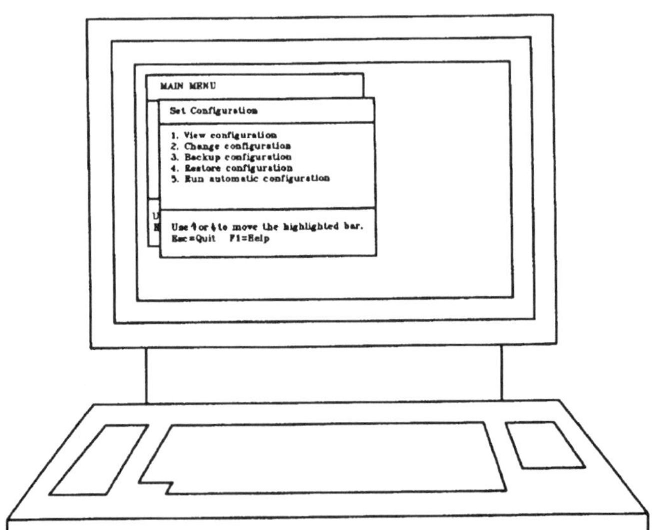

Figure 4.12 The SET CONFIGURATION Menu for IBM PS/2 systems.

Some adapters have greater flexibility for system resource selections than do others. Figure 4.13 gives an example of an adapter with fixed resource requirements. The IBM 3270 Connection™ Version A offers no flexibility in using system resources. If these resources are not available, the adapter card simply will not work. The resources used by other adapters in the system must be reassigned if possible. Because of the way that the configuration utility functions, devices with fixed resource requirements should be placed in lower-numbered slots. Devices with the greatest configuration flexibility should be placed in the higher-numbered slots. During automatic configuration, the system configuration utility program does not attempt to alter the choices for previously installed items that reside in lower-numbered slots. In cases involving fixed resource allocations, most conflicts can be resolved by swapping the positions of the devices with the one with the least flexibility placed in the slot with the lowest number. An alternative method for conflict resolution is to edit the adapter description file in order to resolve the conflict. (Maybe one day IBM will decide to modify the system configuration program so that it's a little smarter!)

While we're on the subject of conflicts, the address space below 1 MB used by memory-mapped adapters and EMS memory is getting very crowded. "RAM cram" is a cute little phrase has been coined to describe this problem. The entire portion of the memory reserved for this purpose in the DOS memory map is only 128 KB. The combination of some devices with fixed memory assignments, EMS requirements for contiguous memory addresses, and some memory "hogs" can cause the system configuration utility to fail. An examination of the ADF files for the devices can at least give you a clue as to what the problem might be. If repositioning the devices or editing the ADF files is not feasible, resolution may require more drastic

```
AdapterId 0E7FFh

AdapterName  "The IBM 3270 Connection Version A"

NumBytes 1

NamedItem

       Prompt "Resources Used"

       Choice  "Only Choice"

         pos[0] = xxxxxxxxb
         io 02D0h - 02DFh
         int 2
         mem 0CE000h- 0CFFFFh

   Help

      "These resources are fixed and must be available for this
      adapter.  If they are in conflict, change resources on other
      adapters to resolve the conflict."
```

Figure 4.13 An example of an adapter with fixed resource requirements.

measures. A later version of EMS, a new reference diskette, a new adapter, or a later ADF version may even be required.

Most adapter description files allow a choice of interrupt request lines. As described in Chapter 3, Micro Channel architecture allows the sharing of an interrupt request line by more than one device. However, interrupt response time may be degraded with multiple devices using the same interrupt request line. Wherever possible, a free interrupt request line should be selected.

Figure 4.14 shows the adapter description file for the integrated serial and parallel connectors on the PS/2 system board. Integrated features also allow multiple configuration choices and can be disabled. The capability to disable these

```
AdapterId 0FFAFh

AdapterName "Built In Features"

NumBytes 1

FixedResources
        pos[0]=XXXXXX11b io 03f0h-03f7h  int 6
                                         arb 2
                                         mem 0fffe0000h
                                           - 0ffffffffh
                                            sysmem 1024

NamedItem Prompt "Serial Port"
    choice "SERIAL_1"  pos[0]=XXXX11XXb  io 03f8h-03ffh  int 4

    choice "SERIAL_2"  pos[0]=XXXX01XXb  io 02f8h-02ffh  int 3

    choice "Disabled"  pos[0]=XXXX10XXb

        Help
"The built-in serial port connector can be assigned as
Serial 1, Serial 2, or disabled.  Use the F5=Previous and the F6=Ne:
keys to change serial port assignments if you are in the 'Change
configuration' window.  Conflicting assignments are marked with an
asterisk and should be changed."

NamedItem Prompt "Parallel Port"
        choice "PARALLEL_1"  pos[0]=1001XXXXb  io 03bch-03bfh
        choice "PARALLEL_2"  pos[0]=1011XXXXb  io 0378h-037bh
        choice "PARALLEL_3"  pos[0]=1101XXXXb  io 0278h-027bh
        choice "Disabled"    pos[0]=1000XXXXb

        Help
"The built-in parallel port connector can be assigned as Parallel 1
through Parallel 3 or disabled.  Use the F5=Previous and the F6=Nex
keys to change parallel port assignments if you are in the 'Change
configuration' window.  Conflicting assignments are marked with an
asterisk and should be changed."
```

Figure 4.14 Adapter description file for integrated serial and parallel connectors.

integrated features is used to allow their functions to be replaced by those on adapter cards.

Figure 4.15 shows the adapter description file for the ESDI fixed disk controller on the PS/2 Model 70. This is a DMA slave device that is capable of utilizing variable arbitration levels, DMA Channels. This file also illustrates the use of the

```
AdapterID 0DDFFh

AdapterName  "ESDI Fixed Disk Controller"

NumBytes 2

fixedresources
        pos[1]=00XXXXXXb
        pos[0]=XXXXXX0Xb
        io 3510h-3517h
        int 0eh

nameditem
        Prompt  "Adapter Memory Location"
          Choice "Segment C800"
            pos[1]=XXXX0010b
            mem 0c8000h-0cbfffh
          Choice "Segment CC00"
            pos[1]=XXXX0011b
            mem 0cc000h-0cffffh
          Choice "Segment D000"
            pos[1]=XXXX0100b
            mem 0d0000h-0d3fffh
          Choice "Segment D400"
            pos[1]=XXXX0101b
            mem 0d4000h-0d7fffh
          Choice "Segment D800"
            pos[1]=XXXX0110b
            mem 0d8000h-0dbfffh
          Choice "Segment DC00"
            pos[1]=XXXX0111b
            mem 0dc000h-0dffffh
          Choice  "ROM Disabled"
            pos[1]=XXXX1XXXb

     Help
"To configure this adapter you must choose the memory location the
adapter will use for its BIOS ROM.  There are six memory locations
that can be selected.  Under normal circumstances, select &lt;Segment
C800&gt;."

nameditem
        Prompt  "DMA Arbitration Level"
        Choice  "Level 5"
          pos[0]=XX0101XXb
          arb 5
        Choice  "Level 6"
          pos[0]=XX0110XXb
          arb 6
```

Figure 4.15 An example of an adapter description file with choices for arbitration levels.

```
        Choice   "Level 7"
          pos[0]=XX0111XXb
          arb 7
        Choice   "Level 0"
          pos[0]=XX0000XXb
          arb 0
        Choice   "Level 1"
          pos[0]=XX0001XXb
          arb 1
        Choice   "Level 3"
          pos[0]=XX0011XXb
          arb 3
        Choice   "Level 4"
          pos[0]=XX0100XXb
          arb 4

     Help
"This selects the DMA channel the adapter will use to transfer data
Under normal circumstances, select <Level 5>."

nameditem
        Prompt   "DMA Burst Length"
          Choice   " 8 Word Burst"
            pos[1]=XX01XXXXb
          Choice   "16 Word Burst"
            pos[1]=XX10XXXXb
          Choice   "24 Word Burst"
            pos[1]=XX11XXXXb
          Choice   "Burst Disabled"
            pos[1]=XX00XXXXb

     Help
"DMA transfer burst length.  This is the maximum number of words th
the adapter will transfer in a single DMA transfer.  Under normal
circumstances, select <8 Word Burst>."

nameditem
        Prompt   "Fairness On/Off"
          Choice   "On"
            pos[0]=X1XXXXXXb
          Choice   "Off"
            pos[0]=X0XXXXXXb

     Help
"Bus Arbitration Fairness.  This controls whether the adapter will
release control of the bus when it has been using it exclusively.
Under normal circumstances, select <On>."
```

Figure 4.15 (continued) An example of an adapter description file with choices for arbitration levels.

fairness enable/disable feature, which determines whether or not the device will release control of the bus when it has been using it exclusively. (In reality, the DMA controller is the device that controls the bus on behalf of the DMA slave device.) As the file shows, the burst length for the DMA transfer is also selectable, ranging from zero up to the maximum time that the device can own the bus.

Adapter Description Programs

Some devices require a memory configuration that cannot be handled by the normal adapter description file. This is handled by an adapter description program (ADP) that is loaded and executed by the system configuration utility program. There are two types of ADPs: system memory ADPs and nonsystem memory ADPs. If you like to "snoop," examine the ADF files of your devices and look for the keywords SysMem and Exec. The SysMem keyword is used to indicate that the device contains system memory and that the ADP program is used to configure the device. The Exec key word is used by memory-mapped devices that want to use the address space above 1 MB for mapping. These ADPs are executed before other resources are allocated.

Dynamic System Configurability

Another benefit of POS is to allow system configurations to be altered by using software to manipulate the POS registers. The most likely use is for enabling and disabling adapters in a fault-tolerant application. If one adapter fails, an identical adapter can be enabled to provide the required function. This capability could be used even during program execution. IBM has not supported this capability with its software, but it is anticipated that it will be used for special applications and will be supported by the application software. Examples of environments that could benefit by this capability are automatic bank tellers, stock and commodity trading floor applications. The procedure for its use is described in IBM's technical reference manuals.

SUBSYSTEM CONSIDERATIONS

Subsystem architectures and their implementations are directly affected by Micro Channel architecture. The next part of this chapter discusses the interaction of Micro Channel architecture with the major subsystems of a computer system.

Processor Subsystems

Micro Channel architecture is based on a different structural philosophy from that of the PC, the XT, and the AT. The old architecture assumed that the CPU would be based on an Intel CISC microprocessor architecture compatible with the 80X86 series and that the CPU subsystem would be resident on the system board. Micro Channel architecture does not impose such boundaries on its use: the system master does not have to be compatible with the Intel 80X86 family since the architecture is processor independent. In addition, it can be implemented with the CPU subsystem located on the system board or on an expansion board, sometimes called a "card on board" implementation.

Processor Independence

As discussed earlier in this book, Micro Channel architecture is independent of the microprocessor architecture used in the system. Implementation examples range from the Intel CISC family of 80X86 to the S/370 processor in the Enterprise System/9370. It is also possible to have generically unrelated microprocessors in the same system, each running their own operating system, as was the case in the IBM Academic System/6000™.

Micro Channel architecture isolates the processor technology from the information transfer bus. The system master follows the same rules and has the same interface to the bus as do all Micro Channel participants. Even the CPU built into the PS/2 Micro Channel system board is just a special case of a bus master that is the system master as well as the default master. The default master controls the bus when no other master is designated. It is also used for system initialization or startup. There is no requirement for the system master to be the default master, but it usually is.

It is also possible to change the system master from one located on the system board to a CPU resident on an expansion board. The AOX MicroMaster bus masters described earlier in this chapter are examples that have been used very effectively to upgrade the system master in Micro Channel systems.

System Board and "Card-on-Board" Implementations

In order to implement a "card-on-board" design, it is necessary to specify the slot location of the card that contains the arbitration control logic and the default bus master that is used when the system is started, or initialized. It is not necessary for the central arbitration control point nor the default master to be on the system board or in any specific expansion slot. In fact, it would be possible to design a fault-tolerant system that supports redundant arbitration control and default master logic for higher reliability. The only requirement is that after the selection process is completed, only one of each be active in the system.

An example of a "card on board" implementation is that of IBM's Electronic Gearbox, an industrial computer made by IBM's Manufacturing Systems Products organization. The "card on board" capabilities of Micro Channel architecture make possible a system design that can use a family of processor cards. This concept enhances manufacturability because of increased parts commonality. In other words, a family of systems can be manufactured whose members differ only by what processor card is installed on the system board. It can also provide increased flexibility and convenient upgradeability to the system owner.

Multiprocessing and Micro Channel Architecture

In order to understand multiple processors and their implementation possibilities in Micro Channel architecture, you have to go back to school to learn some key terms.

Symmetric multiprocessing. An arrangement of two or more microprocessors in which each is a peer of the others. Tasks are allocated based on whichever microprocessor is available.

Asymmetric multiprocessing. An arrangement of two or more microprocessors in which different tasks are executed with each microprocessor according to its capabilities or the functional partitioning by the system software. In other words, not all microprocessors can perform all tasks. The opposite of symmetric multiprocessing.

Micro Channel architecture can accommodate multiple processors in both symmetric and asymmetric designs. In either case, it is recommended that a loosely coupled organization be used. This configuration is one in which each processor has its own private RAM containing an operating system and applications and uses the bus in order to access common I/O devices (Figure 4.16). This avoids the 300 ns overhead of the arbitration cycle and does not force the processor to contend with other masters in order to access memory.

Tightly coupled multiprocessing is probably best implemented using a separate processor complex on a separate bus in order for system memory to be effectively shared between the processors. Using common memory on the Micro Channel bus would reduce performance because of the contention with other masters and the arbitration overhead.

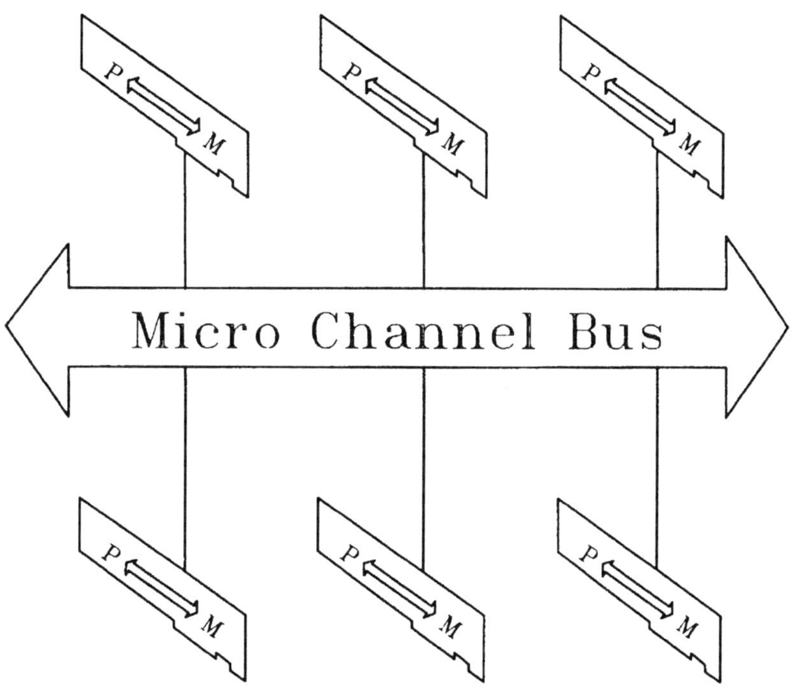

Figure 4.16 Micro Channel architecture makes it possible to implement multiple processor-memory buses.

The role of Micro Channel architecture in multiprocessor configurations is one of a facilitator as opposed to an enabler. Because of the bus master capability, the efficiency of multiprocessor designs is enhanced in accessing common I/O, memory, and other masters when necessary.

One of the best multiprocessing configurations for the Micro Channel bus is one in which tasks are allocated based on the special skills of the microprocessors. For example, a data base, graphics, or arithmetic "engine" as separate masters on the bus could significantly enhance performance in a Micro Channel system. The flexibility and effectiveness of these application-specific arrangements can be very high. For the PS/2 family of systems, this appears to be IBM's general direction for multiprocessing, perhaps for these reasons.

Multiple Bus Implementations

Micro Channel architecture also does not preclude subsystem buses and dual-bus implementations that give rise to processor/memory complexes operating on a separate bus. IBM's PS/2 Model 90 and Model 95 have separate bus implementations. It is also possible for several of these separate buses to exist on bus master adapters in the same system as is shown in Figure 4.16.

While separate processor-memory buses are not included as part of the architecture, it is important to realize that the architecture does not preclude their use. Because of the multiple master capability of the architecture, implementations of processor-memory complexes on expansion boards is actually facilitated.

While we are on the subject of multiple buses, remember that it is possible for an entire computer to use the Micro Channel interface to connect it to another Micro Channel system. In this case, the second computer becomes an arbitrating device through a Micro Channel interface. Many different implementations of this concept are possible. An example of a system that has two system units is the Enterprise System/9371 Model 14 in which one is the System/370 processing unit with an S/370 processor implemented on a card and the other is a PS/2 processing unit with an i386 microprocessor implemented on the system board. The ES/9371 systems will be described further in the next chapter.

I/O devices, memory, and other special functions residing on the system board may or may not be attached to the Micro Channel bus directly. If they are not directly attached to the bus, they are accessed through the CPU subsystem's interface logic. If they are directly attached, they follow the requirements of Micro Channel architecture. It is also possible for a system to be designed with video on a local processor-memory bus in order to gain additional performance at a reduced cost. Some of the tradeoffs involved in these choices are cost, performance, and flexibility.

Memory Subsystems

As previously discussed, Micro Channel architecture can address up to 4 GB of memory. It supports both system and nonsystem memory implementations on the Micro Channel bus.

The flexibility that Micro Channel architecture provides for using memory is one of its most important features. A limitation that is often expressed regarding memory characteristics is that Micro Channel memory that resides on the Micro Channel bus is necessarily slower than is system board memory. This is generally based on the assumption that the data rate to and from channel-attached memory is that of the basic data transfer rate. In the case of a 32-bit implementation, this corresponds to a rate of 20 MB/sec using the 200 ns basic cycle time plus the arbitration overhead if required. This rate is slower than that of most DRAM access cycle times and is significantly slower than SRAM.

In order to compensate for this, the architecture enables higher speed transfers, using the matched-memory procedure or the streaming-data procedures. First of all, the optional matched-memory procedure enables the use of a minimum cycle time of 125 ns, which corresponds to a maximum data rate of 32 MB/sec. This procedure was implemented on the 20 MHz versions of the IBM Personal System/2 Model 80. This is a system-specific solution in which the capabilities of the channel memory device must be matched to those of the processor complex utilizing the matched-memory procedure. In the case of the Model 80 implementation, the 386 processor complex located on the system board was designed to use the matched-memory procedure.

The streaming-data procedures offer a more versatile solution to the utilization of high speed memory. These procedures can be enabled to function between expansion boards as well as between expansion boards and system boards. The streaming-data procedures can increase the speeds for memory transfers in 32-bit devices from 20 MB/sec to 80 MB/sec. For 16-bit devices, the data transfer rate can be increased from 10 MB/sec up to 20 MB/sec. Because of the versatility of the procedures, it is anticipated that most memory cards will utilize the streaming-data procedures instead of the matched-memory procedures. However, the effectiveness of the streaming-data procedures are reduced in the cases of small information transfers or nonsequential information transfers as described earlier in the chapter.

I/O Subsystems

Perhaps the biggest boost to the performance of most Micro Channel systems lies in its use of intelligent I/O subsystems. The use of bus masters with direct memory access to manage I/O subsystems can add to the effective CPU power of systems, both directly and indirectly. Directly, many of these intelligent subsystems have processing power rivaling that of earlier personal computers. For example, the use of Intel's 186 microprocessor as the intelligence on Micro Channel expansion boards used as storage and communication controllers is common. Indirectly, they offload some of the functions traditionally done by the system master and reduce interrupts. As a result, bus masters used in intelligent I/O subsystems can result in performance enhancements for both CPU-intensive and I/O-intensive applications.

In the original DOS world, only rudimentary multitasking existed (for example, print spooling). OS/2, UNIX-based operating systems, and operating systems using the 386 virtual mode (for example, Windows™ 3.0 and VM/386™) are able to utilize Micro Channel's intelligent subsystems for concurrent operations. In some applications, it is possible for an entire application to be running on one of these intelligent subsystems in the background without affecting the performance of the foreground task. An example would be a fax server application running in the background on a bus master designed for that purpose without dedicating an entire system for that purpose.

The performance benefits of Micro Channel architecture are not limited to bus masters, however. The higher speed transfers and the faster and more efficient DMA operations are also beneficial. Storage and communications are some excellent examples of subsystems that have utilized Micro Channel's features to increase performance.

Storage Subsystems

In order to appreciate the role of Micro Channel architecture in storage subsystems, a little history is helpful. In the IBM PC XT, the 10 MB fixed disk drive had an access time in excess of 100 ms and a data rate of 0.05 MB/sec. The 5 Mb/sec data rate of the ST-506 interface and the 1 MB/sec PC XT bus data rate were quite adequate for the system since the disk drive was the bottleneck for performance. However, the 40 ms drives used for the AT were considerably faster and could transfer data faster than even the 16-bit AT bus could accept it.

Disk Interleaving. The solution was to organize sequential sectors or blocks of information with skips in between. This is called interleaving. In the case of the AT, three rotations were required before all of the data stored on a track could be read or written, referred to as a 3:1 interleave factor. Some manufacturers solved this problem by adding extensive buffering in the disk controller and slowly transferring the data to the AT bus. This provided the ability to store sequential data on the track without interleaving (a 1:1 interleave factor), but the AT bus still limited the data transfer characteristics. The DMA operations were too slow, and programmed I/O operations had to allow for overhead and slower devices, some of which had critical service time dependencies.

Micro Channel architecture's higher speed transfer and burst capabilities allow 1:1 interleave without extensive buffering. A full track of data can be read or written with only one revolution of the drive. The data rates of disk drives are a function of the amount of information on a track and its rotational speed. Both of these attributes are increasing rapidly. The fast data transfer characteristics of Micro Channel architecture will be adequate for these advances in drive technology for the foreseeable future.

Faster Disk Controllers. Micro Channel architecture can take full advantage of advances in disk interface and controller technology in the form of the ESDI (Enhanced Small Device Interface) and SCSI (Small Computer System Interface). Not only can these interfaces support higher data rates than the ST-506 interface, but they can also support multiple devices per controller. This combination of faster drives, multiple drives controllers, and faster interfaces effectively impose higher data rate requirements for I/O buses.

ESDI can attach up to seven devices per controller, but is typically used to control two drives. The maximum data rate is 10 Mb/sec. The SCSI bus can support up to 64 devices, but is typically used for seven devices. Today's maximum data transfer rate is 5 MB/sec. (With SCSI-2, 40 MB/sec are possible. On the horizon is SCSI-3, which uses fiber optics). ESDI and SCSI controllers typically have onboard hardware caches or buffers and may or may not be used with software caches. Using these high speed caches and buffers, information can be transferred even faster than the maximum data transfer for ESDI or SCSI. The result can be much faster and more effective data rates. Micro Channel's faster data transfer rates directly influence performance in these environments in both DMA slave and bus master implementations.

Bus master implementations are especially effective in storage subsystems. The ability to overlap commands, to manage multiple disk accesses, and to control data transfers simultaneously with an intelligent bus master device significantly improves performance. The DMA capability of a bus master is used very effectively in such operations since most information transfers are between disk subsystems and memory.

IBM has used ST-506, ESDI, and SCSI in its PS/2 Micro Channel systems. The SCSI implementations have been bus masters. The ST-506 and ESDI disk controller implementations have been DMA slaves. Appendix G contains a summary of IBM PS/2 fixed disk drive characteristics.

Communications Subsystems

The features of Micro Channel architecture are very important in communication subsystems. Onboard intelligence combined with Micro Channel's bus master capability provides significant benefits. For example, expansion boards that support multiple communications devices or do protocol conversion can reduce the load on the system master by performing these activities. Micro Channel's data integrity and RAS features also take on added importance in communication subsystems.

In the LAN environment, it is often the LAN adapter that limits response time and throughput. Adding additional LAN adapters to configurations and choosing bus masters can greatly improve performance as well as the capacity of the LAN (number of users supported) in these applications.

High-speed communication adapters such as FDDI (Fiber Distributed Data Interchange) can support data transfer rates of 100 Mb/sec today and even higher in the future. In order to fully utilize these high speed devices, a very fast bus is an absolute requirement.

At the opposite end of the communications spectrum is the lowly serial port. It is tragic to have a very powerful computer remain idle while waiting for serial devices to transfer data. The use of multiport devices like the ARTIC card eliminates this ridiculous situation through the use of its onboard intelligence and its bus master capability.

There is one very important feature of Micro Channel architecture that we haven't discussed very much yet, the peer-to-peer capability. The peer-to-peer capability is defined as information transfers that occur between two masters. Either bus master may be the controlling master with the other bus master acting as a slave. In order to illustrate the importance of peer-to-peer information transfers, Figure 4.17, illustrating a Micro Channel LAN bus master and a disk controller bus master adapter, is useful. In this example, information can be transferred directly between the storage subsystem and the LAN adapter. This type of capability is also useful for supporting LAN bridges (Figure 4.18) or LAN gateways (Figure 4.19).

In order to effectively use the power of the peer-to-peer capability and the capabilities of intelligent bus master devices, some kind of standardization was needed in programming interfaces and structure. In effect, these "guys" needed a standard way of communicating commands, data, and status if these kinds of transfers were going to work. These conventions and services are provided by the Subsystem Control Block Architecture described in the next section.

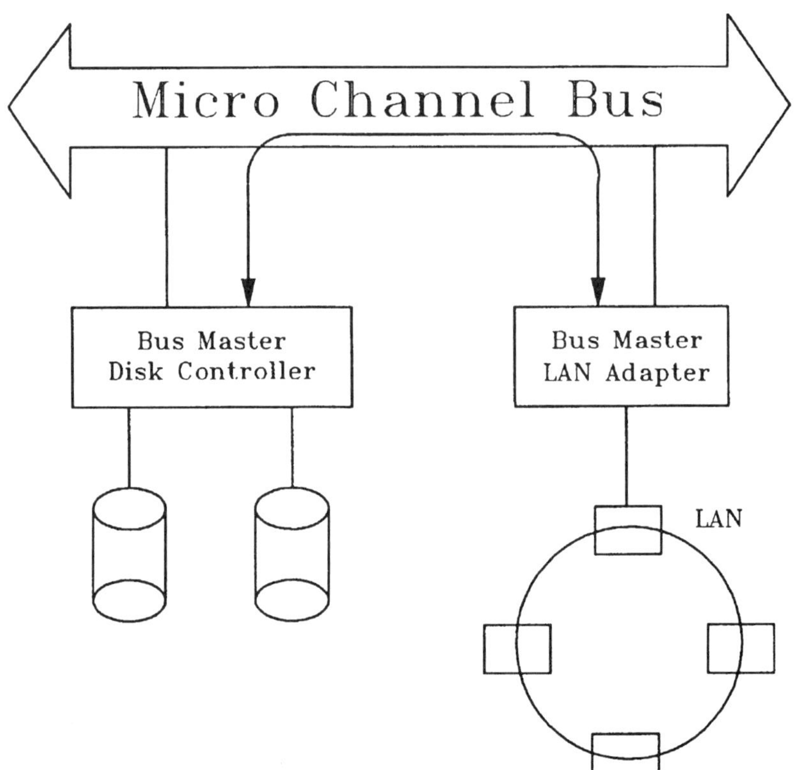

Figure 4.17 The use of peer-to-peer information transfers is beneficial between LAN bus masters and bus master disk controllers.

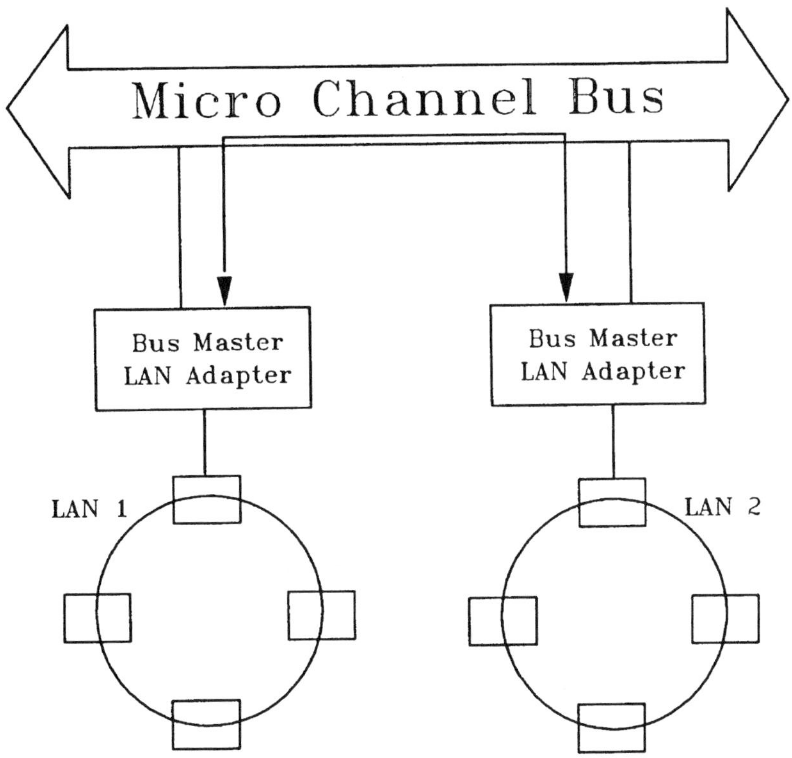

Figure 4.18 LAN bridges using peer-to-peer transfers.

SUBSYSTEM CONTROL BLOCK ARCHITECTURE

In late 1989, IBM announced the Subsystem Control Block Architecture (SCB Architecture™), the hardware and software architecture that defines the communications structure and interfaces between the system master and bus masters and between bus masters. While technically not part of Micro Channel architecture, it is the architecture that is used to support Micro Channel's multiple master capabilities. It provides a consistent method of managing complex information transfers between masters and provides a structure for the independent execution of work in systems.

SCB Architecture provides a high-level interface for use between device drivers and I/O subsystems that is independent of the type of hardware platform and the operating system. The architecture is far more sophisticated than the normal device drivers that open and close files and read and write small amounts of information. In the original IBM personal computers, many applications were written directly to the hardware, using low-level programming. This was especially true in graphics applications because it was a way to increase performance of these slower systems. However, incompatibilities resulted whenever the hard-

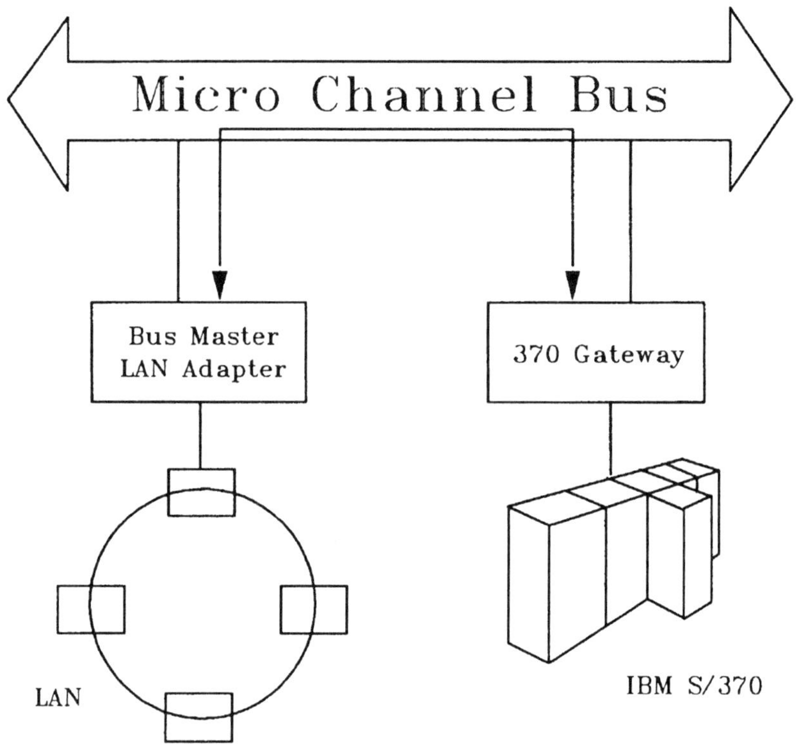

Figure 4.19 Peer-to-peer transfers in a LAN gateway application.

ware was changed. In addition, applications programmers spent a great deal of their time programming hardware instead of writing applications. As performance of the underlying hardware improved, application developers broke this bad habit and started using standard programming interfaces like the system's BIOS for DOS and ABIOS for OS/2. The next step in this evolution is the SCB Architecture, which provides high-level commands and a delivery service between masters that is independent of the microprocessor architecture, the device hardware, and the operating system. While the SCB Architecture is a perfect fit for exploiting Micro Channel's multimaster capabilities, it is also applicable to other bus architectures.

Because of the intelligence of today's devices and their processing power, they are capable of executing complex commands that enable something akin to program execution. These "programs" are what SCB Architecture is all about. What the SCB Architecture provides is the capability for multiple "programs" to be running in the same system at the same time, using different masters to execute them.

Up to this point, we have pretty much used the term information transfer as a synonym for data transfer. Now it's time to separate them. In the SCB Architecture, the location of the control information is separated from the location of data.

The term control block refers to a storage area used by a computer program to hold control information.

The SCB procedure begins with the preparation of a subsystem control block by a program that is stored in system memory. The system issues a request to a program in the bus master, indicating the location of the subsystem control block in system memory. The bus master arbitrates for the bus and transfers the subsystem control block from system memory into its own memory and executes the operation, or "program." Depending on the "program," the subsystem may or may not interrupt the system master with the results upon completion of the operation. Multiple control blocks can be executed, in which case one control block would point to the next one to be executed. When all the subsystem control blocks have been executed, the subsystem notifies the system master. In this way, very complex sequences of commands may be carried out with effort expended by the system master, a process called "command chaining." Similarly, the actions could be accomplished between two bus masters.

A useful analogy is one of a building contractor telling his foreman to prepare a foundation for a building. This operation consists of a number of steps: build a form for the foundation according to a given set of instructions, pour the concrete for the foundation, add the reinforcing rods, and finish the surface. Each of these steps consists of a series of activities, and the steps must be completed in the specified order. In this analogy, the building contractor is like the system master giving a series of SCBs to a subsystem, the foreman in our analogy. The contractor may require that the foreman report back after the completion of each step or may give him all the steps and their appropriate execution sequence, depending on the abilities of the foreman. In other words, it is as if the contractor tells the foreman: "Let me know when you finish each step and I'll give you additional instructions." Or, "I want you to pour this foundation and don't bother me until it is completed, unless you run into problems." In either case, the contractor is working more efficiently than if he is personally supervising the work.

A subsystem that can use the SCB Architecture consists of an intelligent subsystem interface that has bus master capabilities. It also may have multiple devices of the same type or of different types attached to it (Figure 4.20). These subsystems must have the ability to manage information transfers between devices that make up the subsystem and between the various Micro Channel participants. In order to manage these complex subsystems, the subsystem master must have sufficient processing power and local memory to execute these SCB "programs."

A client/server model is useful in describing the SCB Architecture. In our example, the client is a program requesting a command to be processed, and a server is a program executed by the bus master. The request can be made from the application program, the device driver, or the BIOS/ABIOS. In order to use the SCB Architecture, a subsystem must have five or six I/O ports for communication purposes. The function of these ports is:

1. To advise the subsystem that a request has been made by a client and is ready for processing;

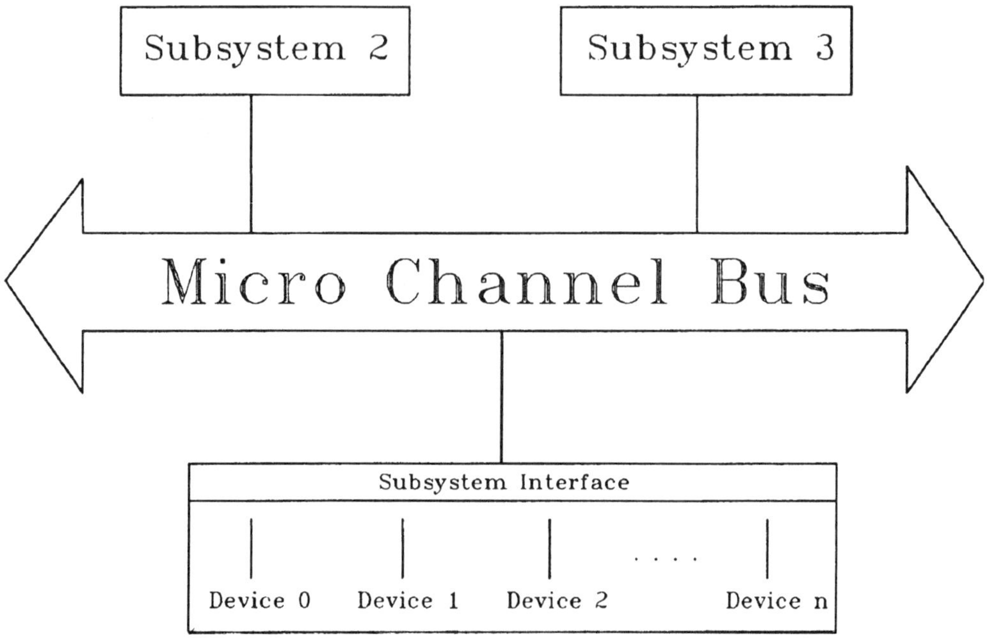

Figure 4.20 Micro Channel subsystems may have multiple devices.

2. To indicate whether or not the subsystem is busy or unavailable to accept other requests;
3. To transfer the physical address of an SCB from the system to the subsystem;
4. To advise the system which devices within a subsystem have interrupts pending;
5. To present interrupt data to the system from the subsystem; and
6. To provide hardware control of several subsystem functions, such as enabling the subsystem to do a DMA operation.

A good example of how the SCB Architecture could be used by an SCSI bus master is the reading of an entire file of information from a disk drive and writing it into system memory. Commands can be grouped together, a technique called "command chaining," so that the process becomes very efficient with little overhead and few interrupts associated with it. This type of operation has traditionally been done by transferring very small amounts of information at a time and interrupting the system master to advise that the transfer has been completed. The process is repeated with additional interrupts until the entire file has been transferred to system memory, a very inefficient process at best.

Similarly, an entire disk drive can be backed up with a tape drive using SCBs in what amounts to a macro operation. Or a file can be transferred to a local area network requester from the servers disk subsystem directly to the LAN adapter for delivery, as was shown in Figure 4.17. In our building analogy, this would correspond to the foreman communicating directly with the foreman responsible for the next step after the foundation is completed without advising the contractor. Obviously, this is quicker than the foundation foreman advising the contractor that the work is completed and the contractor advising the other foreman that the foundation is completed.

The future applications of the SCB Architecture are very exciting. In addition to the powerful capabilities it enables in I/O subsystems, this is the architecture that defines resource sharing and status reporting among multiple processors using the Micro Channel architecture. These techniques have been defined for IBM's mainframe architecture for many years. Bringing this capability to small systems will enable great performance benefits and will allow them to exploit Micro Channel's capabilities.

SUMMARY

This chapter has provided an in-depth examination of four of the most important features of Micro Channel architecture: bus master support, direct memory access, streaming-data procedures, and the Programmable Option Select feature and related procedures. In addition, the effect on subsystem architectures has been described along with the very powerful Subsystem Control Block Architecture. In the next chapter, you will learn about some of the implementations of Micro Channel architecture and some of the solutions that it provides for today's and tomorrow's application environments.

QUESTIONS

1. Do you think Micro Channel architecture will replace the channel architecture of IBM's mainframes? Why or why not?
2. What are some bus masters that would be useful in your application environment?
3. How can the streaming-data features be implemented without losing compatibility?
4. List the functions of POS.
5. Trace the steps used in automatic system configuration.
6. What is the function of NVRAM in configuration with POS?
7. What are some techniques used by designers to balance the data transfer characteristics of I/O devices and buses?
8. What are some applications that could benefit from peer-to-peer transfers?
9. What are some examples of command chaining that would be useful in your application environment?

5

Micro Channel System Implementations and Applications

In Chapter 1, you learned that there was a significant difference between an architecture and its implementations. Up to this point, we have been concerned only with Micro Channel architecture. In this chapter, some representative system designs that utilize Micro Channel architecture are described. These designs are included to represent the range of implementation possibilities and to illustrate the use of key features of the architecture. The chapter is not intended to serve as a comparison of basic system functionality nor to describe these systems in detail. The focus in on the use of Micro Channel architecture by these systems. IBM systems and those of other manufacturers are described.

The later part of the chapter describes several major application areas and how Micro Channel products address their requirements in order to provide innovative solutions. These application areas were chosen to illustrate the power and advantages of Micro Channel architecture in today's (and tomorrow's) environment.

IBM SYSTEMS

Micro Channel architecture is currently used in the following IBM system families:

- IBM Personal System/2 (Models 50 and higher);
- IBM RISC System/6000;
- IBM Enterprise System/9371 (Models 10, 12, and 14);
- IBM Gearbox 800 System; and
- IBM 3172 LAN Controller.

The first three of these will be described in this chapter.

IBM Personal System/2

In 1987 IBM introduced the Personal System/2 family. It would have been far easier for the writers of the world and their readers if the term Personal System/2 was used only to identify Micro Channel systems. But, alas, IBM has never been known for simple naming conventions! The PC, AT, and Micro Channel buses are used in PS/2 systems. However, only the Models 50 and higher are Micro Channel systems.

All PS/2 models come with numerous built-in features—features that once required expansion boards. (Specific models have additional integrated features.) These integrated features include:

- A serial port (RS-232 interface) used to attach asynchronous devices like modems and some plotters.
- A parallel port for printers and other devices.
- A pointing-device port. (This is a euphemism for a mouse port.)
- A graphics adapter for display attachment. The characteristics of this adapter are model-dependent.
- The diskette drive controller, which can support two diskette drives. All systems with a fixed disk drive include a fixed disk drive controller.
- System-board memory in the form of memory modules.

As Figure 5.1 shows, there are six different external types of these systems, including the briefcase portable, three desktop types, and two floor-standing types. Table 5.1 summarizes the significant features of these systems. (Not all models described in the following sections are available worldwide. You should check with your local authorized IBM dealer to determine the availability of these systems.)

Additional information regarding IBM PS/2 systems is contained in the following publications available from IBM:

IBM Personal System/2 Reference Guide (G360-2669)

IBM Personal System/2 Facts and Features (G360-2832)

Model 50 and 50Z

The Model 50 was one of the original Micro Channel systems announced in 1987. It has since been replaced by the Model 50Z (Figure 5.2). The most significant difference in the two models is the slower memory (120 ns) used in the Model 50, which required a wait state to be added for the system master access to the system board RAM. The original Model 50 also had a 20 MB fixed disk drive instead of the 30 and 60 MB drives of the Model 50Z.

The Model 50Z is the entry Micro Channel system in the PS/2 family. This small desktop system is used primarily for personal productivity applications such as text processing and spreadsheets or small business and commercial applications. Operating system support includes DOS and OS/2.

The system is based on a 10 MHz 80286 microprocessor with zero wait states for accesses to 85 ns system-board RAM. It comes standard with 1 MB of memory and can accommodate a maximum of 2 MB on the system board. Maximum memory addressability is 16 MB. Also included is a 30 MB fixed disk drive with

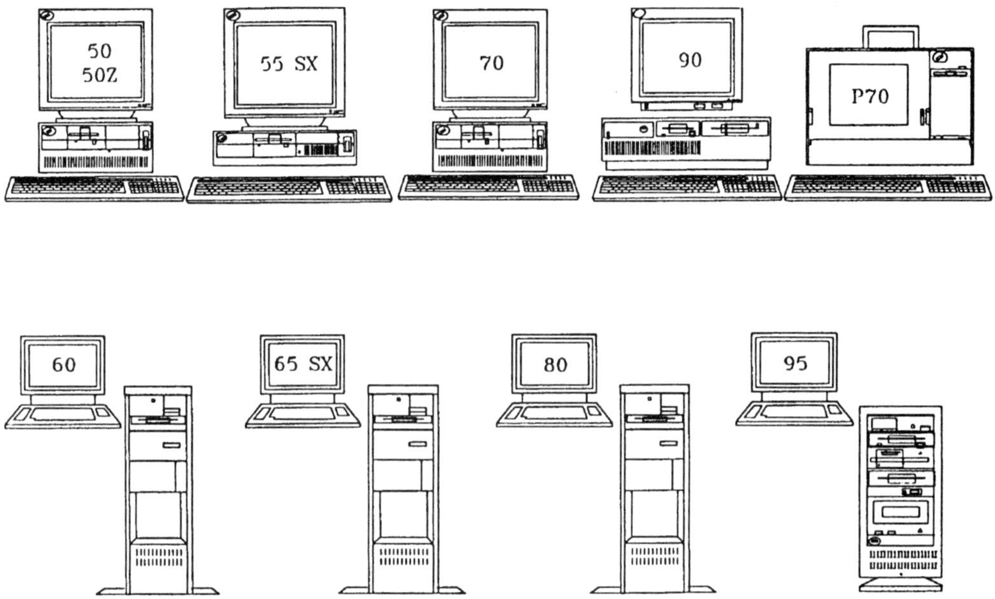

Figure 5.1 IBM PS/2 Micro Channel systems.

an ST-506 controller or a 60 MB fixed disk drive with an ESDI controller. **Video Graphics Adapter (VGA),** which provides a maximum resolution of 640 x 480 (16 colors) and up to 256 colors (320 x 200) resolution is also provided. The system has a 94-watt power supply.

Internal expansion capabilities include the ability to add one additional 1.44 MB 3.5-inch diskette drive or a tape backup unit that uses the diskette controller. There are three Micro Channel expansion board connectors: two 16-bit standard connectors and one 16-bit connector with video extension. The video extension is used to access the system board VGA function for graphics upgrades.

A block diagram of the system board layout for the Model 50 Z is shown in Figure 5.3. On the surface, this looks quite a bit more complicated than our earlier diagrams. However, if you look at it closely, you will see that it is fundamentally the same representation as our earlier bus diagrams. The only difference is that all the system board I/O devices, additional controllers, and buffers are included. The data, address, and control signals are shown separately to indicate their relationship to the various bus participants.

In this single bus design, the system master has to contend with other devices for the use of the Micro Channel bus. When another master owns the bus, the system master must wait to use it, even to access its own memory. However, the 80286 microprocessor does have a small buffer that allows sequential instructions to be prefetched from memory (a very common operation) to relieve some of this contention for the bus. The buffer is refilled as needed. The effect is to allow the system master to do some operations while another master owns the bus.

TABLE 5.1 IBM PS/2 MICRO CHANNEL MODEL COMPARISONS

Model	Configuration	Processor	Speed MHz	Graphics	Expansion Slots Available	Storage Bays
50 Z	Desktop	80286	10	VGA	3	3
55SX	Desktop	80386SX	16	VGA	3	2
60	Deskside	80286	10	VGA	7	5
65SX	Deskside	80386SX	16	VGA	7	6
P70386	Portable	80386	16 20	VGA	2	2
70 386	Desktop	80386/i486	16 20 25	VGA	3	3
70 486	Desktop	i486	25	VGA	3	3
80 386	Deskside	80386	16 20 25	VGA	7	6
90	Desktop	i486	25 33	XGA	3	4
95	Deskside	i486	25 33	XGA	6	7

Figure 5.2 IBM PS/2 Model 50Z computer. (Courtesy of International Business Machines Corporation)

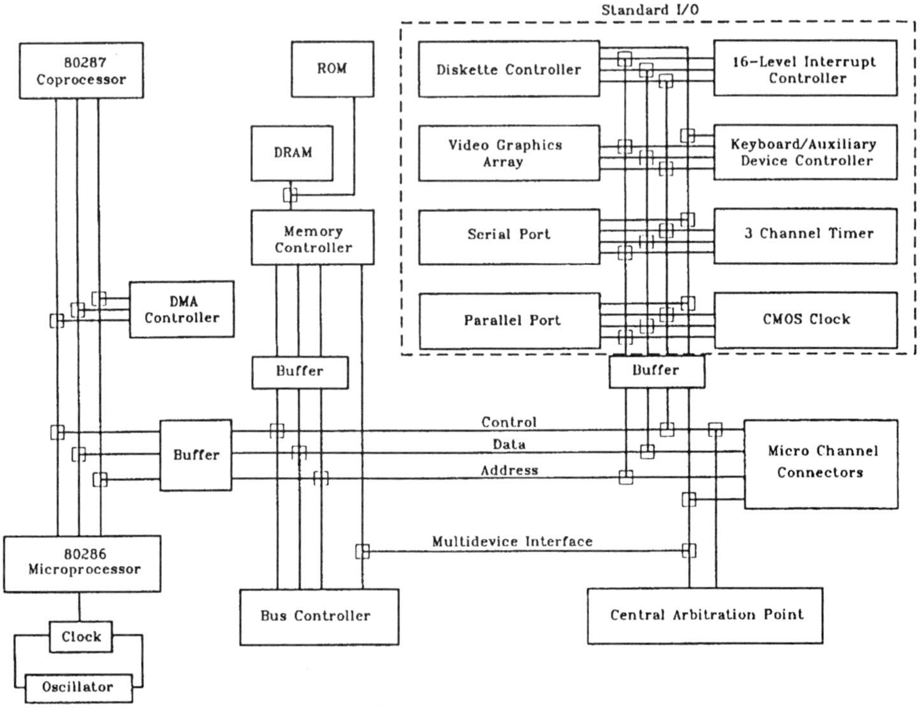

Figure 5.3 The IBM PS/2 Model 50Z system board. (Courtesy of International Business Machines Corporation)

While this bus contention may seem undesirable, the reality is that it probably doesn't affect performance in most of the uses of the Model 50Z. The Micro Channel bus just isn't very busy anyway. Most of the I/O activity is printing, disk reads and writes, and communications using devices slower than the bus data rates. In a single-tasking environment, however, the system master must wait for these operations to be completed, but not because of bus contention. The real productivity gains come from the use of multitasking system software like OS/2 (or even a print spooler). The lesson here is that theoretical considerations do not necessarily translate to user productivity gains.

In all of the PS/2 implementations of Micro Channel architecture, the system master is also the default master. The default master has the lowest priority on the bus. The rationale for this, if it escapes you, is that it eliminates the 300 ns arbitration overhead that the system master would experience if it were not also the default master.

The specifications for the Model 50Z cycle times are shown in Table 5.2. As you can see, the cycle times for the system master to access system board memory and channel memory are both 200 ns. However, the arbitration overhead of 300 ns must be added for channel memory access. In addition, memory refresh must be performed every 15.1 microseconds, which further reduces the true data transfer rate of the 50Z as well as other systems. The data rates previously quoted for Micro Channel transfers were "burst" rates rather than the true data transfer rates because they did not include the arbitration time nor the memory refresh time.

For DMA transfers, the cycle times shown in Table 5.2 are for serial operations between memory and I/O devices. The total time required is the arbitration time plus the sum of the I/O and memory access times for a single transfer. For burst transfers, the sum of the I/O and memory access times must be multiplied by the number of transfers in the burst.

Model 55 SX

The Model 55 SX is a small desktop system with a lower profile and a slightly larger footprint than the Model 50Z (Figure 5.4). The system is capable of supporting DOS, OS/2, and AIX operating systems. Its 16 Mhz 386SX microprocessor allows it to support Windows 3.0 and VM/386 applications by using its virtual 8086 mode. As was described in Chapter 1, the 386SX chip has 32-bit "internals" and 16-bit "externals." The Model 55 SX is designed as a personal productivity workstation in which performance requirements are somewhat greater those for the 50Z. "Run your business" applications such as accounting and inventory, large spreadsheets, and concurrent communications sessions are examples. This system was an industry leader almost from the beginning because of its attractive price, excellent performance, and function.

The system comes with 2 MB of memory standard on the system board expandable to 4 MB, using an additional 2 MB memory module. Up to a total of 16 MB of memory is supported using memory expansion boards. Also included are VGA graphics, a 30 MB fixed disk drive with an ST-506 controller (Model 55-031) or a 60 MB fixed disk drive with an ESDI controller (Model 55-061). These disk drive

TABLE 5.2 MODEL 50 Z CYCLE TIMES (Courtesy of International Business Machines Corporation)

Devices	Wait States	Cycle Time (ns)
Bus Master Access to System Board RAM		300 (min)
Microprocessor (10 MHz) — 100 ns Clock):		
Access to System Board RAM		
85 ns Memory	0	200
120 ns Memory	1	300
Access to System Board ROM	1	300
Acces to Channel:		
Default Transfer Cycle:		
I/O Access	1	300
Memory Access	0	200
Synchronous Extended Transfer Cycle	1	300
DMA Controller (10 MHz — 100 ns Clock):		
System Board Memory Access		
85 ns Memory		200
120 ns Memory		300
Default Transfer Cycle:		
I/O Access		300
Memory Access		200
Synchronous Extended Transfer Cycle		300
Single Transfer: 300 + I/O Access + Memory Access		
Burst Trnasfers: 300 + (I/O Access + Memory Access)N*		

*N is the number of transfers in the burst.

subassemblies also include the controller and connector for directly attaching them to the Micro Channel bus. A Micro Channel slot is not required. The power supply is 90 watts.

The Model 55 SX has limited internal expansion capabilities. It is not designed to add a second fixed disk drive to this system. There are three 16-bit expansion slots, one with the video extension. The expansion boards are installed horizontally rather than vertically, as is the case with the Model 50Z.

The memory management of the 55 SX system uses what is called **paged memory**. Paged memory management is a technique that reduces or eliminates wait states for memory accesses within a segment or page (called a **page hit**). The 386SX, the i386, and the i486 chips have this capability in which memory can be divided into pages (large segments of contiguous memory) instead of the small 64 KB segments of the 8086 and 80286. If the memory is in the same segment, the memory access does not require a wait state. If the memory address is not within the same memory segment, a **page miss** results and two wait states are required. Table 5.3 shows the effects of paged memory on cycle times for the Model 55 SX.

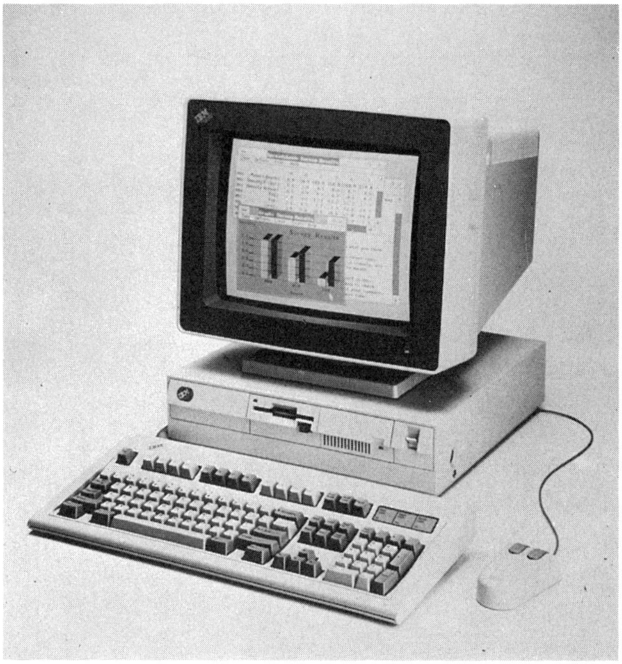

Figure 5.4 The IBM PS/2 Model 55SX computer.

Model 55 LS

This system is what is generally called a **medialess** machine. It is used in a LAN environment as a requester. It has no fixed disk or diskette drives, but is equipped with a standard LAN adapter. A technique called **remote IPL** (Initial Program Load) is used to start the system. All the software and data needed by the medialess system is on the server.

The two most important advantages of medialess systems are security and economy. In terms of security, all the data resides on the server and access can be carefully controlled. You don't have to worry about unauthorized changes or theft of sensitive information at the workstation since you can't even start the system or copy any data. In addition, there can be more control over other aspects of data security such as backup procedures by the server.

Medialess systems differ from **nonintelligent workstations** (dumb terminals) in that they provide local processing capability instead of relying on a host system to supply their "smarts." Since they are medialess, however, their purchase price is less than that of other systems, but more than that of nonintelligent workstations.

The Model 55 LS is a medialess version of the 55 SX. It also includes either a Token Ring or an Ethernet LAN adapter. It is designed to be upgraded if you later decide that you would like to have a 1.44 MB diskette drive or a 30 MB or 60 MB fixed disk drive.

TABLE 5.3 MODEL 55 SX CYCLE TIMES (Courtesy of International Business Machines Corporation)

Devices	Wait States	Cycle Time (ns)
Bus Master Access to System Board RAM		300 (min)
Microprocessor (16 MHz — 62.5 ns Clock)		
Access to System Board RAM:		
Memory Read (Page Hit)	0	125
Memory Read (Anticipated Page Miss)	1	187.5
Memory Read (Page Miss)	2	250
Memory Write(Page Hit)	1	187.5
Memory Write (Anticipated Page Miss)	1	187.5
Memory Write (Page Miss)	2	250
Access to Channel:		
Default Transfer Cycle	2	250
Synchronous Transfer Cycle	4	375
Access to ROM	3	312
DMA Controller (8 MHz — 125 ns Clock):		
System Board Access		375
Default Transfer Cycle		250
Synchronous Extended Transfer Cycle		375
Single Transfer: 375 + I/O Access + Memory Access		
Burst Transfers: 375 + (I/O Access + Memory Access)N[*]		

[*]N is the number of transfers in the burst.

Some application environments that use medialess systems are travel agencies, banks, financial brokerages, and insurance agencies.

Model 60

The Model 60 is a 10 MHz 286 floor-standing system designed for applications that require additional I/O devices and storage compared to the Model 50Z. Some examples are desktop publishing, small to medium network LAN server (shared resources), and multi-user host (shared logic) applications. Operating system support includes DOS and OS/2. This system was also one of the original systems announced in 1987. It is no longer in manufacture, having been replaced by the Model 65 SX.

The system comes standard with 1 MB of memory. Additional memory must be added via memory expansion boards. Maximum memory addressability is 16 MB. Also included is a 44 MB fixed disk drive with an ST-506 controller (Model 60-041) or a 70 MB (Model 60-071) fixed disk drive with an ESDI controller. VGA graphics is integrated on the system board in both models. The power supply is 207 for the Model 60-041 or 225 watts for the Models 60-071. Internal expansion capabilities include the ability to add an additional 1.44 MB 3.5-inch diskette drive or an internal tape backup unit, using the integrated diskette controller. A second 44 MB fixed disk drive can also be added to the Model 60-041, or a 70 MB or 115 MB drive can be added to the Model 60-071. The system will also accommodate a 5.25-inch internal diskette drive or an internal optical disk drive if the second fixed disk drive is not added. There are eight 16-bit Micro Channel expansion board connectors, one of which is occupied by the fixed disk drive adapter. One of the connectors has an auxiliary video extension. Table 5.4 summarizes the system's cycle times. The Model 60 comes with 125 ns memory instead of the 50Z's 85 ns memory, which adds one wait state to memory accesses by the system master.

Model 65 SX

This 16 MHz 386SX system is a floor-standing system with lots of expansion capabilities and features an SCSI bus master adapter. It is designed for essentially the same type of applications as the Model 60 but with additional performance requirements because of its 386SX microprocessor. The system is capable of supporting DOS, OS/2, and UNIX as well as virtual 8086 applications.

The system includes VGA graphics and comes standard with 2 MB of 100 ns memory on the system board and can support up to 8 MB. Total system memory supported is 16 MB, using a memory expansion board. The three models include the Model 65-061 with a 60 MB fixed disk drive, the Model 65-121 with a 120 MB fixed disk drive, and the Model 65-321 with a 320 MB fixed disk drive. The power supply is 250 watts.

TABLE 5.4 MODEL 60 CYCLE TIMES (Courtesy of International Business Machines Corporation)

Devices	Wait States	Cycle Time (ns)
Bus Master Access to System Board RAM		300 (min)
Microprocessor (16 MHz — 62.5 ns Clock)		
Access to System Board RAM:	1	300
Access to System Board ROM:	1	300
Access to Channel:		
Default Transfer Cycle		
I/O Access	1	300
Memory Access	0	200
Synchronous Extended Transfer Cycle	1	300
DMA Controller (10 MHz — 100 ns Clock):		
System Board Memory Access		300
Default Transfer Cycle		
I/O Access		300
Memory Access		200
Synchronous Extended Transfer Cycle		300
Single Transfer: 375 + I/O Access + Memory Access		
Burst Transfers: 375 + (I/O Access + Memory Access)N*		

*N is the number of transfers in the burst.

Also included is a 16-bit SCSI bus master I/O adapter that lets you add up to seven different SCSI peripherals. Up to four SCSI adapters per system are supported, which allows you to add a total of 28 SCSI devices. This industry standard interface is supported by numerous IBM and non-IBM SCSI devices ranging from fixed disk drives, CD ROM drives, tape backup units, and printers.

The system can accommodate a second 1.44 MB diskette drive or tape backup unit internally. There is also room and adequate power for up to three additional 3.5-inch 60 MB, 120 MB, or 320 MB IBM fixed disk drives. Numerous other options are supported, including an internal CD ROM drive. The system features eight 16-bit expansion slots, one of which is occupied by the SCSI adapter. There are seven 16-bit base slots and one slot with the video extension.

Model P70 386

This "lovable luggable" system is a real powerhouse and is loaded with features. Loaded enough to make it a little heavy (weighing in at almost 21 lbs.) however. The good news is that when you get to where you're going with it, it does everything you want it to do—fast!

The system is designed for people that need portable power, such as accountants, auditors, engineers, contractors, and sales professionals. It includes a detachable full-size 101-key keyboard complete with numeric keypad for these applications.

Two of the models are essentially clones of the 20 MHz Model 70 386-061 or -121 and include 4 MB of RAM on the system board with a maximum of 8 MB. The truth is that these models are just a "tad" faster than their bigger brothers on some applications.

Another member of the P70 family is a 16-MHz Model with a 30 MB disk drive and includes 2 MB of RAM with a maximum of 4 MB on the system board. (No, the lower capacity drive and less memory doesn't make it lighter!) A maximum of 16 MB of RAM is supported in all models.

The systems include a 1.44 MB diskette drive and VGA graphics. The VGA supports the high-resolution gas-plasma display as well as other displays in the PS/2 family. It does not support the higher resolution displays like the Model 8514 (1024 x 768), except in VGA modes. The gas plasma display is a 16-gray-level gas plasma with a high-contrast ratio and a dark background. There are two expansion slots available: one 16/32-bit full-size and one 16-bit half-size. The half-size slot is perfect for the IBM 300/1200/2400 Internal Modem/A. Since there is no video extension, graphics upgrades with the higher resolution 8514/A or the use of other adapters that require the extension are not possible.

In addition to the usual built-in serial, parallel, and mouse ports, there is an external storage device port controlled by the diskette controller. This can be used for the attachment of an external diskette drive or other devices designed to work with the diskette drive controller. A nice touch is the optional Hartmann carrying case made of belting leather.

This system is not battery powered because of the power requirements of the gas-plasma screen. It includes an 85-watt internal power supply.

Model 70 386

The Model 70 is a high-performance desktop system with the same external appearance as the Model 50Z. It is designed for applications that require significant processing power such as very large spreadsheets, desktop publishing, high speed concurrent communications sessions, graphics, and the host for a multi-user system. (The system is somewhat limited in its I/O capabilities by it three slots, however.) It is capable of supporting DOS, OS/2, and AIX and virtual 8086 applications.

The five models include:

- Model 70-E61, a 16 MHz 386 system with a 60 MB ESDI fixed disk drive.
- Models 70-061 and -121, 20 MHz 386 systems with either a 60 or a 120 MB ESDI fixed disk drive.
- Models 70-A61 and -A21, 25 MHz 386 systems with either a 60 MB or a 120 MB ESDI fixed disk drive. These include a 64KB static RAM memory cache and can also be upgraded to a 25 MHz 486 system.

All the models include VGA graphics and have 2 MB of memory standard on the system board. The Models 70-E61, -061, and -121 can be expanded to 6 MB on the system board. The Models 70-A61 and -A21 can be expanded to 8 MB on the system board.Using memory expansion boards, all models can be expanded to 16 MB total memory. The systems have 132-watt power supplies.

In terms of internal expansion, a second 1.44 MB diskette drive or an internal tape backup unit can be added. No additional internal fixed disk drives can be added. These systems have two 32-bit Micro Channel slots and one 16-bit slot with the video extension.

The hardware memory cache of the Model 70-A61 and -A21 allow the system master to access its contents at the same time as the Micro Channel bus is in use. This dual bus design benefits performance by reducing the bus contention discussed earlier and also by reducing the memory access times if the desired information is in the cache as Table 5.5 shows.

Through the use of an option that IBM calls the 486/25 Power Platform, the Models 70-A61 and -A21 can be upgraded to systems that are equivalent to the Model 70-486. The 486/25 Power Platform is used to replace the 386 microprocessor, the 387 math coprocessor, and support chips (Figure 5.5). The upgrade physically replaces the 386 processor complex, which may be returned to IBM for credit.

Model 70 486

This desktop model has the same external appearance as the other Model 70s, but what a difference under the cover! The system contains the extremely powerful 25 MHz i486 microprocessor with its internal 8 KB memory cache and integrated math coprocessor. It is almost twice as fast for business applications and up to three times faster for CPU-intensive tasks. It would be a good selection for engineering and scientific applications, graphics, desktop publishing, or as a data base server or multi-user host. The system is capable of supporting DOS, OS/2, and AIX and virtual 8086 applications.

TABLE 5.5 MODEL 70–A21 CYCLE TIMES (Courtesy of International Business Machines Corporation)

Devices	Wait States	Cycle Time (ns)
Bus Master Access to System Board RAM		300 (min)
Microprocessor (25 MHz — 40 ns Clock)		
Access to System Board RAM:		
Memory Read (Cache Hit)	0	80
Memory Write (Cache Hit)	0	80**
Memory Read (Cache Miss, Page Hit)	0 – 2	80 – 160
Memory Write(Cache Miss, Page Hit)	1	80**
Memory Read (Cache Miss, Page Miss)	3 –5	200 – 280
Memory Write (Cache Miss, Page Miss)	0	80**
Access to Channel:		
Default Transfer Cycle	4	240
Synchronous Extended Transfer Cycle	7	360
DMA Controller (10 MHz — 100 ns Clock):		
System Board Access		300
Default Transfer Cycle		200
Synchronous Extended Transfer Cycle		300
Single Transfer: 300 + I/O Access + Memory Access		
Burst Transfers: 300 + (I/O Access + Memory Access)N*		

*N is the number of transfers in the burst.

Figure 5.5 The 486/25 Power Platform is used to upgrade the performance of the Model 70-A21 or Model 70-A121. (Courtesy of International Business Machines Corporation)

The system comes standard with VGA graphics and 2 MB of memory on the system board and is expandable to 8 MB. Up to 16 MB of total system memory can be supported using a memory expansion board. Also included is a 60 MB fixed disk drive and ESDI controller (Model B-61) or a 120 MB fixed disk drive and ESDI controller (Model B-21). The system has a 132-watt power supply.

A second 1.44 MB diskette drive or tape backup unit can be added internally. No additional internal fixed disk drives can be added, however. There are two 32-bit expansion slots and one 16-bit expansion slot with a video extension.

Model 80 386

The eleven members of this family are 386 floor-standing systems that provide a full range of performance and expansion capabilities for almost any application. The Model 80 386 makes an ideal network server, LAN gateway to a host, or multi-user host. Its higher performance members are suitable for engineering and scientific applications and as graphics workstations. The systems that include the SCSI adapter are excellent choices for desktop publishing and multimedia applications because of the variety of I/O devices supported (CD ROM for example).

These systems have been popular since the first ones were introduced in 1987. IBM has continued to enhance these systems including the addition of new models in March and October of 1990. If you examine the features of the family, it's hard to find very much in common except the 386 microprocessor, the 1.44 MB diskette drive, and the VGA.

The members of the family include:

- Model 80-041, a 16-MHz 386 system with 1 MB of RAM, an ST-506 fixed disk controller, and a 44-MB fixed disk drive.
- Model 80-071, a 16-MHz 386 system with 2 MB of RAM, an ESDI fixed disk controller, and a 70-MB fixed disk drive.
- Model 80-081, a 20-MHz 386 system with 2 MB of RAM, a 16-bit SCSI bus master adapter, and an 80-MB SCSI fixed disk drive.
- Model 80-111, a 20-MHz 386 system with 2 MB of RAM, an ESDI fixed disk DMA slave controller, and a 115-MB fixed disk drive.
- Model 80-121, a 20-MHz 386 system with 2 MB of RAM, a 16-bit SCSI bus master adapter, and a 120-MB fixed disk drive.
- Model 80-161, a 20-MHz 386 system with 2 MB of RAM, a 16-bit SCSI bus master adapter, and a 160-MB SCSI fixed disk drive.
- Model 80-311, a 20-MHz 386 system with 2 MB of RAM, an ESDI fixed disk DMA slave controller, and a 115-MB fixed disk drive.
- Model 80-321, a 20-MHz 386 system with 2 MB of RAM, a 16-bit SCSI bus master adapter, and a 320 MB fixed disk drive.
- Model 80-A16, a 25 MHz 386 system with a 64-KB memory cache and 4 MB of RAM, a 16-bit SCSI bus master adapter, and a 160-MB SCSI fixed disk drive.
- Model 80-A21, a 25 MHz 386 system with a 64-KB memory cache and 4 MB of RAM, a 16-bit SCSI bus master adapter, and a 120 MB SCSI fixed disk drive.

- Model 80-A31, a 25-MHz 386 system with a 64-KB memory cache and 4 MB of RAM, a 16-bit SCSI bus master adapter, and a 320-MB SCSI fixed disk drive. This 3.5-inch drive features a 12.5 ms access time.

The systems have eight expansion slots, with one of the 16-bit slots occupied by the ESDI fixed disk controller or the SCSI adapter. All models except the 80-A16, 80-A21, and 80-A31 have four 16-bit slots and three 32-bit slots. These models have three 16-bit slots and four 32-bit slots. In terms of memory expansion, the 25 MHz models can accommodate up to 8 MB on the system board. The 20 MHz models are limited to 4 MB and the 16 MHz models are limited to 2 MB. In all cases, the maximum memory addressability is 16 MB. All the systems have 225-watt power supplies, with the exception of the A16, A21, and A31 models, which provide 242 watts.

The 16 MHz Model 80s do not use paged-memory management, but the comparable Model 70s do. The result is a slight performance edge for the 16 MHz Model 70s. The other members of the Model 80 family use paged memory. The specifications for the 16 MHz models are shown in Table 5.6.

Model 90 XP 486

This powerful desktop system is a completely new system inside and out (Figure 5.6). Its power, flexibility, graphics, expandability, and upgradeability are extremely impressive. It is designed as a high-performance workstation for scientific calculations, spreadsheets, financial applications, or computer program development. Its advanced graphics provide a suitable platform for desktop publishing, multimedia applications, presentation graphics, and computer-assisted design. It

TABLE 5.6 MODELS 80–041 AND 80–071 CYCLE TIMES (Courtesy of International Business Machines Corporation)

Devices	Wait States	Cycle Time (ns)
Bus Master Access to System Board RAM		300 (min)
Microprocessor (16 MHz — 62.5 ns Clock)		
Access to System Board RAM:	1	187.5
Access to System Board ROM:	1	187.5
Access to Channel:		
Default Transfer Cycle	2	250
Synchronous Extended Transfer Cycle	4	375
DMA Controller (8 MHz — 125 ns Clock):		
System Board Memory Access		375
Default Transfer Cycle		250
Synchronous Extended Transfer Cycle		375
Single Transfer: 375 + I/O Access + Memory Access		
Burst Transfers: 375 + (I/O Access + Memory Access)N*		

*N is the number of transfers in the burst.

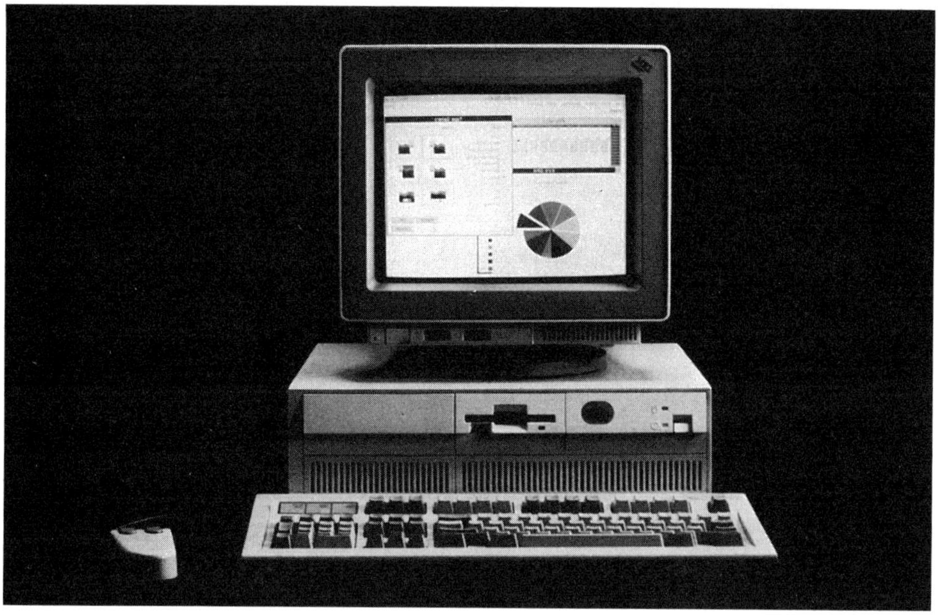

Figure 5.6 IBM PS/2 Model 90 XP 486 computer. (Courtesy of International Business Machines Corporation)

is also useful as a data-base server because of its processing power.

A summary of its features is shown in Figure 5.7. Perhaps its most outstanding feature is its state-of-the-art upgradeable processor complex providing 486 power in two flavors—25 and 33 MHz versions. The processor complex resides on a specially designed adapter card that can be removed and a higher performance version installed. This opens the door for a completely new design concept for IBM's systems in the future. As more powerful microprocessors become available, systems can be easily upgraded to take advantage of them. The Model 95 XP 486 (Figure 5.8) also accepts the same processor complexes.

IBM has introduced its long-awaited high-resolution graphics as a standard feature of this system. Christened XGA, the new graphics adapter provides 1024 x 768 resolution and 16 colors with the standard 512 KB of video RAM (a type of memory that can be read by the video graphics controller at the same time the system is writing to it) or 256 colors with an additional 512 KB of video RAM. The Model 90's bus master implementation of XGA graphics is considerably faster than VGA graphics in earlier PS/2 systems. It is a 32-bit bus master compared to VGA's 8-bit memory-mapped implementation.

There are three models:

- Model 90 XP 486-0J5, which features a 25-MHz 486 processor complex and an 80-MB SCSI fixed disk drive;
- Model 90 XP 486-0J9, which features a 25-MHz 486 processor complex an a 160 MB SCSI fixed disk drive; and

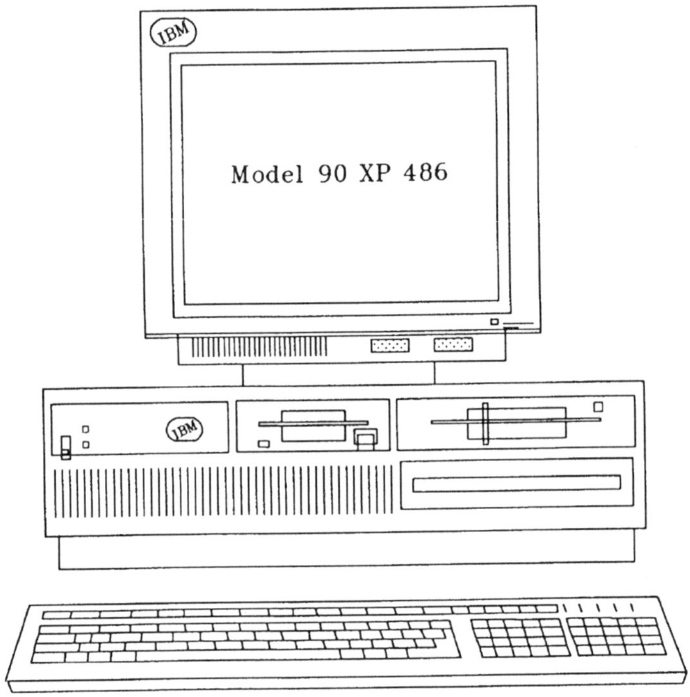

- 25-MHz or 33-MHz i486 microprocessor
  (25 MHz upgradeable to 33 MHz)
- 4 MB 70 ns memory expandable to 32 MB on system board
- 32-bit SCSI adapter
- Four storage bays (960 MB maximum fixed disk storage)
- 3.5" or 5.25" storage device options
- XGA graphics
- Three available slots
- Two DMA serial ports

Figure 5.7 Model 90 XP 486 features.

- Model 90 XP 486-0KD, which features a 33-MHz 486 processor complex and a 320-MB SCSI fixed disk drive.

The systems have considerably more expansion capabilities than the Model 70 desktop systems. They include four 32-bit Micro Channel slots, one of which is used by the standard 32-bit bus master SCSI adapter with its 512 KB of on-board cache. One of the slots also has an auxiliary video extension that can be used by other video adapters such as the M-Motion card (described later in this chapter). The SCSI adapter can be used to add additional internal as well as external storage options. Up to four SCSI adapters can be installed in the system, supporting up to 28 devices.

A 1.44-MB diskette drive and a fixed disk drive come standard with the system. There are two additional **bays** (a storage device compartment) within the system.

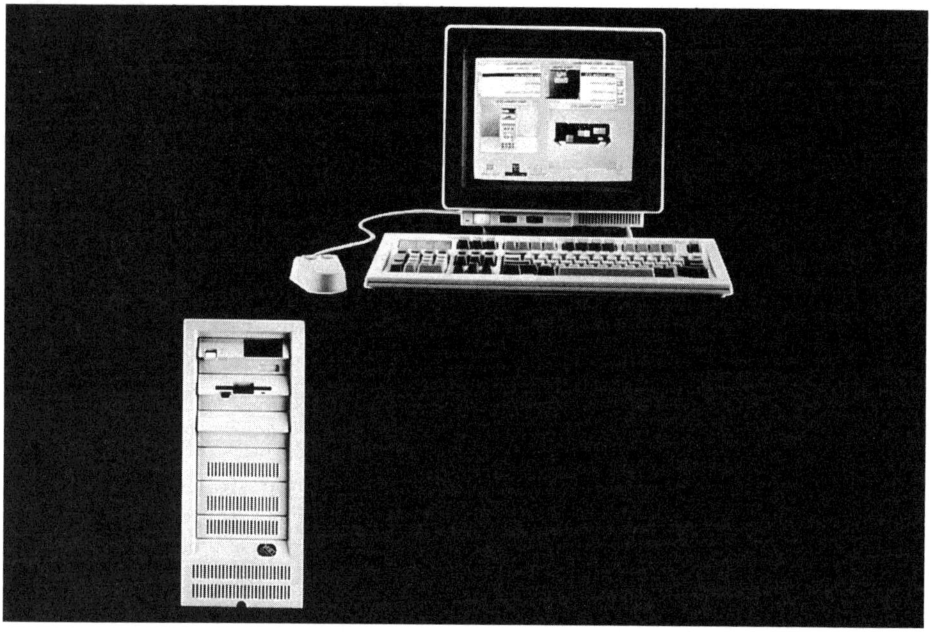

Figure 5.8 The IBM PS/2 Model 95 XP 486 computer. (Courtesy of International Business Machines Corporation)

One bay can accommodate 3.5-inch devices and the other 3.5-inch and 5.25-inch devices. The 3.5-inch bay permits the installation of a second 1.44-MB diskette drive, an additional 3.5-inch fixed disk drive, or an internal tape backup device. The 5.25-inch bay can accommodate a 5.25-inch diskette drive or a 5.25-inch CD ROM drive or any of the 3.5-inch device types. This means that up to 960 MB of storage can be installed internally. The system includes a 194-watt power supply.

In terms of memory, 4 MB of 70 ns memory come standard, with the system expandable to 32 MB on the system board. IBM has stated that 8 MB memory modules can be accommodated in the system, providing a total capacity of 64 MB when they become available. The memory controller is unusually smart since it allows 1-MB, 2-MB, or 4-MB memory modules to be installed in the system.

The systems also include two serial ports that are DMA devices, compared to the single I/O slave implementations of the previous systems. This should provide a performance boost since the DMA controller can offload the system microprocessor.

IBM has changed its philosophy for BIOS implementations in this system and in the Model 95 XP 486. In the earlier systems, BIOS was implemented as ROM microcode on a system-unique hardware module. In the new systems, POST in ROM resides on the processor complex. In addition, the BIOS resides on the fixed disk drive, allowing it to be easily upgraded from a diskette. The reference diskette information is provided both on a diskette and the fixed disk drive, allowing system diagnostics and setup to be run from either. This is a real convenience compared to the earlier systems, which required the reference diskette (only somehow, it always seemed to get lost) to change the configuration or run the diagnostics.

Both Model 90 XP 486 and 95 XP are capable of supporting the DOS, OS/2, and AIX operating systems.

Model 95 XP 486

The floor-standing Model 95 XP 486 has numerous features in common with the Model 90 XP 486, as is shown in Figure 5.9. In addition to the applications described above for the Model 90 XP 486, it provides a powerful platform with additional capacity and expansion for a large number of users for host applications and as a LAN server.

There are three models:

PS/2 Model 95 XP 486

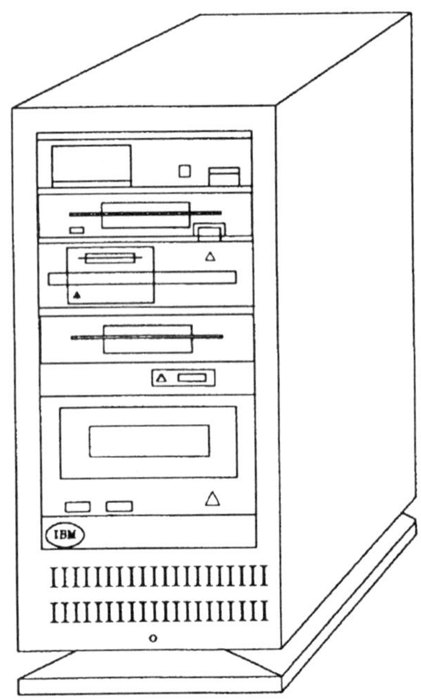

- 25 MHz or 33 MHz i486 microprocessor (25 MHz upgradeable to 33 MHz)
- 4 MB 70 ns memory standard expandable to 32 MB on system board
- 32-bit SCSI adapter standard
- XGA standard
- Six available slots
- Seven storage bays (maximum 1.6GB)

Figure 5.9 Model 96 XP 486 features.

- Model 95 XP 486-0J9, which features a 25-MHz 486 processor complex and a 160-MB SCSI fixed disk drive;
- Model 95 XP 486-0JD, which features a 25-MHz 486 processor complex and a 320-MB SCSI fixed disk drive; and
- Model 95 XP 486-0KD, which features a 33-MHz 486 processor complex and a 320-MB SCSI fixed disk drive.

Standard features include the same 32-bit SCSI adapter used in the Model 90 XP 486 and 4 MB of 70 ns memory. The system board can accommodate up to 32 MB of memory, using 4-MB memory modules, and up to 64 MB, using 8 MB memory modules when they become available. The system uses the same flexible memory controller as the Model 90 XP 486. A single DMA serial port is included in addition to the standard DMA parallel port.

There are eight 32-bit Micro Channel adapter slots, including one occupied by the SCSI adapter and an XGA graphics adapter, leaving six available slots. The slot layout is shown in Figure 5.10. The XGA graphics adapter is not integrated in the system board. The slot occupied by the XGA adapter has a new base video

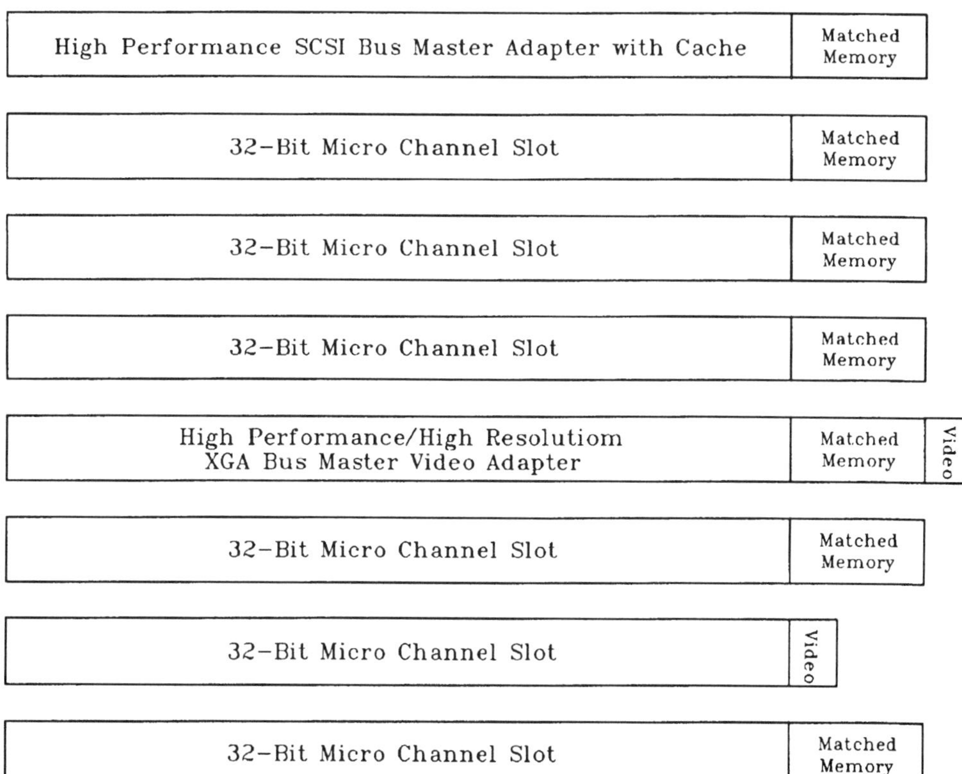

Figure 5.10 Model 95 XP 486 slot layout. The system features a new base video extension in addition to the auxiliary video extension.

extension. One of the slots also has the auxiliary video extension. The purpose of the new base video extension is to provide a signal path between the XGA and another video adapter that utilizes the auxiliary video extension. This is required since there is no video adapter on the system board.

The storage options for these systems are very impressive and should satisfy even the most demanding users, at least for awhile. The system features seven bays of various sizes and shapes, as is shown in Figure 5.11. The system comes standard with a 1.44-MB diskette drive. A second 3.5-inch 1.44-MB diskette drive or a tape backup may be added to the system in the second bay. The third bay can accommodate either 3.5-inch or 5.25-inch storage options, including fixed disk drives, tape backup devices, or CD ROM drives. In addition, a 5.25-inch 1.2-MB diskette drive can be installed.

The fourth and fifth bays can support either two half-high storage devices or one full-high storage device. Both 3.5-inch and 5.25-inch devices can be installed. Some examples of combinations that can be supported are one 5.25-inch fixed disk drive or two 3.5-inch fixed disk drives or two 5.25-inch CD ROM drives. The sixth and seventh bays can also support two 3.5-inch fixed disk drives or one 5.25-inch fixed disk drive. The drive that is standard in the system is installed in the seventh bay. If a full-high drive is installed in the sixth and seventh bay, the standard drive must be moved to the third bay. The system features a hefty 329-watt power supply.

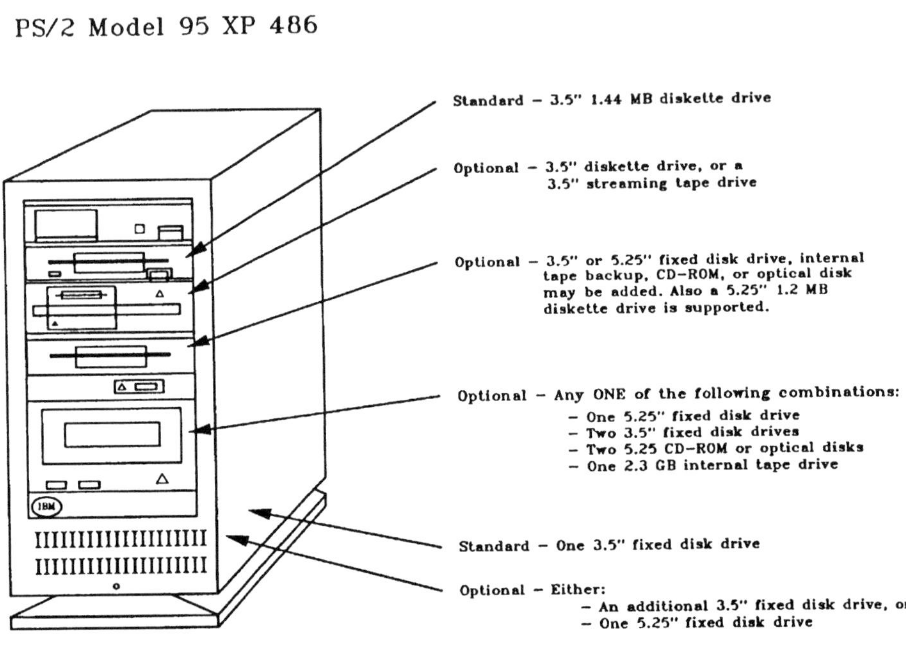

Figure 5.11 Internal storage options for Model 95 XP 486.

After all this talk of bay after bay, you're probably seasick by now! The net result is that the system can accommodate a maximum of 1.6 GB (gigabytes) internally, using 320-MB fixed disk drives.

IBM has also introduced an external storage enclosure, the PS/2 3511, in which up to seven SCSI 320-MB fixed disk drives can be added using the SCSI adapter.[1] Up to 28 SCSI devices can be supported by using four of these external enclosures containing drives, the internal drives, and three additional SCSI adapters. In terms of software support, OS/2 takes care of 24 fixed disk drives for a total of 7.68 GB. DOS users will have to be satisfied with support for 7 drives for a total of 2.24 GB for now.

Model 90 XP 486 and 95 XP 486 Processor Complexes

The Model 90 XP 486 and 95 XP 486 processor complexes provide a quantum leap in performance and flexibility for IBM's Micro Channel systems. The features of the processor complex include a 64-bit data path to system memory, a highly flexible memory configuration capability, an external memory cache, and a unique memory management design that is optimized for both the i486 and Micro Channel architecture's multiple master capability.

Figure 5.12 is a block diagram of the processor complex and the system memory arrangement. There are two separate banks of system memory that can be accessed alternately, or **interleaved,** to provide the retrieval of 64 bits of memory at a time. The way this works is that the 32 bits in the Bank A buffer are transferred to the 486 while the 32 bits from Bank B are being stored in the Bank B buffer. Next, the contents of the Bank B buffer are transferred to the 486.

The result of this is to reduce the apparent memory access time. A performance feature of the i486 microprocessor architecture is its ability to accept 16 consecutive bytes of data by filling its internal cache and its instruction prefetch buffer. The processor complex takes advantage of this capability by using its interleaved arrangement to transfer data in a burst of four 32-bit data transfers with half the wait states for memory access that four independent memory read cycles would require. Using the noninterleaved memory arrangement of the Model 70 486 and the 486 Power Platform architecture, the i486 must wait for a memory access on each of the four cycles (Figure 5.13).[2] The interleaved arrangement only requires waiting for memory access on two of the four cycles.

Even though the processor complexes are not part of Micro Channel architecture, their designs are complementary to its features. The design allows the system master to access system memory while another master has control of the Micro Channel bus. In the earlier systems like the Model 70 486, the i486 microprocessor had to wait its turn in order to access system memory if another

[1]The PS/2 external storage enclosure for SCSI devices can be used as a storage tower for all Micro Channel PS/2 systems equipped with an SCSI adapter.

[2]Remember that the i486 microprocessor has an internal cache. If the required data is in this cache, which is probable, there are no wait states. If this is the case, the cache memory access time is 40 nanoseconds for the 25-MHz 486 and 30 nanoseconds for the 33-MHz 486.

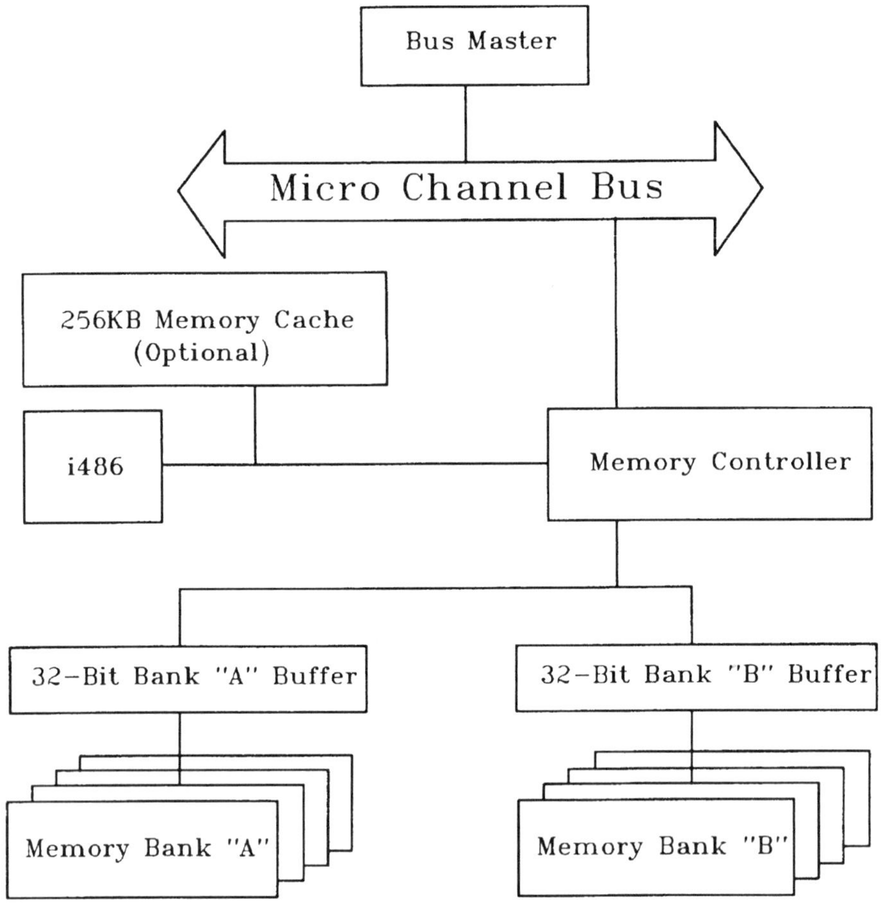

Figure 5.12 The PS/2 Model 90 XP 486 and Model 95 XP 486 processor/memory architecture.

master had control of the bus. In addition, the new processor complex design allows alternating memory accesses by the i486 and a bus master.

The memory controller is designed to allow a variety of memory modules with different characteristics to be used in the system. These must be installed in pairs, but a system may have several types. This capability is important for upgrading memory and minimizing the need to remove one type of memory in order to use another type. In most cases, this prevents "parts on the floor," as was the case for previous systems. This very flexible design allows faster and denser memory to be utilized as it becomes available and gives the ability to mix or match memory types.

Another feature of the memory controller design is that it allows the system to adjust to the speed of a memory module on a cycle-by-cycle basis so that the whole system is not slowed down to the slowest memory module installed.

Even though the i486 has an internal cache, the addition of the optional 256-KB

TABLE 5.7 MODELS 90 XP 486 AND 95 XP 486 (25 MHZ) CYCLE TIMES (Courtesy of International Business Machines Corporation)

Devices	Number of 486 Cycles	Cycle Time (ns)
Microprocessor (25 MHz — 40 ns Clock)		
Access to System Board RAM:		
Memory Read (Cache Hit)	2	80
Memory Write (Cache Hit)	2	80
Memory Read (Cache Miss, Page Hit)	5–1–3–1**	400
Memory Write(Cache Miss, Page Hit)	5	200
Memory Read (Cache Miss, Page Miss)	9–1–3–1**	540
Memory Write (Cache Miss, Page Miss)	9	360
Access to Channel:		
Default Transfer Cycle		240
Synchronous Extended Transfer Cycle		320
Refresh Cycle Time:		
Approximately every 15.1 microseconds		
Bus Master:		
Access to System Board RAM:		
Default Transfer Cycle (Page Hit)		340
Default Transfer Cycle (Page Miss)		500
DMA Controller (10 MHz — 100 ns Clock):		
System Board Memory Access (Page Hit)		300
System Board Memory Access (Page Miss)		420
Default Transfer Cycle		200
Synchronous Extended Transfer Cycle		300
Single Transfer: 300 + I/O Access + Memory Access		
Burst Transfers: 300 + (I/O Access + Memory Access)N*		

*N is the number of transfers in the burst.
**Numberof 486 Processor cycles required on four consecutive accesses to system board RAM.

SRAM external cache boosts performance further, especially in systems with bus masters installed. Any cycles that are missed in the internal cache may find the desired information in the external cache. A bus master or the DMA controller has exclusive access to the system board memory when the i486 is running out of either its internal or external caches.

The processor complex is a removable, interchangeable card that plugs into the Micro Channel and memory bus using a special connector design. The DMA controller is physically located on the processor complex, but is electrically attached to the Micro Channel bus. The processor complexes and their relationship to the system board components have been obviously chosen to provide maximum flexibility for future upgrades of higher speed processors and other components. They differ significantly from the 25-MHz 486 Power Platform upgrade described previously, which was virtually identical to the 25 MHz 386 processor it replaced.

TABLE 5.8 MODELS 90 XP 486 AND 95 XP 486 (33 MHZ) CYCLE TIMES (Courtesy of International Business Machines Corporation)

Devices	Number of 486 Cycles	Cycle Time (ns)
Microprocessor (33 MHz — 30 ns Clock)		
Access to System Board RAM:		
Memory Read (Cache Hit)	2	60
Memory Write (Cache Hit)	2	60
Memory Read (Cache Miss, Page Hit)	4–1–2–1**	240
Memory Write(Cache Miss, Page Hit)	4	120
Memory Read (Cache Miss, Page Miss)	8–1–2–1**	360
Memory Write (Cache Miss, Page Miss)	9	240
Access to Channel:		
Default Transfer Cycle		210
Synchronous Extended Transfer Cycle		330
Refresh Cycle Time:		
Approximately every 15.1 microseconds		
Bus Master:		
Access to System Board RAM:		
Default Transfer Cycle (Page Hit)		300
Default Transfer Cycle (Page Miss)		420
DMA Controller (10 MHz — 100 ns Clock):		
System Board Memory Access (Page Hit)		300
System Board Memory Access (Page Miss)		420
Default Transfer Cycle		200
Synchronous Extended Transfer Cycle		300
Single Transfer: 300 + I/O Access + Memory Access		
Burst Transfers: 300 + (I/O Access + Memory Access)N*		

*N is the number of transfers in the burst.
**Number of 486 processor cycles required on four consecutive accesses to system board RAM.

IBM PS/2 Micro Channel System Performance Summary

The preceding sections have contained numerous references to performance in the IBM PS/2 family of systems. Several tables summarizing performance "specifications" for systems were also included. Actual performance results depend on a number of very complex relationships that are heavily dependent on the environment (standalone workstation vs. LAN File server, for example), system configurations, and applications.

Figures 5.14 and 5.15 summarize the mean relative performance of IBM PS/2 Micro Channel systems used as standalone workstations in a DOS-based and OS/2-based environment. The figures are the unweighted averages of a large number of applications that produced a broad range of results for each of the systems tested. For example, the factors that influence spreadsheet performance

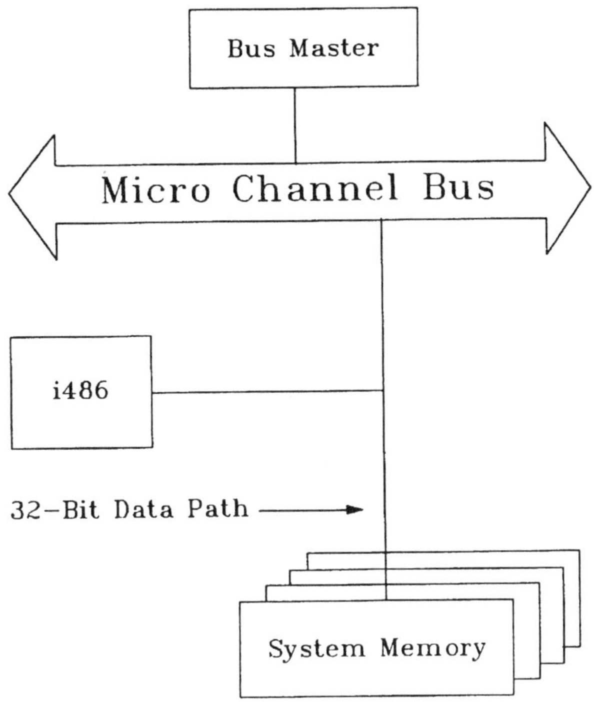

Figure 5.13 The PS/2 Model 70 486 processor/memory architecture.

are greatly different from those that affect graphics performance. Addition of various options, different device drivers, and alternative configurations could radically alter these results.

The *IBM Personal System/2 Performance Guide* (G326-0041) is a full report on PS/2 performance. This excellent report contains relative performance indices for a number of environments and popular applications.

IBM PS/2 Micro Channel Features

PS/2 systems implement several of the optional features of Micro Channel architecture. Most of the 32-bit PS/2 Micro Channel systems support 40 MB/sec streaming-data transfers between expansion boards that also support these features. However, none of the PS/2 systems manufactured to date support streaming-data transfers to or from the system microprocessor or system board memory. IBM's wording when the enhancements to the architecture were announced in September 26, 1989 implied that systems that were in current manufacture supported the advanced features between expansion boards, although it was not clear which models or serial numbers were included.

To put this "limitation" in perspective, there are no devices available that require these higher data rates in today's PS/2 environment. Because of the characteristics of Micro Channel architecture, the higher data rate devices can remain compatible when they become available, however.

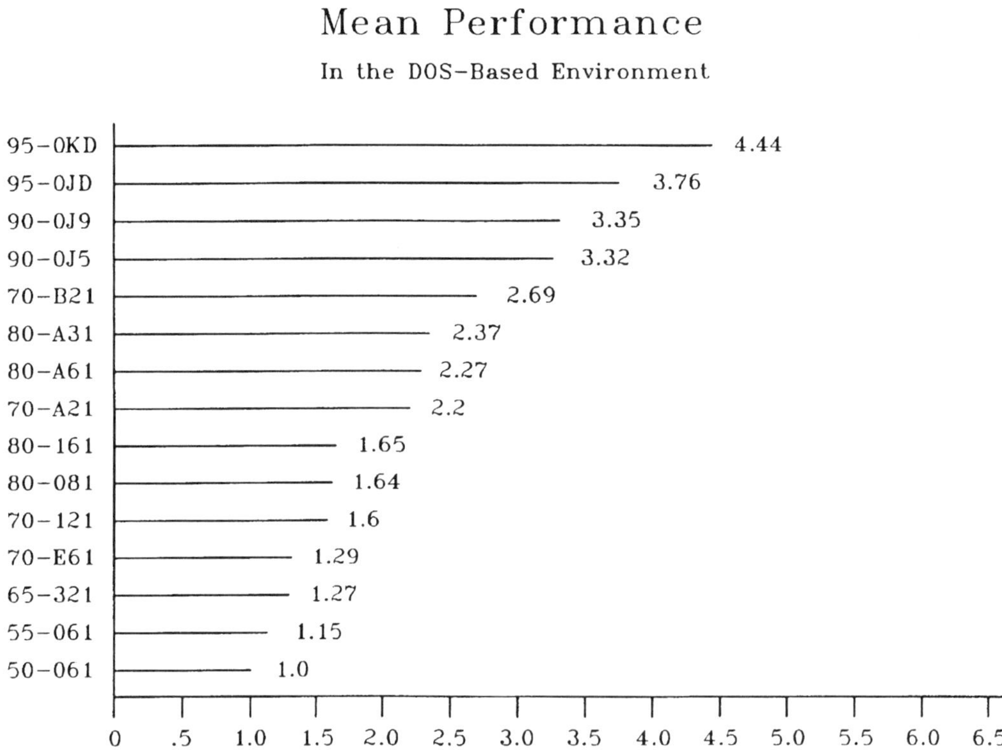

Figure 5.14 Mean Performance of PS/2 Micro Channel systems in the DOS environment.

In the case of the Model 90 and Model 95, all the models support data and address parity, and up to 80 MB/sec streaming-data transfers for peer-to-peer transfers between supporting devices. For transfers to and from the processor complex, the existing processor complexes do not support these optional features. However, future processor complexes may be capable of support between their components and other supporting devices.

Current 386 and 486 PS/2 systems can address a maximum of 16 MB of system memory with operating system support. This is indirectly a consequence of the 16-bit DMA controller with its 24 address lines used in these systems. Even though bus masters in these systems can address up to 4 GB of system memory, current versions of OS/2 do not allow for mixed addressability limits nor support of 4 GB of system memory. IBM has not announced its intentions regarding mixed addressability support in its forthcoming 32-bit version of OS/2, although it is technically feasible.

PS/2 Micro Channel systems are designed to support asymmetric, but not symmetric multiprocessing. Microprocessors in Micro Channel expansion slots cannot access (control) the system I/O devices (such as the serial and parallel devices and the keyboard). This has no basis in Micro Channel architecture, but is, in fact, the way it has been implemented in most PS/2 systems. However, asymmetric multiprocessing is probably more appropriate for the application environment of most personal computers, anyway.

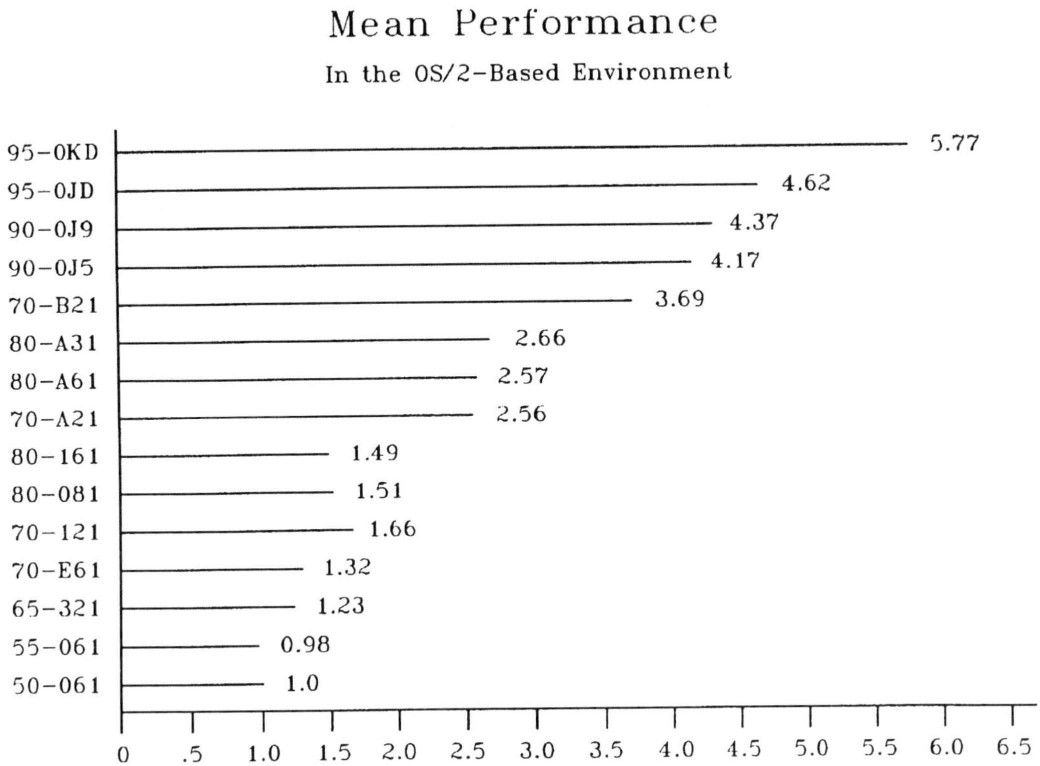

Figure 5.15 Mean Performance of PS/2 Micro Channel systems in the OS/2 environment.

IBM RISC System/6000 Family

In early 1990, IBM introduced the RISC System/6000 computers, a powerful new family of RISC-based UNIX workstations and servers. These systems feature a revolutionary new processor architecture that IBM refers to as POWER, an acronym that stands for Performance Optimization With Enhanced RISC.

These systems represent state-of-the-art implementations of Micro Channel architecture. Many of the optional advanced features are included in these systems and a large number of high-function expansion boards are also provided.

The systems include desktop, floor-standing, and rack-mounted models, providing a broad range of configurations suitable for workstations **(POWERstations)** and servers **(POWERservers)** in technical and business environments. The servers are designed for both multi-user host applications as well as network servers. These UNIX platforms are supported by IBM's AIX. The systems also emulate an Intel 8086 and can run DOS applications faster than the AT could.

RISC System/6000 Overview

There are six models of the workstations and servers and one LAN station model. The systems are illustrated in Figure 5.16. Table 5.9 is a summary of the characteristics of the family members.

The system units include the following features:

- Keyboard port.
- Mouse port.
- Tablet port.
- Parallel port.
- Two serial ports.
- High-speed serial port. (An optical link included in all systems except the 320, designed to connect other RISC System/6000s. It is projected to run at approximately 220 Mb/sec.)
- 1.44-MB diskette drive.
- An SCSI adapter (except the POWERstation 320).
- A fixed disk drive.

The POWERservers are supplied without a graphics adapter, which is not a requirement for server applications. However, all of the systems support a wide range of graphics adapters (except the POWERserver 930) and communications options.

The systems also support a wide range of communications options.

Figure 5.16 The RISC System/6000 family. These powerful Micro Channel systems represent state-of-the-art implementation of RISC and Micro Channel architecture. (Courtesy of International Business Machines Corporation)

TABLE 5.9 CHARACTERISTICS OF THE RISC SYSTEM/600 FAMILY

Model	320	520	530	540	550	730	930
Configuration	Desktop	Deskside	Deskside	Deskside	Deskside	Deskside	Rack
Clock (MHz)	20	20	25	30	41	25	25
Memory							
Standard (Mbytes)	8	88	16	64	64	16	16
Maximum (Mbytes)	128	512	512	256	512	512	512
Memory Bus Width (Bits)	64	64	128	128	128	128	128
Internal hard disk							
Standard (Mbytes)	120	355	355	640	800	355	670
Maximum (Mbytes)	640	2,571	2,571	2,571	2,571	2,571	11,998
Micro Channel Slots	4	8	8	8	8	8	8
Parallel port	1	1	1	1	1	1	0
Serial ports	2	2	2	2	2	2	2

POWERstation 320

This is an entry-level desktop unit that can be operated in either a vertical or horizontal position. It is roughly the size of the PS/2 Model 90 XP486 (Figure 5.17). It comes equipped with a 20-MHz CPU and 8 MB of 80-ns memory. The CPU plugs into a slot on the system board. Also on the system board are four 32-bit Micro Channel slots and two memory card slots. A maximum of 128 MB of memory using 4-MB memory modules can be supported. The memory controller in this system and others is designed to use denser memory modules as they become available. Figure 5.18 is an illustration of the system board of the POWERstation 320. The system accommodates one or two fixed disk drives, and comes standard with the same 120-MB ESDI fixed disk drive used in PS/2 models. The system also supports the 320 MB SCSI drive used in PS/2 models using the optional SCSI adapter. Two of these drives are used to provide a maximum internal storage capacity of 640 MB. A 5.25-inch diskette drive can also be added.

POWERstation 520 and 530.

The POWERstation 520 is an entry floor-standing system with the same 20-MHz CPU complex as the Model 320 (Figure 5.19). The POWERstation 520 comes standard with 8 MB of memory on the system board. The POWERstation 530 has a different CPU complex chip set that runs at 25 MHz and includes additional data cache and memory bandwidth. It comes standard with 16 MB of memory. The POWERstation 520 is upgradeable to the POWERstation 530.

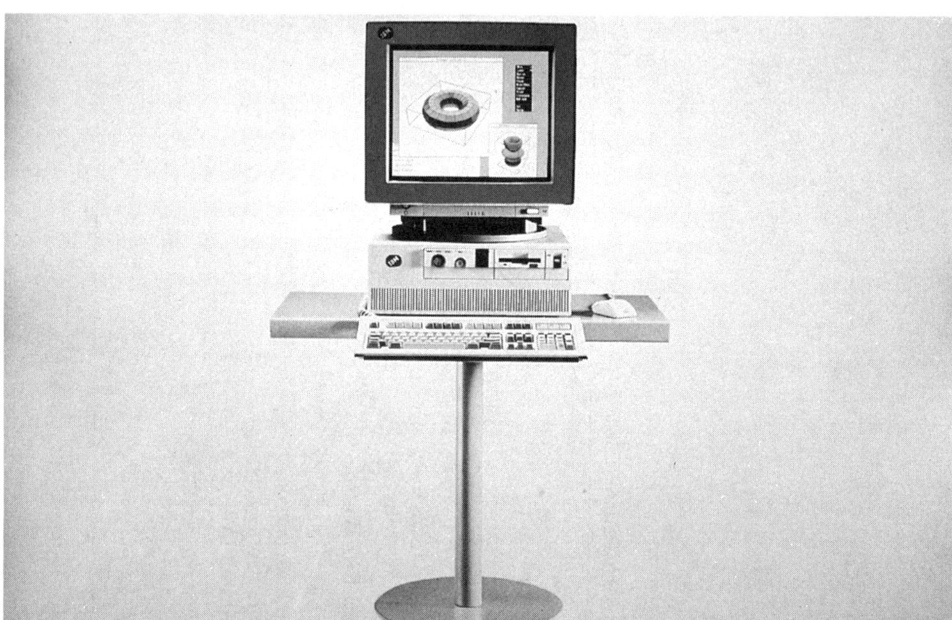

Figure 5.17 The RISC System/6000 station 320 computer. (Courtesy of International Business Machines Corporation)

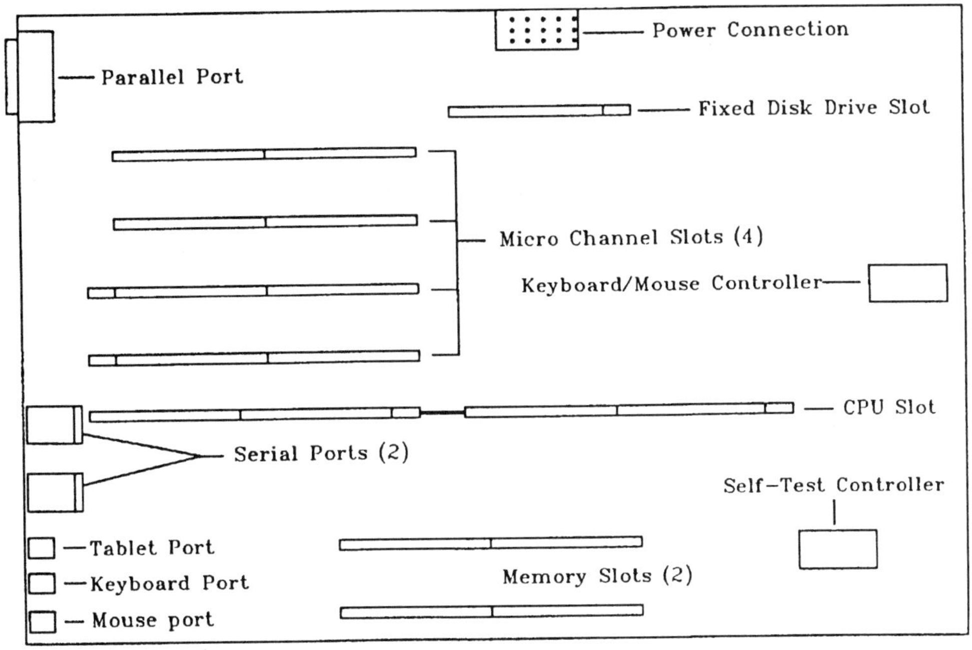

Figure 5.18 The POWERstation 320 system board.

These larger systems provide greater expansion capabilities than their desktop brother, however. In terms of memory expansion, up to 128 MB of system memory using 4-MB memory modules can be accommodated. There are eight Micro Channel slots, one of which is occupied by the 32-bit SCSI bus master adapter.

The system includes a 5.25-inch SCSI 355-MB fixed disk drive and has a maximum internal storage capacity of 2.5 GB.

POWERserver 540 and 550

The POWERserver 540 and 550 are floor-standing systems that feature a 30-MHz CPU complex and a 41-MHz CPU complex, respectively. The 540 system is supplied with 64-MB standard memory that can be expanded to 256 MB, using 4-MB memory modules. The 550 system comes standard with 64 MB of memory that can be expanded to 512 MB, using 4-MB memory modules. The systems use the same external enclosure as the POWERstations 520 and 530. There are also eight Micro Channel slots, one of which is occupied by the SCSI adapter. In terms of fixed disk storage, two 3.5-inch SCSI 320 MB fixed disk drives are the standard configuration, with a maximum internal storage capacity of 2.5 GB.

POWERstation 730

This powerful floor-standing system is designed as a high-performance graphics workstation for such applications as solid modeling and graphics animation (Figure 5.20). Its enclosure is the same height as the other floor-standing systems, but it is

Figure 5.19 The IBM RISC System/6000 POWERstation 520 computer. (Courtesy of International Business Machines Corporation

wider and has a 950-watt power supply. It includes what IBM calls the Supergraphics Subsystem, with outstanding resolution, color, and performance capabilities.

It is supplied with the 25-MHz CPU and 16 MB of memory expandable to 512 MB, using 4-MB memory modules. The system includes a 5.25-inch 355-MB SCSI fixed disk drive and has a total storage capacity of 2.5 GB. There are six available Micro Channel expansion slots.

POWERserver 930

This rack-mounted system looks like a baby mainframe and is considerably larger than the other floor-standing systems in the family (Figure 5.21). It features a 25-MHz CPU implementation with 16 MB of standard memory and can accommodate a maximum of 512 MB, using 4-MB memory modules. There are seven available Micro Channel slots. One storage drawer is standard, and the system can include up to three disk drive drawers. Each drawer can have up to four full-high storage devices or eight half-high devices. The system includes a 670 MB SCSI drive and can provide almost 12 GB of internal storage. It also has a battery backup capability that allows the system to continue operating during a power failure.

Xstation 120

This is not one of the POWER systems, but is a high-function LAN station (Token-ring or Ethernet) designed to attach to one of the POWERservers in order

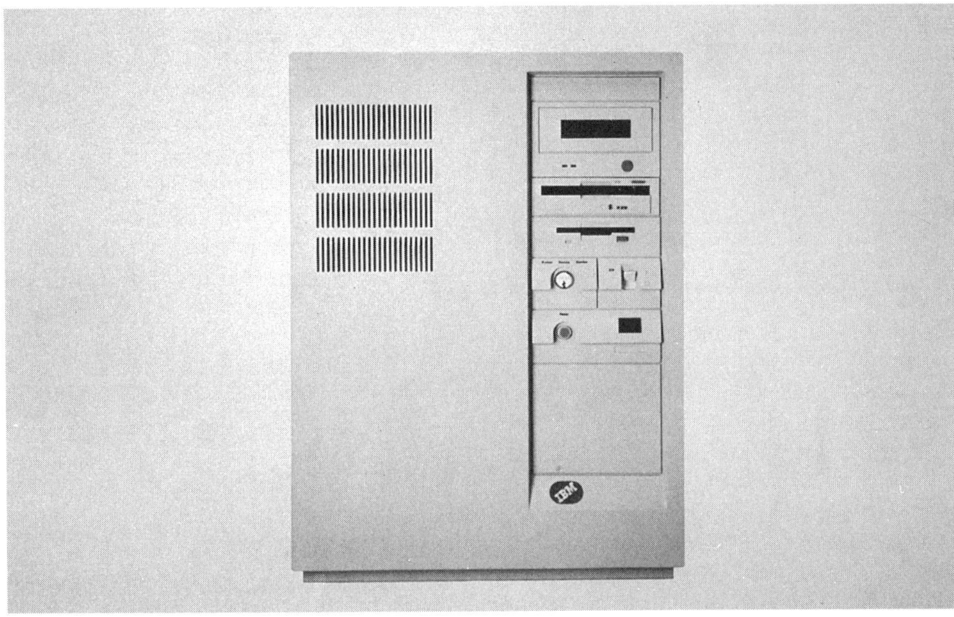

Figure 5.20 The IBM RISC System/6000 POWERstation 730. (Courtesy of International Business Machines Corporation)

to provide a low-cost multi-user solution. The Xstation 120 provides users with a windows-oriented user interface that supports the X-Windows System™ protocol (Figure 5.22). The system requires a host machine to run it applications, but is a good example of cooperative processing by using the power of the network server and the graphics capabilities of the LAN station.

The Xstation 120 includes an I/O subsystem controlled by an 80186 microprocessor and a video subsystem controlled by a graphics processor that executes the display server code. This design frees up the video subsystem from managing the communication tasks to and from the server and other I/O devices. The Xstation 120 supports a wide range of monitors including low-cost monochrome displays to high-resolution, full-color monitors.

RISC System/6000 Architecture

Figure 5.23 is a block diagram of the RISC System/6000 architecture. It consists of three basic elements: the processor/memory subsystem, the system I/O bus, and the I/O subsystem. The Micro Channel bus is part of the I/O subsystem. The two high-speed serial links are also part of the I/O subsystem. System memory is not on the Micro Channel bus, but is part of the processor/memory subsystem. Access to the system bus by the I/O subsystem is controlled by the **I/O channel controller** (IOCC). This two bus system (Micro Channel bus and system I/O bus) provides significant performance benefits.Let's examine these elements a little closer.

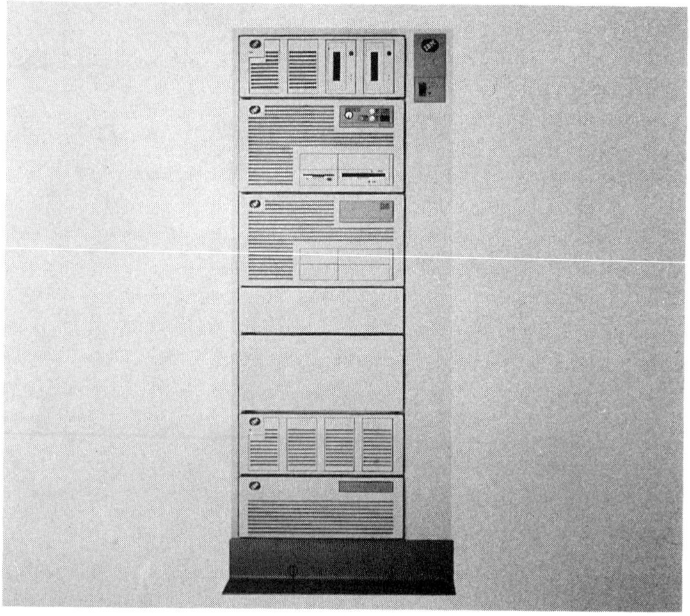

Figure 5.21 The IBM RISC System/6000 POWERstation 930. (Courtesy of International Business Machines Corporation)

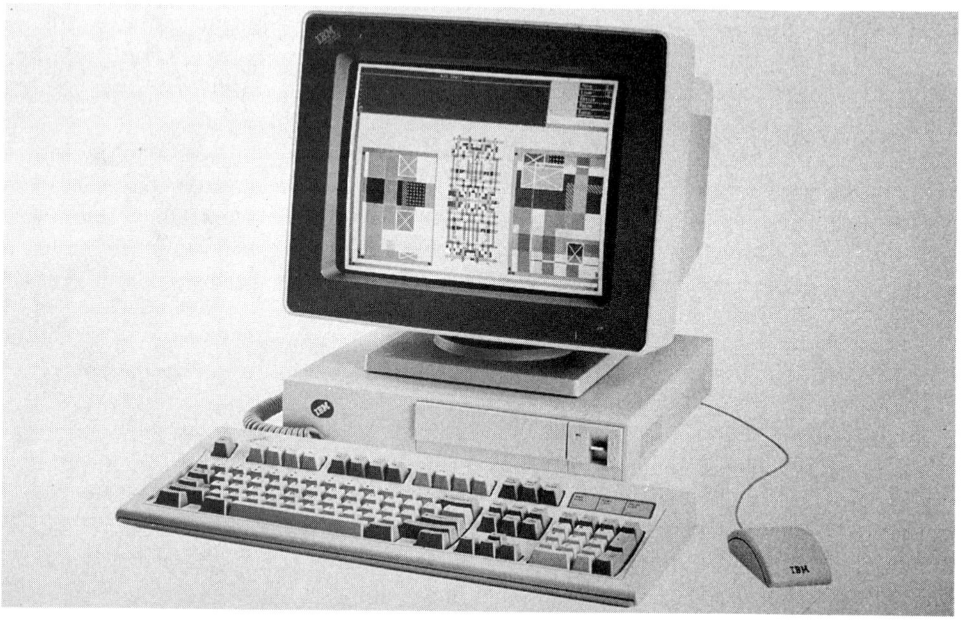

Figure 5.22 The IBM RISC System/6000 Xstation 120. (Courtesy of International Business Machines Corporation)

Micro Channel Implementation. The Micro Channel implementation includes the base 32-bit architecture and support for up to 40 MB/sec data rates between the Micro Channel and the I/O channel controller, using the streaming-data procedure. The systems can also support up to 80 MB/sec data rates between expansion boards that are designed to support the higher rates, although none are available at this time. Also included is support for data and address parity, and synchronous channel check, a procedure that provides an exception signal during the same bus cycle in which the exception occurs. The later capability simplifies error recovery. As was previously discussed in Chapter 3, the RISC System/6000 Micro Channel expansion boards may be a different size and require greater power than the Micro Channel cards designed for the PS/2 in order to meet the requirements of some of the higher-function I/O devices.[3] The PS/2 Micro Channel boards can, of course, be used in the RISC System/6000 systems if supported by the required software, diagnostics, and setup instructions.

The I/O channel controller generates the Micro Channel interface. It supports all Micro Channel data transfer mechanisms and controls all transfers between the I/O devices and the CPU complex. It also includes the DMA controller, the interrupt controller, the central arbitration logic, and memory refresh control. Up

[3]The larger boards are called Type 5 cards. The smaller boards are called Type 3 cards.

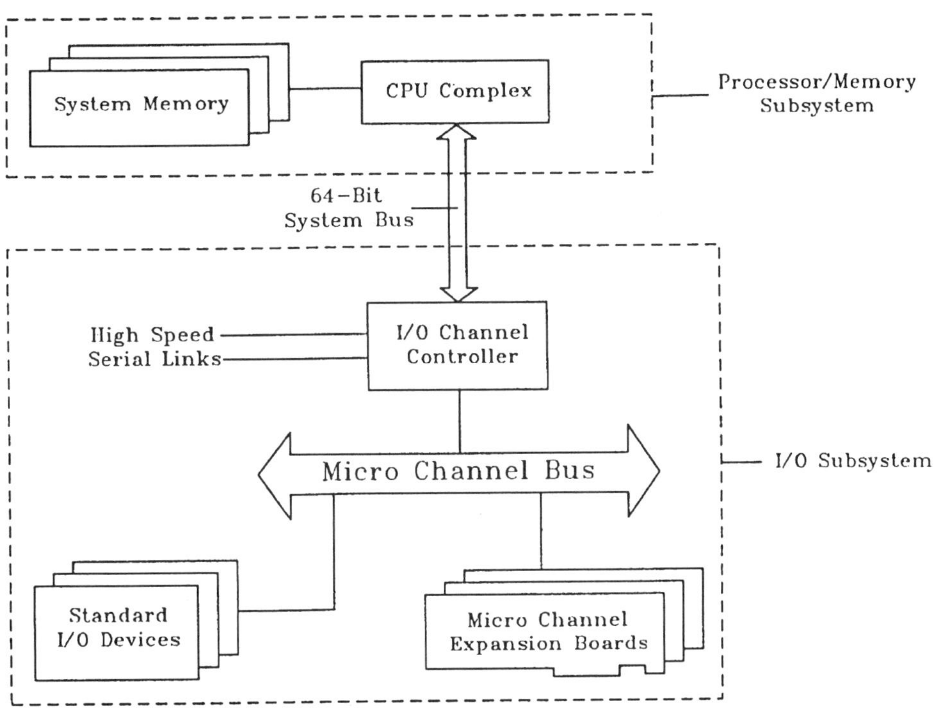

Figure 5.23 The RISC System/6000 basic architecture.

to 15 DMA channels and 16 levels of interrupts are supported by the IOCC. When a bus master has control of the Micro Channel bus, the IOCC acts as a 32-bit memory slave for transfers to the system bus. This incredibly complex controller is truly at the heart of the RISC System/6000 architecture.

Processor/Memory Architecture We can't leave a discussion of the RISC System/6000 family without a quick look at the memory and CPU architecture. The memory cards implement a four-way-interleaved design. Depending on the model, the memory bus from the memory cards to the processor is 64 or 128 bits wide. The design is similar to that of the PS/2 Model 90 XP 486 and Model 95 XP 486 memory architecture, except much more sophisticated.

The RISC CPU architecture is the really big news in these systems. The second generation RISC processors are a far cry from IBM's RISC implementation in the IBM RT. The goal of the designers was to achieve an execution rate of less than one cycle per instruction by providing a design with a high degree of parallel processing. The result was that up to four instructions can be executed in a single cycle.

Figure 5.24 is a block diagram of the RISC CPU architecture. There are three separate processor chips: the ICU (the instruction cache unit), the FXU (the fixed point unit), and the FPU (the floating point unit). (Fixed point refers to integers and floating point refers to numbers expressed with exponents and fractions.) The role of the ICU is to supply instructions to the FXU and the FPU and to manage branching. It is designed to do several of these activities simultaneously. These hungry chips are fed by a high-speed memory cache subsystem.

The net result of the RISC System/6000 systems is incredible performance that has established IBM as the technical leader in the workstation market.

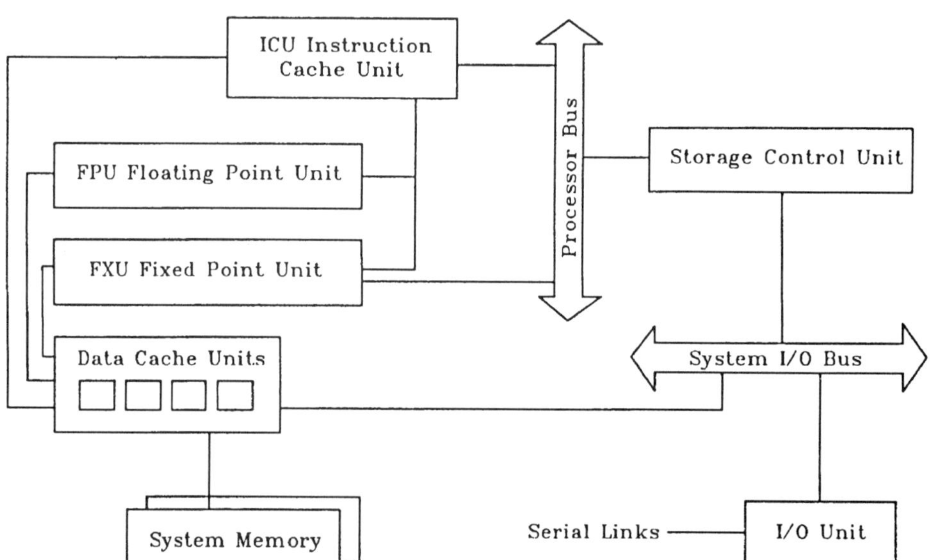

Figure 5.24 The RISC System/6000 CPU architecture.

RISC System/6000 Expansion Boards

A number of Micro Channel expansion boards were announced with these systems. These are described in Appendix E of this book and include several bus masters, such as a multiprotocol communications controller, a high-performance token-ring network adapter, a high-performance Ethernet network adapter, a System/370 host interface adapter, a number of graphics adapters, and an SCSI bus master adapter. The System/370 interface adapter is used to provide a high-speed connection to a System/370 channel. The SCSI adapter is designed specifically for the RISC System/6000 family and is not the same as either of the SCSI bus master adapters used in the PS/2 Micro Channel systems.

The RISC System/6000 computers support a wide range of graphics adapters. There are five different graphics offerings available, providing various levels of performance and functionality. These range from grayscale adapters all the way to the integrated graphics subsystem of the Model 730. All of IBM's graphics adapters for these systems are bus masters.

RISC System/6000 System Packages

IBM has chosen to provide a number of system packages based on the RISC System/6000 family that are designed to meet a broad range of customer requirements. There are workstation packages, LAN server packages, and multi-user packages. They are made up of a variety of models, graphics features, displays, memory, storage, backup/restore devices, connectivity options, and AIX system software. The system packages are designed for ease of installation and configuration. One of the customer options for software distribution is a preloaded fixed disk, for example.

Enterprise System/9371[4]

In early 1990, IBM introduced a family of systems that represents a union of System/370 processor architecture and Micro Channel architecture. These entry level additions to the System/370 mainframe line feature a native 370 processor, the Micro Channel bus, and one or more PS/2 Model 80 system boards with a 386 microprocessor used for I/O processing or for running applications. In these implementations, selected Micro Channel adapters are supported with microcode, which allows the Micro Channel attached devices to operate like S/370 channel-attached devices.

The ES/9371 family heralds the future convergence of mainframe and PC architectures. The ability to utilize common hardware and software and to transfer data and instructions between processors by using Micro Channel architecture as a single hardware interface between the two system families provides a degree of commonality and compatibility for true interoperability.

---

[4]The Enterprise System/9371 family has recently been renamed the Micro Channel 370™ family. For consistency with the expansion boards described in Appendix E, the Enterprise System/9371 designation is retained in this book. The new model designations are the Micro Channel 370 Models 110, 112, and 114, instead of the ES/9371 Models 10, 12, and 14.

ES/9371 Model 10 and Model 12

The ES/9371 Model 10 has the following standard features:

- System/370 processor;
- Processor memory (4, 8, 12, or 16 MB);
- Bus control unit;
- An I/O processor (20-MHz 386) with 2 MB of memory;
- A 1.44-MB 3.5-inch diskette drive;
- Two 295-MB fixed disk drives (expandable to six, yielding a total capacity of 1.77 GB);
- A 32-bit SCSI bus master adapter;
- Console keyboard and display ports;
- A parallel and serial port;
- A multiprotocol communications adapter to support remote support facilities; and
- Three available Micro Channel expansion slots.

The ES/9371 Model 12 includes all of the features of the Model 10 but adds a second PS/2 Model 80 system board and associated bus control unit that provides seven additional Micro Channel expansion slots, and an additional serial and parallel port. The i386 microprocessor serves as an I/O processor and cannot be used to run applications in these models.

The 370 processor and memory complex is on a separate bus and occupies two Micro Channel slots, using only the power and ground pins. The processor/memory complex is connected to the Micro Channel bus, using a bus control unit in a third Micro Channel slot, which supplies the interfaces to the two buses, required buffers, and miscellaneous control logic.[5] In the case of the Model 12 and Model 14, an additional bus control unit is also attached to the second Model 80 system board.

The SCSI and multiprotocol adapters occupy the fourth and fifth slots in these systems. This leaves three available slots in the Model 10 and ten in the Model 12.

ES/9371 Model 14 BiProcessor

This system functions almost like two separate systems. Its two personalities include a System/370 and a PS/2 Model 80. Two Model 80 system boards are included with the first, serving the same function as in the Model 10. The second Model 80 system board provides the capability of running native i386 applications under DOS and OS/2, for example. The optional Data Exchange Adapter provides a high-speed Micro Channel connection between the Intel processor and the 370 processor that allows for transfer of data between the "two" systems.

The ES/9371 Model 14 includes all the features of the Model 12 and what is functionally a PS/2 Model 80 386. The PS/2 features include:

- An i386 20-MHz microprocessor;
- 2 MB of memory, expandable to 16 MB;
- A 1.44-MB 3.5-inch diskette drive;

[5]The bus control unit serves as a memory slave in Micro Channel parlance.

- Keyboard and VGA display port;
- A parallel and serial port;
- A mouse port; and
- Eight slots.

In addition, a virtual console feature allows a single keyboard/display to be switched between the two processors.

One example of how the Model 14 with the Data Exchange Adapter is used is as a network file server (running Netware 386, for example) as well as 370 multi-user applications and host communications.

ES/9371 Micro Channel Expansion

All three models use the Micro Channel bus. However, on the Models 10 and 12, and the first system board of the Model 14, the Micro Channel slots act like S/370 channel-attached devices and are only recognized by S/370 software. Supported Micro Channel adapters include those providing SCSI, token ring, Ethernet, Communications (via the ARTIC card), X.25, 5080 graphics, 3270 terminal/printer, and high-speed printer attachments. In the Model 14 PS/2 system board, Micro Channel boards are supported that can be used in the PS/2 Model 80.

OTHER MICRO CHANNEL SYSTEMS

As discussed in Chapter 2, there are a number of large and small companies that offer Micro Channel systems. Some of these systems are developed and manufactured from the ground up by these companies, while others are little more than a company's logo added to another company's system. (This "rebadging," as the industry calls it, is not unique to Micro Channel systems, however!) At last count, there were 27 vendors manufacturing 81 models of Micro Channel systems.

When these Micro Channel systems first began to appear, there were a number of incompatibilities. Some of these related to other elements of the system (BIOS implementations, for example) rather than Micro Channel board compatibility. Some chose not to implement POS (which is *not* an optional feature of the architecture). However, most systems built today do not have the compatibility problems of some of the earlier models.

In the following section, representative systems developed and manufactured by some of the larger companies are described. There are numerous excellent systems available from other suppliers that could not be included, however. What follows is a brief description of systems offered by ALR, NCR, and Olivetti. Because of the number of new systems constantly being introduced, you should consult the specific companies to obtain the most current information on their product offerings.

Advanced Logic Research®, Inc.

ALR offers a number of Micro Channel systems with a variety of processor and storage choices. Perhaps the most outstanding feature of ALR systems is their processor/memory complexes. In both the 386 and 486 systems, ALR has incorporated a very fancy architecture, using their own custom cache controllers. Both desktop and floor-standing systems are available.

The MicroFlex 7000 is a 25-MHz 386 floor-standing system offering excellent performance and expandability. Its MicroFlex architecture includes 64 KB of 25-ns SRAM that delivers a 64-bit bus between the cache and main memory.

The ALR MicroFlex 3300 is a 33-MHz 386 system available in a desktop or floor-standing configuration (Figure 5.25). Desktop models include a choice of 80 or 120 MB ESDI fixed disk drives. Floor-standing models are available with 150-MB, 340-MB, and 650-MB ESDI fixed disk drives. Its FlexCache™ architecture has 128 KB of high-speed SRAM with a dual 64-bit design.

ALR's 486 systems feature the PowerCache™ 4 cache controller, which utilizes the 128-bit burst capability of the 486 microprocessor. The PowerCache 4 systems (Figure 5.26) include a dual external cache design made up of two blocks of 64 KB of 25-ns SRAM in order to satisfy the appetite of the 486. Figure 5.27 is a diagram of the PowerCache 4 processor memory/subsystem.

The ALR Modular Processing System, with processor options ranging from 33-MHz 386 to 33-MHz 486 choices, offers high-performance upgrades for some of ALR's models. The CPU complex of these systems is mounted on a special expansion board, not the system board.

Figure 5.25 The ALR MicroFLex 3300 computer (Courtesy of Advanced Logic Reasearch, Inc.)

Figure 5.26 The ALR Power Cache 33/4 computers. (Courtesy of Advance Logic Research, Inc.)

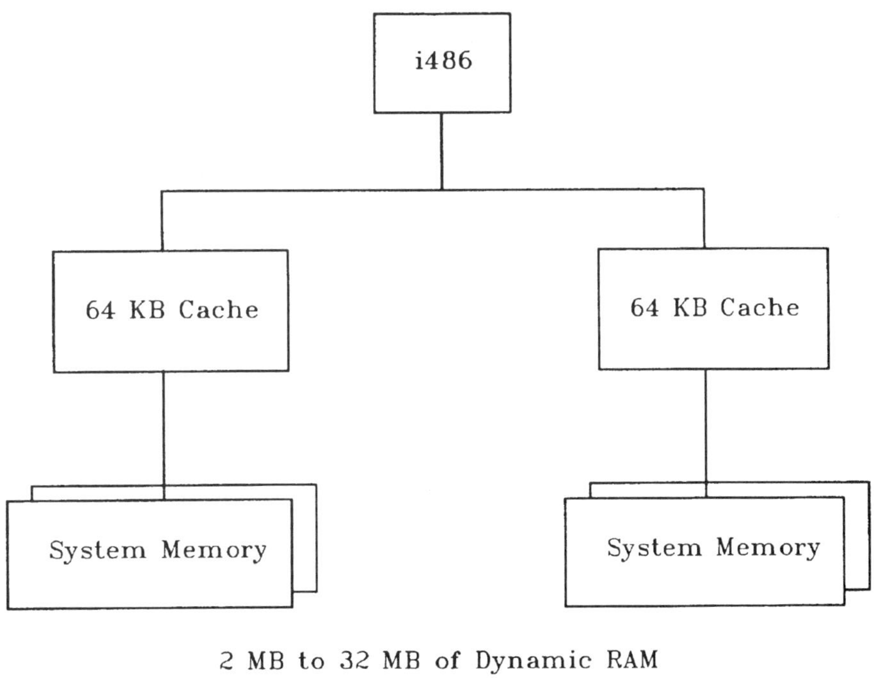

Figure 5.27 The ALR PowerCache 4 processor/memory subsystem.

NCR Corporation

NCR offers a range of Micro Channel systems designed to meet the requirements of a broad range of users. From the looks of their product line, it appears that NCR is firmly committed to Micro Channel architecture.

There are 386SX, 386, and 486 Micro Channel systems in NCR's offerings. Each of these systems include an SCSI controller, a Super VGA video display adapter (800 x 600 resolution), and a wide range of storage options. The desktop systems make extraordinary use of space using NCR's VLSI skills, and provide as many as five Micro Channel expansion slots. The NCR Micro Channel lineup looks like this:

- PC386sx/MC™. This is a 16-MHz 386SX entry desktop model that includes 1 MB or 4 MB of memory expandable to 16 MB, using a memory expansion board. It includes three internal 3.5-inch disk drive positions.
- PC386sx/MC20™. This 386SX desktop unit is one of the first 20-MHz systems in the industry. It is a solid performer featuring a 16-KB memory cache and 2 MB of 80-ns memory standard and up to 16 MB on the processor board. Also offered for the PC386sx/MC20 is the i486 Technology Upgrade, which includes a 25-MHz 486 and a unique buffer and logic arrangement designed to incur no wait states for writing data to memory.
- PC486/MC™. This 25-MHz desktop system features two identical cache controllers with a total of 128 KB of high-speed cache memory. These two caches run in parallel, providing a 64-bit data path, and represent an interleaved design. The design is another example of how the industry is designing to use the 128-KB burst capability of the i486 microprocessor. The system is supplied with 2 MB of memory and is upgradeable to 16 MB.
- PC486/MC33™. This 33-MHz version has a unique Micro Channel chip set that, in addition to providing the standard Micro Channel interface, includes a bus controller and a dual-ported memory controller, allowing simultaneous access to memory by the system master and other masters. The system comes standard with 4 or 16 MB of 80-ns memory and can accommodate up to 64 MB of memory. Also featured is a high-performance SCSI bus master that provides a data transfer rate of 10 MB/sec compared to 5 MB/sec in other implementations. Figure 5.28 and 5.29 are photographs of the PC486/MC_{33}.
- S486/MC_{33}. This powerful floor-standing system is designed to support a wide range of network solutions. It can also be used as a power workstation for CPU-intensive applications that require more expansion than the PC486/MC_{33} desktop system. It features the same processor/memory architecture as that of the PC486/MC_{33} and the SCSI II controller. In terms of expansion capabilities, the system features seven Micro Channel slots (one 16-bit slot with video extension and six 32-bit slots). There are also four additional slots for

Figure 5.28 The NCR PC486/MC33. (Courtesy of NCR Corporation)

memory expansion of up to 64 MB. Figure 5.30 shows the outstanding expansion characteristics of this system.

NCR has also announced that it plans to build "mainframe-class" computers, utilizing the Intel 80x86 architecture with scalable multiprocessor offerings and Micro Channel architecture. Figure 5.31 is an illustration of prototypes of these systems.

Olivetti

Olivetti offers a range of Micro Channel systems in the medium- to high-performance category. Both desktop and floor-standing systems are available. Let's take a look at some of the models.

- P500. This is a 16-MHz 386SX system that meets the requirements for most business users with its five free Micro Channel expansion

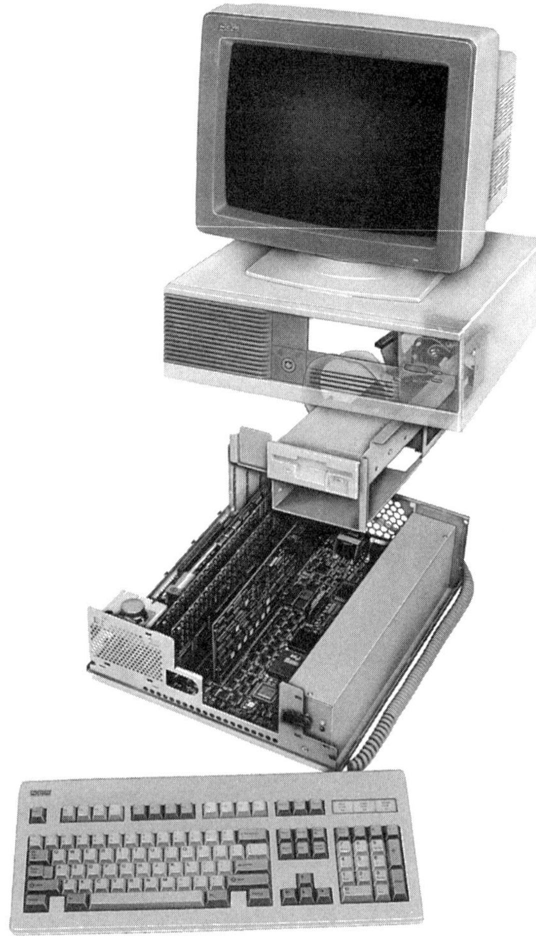

Figure 5.29 Exploded view of the NCR PC 486/MC33.(Courtesy of the NCR Corporation)

slots, its support for up to 16 MB of memory, and its OVC, Olivetti's VGA compatible controller.

- P800. This floor-standing systems provides a 25-MHz 386 power for server and workstation applications. Important features are its OVC video controller, eight expansion slots, a 64-KB memory cache, and 4 MB of standard memory expandable to 32 MB. Up to five storage devices can be accommodated inside the system. It also includes a battery backup in case of a power failure. Figure 5.32 is a photograph of the system.

Reply Corporation

Reply Corporation is a relative newcomer as a Micro Channel system vendor. Their systems have a design concept that includes a separate processor module containing either a 286 or 386SX microprocessor. This TurboProcessor™ Module, as it is

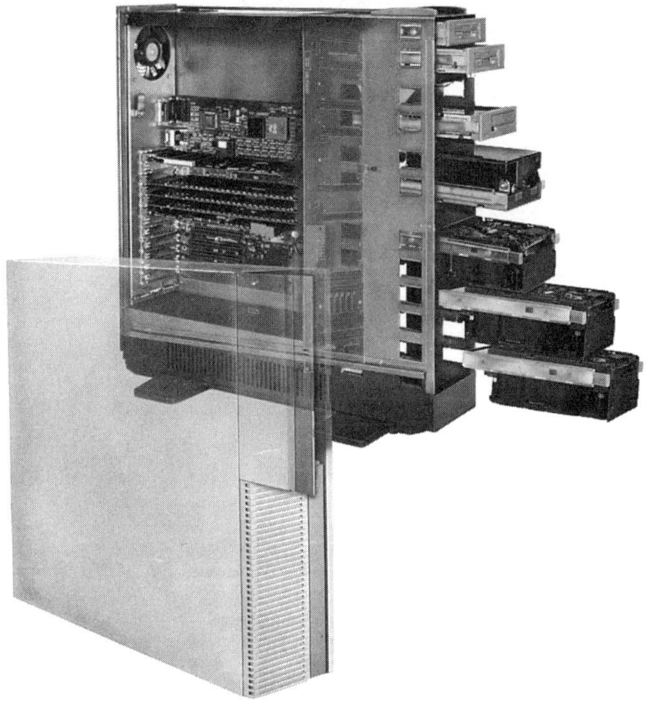

Figure 5.30 The NCR S486/MC33 features the expandability of a minicomputer. (Courtesy of NCR Corporation)

called, provides a mechanism for customers to upgrade their systems for higher performance. The six models come standard with 1 MB of RAM and can accommodate up to 8 MB on the system board. They also include five 16-bit Micro Channel expansion slots and five drive bays. Super VGA, two parallel and two serial ports, and a pointing device port are integrated with the system board. The TurboProcessor options include 16- and 20-MHz 286 and 386SX versions. The 386SX TurboProcessor option is also available with a cache. The ESDI fixed disk drive choices range from 30 to 760 MB.

This flexible design using a common system board that is highly upgradeable has many advantages. The Reply systems with their TurboProcessor options are excellent examples of the timing flexibility of Micro Channel architecture.

MICRO CHANNEL EXPANSION BOARD RELATIONSHIPS

With the number of systems based on Micro Channel architecture, you may wonder if expansion boards from one system family can be used in other system families. The answer is yes, but...

Let's begin with the hardware. The large majority of expansion boards are portable from system to system. However, the larger system boards used in the RISC System/6000 are not designed for use in the PS/2 systems and similar products due to

Figure 5.31 The NCR 3550 has incremental performance options of two to eight Intel i486 50-MHz microprocessors, offering 80 to 320 MIPS and 16 Micro Channel slots. The cabinet is 29 inches high, 17 inches wide, and 29.5 inches deep. (Courtesy of NCR Corporation)

their spatial and power requirements. The same is true of the System/370 processor/memory subsystem used in the ES/9371 Micro Channel systems.

As we learned in Chapter 2, not all systems support all features of Micro Channel architecture, such as address and data parity. However, the architecture requires that those expansion boards that implement the optional features be compatible with systems that do not.

In terms of software, however, the hardware device drivers vary from system family to system family. Device drivers are designed to utilize system strengths and cannot be optimized across system families. Some of their programming elements are written in a fairly low level language, making device drivers hardware-dependent. In addition, different device drivers are required for different operating systems. The result is that device drivers vary in both structure and language.

Since each system type requires a different reference diskette and a slightly different setup procedure because of its BIOS and diagnostics, the required software is also different for the three system families. However, IBM and other developers have usually elected to provide the supporting software for those systems where a customer requirement exists. Two good examples of expansion

Figure 5.32 The Olivetti Personal Computer P800. (Courtesy of Olivetti Office USA)

boards used in many system families are the ARTIC programmable communications coprocessors and the PS/2 X.25 network support adapter. In these cases, the hardware part number is the same across the system families, but the feature number is unique because of the software differences.

In terms of Micro Channel clones, the current ones are closely related to the IBM PS/2 systems in terms of expansion board usage. Most of these systems are designed to function identically in terms of their acceptance of hardware and software. A different reference diskette is required, however, so that those devices whose configuration files appear on the reference diskette of one system must be ported to the other systems in order to use the expansion board. Most devices, however, have their adapter description files on a separate diskette, which allows them to be used across the various systems.

A word of caution: Some developers have developed Micro Channel expansion boards without using the POS feature. If you really love to set DIP switches, you will like these products. However, you may get into some horrendous resource conflicts without adequate documentation to resolve them.

MICRO CHANNEL SOLUTIONS

Up to this point, we have focused primarily on the architecture and its system implementations. Now it's time to broaden our scope and look at some of the unique applications provided by Micro Channel architecture. The following section is devoted to the examination of some key areas that illustrate the unique benefits of Micro Channel architecture: image processing, multimedia, server applications, and investment protection. It would be possible to devote an entire book to the subject of Micro Channel solutions, but these areas were chosen because of their current and future importance. They are also applications that utilize many of the advanced features of Micro Channel architecture.

Because of the broad applicability and the number of potential users, the focus is on the use of personal systems based on Micro Channel architecture. Solutions incorporating the RISC System/6000 family and the ES/9371 systems are not included. Application-oriented solutions using these systems are provided as customized packages, and information regarding them may be obtained from IBM and appropriate remarketers.

Image Processing

Image processing is defined as the use of some form of electronic manipulation for managing information that has typically been on paper. We live in a world inundated by paper. The ability to electronically store, retrieve, manipulate, and transmit all the information currently stored on paper would be one of the greatest productivity improvements in the history of mankind! In addition, the environmental benefits would be enormous. Most of our garbage is paper, for example.

Vast sums of time and money are spent by all of us handling paper, storing it in warehouses, mailing it, and just trying to find it when we need it. Image processing provides the ability to virtually eliminate paper as a storage and communications media. Regardless of its obvious benefits, however, most information still resides on paper today. UNNECESSARILY! The hardware and software technology is here today that provides image-processing solutions that could produce these enormous productivity benefits.

Image processing demands a great deal of processing power from systems and subsystems. Performance and capacity in graphics, storage, and communications subsystems are particularly important. Most of us are quite impatient in our performance expectations of our computers, demanding subsecond response times for almost everything. Image processing is an application environment that utilizes a number of the benefits of Micro Channel architecture. But before we look at some of the specific Micro Channel solutions, you need to learn some basics about image processing.

An Image-Processing System

Figure 5.33 is a typical image-processing system. The first step in image processing necessarily begins with getting the image into a computer from its original form. Its original form may be on paper, a photograph, or even on videotape. (We

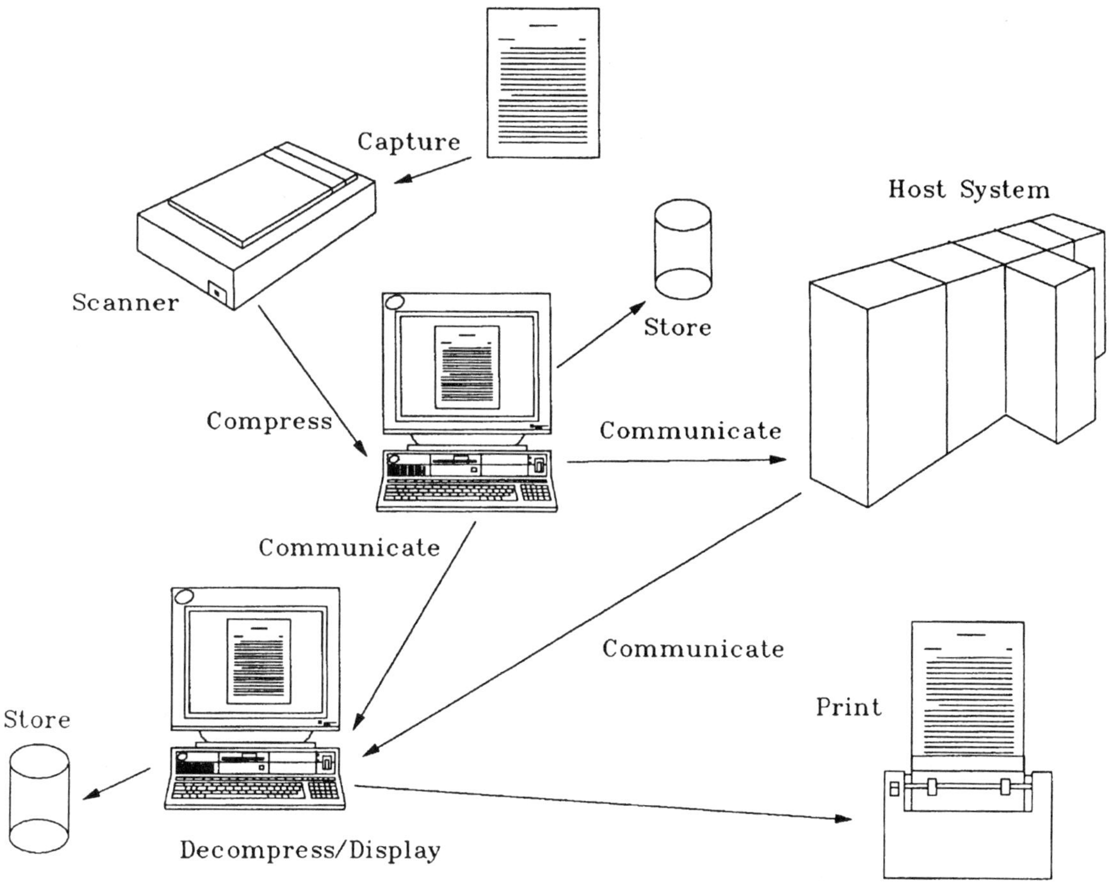

Figure 5.33 A typical image processing system.

stretched our original definition of image a bit, but you get the idea.) There are two basic methods of image capture in common usage: scanning and video digitizing. These capture tools are commonly available in the form of an office scanner or a video camera attached to a video digitizer adapter in a personal computer. A special case of an image capture device that we are all familiar with is a FAX (or facsimile) machine.

The second step in an image-processing system is compression of the image. This is required in order to reduce the amount of data so that it can be readily communicated, manipulated, and stored. The compression process does not alter the image, however. It just makes it more manageable. Image compression requires a significant amount of processing power. Just a few years ago, image compression and decompression required systems in the $250,000 range. Today it can be achieved at the workstation in systems costing less than $10,000 by using a special image-processing adapter.

The next step in image processing may be storage or communication to another system. A compressed image of a page of printed text requires about 25 KB of storage compared with about 3 KB for a coded version of the same information. That's quite a bit, but not unmanageable using today's huge disk drives and optical storage devices. Since a great deal of potential image applications involve a common form, storing the form numerous times is not necessary. Only the data on the form is different. The ability to recreate the form and add text data to its image further reduces image size and storage requirements.

Being able to store and retrieve images rapidly is also possible at the workstation. A combination of magnetic and optical storage technology usually meets this requirement. Magnetic storage is used for frequently accessed images because of its superior performance characteristics and optical storage for longer term storage. Either device is faster than going to the warehouse and trying to find a stored document, however!

The next step in our image-processing system probably involves transferring the image from where it was originally captured or stored to another system. Properly configured, today's workstation network communication capabilities are adequate for most image applications. In addition, fiber optic LANS and ISDN are providing the foundation for even faster communications. The host system may be a mainframe computer, a midrange system, or a network server, depending on the particular application.

When the image arrives at its next stop, it may be decompressed for display, stored, or printed, depending on the requirement. The benefits of the image-processing system described above are obvious and can be useful in almost any environment.

The IBM ImagePlus System

IBM's ImagePlus® system is an excellent example of a cost-effective image solution. Let's look at some of the requirements used to develop the ImagePlus system:

1. Image capture—A 10-page-per-minute image capture rate;
2. Image display—A full-page image displayed within one second after receipt from the host system;
3. Image printing—A six-page-per-minute image printing capability;
4. Image communication—At least a 100 KB/sec host communication;
5. Text and image overlay capability; and
6. Cost—The price of an entry business DOS workstation.

Figure 5.34 shows the hardware arrangement chosen for this powerful system. Surprisingly, the ImagePlus system uses the humble IBM PS/2 Model 50Z for its low-cost workstation, paired with a System/36™, an AS/400, or a System/370 system if required.

The Model 50Z computer was equipped with the IBM Image Adapter/A. This adapter with its onboard RISC processor handles compression and decompression and also serves as the graphics adapter for the high-resolution display (the IBM 8506 or 8508) used in the system. Since the system is also able to receive the image

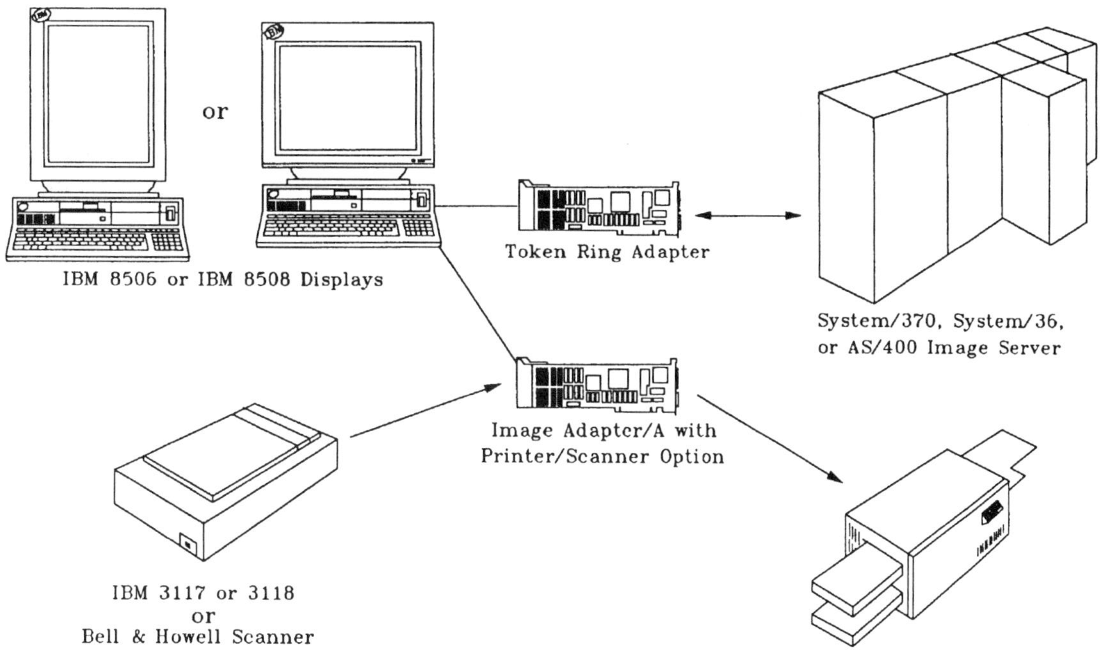

Figure 5.34 The hardware used in the IBM ImagePlus system.

data using its 10 MHz 80286 microprocessor at the same time the Image Adapter/A is doing its business, performance is excellent.

The Image Adapter/A is a bus master capable of driving resolutions up to 1600 x 1200, with up to 16 shades of gray. It also has a printer/scanner attachment (a "daughter" card, as it is called), which enables it to attach printers and scanners directly to it. The net result is that images can be captured, compressed, decompressed, displayed, or printed using the Image Adapter/A at the same time document pages are being received.

The outstanding software used in our image-processing system is the ImagePlus Workstation Program. Its function is to manage the workstation and host communication, execute all the image-processing functions including capture, display, and printing, and provide the end-user interface. Bear in mind that this is a DOS workstation (with all its 640-KB memory constraint) that is generally working with an uncompressed image of almost 500 KB, a typical page. In March 1990, IBM announced that an OS/2 version of the ImagePlus Workstation Program is planned for the future that will enable additional workstation productivity.

The ImagePlus system is a very powerful example of how Micro Channel architecture delivers high-performance solutions even in the DOS environment.

Although not officially part of the ImagePlus system, IBM's SCSI adapter plays a very important role in current and future image applications. High-capacity optical storage devices such as CD ROM and read/write optical drives use the SCSI interface in IBM's Micro Channel systems.

The Image Adapter/A is also offered separately as an option for IBM PS/2 Micro Channel systems for high-performance, high-resolution graphics[6] used in technical workstation applications and desktop publishing. Popular programs such as AutoCad and Pagemaker™ are supported. The Image Adapter/A delivers outstanding performance in a graphics environment and can also be used to accelerate standard graphics (VGA and XGA). It outperforms many graphics adapters sold for technical workstations and is available at a far lower cost.

A good source of additional information about IBM's image products is a special issue of the **IBM Systems Journal, Vol. 29, No. 3, 1990,** which is devoted to image processing. There are also several examples of other products that provide image solutions in the Appendix of this book and in the *Catalog of Micro Channel Adapters,* described previously.

Multimedia Solutions

Almost the entire history of computers has been dominated by alphanumeric characters. The exclusive use of letters and numbers in spreadsheets, data base, and word processing applications is rapidly giving way to the use of graphics in these traditional applications.

Desktop publishing has completely altered our idea of document preparation by adding all kinds and sizes of fonts and illustrations to our word processing. The graphical user interface of products like Microsoft's Excel™ has greatly enhanced the usability of spreadsheets.

In the late 1980s, sophisticated 2D- and 3D-graphics programs became a reality on reasonably-priced workstations due to their processing power and display capabilities. As we have seen, advanced systems based on Micro Channel architecture have contributed to this capability.

The next step in this logical evolution of text to text merged with graphics is the addition of image, animation, sound, and video (Figure 5.35). This is how the term multimedia is generally used, although it's nearly impossible to get a consistent definition. Most computers do okay on text processing and basic sound effects. Graphics represent a somewhat greater challenge depending on the requirements. But the real stretch is to high-quality audio, animation, and video. It is in these applications that Micro Channel systems demonstrate their enormous potential.

The equipment requirements have been pretty pricey for video capture and editing, mixing graphics or text with audio and video, and other mixed media manipulations. In addition, the software requirements for multimedia systems have been designed for technical professionals in the media business rather than for just regular people. The authoring tools, as they are called, required users to spend so much time and energy with the technical aspects that the creative process became secondary.

[6]**Image** is distinguished from **graphics** in that images are captured and graphics are created.

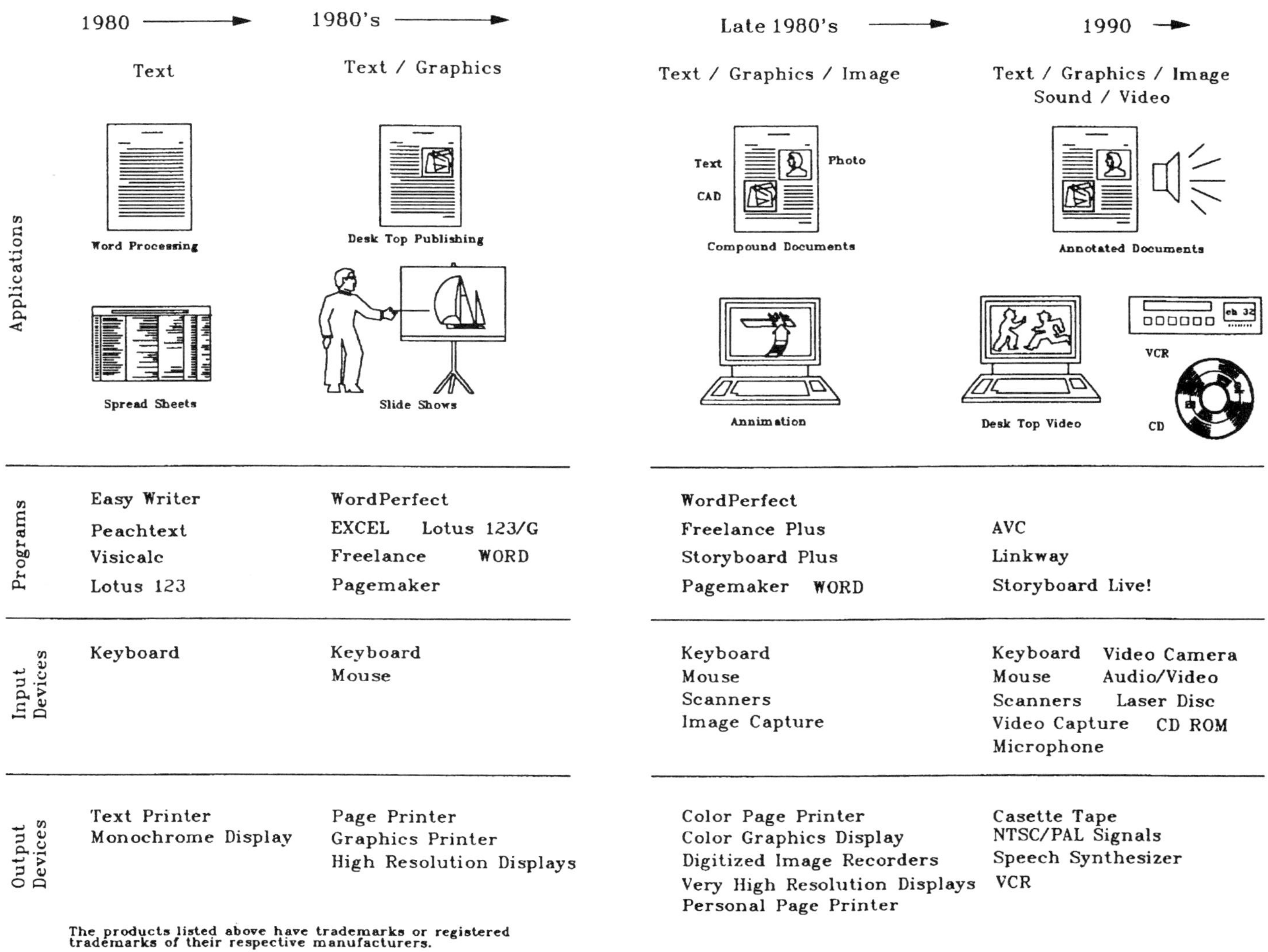

Figure 5.35 Personal computing media progression. The intersection of sound and video with text and graphics is inevitable.

"Few to Many"

The result of the high entry and skill requirements of multimedia products has been limited authorship to professionals. The multimedia industry calls systems that require a professional authoring system "few to many." In this case, some kind of "mastering" process is required that produces multimedia applications in high volumes and low cost. An example is a CD-ROM application using stamped media. The playback system is one that many people can use and afford. The bulk of multimedia applications today are of the "few to many" type.

The second kind of multimedia system is referred to as "many to few." These applications are not in common usage today because easy-to-use authoring tools have not been available and equipment costs have been too high. However, today's workstation is capable of delivering the equipment for these applications at a reasonable cost. In addition, the authoring tools are becoming much simpler to use.

Opportunities for using multimedia are numerous. In almost every environment, there is a requirement for education, training, or business presentations that could incorporate multimedia. In addition, the use of voice and video combined with traditional reports and documents could certainly enhance them. Sounds a lot more exciting than just letters and numbers, doesn't it!

What is occurring today is a migration of multimedia applications from the "few to many" toward the "many to few." Several Micro Channel hardware products are available today that make these exciting new applications a reality.

IBM has produced a number of excellent Micro Channel products, supporting software, and authoring tools for multimedia applications. There are basically three product groups: the AVC™ group, the M-Motion group™, and the ActionMedia™ group.

Audio Visual Connection

AVC is short for Audio Visual Connection®, a program product that lets you produce sound and image presentations. The AVC program and the video and audio capture adapter cards let the novice user (or the expert, for that matter) capture and edit sound and image to produce exciting visual and sound effects for a variety of applications.

The Video Capture Adapter/A is used to capture images from a variety of sources, such as a video camera, a videodisc, or a videotape. Its onboard processor digitizes the analog input signal so that it can be processed for later use. For example, the captured image can be stored, compressed, edited, or mixed with audio. The card also includes output connectors that allow you to view the live or captured image. The Video Capture Adapter/A uses the Micro Channel video extension slot.

The Audio Capture and Playback Adapter/A is used to capture sound from standard audio equipment like cassette tape players, CD players, or a microphone. The card is also used to provide compression and decompression for storage and playback, using the AVC software. The video capture card is not required for playback of the presentation.

Using the AVC tools and the two adapters results in a highly sophisticated presentation of sound and video merged with text and graphics that a novice can produce. The playback requirements are minimal, which "many" can use.

The AVC program supplies the graphics and text editing, the audio capture and editing, the video capture and editing, and a file management system. The program also provides the ability for the user to branch to other segments of the "show" rather than the serial format required by the slide shows of earlier programs. Both DOS and OS/2 versions of the Audio Visual Connection are available.

Let's Get Moving!

The M-Motion products include the IBM M-Motion Video Adapter/A and the M-Control™ Program. These products are designed to display and manipulate full-motion video instead of still images, using analog input and output. The hardware and software allow input from up to three different sources, including videodisc players, VCRs, or video cameras. Full-motion interactive color video and audio presentations are the result. The M-Motion card uses the Micro Channel video extension slot.

In terms of application support, IBM has recently announced Storyboard Live!™ Storyboard Live! is the latest evolution in the Storyboard line of multimedia products for DOS users that incorporates drawing, painting, animation, motion video, music, and voice.

An outstanding editing and post-production system for M-Motion applications is Media-Link/PM™ from RGB™ Corporation, running under OS/2 with a Presentation Manager interface. Two video picture inputs and one video picture output can be displayed simultaneously. Up to 13 source video tape recorders are supported. This powerful, easy-to-use system meets the needs of video editing professionals as well as users with limited video experience. In the past, a video-editing system such as this would have cost hundreds of thousands of dollars.

Another type of multimedia product using Micro Channel architecture is an expansion board capable of merging graphics with video (a capability called videographics) and outputting the signal to videotape or TV. The Vidtech MediaMaster™ is a Micro Channel adapter that is used to mix data from a computer with video and output the combination as an S-Video signal or RGB in either NTSC or PAL video standards. The computer-generated information is normal text and graphics data that is combined with the video from a number of sources, such as a VCR or a video camera. The resulting signal can be taped or broadcasted. Truevision® offers a similar product, the TARGA+™, with a wide range of supporting software.

Lights, Camera, Action!

The final Micro Channel multimedia solutions are the ActionMedia products. These products came out of a joint development activity between Intel and IBM. There are two adapters in this system—one for capture and one for delivery. The function of the capture board is to produce digitized audio and video. The delivery board serves to display the video and audio from storage media, including CD ROM.

The technology used in the ActionMedia system is called **Digital Video Interactive,**™ or **DVI**. DVI is used to join computer and TV technologies in order to capture and display full-motion video with TV quality at a very high rate. The standard TV format, NTSC, displays video signals with 512 by 482 resolution in millions of colors at 30 frames per second.

The advantage of DVI technology over that of the M-Motion approach lies in its digital nature and its exceedingly high compression capabilities (160 to 1, for example). The ActionMedia playback adapter is able to decompress these huge amounts of information contained in each video frame in real time and display it using computer graphics. The adapter also uses Micro Channel's video extension. While the first version of the ActionMedia boards are not bus masters, it is likely that the next generation of products will be.

Server Solutions

Micro Channel architecture provides definite advantages for shared-logic and shared-resource server solutions. Earlier in the book, we learned of the many RAS and data integrity benefits of the architecture that are especially important in server applications. The following sections focus on uses of Micro Channel architecture implementations in multi-user environments.

Shared-Logic Solutions

What we mean by shared-logic is illustrated in Figure 5.36. This was, perhaps, the most common application environment for computers prior to the introduction of personal computers. The classic example of this environment is an S/370 system providing the intelligence for a number of nonintelligent terminals. In today's world, the host or server in this environment is likely to be a personal computer or workstation. Such applications are common in small, medium, and large business operations.

The key to many of these applications are programmable communications coprocessors like the ARTIC Portmaster Adapter/A (ARTIC is an acronym for A RealTime Interface Coprocessor) combined with server-class Micro Channel systems like the IBM Model 95 XP 486. More modestly priced solutions are based on systems like the IBM Model 65 SX or the Model 80 family members and the ARTIC Multiport/2, a DMA slave adapter.

The ARTIC adapters, with their 12.5 MHz or 7.37 MHz Intel 80186 microprocessors and up to 2 MB of memory, function as very powerful computers in their own right. Their use allows a very low-priced system to serve as the host for shared-logic applications, which used to be done with much larger systems. Bus master programmable communications coprocessors are especially effective at leveraging processing power in inexpensive servers. These devices can transfer information to and from other I/O devices and memory without interrupting the

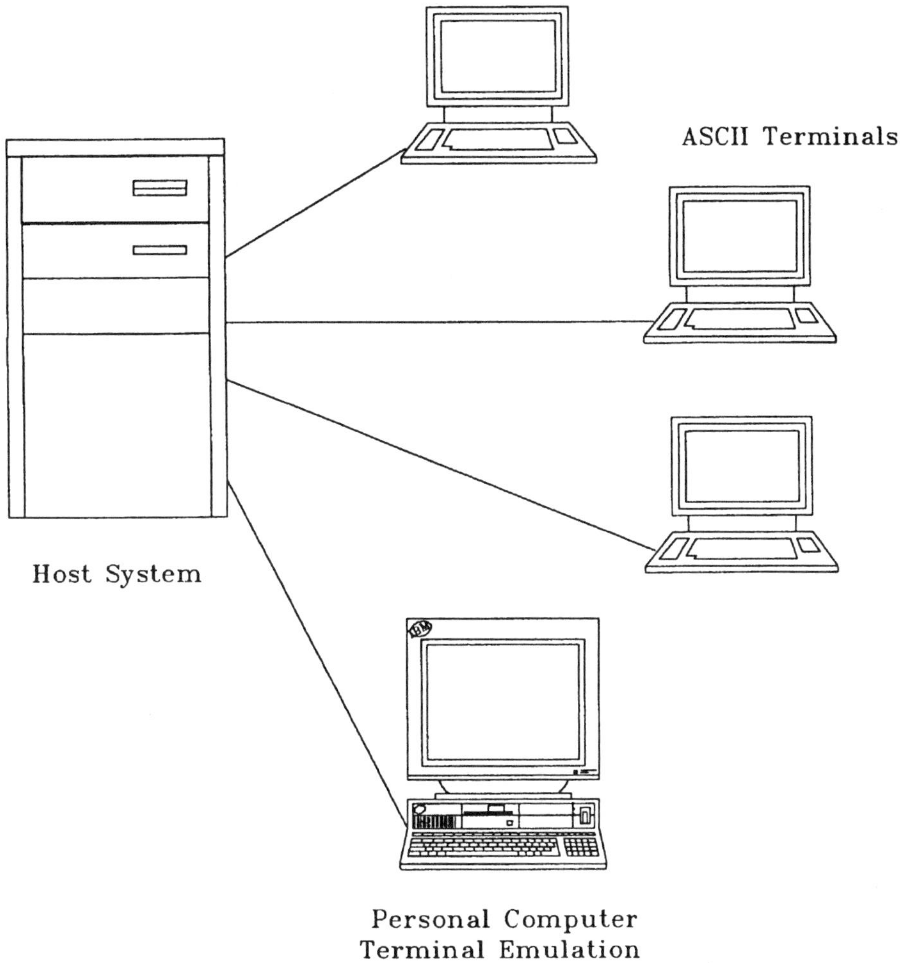

Figure 5.36 A shared-logic server environment. The server provides the intelligence for the attached ASCII terminals. The RPG II Application Platform is a good example of this environment.

system unit processor. In a multitasking environment, the system has plenty of processing power left over for other applications.

Some typical configurations are shown in Figure 5.37 and Figure 5.38. The use of multiple terminals attached to a Micro Channel system via the ARTIC card brings solutions to insurance agencies, medical offices, retail stores, warehousing, reservation agencies, legal offices, and almost any environment you can imagine.

Another very important group of applications is available by using the RPG II Application Platform™, which allows up to 16 users to execute IBM System/36 general business and industry solutions on a PS/2 Micro Channel system as a

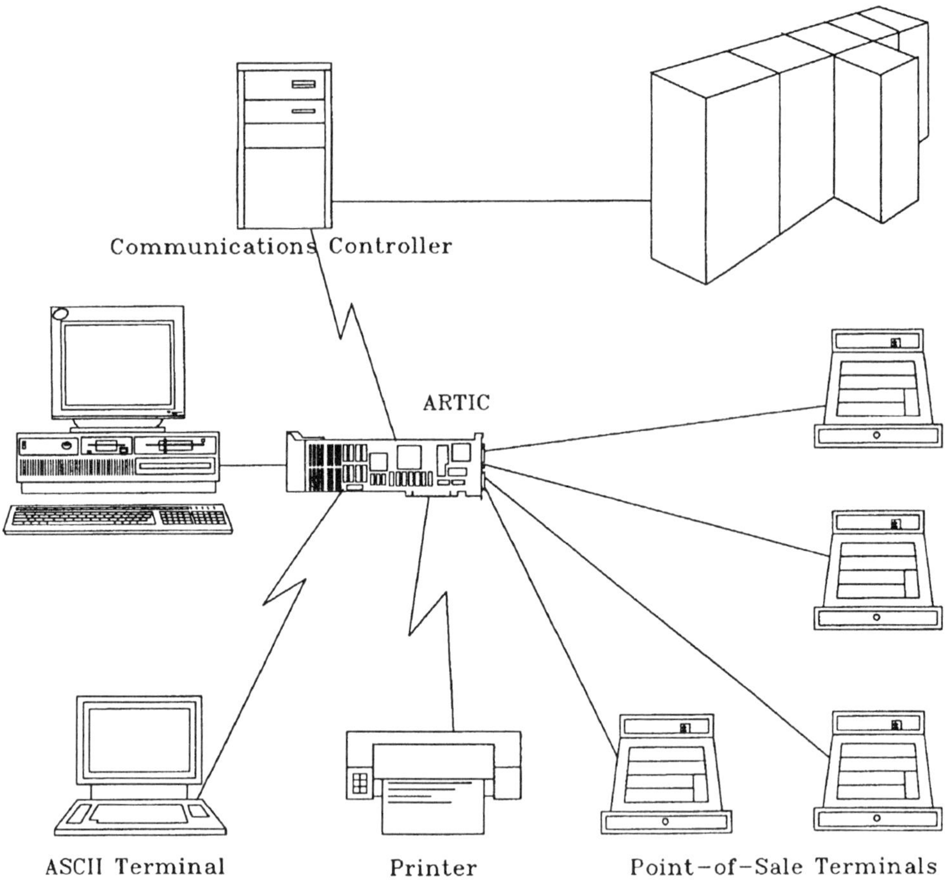

Figure 5.37 A terminal controller application. This arrangement is very common in point-of-sale applications or reservations systems.

server running OS/2. IBM 3151 ASCII Display terminals and PS/2 systems can be used as workstations for this multi-user solution.

Server solutions using the ARTIC card are also available for the RISC System/6000 and the ES/9371 families described earlier in this chapter. A good reference to the many software solutions using the ARTIC adapter is available from IBM sources.

LAN Server Solutions

Micro Channel architecture delivers numerous benefits to the LAN server environment. Many Micro Channel systems suitable for LAN server applications have been described earlier in this chapter. The following section provides a description of two innovative solutions that illustrate the broad range of potential for Micro Channel network server solutions.

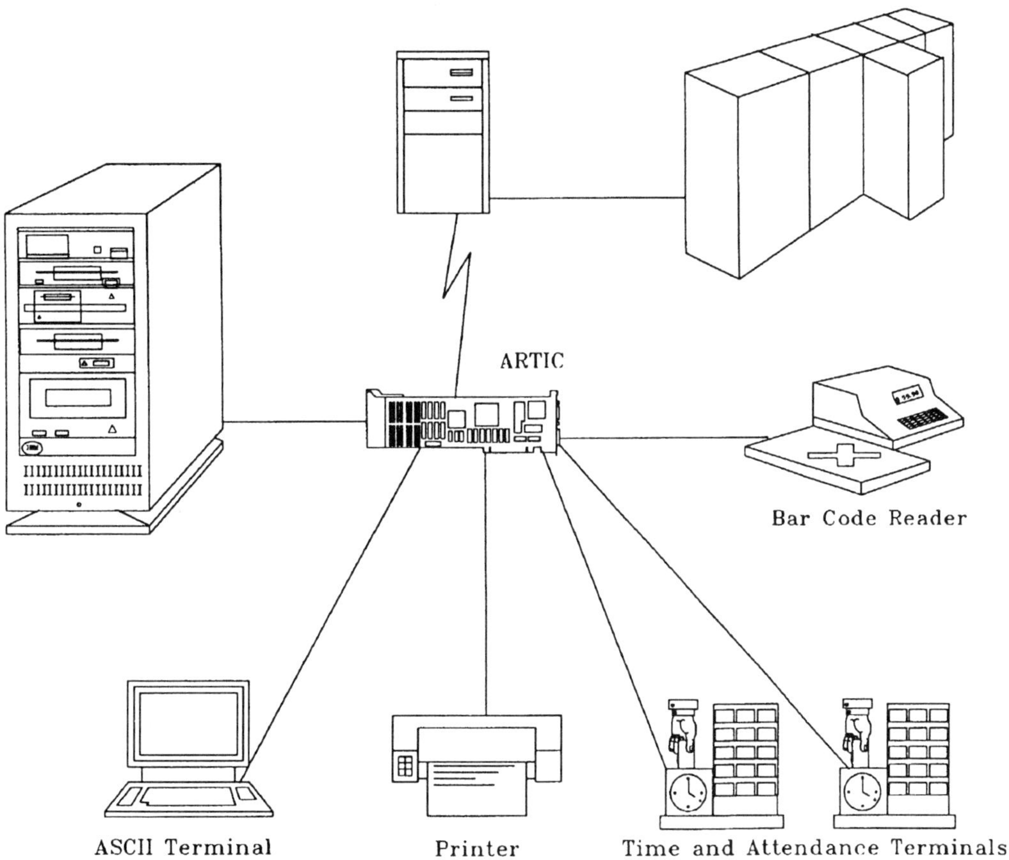

Figure 5.38 A wide variety of RS-232 and RS-422 devices can be attached to systems using the ARTIC Micro Channel products or similar adapters.

Micro Channel "Super Server"

The term "super server" is one that IBM uses to refer to a number of possible application-specific LAN server configurations. The configurations are a combination of hardware and software products designed to deliver maximum performance for PS/2 Micro Channel systems in server applications.[7]

One of these potential solutions that IBM has shown in business shows as a technology demonstration is based on the PS/2 Model 95 XP 486, combined with several high-performance bus master adapters and OS/2 system software. It uses an asymmetrical multiprocessor implementation with a unique function split between the 486 microprocessor of the base system and a second processor, the Aox MicroMaster 486. The configuration features a huge amount of both internal and

[7]In this section, the technology demonstrations described include some hardware and software products that are not currently available from IBM.

external storage capacity using SCSI bus master adapters, 3.5-inch 320-MB disk drives, and the PS/2 3511 external enclosures.

Figure 5.39 illustrates one of the possible IBM "super server" configurations that was demonstrated as a technology in business shows in 1990. There were six bus master adapters in the system: two 32-bit SCSI boards, two 16/4 Token Ring adapters, one Ethernet board, and the Aox associate processor. The software included OS/2 Extended Edition 1.2 and a customized version of 32-bit LAN Server designed to support the two 486 microprocessors.

The SCSI bus masters used SCB architecture to provide chaining of commands. Up to 16 commands could be chained together and sent to the SCSI adapter for execution. The adapter also supported **scatter-gather** operations, which permitted the data to be scattered anywhere in memory and gathered by the SCSI adapter into its cache for execution. This process reduced the overhead required for data transfers by eliminating a number of steps. The LAN adapters used are also capable of command-chaining and scatter-gather operations.

In the demonstration, each of the 486 microprocessors in the system had a copy of OS/2 loaded onto it. The associate processor was responsible for managing the file system portion of the OS/2 kernel and the LAN requests. The system board

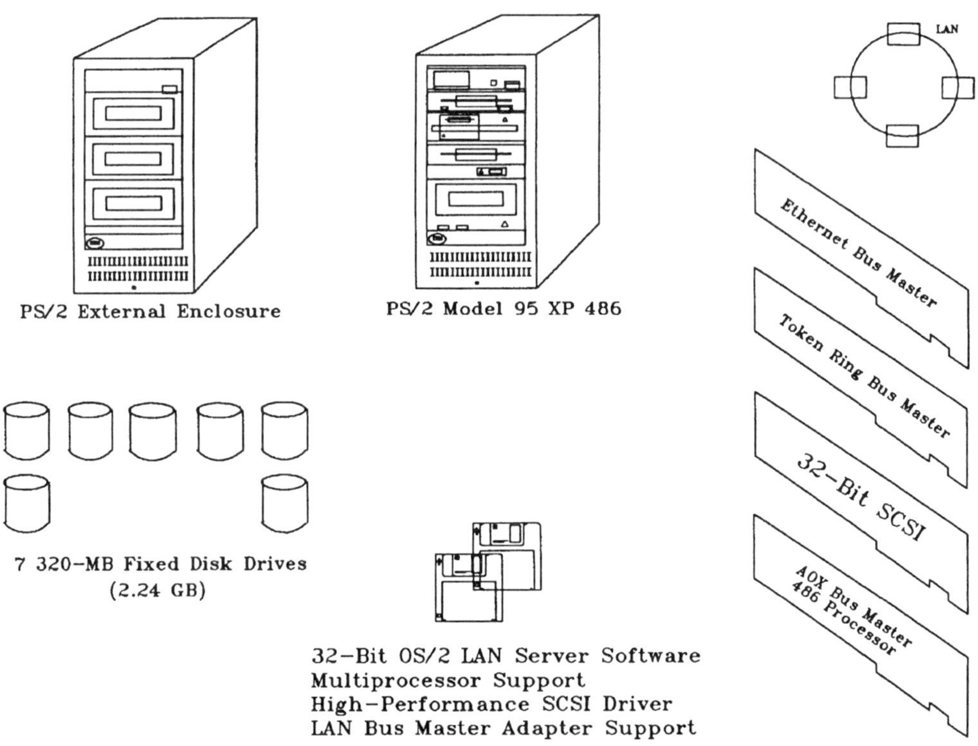

Figure 5.39 This "Super Server" configuration utilizes many of the capabilities of Micro Channel architecture.

processor ran the Presentation Manager portion and user applications. The implementation also supported medialess workstations by loading OS/2 in the memory of the workstation.

In another technology demonstration, another "super server" configuration connected two servers to the same disk array, illustrating the ability to recover from a failing disk drive or a failing server. In addition, a PS/2 Model 95 was configured with four additional 33-MHz 486 microprocessors on expansion boards to provide even higher levels of performance.

The "super server" configuration shown in Figure 5.39 has been used to demonstrate transaction processing and large blocks of color image data. Another application demonstrated by IBM has been full-motion video across the network at 30 frames per second to each of four workstations, using DVI-based digitizing, compression, and display technology.

This powerful combination of Micro Channel hardware and supporting software delivered excellent performance. However, it is possible to build your own "super server" configuration if you understand the bottlenecks in your application environment. You can use Micro Channel adapters to deliver the maximum possible performance for the least amount of money if you understand some important principles and your application environment.

Increasing performance involves the systematic removal of the bottlenecks in your system. You must understand where these bottlenecks occur and start removing them one by one. You can spend a great deal of money and not improve performance unless you work on the right areas.

The first step in building your "super server" is to characterize your applications as **compute-intensive** or **I/O-intensive**. Perhaps the most common examples of compute-intensive environments for network servers are data base applications. In order to enhance performance in such an environment, increasing the effective CPU power is a requisite step. We have seen many examples of how Micro Channel bus masters increase computing power directly and indirectly. Directly, additional processing power may be added to systems through processor upgrades and additional processors. Indirectly, the use of bus master LAN adapters and storage controllers with onboard processors increase compute power.

In an I/O-intensive environment, increasing computing power will have little or no effect until you remove the primary bottlenecks to performance. File servers accessing medium to large files are examples of I/O-intensive environments. The characteristics of the storage subsystem are probably the most important variables in this performance equation. Focusing on reducing mechanical delays by utilizing faster drives, caches, and an operating environment in which disk accesses can be overlapped is fundamental.

Less obvious ways to improve performance are to utilize multiple storage subsystems and LAN adapters. The Micro Channel bus is able to support much higher data transfer rates than what a single LAN adapter or storage controller can provide. Consider a typical token ring adapter, which has a burst data rate of 16 Mb/sec (2 MB/sec). Such a configuration is only able to use a small part of the capability of the bus. Purchasing another network adapter and distributing the nodes on two networks is an excellent way to get a performance boost.

The absolute best approach to gaining the maximum performance for the least money is through experimentation of various adapter, device, and software combinations rather than purchasing new systems. The intelligent use of Micro Channel adapters to deliver application-specific performance solutions is all you need to build your own "super server" solutions.

"LAN-IN-A-BOX"

Perhaps the ultimate implementation of Micro Channel server technology lies in something yet to come, a "LAN-IN-A-BOX." This is a concept that IBM demonstrated as a technology in November 1989 at COMDEX, one of the computer industry trade shows. The concept involved using the Micro Channel bus as a very high speed LAN.

You may have noticed that many Micro Channel boards are really small computers. The "LAN-IN-A-BOX" prototype took this a step further by putting what amounted to a 386SX computer on a Micro Channel board, including memory, VGA, keyboard controller, and other standard I/O. Cabled to the card was a display and keyboard that could be approximately 100 feet away from the system. Several of these "55 SX" boards were installed in an IBM Model 80 386, using the Micro Channel bus as a LAN. Each "computer" on the "LAN" could access the I/O devices of their "server." In this case the "clients" just happened to reside inside the server! This is truly the ultimate medialess solution. Figure 5.40 is an illustration of this concept.

The peer-to-peer capability and SCB Architecture are particularly suitable for this arrangement. The "clients" in this concept are bus masters, of course, with all the rights and privileges that go with bus ownership.

Although there are no products of this type currently available, it is anticipated that either IBM or industry developers will implement them in the future.

Investment Protection Solutions

One of the benefits of Micro Channel architecture described earlier in this book was the investment protection and extended system life of Micro Channel systems. There are four elements of systems that generally require upgrading: CPU power, memory, storage, and graphics. Let's look at an example of how the IBM PS/2 Model 50, announced in 1987, can be upgraded to meet today's environment.

The Model 50 has three 16-bit slots, one of which has a video extension. It was provided with 1 MB of memory on the system board, which could not be increased (except by using memory expansion boards). The original disk drive had an access time of 80 ms and a capacity of 20 MB. VGA graphics were integrated with the system board. As is, this system is useful only as a low-end DOS workstation. What you would like is a new 386 system with high-resolution graphics, a faster disk drive with more capacity, a CD ROM drive, a tape backup unit, and enough memory for Windows 3.0 or OS/2. Amazingly, this system can be upgraded to meet these requirements.

The system can be upgraded with 20-MHz, 25-MHz, or 33-MHz 386 power, using

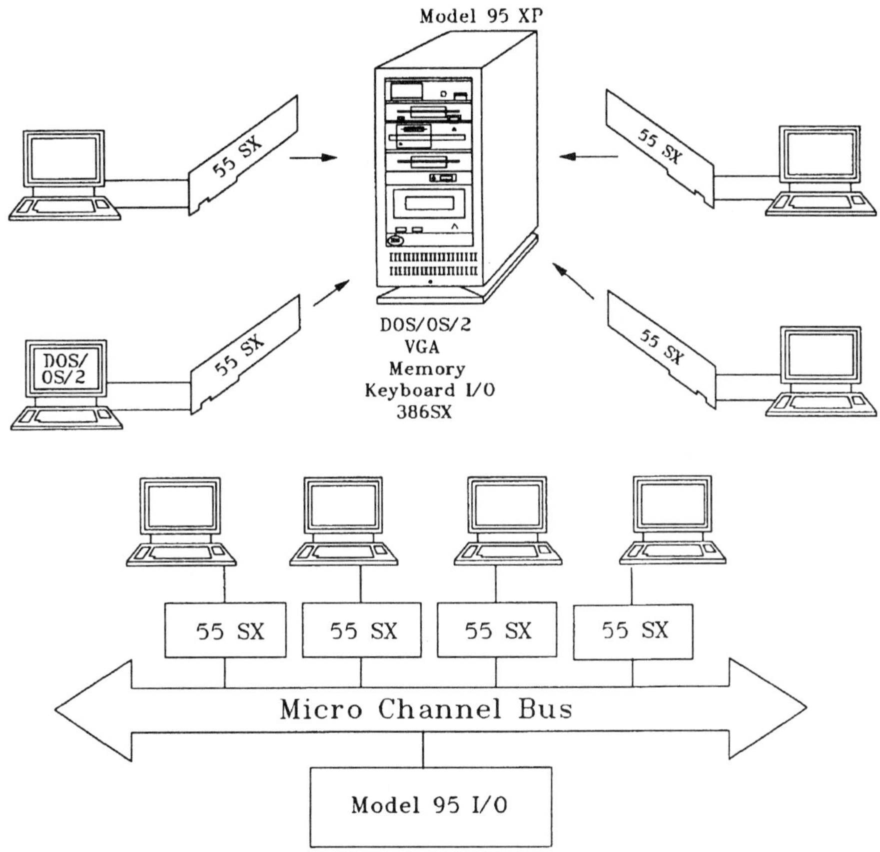

Figure 5.40 The "LAN-IN-A-BOX" concept is an innovative concept of the Micro Channel bus as a high-speed network pathway.

the Aox MicroMASTER 386. If you choose the 33 MHz version, you can increase the speed of your Model 50 about six times. Up to 8 MB of memory can be installed on this board, using 4-MB memory modules. The adapter can cache all RAM, ROM BIOS, and video ROM, which ensures the effectiveness of the upgrade. Since the i386 microprocessor becomes the system master with this upgrade, you are now capable of running Windows 3.0 or 32-bit OS/2 when it becomes available. That takes care of one of the Model 50's slots, however.

Now for the graphics. Several graphics upgrade cards are available in the industry that use the video extension slot. The IBM PS/2 Display Adapter 8514/A provides 1024 x 768 resolution and 256 colors if that's your choice. Two slots used, and only one to go, however.

The best choice for the last remaining slot is the SCSI bus master adapter. Using this powerful adapter, you can expand your system with up to seven mix and match SCSI devices available from industry sources, including some of the fastest disk drives in the industry. There are several options for SCSI enclosures also available, including the IBM PS/2 3511.

If you still need an additional slot for a communications card and would prefer to have your disk drive installed internally, another option is available. One company that has focused on storage upgrades is CORE International. Using their products, it is possible to add a fast 44- or 80-MB drive and also keep the original 20-MB drive. The best news is that the upgrade does not use a slot. Adding one of the bus master LAN adapters like the Cypress/2 from Lantana should complete the upgrade. Okay, so you've spent some money. But the result is an extremely powerful system that would cost you much more if you purchased a new one.

Let's try another example. Suppose you purchased an IBM PS/2 Model 80-041 a few years ago. You would like to have a fast new 486-based system with a high capacity disk drive to use as a data base server, but you can't afford it. Upgrading your current system is a real possibility, with the 25 MHz AOX MicroMASTER 486 serving as the data base "engine." The card and its onboard memory are designed to utilize the burst mode of the i486 microprocessor and support full 32-bit operations. In terms of the storage requirement, the Model 80-041 has plenty of room to add fast, high-capacity disk drives, such as the 16-ms 650-MB ESDI drive from CORE. Using a high-performance ESDI bus master controller, it is possible to have a state-of-the-art storage subsystem. Adding a faster network adapter completes the upgrade. For the Ethernet contingent, Novell's™ 32-bit Micro Channel adapter is an excellent choice.

The above examples are just a few of the many investment upgrade options that Micro Channel architecture makes possible. Other systems may be upgraded in a similar fashion, using the bus master features and the video extension slots. As we learned earlier in this chapter, some systems feature processor-complex upgrades as part of their basic design.

(To contact the companies mentioned in this section, consult the Micro Channel catalog mentioned earlier.)

SUMMARY

In this chapter, you have been introduced to a number of system implementations based on Micro Channel architecture. You have seen computers ranging from low-priced 16-bit systems up through minicomputers and "baby mainframes." Some of the outstanding products available from companies other than IBM were described.

The ins and outs of the various Micro Channel implementations and the use of some of its advanced optional features should give you a good flavor of products currently available, as well as what some future products may look like.

Finally, several solutions were described that use Micro Channel features in various application environments. Hopefully, this chapter has served its purpose: bringing the esoteric subject of computer architecture down to something useful in your environment.

QUESTIONS

1. Under what circumstances would the bus contention in the Model 50Z lead to a performance degradation?
2. What are some applications of medialess systems? How do you think the POST and setup routines are conducted on medialess systems?
3. Why is the maximum memory addressability of current PS/2 implementations of Micro Channel architecture limited to 16 MB?
4. What are some features of Micro Channel architecture that enhance SCSI adapter implementations?
5. How does the processor complex of the IBM PS/2 Model 70 486 differ from that of the PS/2 90 XP 486?
6. How does the separation of the I/O bus from the processor/memory bus affect bus master access times to system board memory?
7. What is the role of the IOCC in the RISC System/6000 systems?
8. Discuss the portability of Micro Channel expansion boards from system to system.

6

Bus Wars: EISA and Other Warriors

In this chapter, Micro Channel architecture will be compared to other bus architectures used in microcomputers. The objective of this chapter is to sort out some of the confusion present in the microcomputer industry. And a very confused industry it is! With a broad range of system designs using the various versions of the AT bus, systems based on the Extended Industry Standard Architecture (EISA), and Micro Channel systems with enhanced features of the architecture, it is no wonder decision makers have their hands full these days.

"Which bus to take?" is a prime topic for discussion in almost every organization, and continues to be the subject of numerous articles in the trade press. This decision will form the basis for the purchase of billions of dollars of equipment in the 90s and will affect almost every aspect of information management in the coming decade. In the beginning of this book, we stated that one of our goals was to remove this confusion and to sort out some of the issues and transition challenges. The next two chapters are designed to help you answer the question: "What is the best choice for microcomputer bus architecture in our organization and how can we manage the change?"

WHY CHOOSE?

At this point, you may be asking yourself, "Why even make a choice?" The answer to this question is driven by a number of factors that relate to how computers are used, as well as technology advances. There are a number of forces in the early 1990s that will drive a change from earlier personal computer buses:

1. 386, and later 486, systems will replace 286 and 386SX systems as the entry level workstation. (You don't have to look very far into the future to see this one!)

2. High-frequency (>25 MHz) 32-bit systems will dominate the mid-range, technical workstation, and server arena with increasing presence of RISC processors.
3. Multitasking 32-bit operating systems (OS/2, UNIX) will utilize and require the features of advanced I/O bus architectures, delivering significant performance benefits.
4. I/O-intensive applications such as page printing, multimedia, and image processing will drive 32-bit I/O requirements at the personal workstation level.
5. Migration of function from mainframe systems to "personal computers" (both standalone and networked) and advanced workstations will impose stringent reliability, data integrity, and fault-tolerant requirements.

These trends are already present to some degree. It is clear that today's purchase decisions should be made with these directions in mind if at all possible. Even though the majority of systems in use today are based on the AT bus, they are simply not capable of addressing these directions adequately. A choice must be made. What the best choice is and when and how it should be made are the real questions.

THE CONTENDERS

The list of major contenders includes Micro Channel architecture, 32-bit AT systems[1], the Extended Industry Standard Architecture, and Apple's NuBus. Figure 6.1 is a composite estimate of 32-bit system sales projected by bus architecture for IBM compatibles in 1993. By the numbers, Micro Channel architecture is expected to have the highest share in this environment.

One of the most striking things about the chart is that a significant number of AT-bus systems are still predicted to be sold. There is no question that AT-bus systems will be around for awhile. These systems will continue to be used for traditional personal productivity applications in a single-tasking environment at home and in the office. However, the need for some AT expansion boards will shrink since most of the necessary I/O devices required for the bulk of personal productivity applications will be integrated with the system board.

The conclusion from these projections and other forecasts is that no one bus architecture will dominate the market, but most projections give Micro Channel systems the edge in the 32-bit world. However, these projections may be more closely related to choice of vendor rather than choice of bus architecture!

Let's get out of projections and examine the offerings of system vendors today. These should give some clues about their directions. Apple is already heavily focused on NuBus. The group of vendors with systems growing out of the IBM AT architecture present a more difficult pattern for projections.

[1]These systems are those with 32-bit microprocessors (such as the 386SX, i386, and i486) and 16-bit I/O buses.

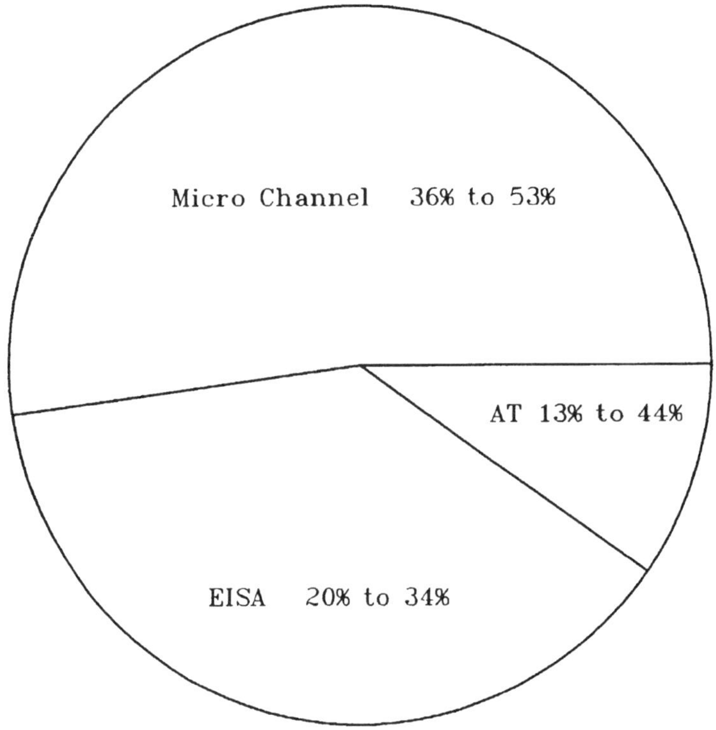

Figure 6.1 Composite estimate of 1993 shipments based on various bus architecture.

The bus strategy of most of the EISA vendors seems to offer systems based on the AT bus for the traditional PC applications and EISA systems for the high end, positioned closer to the minicomputer and technical workstation market. Compaq, however, is beginning to build lower-priced EISA systems in the midrange and appears to be moving away from the AT bus. Some of the system vendors are building products based on all three buses.

IBM seems to have a strategy of offering the AT bus for entry PC applications, but with much more overlap of Micro Channel systems in the lower price ranges. (There are 16-bit Micro Channel systems but no 16-bit EISA systems offered today.) In the other direction, IBM has extended Micro Channel architecture much further up the price/performance ladder with the RISC System/6000 and ES/9371 systems.

The 32-bit bus market for add-in board vendors is split into three primary segments: Micro Channel, NuBus, and EISA systems. At this time, Micro Channel boards constitute the largest segment and NuBus is second.

In terms of opportunity, there is no doubt that Micro Channel systems offer a more attractive business case for third-party developers than do the other two bus architectures at this time. NuBus boards are offered by fewer vendors than Micro Channel, but many develop only NuBus boards. In the world of IBM and compatibles, it is not unusual to find vendors developing boards for the AT, Micro Channel, and EISA buses.

In terms of EISA board development, third-party activity is fairly small at this time but is growing as the installed system base increases. Several of the EISA boards are being developed by the system vendors for their own products and are not available for other systems. Examples include Compaq's intelligent disk array (IDA) controller and Zenith's high performance ESDI disk controller.

You could safely conclude from the preceding discussion that current hardware development activities are focused heavily toward advanced bus architectures. System software development is also targeted toward the 32-bit platforms. What all this points to is that 32-bit systems with 32-bit buses and 32-bit software will rapidly become the desktop and server standard. Because of these obvious directions, it makes sense to plan your current purchases with an eye toward the future.

DISPOSABLE COMPUTERS?

One aspect of this discussion that may be bothering you is the rate of obsolescence of equipment. Why not buy the cheapest systems available and "throw them away" in a couple of years? Why plan for the future with today's purchases? You probably already know the answers. Look around and you will see that all that "obsolete" equipment is still with you. You really don't throw it away, you just live with it. That's why it's so important to purchase equipment that complements your future directions instead of inhibiting them.

WHICH BUS TO TAKE?

Part of the answer to this question lies in the technical merits of the various choices. What follows is a relatively technical discussion of the contending bus architectures. The primary focus will be on the AT bus architecture and EISA. A brief comparison of Micro Channel architecture with NuBus and Futurebus is also included.

Micro Channel Architecture vs. the AT Bus

Throughout this book we have made repeated references to the AT bus design. Chapter 2 contained a brief description of the history of the AT bus and its features. To avoid repetition, only a brief overview will be presented in this chapter, with emphasis on the differentiating features. Some of the specific attributes of the AT bus are compared to those of other bus architectures in Table 6.1.

As we learned earlier, the AT bus was a synchronous design that supported 8- and 16-bit data transfers and was capable (although rarely used) of addressing up to 16 MB of memory. It was designed primarily as an I/O bus to support the 80286 microprocessor of the AT. There was no provision for the accommodation of the

TABLE 6.1 BUS ARCHITECTURE FEATURE COMPARISON

Feature	AT (8 MHz)	EISA	NuBus	MC
Superior/Subordinate Structure	Yes	Yes	No	No
Number of Signals	98	188	96	178
Number of Ground Pins	4	21	22	27
Number of Power Pins	6	15	23	18
Address Lines	24	32	32	32
Memory Addressability	16 MB	4 GB	4 GB	4 GB
Data Path Width	8/16	16/32 (EISA Bus)	8/16/32	8/16/32/64
Basic Data Rate	5.3 MB/s	16.7 MB/s	20 MB/s	20 MB/s
Maximum Data Transfer Rate (Published)	8.0 MB/s	33 MB/s	37.5 MB/s	160 MB/s
DMA Channels	7	7	Optional	8 (7 virtual)
16-bit DMA Data Rate (Basic)	1.6 MB/s	4.0 MB/s	NA	5 MB/s
32-bit DMA Data Rate (Stream/Burst)	NA	33 MB/s	NA	10 MB/s
Multiplexed Address and Data Bus	No	No	Yes	No[1]
Bus Master Support	Limited	Yes	Yes	Yes
Arbitration Levels	7	15	# Slots	16
Arbitration	Ctrl	Ctrl	Dstrb	Dstrb
Fairness	No	Round Robin	Always	Optional
Bus Master Priority	N/A	Low	Slot	Flexible
Sync/Async	Sync	Sync	Sync	Async
Interrupt Handling	Edge	Level (EISA Cards)	Level	Level
Interrupt Request Lines	11	11	1	11
Shared Interrupts	No	Yes (EISA Cards)	No	Yes
Audio Bus	No	No	No	Yes
Switchless Setup	No	Yes (EISA Cards)	Yes	Yes

[1]Micro Channel Architecture does not use multiplexed data and address lines to achieve its basic transfer rate. However, multiplexing is used to achieve data rates in excess of 40 MB/sec.

TABLE 6.1 BUS ARCHITECTURE FEATURE COMPARISON (continued)

Feature	AT (8 MHz)	EISA	NuBus	MC
Address/Data Parity	No	Not Defined	Yes	Yes
Adapter ID Number	No	Yes (EISA Cards)	No	Yes
Power Per Slot[2]	N/A	4.5 amp at 5 V	2.0 amp at 5 V	1.6 amp at 5 V
Board Area (sq. in.)	63	63	52	36
Connector Type	Edge	Edge	DIN	Edge

[2]The power per slot is normally a design specification. The values given here are derived from the PS/2 Micro Channel and the Macintosh II system specifications and from the EISA specification. The power specifications for the AT were never published by IBM.

i386 microprocessor, such as wider data paths, greater memory addressability, or faster bus speeds.

Will the Real AT Bus Stand Up?

The AT bus was not really an architecture; it was more of a subset of the AT system design. There were a number of designs that collectively constituted what is generally called the AT bus. IBM itself had three versions: the 6- and 8-MHz AT systems and the 10-MHz PS/2 Model 30 286. To further complicate matters, very little documentation for the AT was published by IBM. What was published was subject to a broad range of interpretations by board vendors and system manufacturers. Because of this diversity, the compatibility of boards from system to system differed significantly. The widely varying characteristics of the implementations of the AT bus and the incompatibilities from system to system certainly could not be called a bus architecture.

So which version of the AT bus do we compare with Micro Channel architecture? The 8- MHz AT Model 339 probably represents the best case for a comparison. There were an enormous number of these systems built by IBM and other manufacturers that centered around this design point. It is probably the most representative of the "industry standard AT" if there ever was one. It is the design point that expansion board vendors generally target for compatibility.

The Fundamental Difference

The fundamental difference between the AT bus and Micro Channel architecture is that the AT bus was designed primarily for a single-tasking single-user environment with a limited number of I/O devices and operations. Performance and flexibility were not primary considerations as they were with Micro Channel architecture. The Micro Channel bus was designed with OS/2 and UNIX in mind, providing many features that support multitasking and multi-user environments. The greater bus band width, enhanced utilization of system resources, improved data integrity characteristics, the method of handling interrupts, more efficient DMA procedures, exception condition procedures, extended address range, and the multimaster capability are examples of Micro Channel architecture features that provide benefits in multitasking and multi-user environments.

One of the most important differences between the AT bus and Micro Channel architecture is the processor-dependent nature of the AT bus. Just as the original PC bus was based on the 8088 microprocessor, the characteristics of the AT bus in IBM's computers were patterned after the 80286. The AT bus signals and frequency were basically the same as the external signals of the microprocessor.[2]

In terms of the structural characteristics, the AT bus is an I/O bus that requires a system board implementation for the system microprocessor. There is no provision for the system microprocessor to reside on an expansion board. It is basically a superior/subordinate structure in which the system microprocessor or the DMA controllers directly or indirectly control all information transfers on the bus. Even though there was a provision for one additional master other than the system microprocessor and the DMA controller, this additional master was not a peer of the other two. In the AT architecture, the DMA controller and the bus master had a subordinate relationship to the system master as was described earlier.

The true bus master capability of the AT bus was rarely used for a number of reasons. It was very difficult, if not impossible, to design an AT bus master that was functional on a number of machines. While the lack of documented timings was a significant problem for AT masters, the absence of a method for changing bus ownership and the lack of a PREEMPT signal were even greater problems. The AT master was required to determine the proper time to release the bus in order for memory refresh to proceed. There was also no effective method for an alternate master to know if a device was requesting a DMA transfer and which DMA channels were available.

The AT's synchronous bus required that transfers to the bus be synchronized to the bus clock rate. This was usually 8 MHz but varied considerably from "industry standard" machine to machine. The result was to substantially slow down bus transfers from an alternate master. Because the Micro Channel bus is asynchronous, an alternate master can transfer data as fast or faster than the system master.

In terms of system resources, the AT bus had two sets of DMA controllers, yielding a total of 8 DMA channels. Four were 8-bit and four were 16-bit channels, one of which was reserved for use only on the system board. In terms of interrupt capabilities, the AT bus had 15 interrupt request lines, 11 of which could be used by expansion boards.

In terms of data transfer rates, the basic data rate for the 8-MHz version of the AT bus was 5.3 MB/sec, assuming a bus cycle time of 375 ns and one wait state.

---

[2]The AT specification also defined a capability for the microprocessor to operate at a higher frequency than the bus. This capability was never used by IBM, but was incorporated in some AT-compatibles made by other manufacturers. This feature was used in high-speed 286 and 386 systems.

With no wait states, a maximum of 8 MB/sec could theoretically be achieved. (The basic data rate for the 10-Mhz version was 6.7 MB/sec, assuming a bus cycle of 300 ns with one wait state.) Micro Channel architecture defines a data rate that approaches 20 times that of the 8-MHz AT's maximum capability (using the 160 MB/sec streaming-data procedure with a 50 ns cycle time). A comparison of these rates with those of the other bus architectures is shown in Table 6.1. (The actual data rates are somewhat less due to the cycles associated with memory refresh and arbitration overhead.) Obviously, the data transfer rates of the AT bus are very slow by comparison to all the other buses.

The AT bus used the edge-triggered method of handling interrupts as compared to the level-sensitive method used by Micro Channel architecture. The former is definitely inferior in terms of data integrity, due to the possibility of lost and false interrupts.

The AT bus has some significant problems in terms of its electromagnetic characteristics, a problem later addressed by Micro Channel architecture. Micro Channel architecture contains 4.5 times the number of power and ground pins than the AT. This increase in pins and their strategic connector locations goes a long way toward removing stray RF-induced signals, a common source of errors on the AT.

Another significant improvement is Micro Channel's POS function. There is nothing comparable to this feature in AT systems. The DIP switches used for selection of system resources in AT systems (as compared to the "software switches" of Micro Channel architecture) were a source of confusion and error. Several other POS functions are also improvements over the AT bus.

"32-Bit AT Systems"

As you may recall from the discussion in Chapter 2, 32-bit AT systems were designed by a number of manufacturers in an attempt to exploit the capabilities of the i386 and i486 microprocessors. These dual bus designs added a separate high-speed 32-bit processor-memory bus while retaining the 16-bit AT I/O bus. Each of these systems is somewhat unique and may require specific memory upgrades from the manufacturer. Unique software may also be required.

Many systems based on these designs have excellent performance capabilities, however. This is especially true in the DOS environment. Why is this? In the discussion in Chapter 2, we showed performance to be definitely influenced by the application environment. Single-user, single-tasking applications do not utilize the concurrency features of advanced bus architectures. As a result, DOS performance is most often affected by the raw CPU power of the system rather than I/O bus characteristics. In addition, most of the AT boards rely heavily on the CPU to move information. Because of these factors, these systems have excellent performance capabilities in a DOS environment with AT boards. However, they were not designed for multitasking.

The DOS performance benefit of these systems is their only advantage over the traditional AT design. All the other limitations of the AT bus described in the previous section still apply.

Conclusions

The capabilities of the AT bus are rudimentary in comparison to those of Micro Channel architecture. Its lack of flexibility, performance limitations, limited system resources, and absence of important data integrity characteristics do not place it in the same league with Micro Channel's technical improvements.

Yet there are currently more AT-bus systems sold than any other type, and this is expected to continue for quite some time. An AT-bus system with moderate CPU power continues to be an acceptable choice for the DOS environment for users with modest requirements. However, you are probably not using your money very wisely buying fast 386 and 486 systems based on the AT bus because the I/O subsystem cannot keep up with higher-speed processors.

If your performance requirements are expected to increase in the future, you should consider a Micro Channel system for its bus master and upgrade capabilities alone. A 16-bit Micro Channel system is a good choice because the price is about the same as an AT-bus system from a comparable manufacturer. As CPU-hungry graphical user interfaces become pervasive, even the least sophisticated users will need faster systems. Micro Channel systems are designed for graphical upgrades with powerful adapters, such as IBM's Image Adapter/A described earlier.

Additional Information

Additional information on the AT architecture may be obtained from the following IBM sources:

IBM Personal Computer AT Hardware Technical Reference (S229–9611)

IBM Personal Computer AT Model 339 Hardware Technical Reference (S229–9608)

IBM Personal System/2 Model 30 286 Hardware Technical Reference (S01F0237)

Micro Channel Architecture vs. EISA

In late 1988, a consortium of companies consisting of AST, Compaq, Epson, Hewlett-Packard, NEC, Olivetti, Tandy, Wyse, and Zenith announced support for a 32-bit extension to the AT architecture called the Extended Industry Standard Architecture (EISA). The primary benefits claimed for EISA have been the absence of control by a single manufacturer and the bus's compatibility with AT and PC expansion boards. Many of the features of EISA bear a strong resemblance to those of Micro Channel architecture, including multimaster capability, automatic setup, and high-speed 32-bit data transfers.

In late 1989, the first EISA systems were announced, led by AST, Olivetti, Compaq Computer, Hewlett-Packard, and Zenith. These systems were targeted toward the high-end server market and high performance desktop applications and have price tags to match. During 1990, many other systems and models by other members of the consortium were announced, a significant number of which featured system boards manufactured by Mylex.

EISA will be described in more detail than the other bus architectures in this chapter because of its relationship to Micro Channel architecture. It is, of course, software-compatible with previous IBM personal computers. EISA and Micro Channel architecture are viewed as direct "competitors," at least in the 32-bit world. Because of this, an in-depth description of EISA architecture is called for.

The source of most of this information is the EISA specification version 3.10. Contained in this massive 430-page document is an overview of the architecture, the EISA bus specification, a description of the system board I/O control functions, EISA system configuration, and over 100 figures. The specification provides complete timings, functional characteristics, electrical requirements, and mechanical designs for both the EISA bus and the AT bus (which is referred to as the Industry Standard Bus, or ISA, in the EISA specification).

There is some irony in that the ISA bus is more completely specified by the EISA documentation than by IBM, the originator of the bus. This was necessary since some old AT boards don't meet the ISA specifications and are not fully compatible with EISA systems. From our earlier discussion, this was not an unexpected problem, since some incompatibilities had always existed among AT boards and the various AT clones.

Overview

It is somewhat difficult to identify what actually constitutes EISA. Since EISA requires compatibility with AT expansion boards, and also requires a separate processor and memory bus, EISA (the architecture) actually consists of three buses, as illustrated in Figure 6.2. These three buses are the EISA bus, the processor-memory complex (vendor-specific), and the AT (or ISA) bus. There is, then, a distinction between EISA architecture and the EISA bus.

The three-bus structure of EISA systems is reminiscent of the split bus architecture that characterized earlier "32-bit AT" systems. Many of the vendors making up the original "gang of nine" actually made AT systems of this type. Their evolution into EISA architecture with its separate processor-memory complex was predictable.

The following is a summary of the major features of EISA:

- Compatibility with most PC and AT expansion boards (called ISA boards in the EISA specification);
- An expansion bus interface supporting both AT and EISA boards;
- 32-bit memory addressing for the CPU, memory, and EISA devices;
- 16- and 32-bit data transfers for EISA attached devices;
- An arbitration procedure that provides for bus ownership by up to 15 arbitrating devices, one of which must be the system CPU;
- Synchronous data transfers, including basic and burst modes;
- Automatic configuration of system and EISA expansion boards;

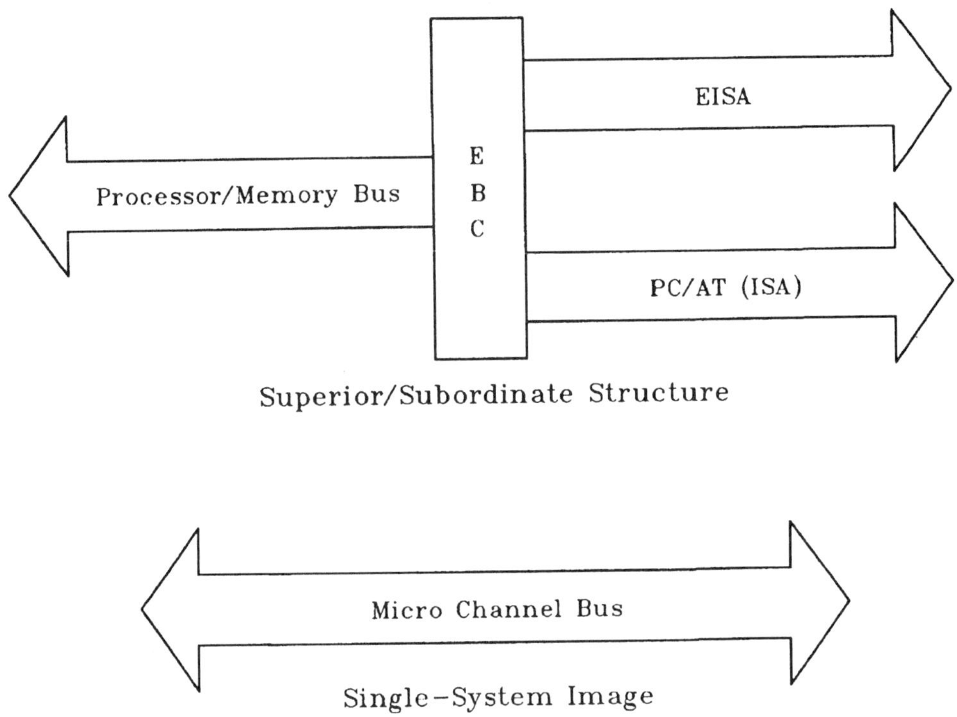

Figure 6.2 EISA versus Micro Channel architecture. Even though some Micro Channel systems have a separate processor/memory bus and a system board implementation, it is not a requirement of the architecture.

- A procedure for translation and transfer of information between EISA and AT (ISA) masters and slaves;
- Faster direct memory access procedures;
- Data transfer rates of up to 33 MB/sec;
- Shared interrupts on the EISA bus; and
- Edge-triggered and level-sensitive interrupt handling.

Sound familiar? There is a strong similarity between Micro Channel architecture and EISA. The major technical features are summarized in Table 6.1. The major differences lie in their different structural philosophies, the degree of processor independence, maximum data transfer rates, and in some missing features (for instance, address and data parity). And, of course, EISA systems can accept AT boards and Micro Channel systems cannot.

Structural Philosophy

Let's return to the simplistic diagram in Figure 6.2. EISA architecture is based on a superior/subordinate structural philosophy as was the AT design. There is an assumption that the CPU is resident on the system board. It is unclear if future

EISA designs will accommodate microprocessors other than Intel's i386 and i486 or future members of the X86 family, although it is feasible.[3]

The system board manages all the translations between the three buses and serves as the "switch" that controls movement of information among the three buses. The processor-memory bus can operate independently from the ISA and the EISA buses, but they cannot operate simultaneously since they share some common signals.

In EISA architecture, the CPU-memory complex, the AT expansion boards, and the EISA expansion boards have different views of the system. This is in contrast to the basic Micro Channel architecture in which there is a single system image, as illustrated in Figure 6.2. Although there are a number of Micro Channel systems that have separate processor/memory buses, each device attached to the Micro Channel bus has the same image of the system and follows the same architectural rules. The point is that EISA *requires* a more complex structure, whereas it is *optional* with Micro Channel architecture.

EISA Connector Characteristics and AT Compatibility

Perhaps the strongest selling point for EISA systems is that they are architected to be compatible with most PC and AT boards. The connectors for EISA boards are a superset of the 16-bit AT connectors. Physically, the PC and AT boards can be installed in the same slots as the EISA boards. A section of this clever connector design is shown in Figure 6.3. The connector is a two-level affair with the 98 upper pins being compatible with the ISA boards and the lower pins keyed in such a way that only the newer EISA cards can make contact with both levels (188 total pins).

An additional compatibility consideration is that some of the older PC and AT cards were designed to work at speeds much slower than the EISA bus basic transfer rate. For example, the original PC boards were designed for the 4.77-MHz 8088 microprocessor. The current vintage of EISA implementations are based on a synchronous design of 8.25 or 8.33 MHz.[4] The conclusion is that some PC and AT boards may not work in EISA systems due to these timing considerations. This limitation may not be significant, however, since most of the slower boards are older and will probably not be migrated to EISA systems.

Participants

Based on the EISA specifications, bus masters, memory slaves, I/O slaves, and DMA slaves are the participants that are allowed to use the bus. Theoretically, information can be transferred from any device on any bus to another device located on its own bus or another bus. However, there are some problems related to the fact that the ISA bus only allows one and two byte transfers, but the host

[3]The EISA bus architecture has a very close relationship to the Intel 80X86 family of microprocessors as did the AT bus. However, it would be possible to accommodate a system CPU with a different instruction set, using fairly complex bus interface logic in order to "translate" the signals. This is analogous to the IBM RT with its RISC processor and AT I/O bus.

[4]The bus speed is a factor of the microprocessor frequency. For example, systems with 25-MHz and 33-MHz microprocessors have bus speeds of 8.33 and 8.25 MHz, respectively.

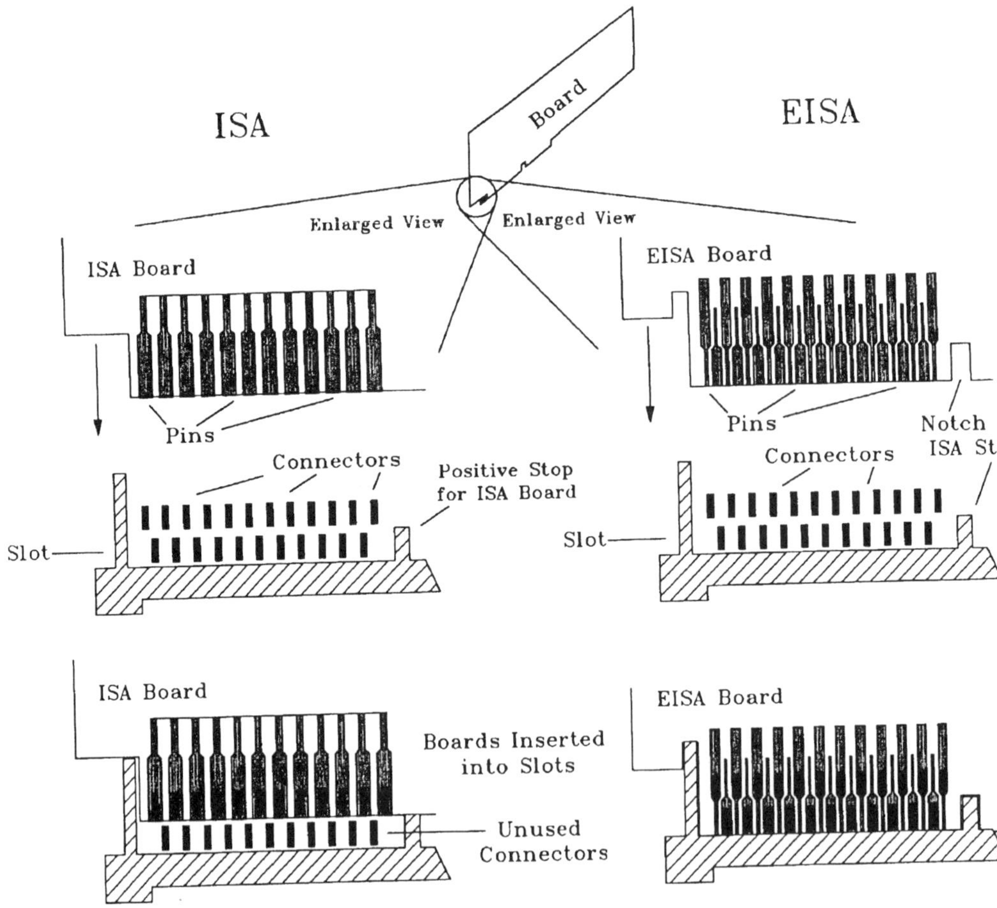

Figure 6.3 The EISA connector design accepts either ISA or EISA boards.

bus and the EISA bus allow one, two, three, and four byte transfers. Because of this alignment problem, the system board is required to manage all transfers, adding some additional overhead. Peer-to-peer transfers between ISA and EISA devices are not enabled by current implementations, but are theoretically possible whenever the alignment problem is solved. Micro Channel architecture does not have this limitation, since its participants are self-aligning and do not require the intervention of the system board logic to manage transfers.

EISA/ISA Signals

A summary of the EISA signals is shown in Table 6.2.[5] There are a total of 188 ISA and EISA pins. EISA requires 64 additional logic signals and another 26 power and ground connections. There are no more than four signal pins between each

[5]The signal definitions for the AT bus were described earlier and are summarized in Table 1-3 in Chapter 1.

TABLE 6.2 EISA SIGNALS

Pin Description	ISA	EISA Added	Total
Ground	4	17	21
+5V	3	8	11
-5V	1		1
+12V	1	1	2
-12V	1		1
Address	27	23	50
Data	16	16	32
Data/Address Control	14	14	28
Additional Control	6	2	8
Interrupt Request	11		11
DMA Request	7		7
DMA Acknowledge	7		7
MFG Specific		4	4
Reserved		5	5
Total	98	90	188

Signal Type	Signal	Function
Address Lines	LA2 through LA16 -LA24 through -LA31	Latchable address bits. Address bits 24 through 31 expand the address range to 32 bits. These lines are driven by the CPU or bus master.
Data Lines	D16 through D31	Data lines 16 through 31 used to expand the data bus to 32 bits. Driven by the CPU, bus master, or slave.
Timing and Control	-BE0 through -BE3	Indicates which of the four data bytes are active. Driven by the CPU or bus master.
	-CMD	Used to indicate a data cycle on the EISA bus. Supplied by the system board.
	-START	Supplied by the system board and used to control the timing of the start of an EISA bus cycle.
	M/-IO	Indicates a memory cycle when high and an I/O cycle when low for EISA cards. Supplied by the CPU or bus master.

TABLE 6.2 EISA SIGNALS (continued)

Signal Type	Signal	Signal Function
	W/-R	Indicates a write cycle when high and a read cycle when low for EISA cards. Supplied by the CPU or bus master.
	-EX16	Driven by an EISA slave to indicate that it can support 16-bit transfers.
Timing and Control	-EX32	Driven by an EISA slave to indicate that it can support 32-bit transfers.
	EXRDY	Driven by an EISA slave to indicate that it needs wait states.
	-SLBURST	Driven by an EISA slave to indicate that it can support burst cycles.
	-MSBURST	Driven by a bus master or the CPU to indicate to a slave that it can perform burst cycles.
	-LOCK	Used to prevent the DMA controller from rearbitrating for the bus. Driven by the CPU or bus master.
	-MREQx	Used by the CPU or bus master to request use of the bus (slot-specific).
	-MAKx	Used to indicate to the EISA bus master in slot x that it may take control of the bus. Driven by the system board.

pair of power and ground pins. This proximity of power and ground pins enhances electromagnetic compatibility and reduces crosstalk between pins. As discussed in Chapter 3, Micro Channel connectors have very similar characteristics in terms of the number of power and ground pins and their distribution.

However, the older AT boards cannot access the additional power and ground pins of the EISA connectors. Because of this, some of the problems of electromagnetic interference in the AT design are transferred to EISA when AT boards are used in EISA systems. While the EISA connector is definitely an improvement over the older design, the electromagnetic interference design problems remain, and the potential for data integrity problems still exists.

The first 98 signals are identical to those of the AT bus. This layout provides for electrical compatibility of the ISA boards used in EISA systems and AT systems. The EISA boards use a number of these signals but not all of them. This is due mostly to the 32-bit characteristics of EISA, the faster timing characteristics of the EISA boards, and the use of unlatched address signals in EISA. As you may recall from Chapter 1, the original PC provided latched address signals. The AT provided for unlatched versions for the bits 17–23. The EISA bus provides for all address signals to be unlatched, including those of the original PC and the eight new bits associated with the 32-bit bus. This is done to provide the address information earlier in the cycle, in order to enhance data rates.

In addition, there are some differences in the characteristics of ISA signals on the EISA bus compared to the way they were used on the AT bus. The most significant difference is in the system clock (BCLK) signal. In the AT, this signal had a fixed 6-MHz or 8-MHz frequency, with a fixed duty cycle. In EISA, the signal frequency is 8.333 MHz at a 50 percent duty cycle or 6 MHz at a 33-percent duty cycle. This is done to provide higher data rates on the EISA bus while retaining compatibility with most of the older boards.

The EISA unique signals are of several varieties. Many of these are required for 32-bit operations and are taken by additional address, data, and control signals. There are also lines used to signal the start and stop of EISA bus cycles, supplied by the system board. There is another line used to signal burst capabilities by masters and slaves. There are also signals for masters to request the bus and to acknowledge to the master that it may take control of the bus. These signals are used for the same purpose as is the arbitration bus in Micro Channel architecture (that is, to pass ownership from one master to another). There are some significant differences, however, in EISA and Micro Channel bus arbitration and prioritization of arbitrating devices. These differences are discussed later in this chapter.

There are no audio bus or audio signals defined by EISA. For systems used as servers, this is probably not an important feature, however. It is more appropriate for the desktop environment. But there is nothing in EISA that is comparable to the video extension signals of Micro Channel architecture. This is the feature that allows graphics boards to access the video capabilities on the system board and paves the way for advanced multi-media applications. Again, this is probably not an important consideration in the EISA server world since graphics capabilities are not as important there.

There are no address and parity signals defined in EISA architecture, a significant difference compared to Micro Channel architecture. This is surprising, since several of the EISA systems introduced to date have been in the high end server arena, where address and data parity checking has been "standard" for many years. There are also no signals defined for anything comparable to the streaming-data procedures of Micro Channel architecture.

There are four EISA signals that can be used for unique functions by a given manufacturer. In addition, there are five reserved pins. The function of these manufacturer-specific signals and reserved pins is open for speculation at this time. One guess is that the reserved pins may be used for implementation of something like the streaming-data procedures defined in Micro Channel architecture or for address and data parity. There do not appear to be enough reserved pins to implement both of these features, however.

Timing Considerations and Data Transfers

The EISA bus is a synchronous bus. Bus cycles use a clock located on the system board as the reference for the transfer. The system board is the source of almost all activity, and has the job of adjusting the bus clock characteristics to achieve the best performance of the CPU and memory. Because of these adjustable clock characteristics, a variety of cycle types that cover a range of speeds and transfer types are provided. There are, of course, numerous types of transfers and timings required for transferring information from one bus to the other and from the many versions of ISA cards to other devices.

At this time, all EISA systems use a set of Intel chips that control all these various transactions. The set of four chips is collectively called the 82350 chip set. Three of these chips are used on the system board and the fourth chip is designed as a bus master interface to be used on expansion boards. These three system board chips support Intel's i386 and i486 processors. There are different versions required for the 25-MHz and 33-MHz microprocessors. The heart of EISA implementations is the EISA BUS CONTROLLER (the EBC). This chip acts as a traffic cop for the movement of information within the system. It provides the interface to the host CPU and the other buses, translates the data bus width to and from the three buses, controls 8-, 16-, and 32-bit masters and slaves, and numerous other functions.

The Intel chip set is almost inseparable from EISA architecture. It is difficult to imagine an implementation of EISA that does not use a very similar design, if compatibility with ISA boards is a part of the architecture. Control of the timings and bus translations is exclusively in its province. The design of the chip set is also directly related to the microprocessor characteristics on the CPU-Memory bus, which is keyed to Intel CISC microprocessors.

Micro Channel architecture contrasts strongly with these fixed characteristics of EISA, if current systems are representative. There is no direct relationship between the type of microprocessor nor its timing characteristics and the timings of the bus cycles because of the processor independent and asynchronous nature of the Micro Channel bus. This is true in the older system as well as in newly designed systems. Existing systems can accommodate higher speed and different types of system masters. Future systems can also be designed with different masters on the system board.

EISA DMA Operations

DMA operations are very similar to those of the AT bus. EISA provides for full 32-bit DMA transfers instead of the 16-bit AT capabilities. The transfers are parallel as opposed to the serial transfers of Micro Channel DMA operations. Thus, DMA operations for EISA are single step if both the source and the target have the same data path width and reside on the same bus. If the data paths are different, however, multiple steps are required. For example, transferring information from 32-bit devices to 8-bit devices requires four steps. The data transfers are conducted at the rate of the slowest participant. Micro Channel's serial DMA capabilities are conducted at the maximum data rates between the participants, which may be different for the serial operations. A complete discussion of serial versus parallel DMA capabilities is contained in Chapter 4.

EISA defines several different types of DMA operations, depending on the characteristics of the various devices. The slowest DMA speeds are designed for the slowest ISA cards. The fastest DMA speeds are used for transfers to and from EISA cards that are designed to support burst transfers. Table 6.3 summarizes the various DMA data rates supported by EISA and Micro Channel architecture. These are maximum data rates as opposed to sustained data rates and do not include any overhead or memory refresh cycles, which would, of course, reduce these numbers.

The two architectures appear to have a different philosophy in terms of the role of the DMA controller in DMA transfers. Micro Channel architecture focuses on the bus master as the prime mover of information to and from memory. The role of the DMA controller is secondary and is there basically for compatibility.

The data rates involving bus master transfers for the two architectures (Table 6.3) show definite advantages for Micro Channel architecture. However, the faster data rate that has been implemented in Micro Channel systems to date is 40 MB/sec. In the case of EISA, the fastest rate is 33 MB/sec.

TABLE 6.3 MICRO CHANNEL AND EISA DATA TRANSFER RATES

Tranfer Type System	**Micro Channel**	**EISA System EISA Cards**	**EISA ISA Cards**
DMA BASIC (MB/sec)			
8-bit	2.5/5.0*	2.0	1.0/1.3/2.0
16-bit	5/10	4.0	2.0/2.6/4.0
32-bit	10/20	8.0	NA
DMA STREAM/BURST (MB/sec)			
8-bit	NA	8.2	NA
16-bit	10/20	16.5	NA
32-bit	20/40	33.0	NA
64-bit	40/80	NA	NA
BUS MASTER BASIC (MB/sec)			
8-bit	5	NA	2.6
16-bit	10	8.2	5.3/8.2
32-bit	20	16.5	NA
BUS MASTER STREAM/BURST (MB/sec)			
8-bit	NA	NA	NA
16-bit	20	16.5	NA
32-bit	40	33.0	NA
64-bit	80	NA	NA

*The lower number is for third-party DMA transfers (two steps). The higher number is for DMA operations using bus masters (one step).

The chart shows that maximum data rates for Micro Channel systems greatly exceed what is currently defined by EISA, but, so far, actual implemented data rates are not greatly different. EISA has not defined any direction for increasing data rates beyond the current 33 MB/sec maximum. While it is possible to increase the clock speed for EISA systems, loss of compatibility with ISA boards may result. There are some other possibilities for increasing data rates in EISA systems, but the currently implemented data rates are probably more than adequate for today's environments.

EISA vs. Micro Channel Arbitration

EISA systems implement a centralized arbitration method (Figure 6.4) as opposed to the distributed method used in Micro Channel systems. In the EISA method, the central arbitration logic actually determines which of the devices is granted control of the bus. This is in contrast to the distributed arbitration method used in Micro Channel systems, in which the arbitrating devices determine ownership.

EISA systems use a rotating arbitration method. Bus ownership priority is established by their position in the rotation rather than the order in which they assert requests. Compatibility with ISA cards imposes certain restrictions on the arbitration priorities for EISA. Because memory cards may reside on the ISA bus, memory refresh cycles must be made available for these cards on a timely basis. In addition, ISA cards that function as DMA slaves must also be served in a timely

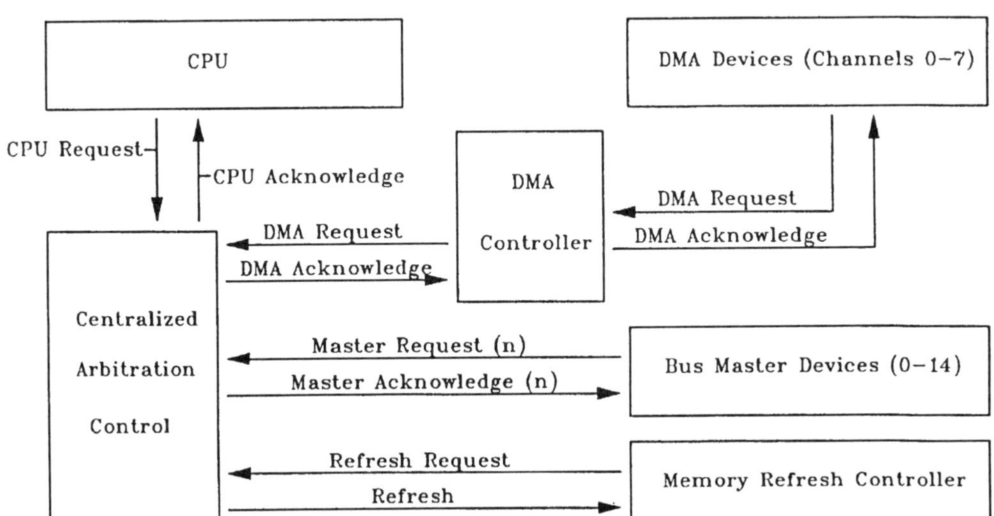

Figure 6.4 EISA arbitration is centralized using the centralized arbitration control logic.

fashion. Both ISA memory cards and DMA devices were designed with highly specific timing characteristics and must be serviced first.

The EISA arbitration scheme is illustrated in Figure 6.5. EISA provides for a fixed DMA priority arbitration sequence and, alternately, a rotating sequence. In the first case, bus access is granted sequentially to the highest priority DMA channel, the refresh controller, and either the system master or a bus master in rotational sequence. In the second case, the only difference is that there is another rotation involving the DMA channels.

The DMA subsystem is given some preference in order to provide compatibility with existing ISA DMA devices, however. The EISA specification devotes several pages to the characterization of the latencies that may be experienced in the various arbitration situations. Some of these latencies can be quite long, requiring extensive buffering to be used on EISA bus masters.

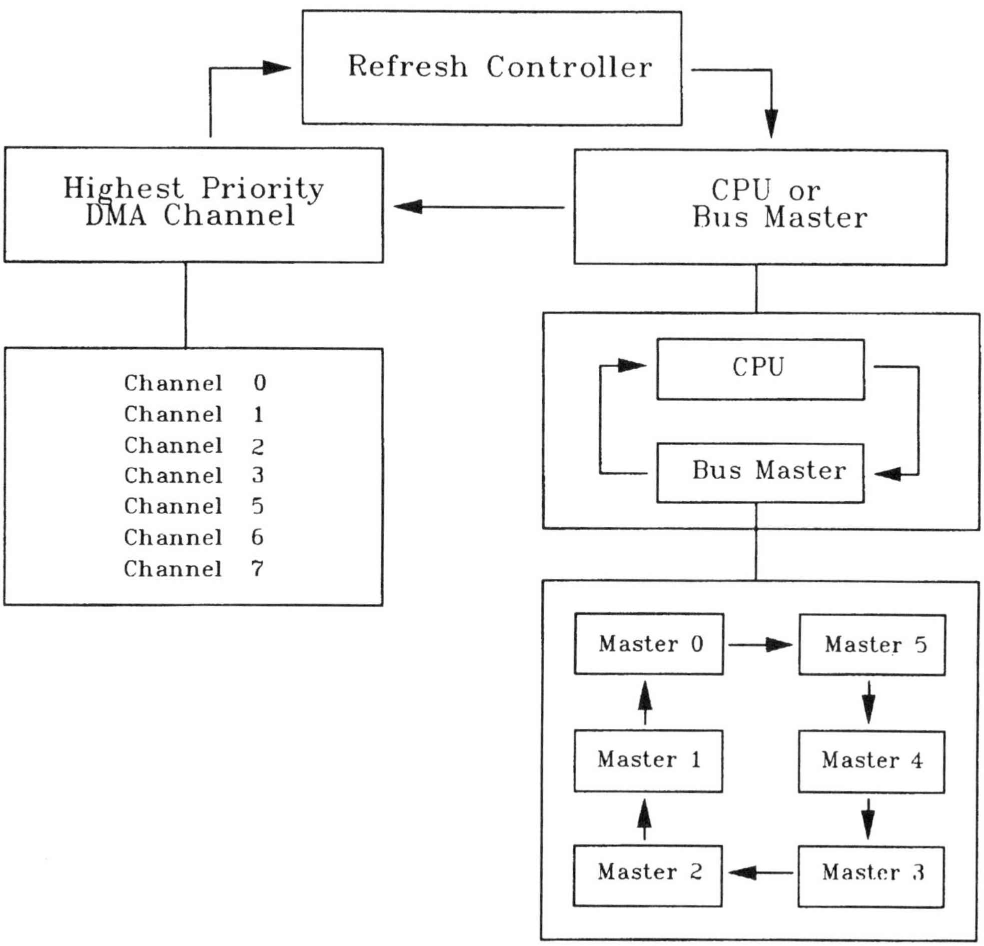

Figure 6.5 EISA arbitration involves a round-robin procedure.

A possible arbitration sequence is shown below:

1. MEMORY REFRESH
2. SYSTEM MASTER
3. DMA CHANNEL 0
4. BUS MASTER 1
5. DMA CHANNEL 1
6. BUS MASTER 2
7. DMA CHANNEL 0
8. MEMORY REFRESH
9. SYSTEM MASTER
10. DMA CHANNEL 4
11. ETC.

The Micro Channel arbitration procedure was described in Chapter 3. The main differences between the two arbitration procedures is the flexibility and programmability of Micro Channel priorities compared to the relatively fixed assignments of the EISA architecture. Thus, priorities can be changed depending on the application environment. In the case of EISA, it is possible for a critical bus master to wait a very long time until it gets serviced, especially when there are many devices requesting the bus. It is also possible for masters on the ISA bus to dominate the bus since there doesn't appear to be a provision for EISA masters to preempt ISA masters.

Micro Channel architecture provides for 16 arbitration levels and EISA 15. The system master "owns" one of these levels in both architectures (DMA Channel 4 for EISA Systems). Micro Channel architecture provides the flexibility to assign all 15 of the remaining levels to be used for any combination of DMA channels and bus masters even though current implementations use eight of these levels for DMA channels. In order to increase EISA DMA channels beyond seven, a physical connector change is required.

Overall, the EISA arbitration scheme is fundamentally sound. It represents a reasonable compromise for bus ownership between ISA and EISA devices. Even though some of the priorities may appear to be reversed in some cases, the difference will probably not be apparent in most EISA systems. The lack of flexibility will be most apparent to designers of EISA boards in the near term and will cause costs to be somewhat higher due to the added buffer requirements.

EISA Automatic System Configuration

EISA systems have a partial method of configuring systems automatically. Devices that exist on the system board (for instance, serial ports, parallel ports and VGA) can be fully configured automatically. EISA expansion boards are given the option of including configuration files with their products that can be used for automatic configuration provided the boards are designed with programmability in mind. EISA and ISA boards that have switches require manual switch setting. There is, of course, no way to make ISA boards fully programmable since they were not designed for this purpose.

EISA uses a slot-specific method for assigning I/O addresses. No two slots have the same I/O address range, so conflicts are avoided for EISA cards. This is similar to the approach used by NuBus described later in this chapter. This geographic addressing, as it is called, provides a simple method for a device to be selected. Micro Channel boards have to be smart enough to determine if they are the selected device.

EISA also includes a product identification mechanism similar to that used for Micro Channel boards. The identifier of each product is selected by the manufacturer and does not need the approval of the other members of the consortium. The numbers are registered with BCPR Services, the legal firm that is responsible for the distribution of the EISA specification. This is in contrast to Micro Channel identification numbers, which are supplied by IBM. In the case of EISA boards, configuration problems are possible if the selection guidelines are not followed. For Micro Channel boards, each one has a unique identification code that cannot be used by another device. Both schemes are workable, however.

For those devices that are programmable for automatic configuration, the process for EISA boards is almost identical to that of Micro Channel boards. A summary of the steps is shown below:

1. The configuration files are read.
2. The system resources are allocated to create a conflict-free system.
3. The configuration information is saved on a diskette.
4. The configuration is then written into the system's nonvolatile memory.
5. The configuration information contained in the system's nonvolatile memory on powering up the system is read, and the expansion boards are "initialized" or are given their resource assignments.

Overall, the most important difference between EISA's and Micro Channel's automatic configuration schemes is that Micro Channel provides a complete solution, allowing all devices to be configured. Only the EISA expansion boards and EISA system devices can participate in automatic setup. One still must manually set the switches on the old boards. In some cases, the allowable switch settings for ISA boards are not readily available, which makes setup difficult to say the least.

Interrupt Handling Procedures

EISA provides for 11 interrupts, which are assigned at setup time. ISA levels are set using switches on the boards and some are hard-wired (cannot be changed). In the case of EISA devices, interrupt handling uses a level-sensitive method similar to that used by Micro Channel systems. ISA devices require edge-triggered interrupt handling. Even though level-sensitive interrupt handling is preferable, there is no way to change the design of the older ISA boards. However, each interrupt line can be programmed for either level-sensitive or edge-triggered mode so that both can exist in the same systems. Because of this, EISA devices can share interrupt lines.

EISA defines a procedure for sharing interrupt request lines similar to that of Micro Channel architecture. Of course, any interrupt lines assigned to ISA cards cannot be shared since there was no provision for sharing for these boards. In addition, some ISA boards are required to use specific interrupt lines, and this could result in unresolvable conflicts.

Technical Summary: EISA vs. Micro Channel Architecture

Let's summarize. The number one technical advantage that EISA architecture has over Micro Channel architecture is its compatibility with AT boards. If this is important, then EISA definitely has the advantage. However, many of these boards were built using older designs and slower logic. Because of the high-end applications that EISA systems are currently targeting, AT boards won't meet the needs, so compatibility may not be as important. This will be especially true after a reasonable number of EISA expansion boards are available.

The price of compatibility is high. The EISA approach is unnecessarily complex because of it, and EISA bus masters have low priorities as a result. The bus speed is not as fast as it could have been if it were not for the ISA compatibility requirement. Some of the EMC problems of ISA cards also carry over to the EISA environment. Automatic configuration and interrupt sharing are limited to EISA boards.

Obviously, both Micro Channel and EISA architectures have many common features and offer significant advantages over the AT architecture. In some cases, EISA offers a partial advantage due to its compatibility with AT expansion boards. Its flexibility and performance capabilities are likewise limited by the same factors.

Based on the available implementations today for systems in the 386/486 category, the apparent technical features in the two buses are not greatly different if only EISA boards are used, although Micro Channel has the edge. What is important is that there are a large number of advanced function Micro Channel boards available today, but very few EISA boards. Over time, this situation may change, but the very large numbers of Micro Channel systems represent a larger opportunity for board vendors, with less risk than the relatively low EISA volumes.

However, the real differences in the two architectures do not lie in today's 386/486 implementations, but in other processor families and future implementations. There is no doubt that Micro Channel is far more flexible, has higher performance capabilities, and is a much richer and broader architecture than EISA. It has superior data integrity features that make it much more appropriate for use in a multitasking or multi-user environment than EISA. These features have already been implemented in the RISC System/6000 family and are anticipated in other systems in the near future.

Additional Information

Copies of the EISA specification may be obtained through BCPR Services, Inc., 1400 L Street N.W., Washington, DC 20005-3502, telephone (202) 371-5921, FAX (202) 371-5922, Bulletin Board (202) 371-5924. An information kit is also available on request. The cost of the complete specification is $450. A partial version is available for $125.

MICRO CHANNEL ARCHITECTURE VS NUBUS

NuBus is an industry standard bus that originated at M.I.T. in the late 1970s. The goals of NuBus were the creation of a simple 32-bit backplane bus that was independent of a particular CPU type and was also suitable for multiprocessor systems. This "bus-based" concept was first described by M.I.T. professors Steve Ward and Chris Terman in 1979 and was later specified and prototyped. Western Digital worked with the M.I.T. group to enhance the original concepts and to refine the engineering. The results of this joint effort was the essence of the present NuBus. In 1983, the work was moved to Texas Instruments, who further pursued its development. (Texas Instruments also owns the trademark and several related patents.) The bus was presented to an IEEE working group with the hope that it could become a "sister" bus to Futurebus, described later in this chapter. Unfortunately, this did not happen, and a separate work group for NuBus was established in 1984. The result of this work group activity is the ANSI/IEEE Std. 1196-1987, the current bus definition.

Today, NuBus in used in the Macintosh II and the Next system. Texas Instruments also used the bus in its System 1500, a multiprocessor system, and the Explorer LX, a system used for artificial intelligence development.

NuBus is an elegantly simple bus. It has only 96 signals, 45 of which are ground and power pins. This small pin count earns it top honors for delivering the most function with the fewest signals (Table 6.4). Part of this simplicity and low pin count is due to its multiplexed data and address bus. The address bus is also used to transfer data similar to Micro Channel's 64-bit streaming-data procedure. However, the multiplexing in NuBus yields 32-bit data transfers.

NuBus has many other features in common with Micro Channel architecture. It is a 32-bit high data rate bus that supports multiple masters with an arbitration bus and fairness algorithm, has automatic configuration capabilities, block move capabilities, superior electromagnetic characteristics, parity features, and operates at 10 MHz. It is a synchronous bus architecture with some of the timing flexibility of an asynchronous bus. The number of clock periods is allowed to vary, providing a range of timings for attached devices.

The multiple master capability of NuBus allows a Mac to do a reasonable imitation of an IBM PC by supporting an expansion board with a 386 microprocessor. Conversely, installing an expansion board with a Motorola 680X0 microprocessor (the Mac II's "engine") in a Micro Channel system allows that system to run Motorola 680X0 applications with the appropriate software support.

Both NuBus and Micro Channel architectures are "democratic" in nature. That is, the expansion board devices are not subordinate to the devices on the system board. In both Micro Channel and NuBus systems (for example, the Mac II), the system microprocessor effectively occupies a "slot" that has the same rights and privileges as the other expansion boards.

TABLE 6.4 NUBUS SIGNALS. NuBus gets top honors for its advanced bus features with a minimum number of signals.

Signal Type	Signal	Function
Address/Data	AD31–AD0	Address and Data Lines (Multiplexed)
Timing and Control	Start	Start
	ACK	Acknowledge
	TM0	Transfer Mode 0
	TM1	Transfer Mode 1
	CLK	Clock
	NMRQ	Non-master request Provides an interrupt mechanism for slaves
Arbitration	ARB3–ARB0	Used for arbitration
	RQST	Request
Parity	SP	System Parity
	SPV	System Parity Valid
Slot ID	ID3–ID0	Slot identification
Electrical	+5VDC	Power lines for various voltages
	+12VDC	
	-12VDC	
	-5.2VDC	
	GND	
Miscellanous	RESET	Resets the system
	PFW	Power Fail Warning
Total	96	

A closer look reveals some significant differences, however. NuBus has no third-party DMA transfers using a DMA controller. Transfers are between bus masters and slaves. As you learned previously, these transfers are more efficient than third-party DMA transactions, anyway.

Another difference lies in the method of handling interrupts, where NuBus interrupt capabilities are limited in comparison to Micro Channel architecture. NuBus defines a single interrupt signal to be shared by all devices. The software must poll the slots to determine the source of the interrupt. Another interrupt procedure requires a device to be implemented with write transactions into an area of memory that is monitored by that processor. This can only be used by a master however. The Macintosh II uses an interrupt handling method that is not defined by NuBus. It adds signals for each slot to be used for interrupts signals to the 680X0.

The absence of DMA capabilities and the method of handling interrupts are some of the reasons why IBM did not adopt NuBus for its 32-bit bus standard. The lack of DMA and the different method of handling interrupts would have prohibited software compatibility with the PC and the AT.

Another significant difference in the two buses lies in the basic philosophy of resource sharing by multiprocessors. NuBus has chosen to manage the sharing of resources such as system memory in the hardware architecture. IBM has chosen to handle resource sharing utilizing software, the Subsystem Control Block Architecture. The use of control block architecture as a programming model in multiprocessor implementations such as the System/370 is a proven approach to resource sharing and one that IBM chose because of its flexibility. Since SCB Architecture can be tailored to fit the varied operating system environments of Micro Channel systems, it is the better choice.

Additional Information

Additional information regarding NuBus may be obtained by contacting NuGroup, 13762 Newport Ave., Suite 204, Tustin, CA 92680, telephone (714) 669-1201. NuGroup is a manufacturer/user group formed to encourage the use of NuBus and to provide technical support for its users. Membership in NuGroup includes a copy of the IEEE-1196 specification and NuBus happenings.

MICRO CHANNEL ARCHITECTURE VS FUTUREBUS

Futurebus has several similarities to NuBus. It is a multiplexed bus that uses the same 32 bus lines for data and address on a single 96-pin connector. As mentioned earlier, the goal was compatibility for the two buses.

Futurebus also has numerous features in common with Micro Channel architecture. It is a multiple master processor-independent architecture featuring a separate arbitration bus, burst mode and streaming-data procedures, and high data rates.

Futurebus is an asynchronous bus, does not require a central clock, and should be able to accommodate faster technologies in the future, while retaining compatibility with slower devices. Sound familiar? Micro Channel's asynchronous characteristics also provide this capability.

Another important attribute of Futurebus is that there is no limitation on its data rate. Since there is no maximum defined, the nod goes to Futurebus on this one compared to Micro Channel's 160 MB/sec, the currently defined maximum. However, the same technology that will allow Futurebus to achieve higher data rates can probably be applied to Micro Channel architecture, with a connector change. The significance of data rates in excess of 100 MB/sec remains to be seen, however, since the bandwidth of either bus is not expected to inhibit performance for a long time.

Futurebus designers have paid very close attention to resource sharing among multiprocessors. One unique aspect of Futurebus is the ability to support three-party transactions involving a master, a slave, and a third-party cache or multiple slaves. This contrasts with Micro Channel architecture, in which there are only two-party transactions, involving a master and a slave. The problem of maintaining valid information in multiprocessor caches residing on the bus is not resolved in Micro Channel architecture. It is not clear how IBM and other Micro Channel manufacturers plan to proceed in this area, but they may choose to extend Subsystem Control Block architecture. However, the consequence of not implementing three-party bus procedures are additional cycles to ensure that all caches have the latest information. In very fast buses, this problem would probably not result in performance losses, however, since the number of bus cycles would not be the limiting factor.

Futurebus also has a number of features that are designed specifically for fault-tolerance. A power cable and procedures are defined that allow the live insertion and removal of a board in an operating system. Another important fault-tolerant feature in Futurebus is that it makes provision for redundant buses. These features are a level above what is currently a part of Micro Channel architecture. The use of redundant boards and dynamic reconfiguration is, however, a key part of Micro Channel architecture. The difference is that there is no provision for the live insertion and removal of cards.

To summarize, Futurebus and the Micro Channel bus have a great deal in common. However, in terms of implementation, Micro Channel systems are far ahead. Most of the advantages of Futurebus truly lie in the future and are not well-defined in terms of implementation. Futurebus is viewed as being a more advanced bus architecture than Micro Channel by many, but there are many unanswered implementation questions. Perhaps Futurebus is an appropriate name!

CONCLUSIONS, TECHNICALLY SPEAKING

The conclusions of almost every technical analyst would give Micro Channel architecture the edge in terms of technical merits over the other contenders, with the possible exception of Futurebus. This author's technical ranking of the architectures would look like this:

Micro Channel

NuBus

EISA

AT

(I have chosen not to include Futurebus in this ranking because of the lack of implementation in systems. While Futurebus has many desirable features, ranking it would be purely rhetorical.)

The above ranking of bus architectures may not be so obvious in today's systems and computing environments, however. This is due to a variety of reasons. Some of these features may not be incorporated in systems built today, for example. Or, the bus data rate does not translate into a performance benefit because the speed of the I/O devices is so slow. Adapter cards may not be available that demonstrate these benefits. Some of the advantages depend on the development of software support in the future. In terms of error rates, the end user may not be aware of the true error rates of these systems because the operating system covers them up.

The framework of this conclusion is strategic, however. In the long term, these differences will become more and more apparent. The pervasiveness of multitasking and 32-bit operating systems and expansion boards in the near future will differentiate these bus architectures. As I/O devices become faster and faster, the data rate differences will become more important. The processor-independent nature of Micro Channel architecture and its asynchronous characteristics will provide technical longevity.

SUMMARY

This chapter was designed to provide a practical approach to choosing a bus architecture for microcomputers for the coming decade. A technical analysis of the major contenders was included using the important concepts developed earlier in the book. Hopefully, the "bits and bytes" approach in this chapter was tempered with a realistic assessment of industry trends.

QUESTIONS

1. What applications do you have that would benefit from a 32-bit I/O bus?
2. Compare arbitration methods in Micro Channel, EISA, and NuBus. What are the ramifications on expansion board design? System board design?
3. What is the function of the EISA bus controller? What is its relationship to the system CPU?
4. Name some features of Micro Channel architecture that EISA and NuBus do not provide. Name some features of EISA and NuBus that Micro Channel lacks.
5. Compare the use of third-party DMA transfers in the three 32-bit bus architectures.
6. How do EISA and NuBus achieve automatic system configuration?
7. What are some of the unique features of Futurebus?

7

Getting Down to Business

Our final chapter is designed to consolidate the information presented earlier and present an orderly view for future directions. In the previous chapter, the technical merits of various bus architectures were discussed. The conclusions were somewhat rhetorical, however. In most organizations, it is not possible to instantly convert to a 32-bit bus standard, regardless of its technical merits. Most environments are a complex mixture of systems based on various bus architectures with widely varying user requirements. How to effectively utilize AT and Micro Channel systems in the same organization and to manage the migration to Micro Channel architecture in the "real world" is the focus of this final chapter.

These topics will be especially interesting for MIS managers and those of you who are responsible for equipment purchases and inventory management.

"AND THE WINNER IS..."

Now that we have explored the technical factors, let's return to the real question: "What is the best long-term strategy for microcomputer bus architecture for your organization?" Remember the list of attributes that were described for the ideal bus architecture in Chapter 1? In case you have forgotten, the list is repeated below:

*Computer Architecture Characteristics**

Affordability	Flexibility
Compatibility	Industry Acceptance
Data Integrity	Investment Protection

Ease of Use	Performance
Expandability	RAS Characteristics
Extendibility	

* Not Prioritized

In order to answer the question regarding the strategic bus architecture choices, you must first rank the importance of these attributes. There is no universal "right" answer, however. What is important to one company or organization may not be at all important to others. In addition, priorities of a given company may change over time. Also, these priorities are certainly different for different application environments.

If affordability is at the top of your list, you would probably choose AT bus entry systems for short-term value. For longer-term value, 16-bit Micro Channel systems are the best choice because of their investment protection features. On the basis of overall technical merits, Micro Channel is the winner. If backward compatibility with AT cards is at the top of your list, EISA is the answer. If Apple compatibility tops your list of priorities, your choice is NuBus.

In terms of IBM's priorities, data integrity was at the top of the list in developing Micro Channel architecture. Nothing is more important than data integrity in computer architecture. There was no room for compromise on this point. Compatibility across multiple platforms for years to come was also high on the list. However, the best news is that Micro Channel architecture provides all the characteristics on the list in both current and future systems.

The other bus architectures provide some of these attributes, of course. There are several outstanding examples of systems based on NuBus, EISA, and AT architecture. But the benefits of Micro Channel architecture are much broader in their scope, affecting many more system implementations and delivering benefits to a much wider range of applications.

DECISIONS, DECISIONS, DECISIONS

In order to better understand how business factors influence the choice of bus architecture, let's examine some typical situations.

Scenario 1

The Tick Tock Watch Company is under extreme cost constraints. They manufacture windup watches, having recently sold their quartz division to another company. Their revenues are flat, and the company is in the process of reducing the number of employees. They have decided to make DOS their strategic operating system for their workstations for the next few years. They have a hodgepodge of XT and AT clones from a variety of manufacturers. The company has a small inventory of AT expansion boards and parts.

Recommendations

This company is in trouble. Because of its obsolete product line, it probably won't be in business in two years unless it can be transformed to a growth business. Obviously, its priorities begin and end with affordability. This is a clear cut case for the purchase of systems based on the AT bus at the workstation level, for several reasons. The existing board and parts inventory can be effectively utilized. The choice of DOS as the operating system and the absence of LANs are also factors.

Because of the large number of system vendors and offerings in the AT marketplace, it may be possible to obtain entry systems at lower prices than the other buses. Vendor selection is extremely important, however. For any new system purchases, this company should focus on vendors whose products have a high resale value and whose staying power in the business is secure. If the company truly goes under in a couple of years, it will be selling all of its data processing assets. Another possibility that should be investigated is leasing equipment instead of purchasing.

Scenario 2

Med Tech, Inc. (a fictitious company) is a small growth company with rapidly increasing revenues, whose primary business is designing and manufacturing innovative medical diagnostic equipment. Most of the profits are reinvested to provide for future growth rather than distributed to the stockholders. Their workstation strategy is to enable automation in every aspect of their business. Most of their employees are technical people who use their workstations for design and functional simulation of their leading edge equipment. They have very high processing requirements at their workstations. They plan to have numerous LAN servers in order to provide electronic mail services and shared graphical files of their complex designs.

Recommendations

This is an easy one. This environment can benefit immediately from standardizing on the Micro Channel bus. Selection of technical workstations and servers from the RISC System/6000 family for their UNIX applications is definitely recommended for Med Tech. Additional servers and workstations in the PS/2 system family or Micro Channel systems from other manufacturers for business and office applications are indicated. This company needs a great deal of processing power and capacity at all levels, and should standardize on 386SX and higher Micro Channel platforms in order to run 32-bit applications. It is clear that performance and current and future compatibility is very near the top of their list of priorities for their strategic bus architecture.

Scenario 3

The two scenarios above are, of course, quite atypical. Most of the time our choices are not so clearly defined. Our final scenario is more representative of most organizations today.

SMI International (a fictitious company) is a medium-sized company whose primary business is life and casualty insurance for United States servicemen. The company's installed base of equipment includes a variety of systems based on the PC and AT bus. They are planning to implement a LAN strategy at the department level, but will continue to use their IBM mainframes as a central data repository. Over the next few years, they recognize that OS/2 has numerous benefits in their environment, but plan to continue with DOS as their primary operating system until the hardware costs for OS/2 are reduced.

A strategic application for their future includes image processing in order to alleviate the vast amounts of paper handling and storage. In addition, a fully automated system using expert programs for policy issuance is planned. The automated system will require an easy-to-use graphical interface and will include a marketing presentation.

Recommendations

SMI International is on the verge of implementing some extremely important applications that will contribute enormously to their productivity and profitability. This forward-thinking company is poised to gain a significant competitive advantage because of their plans for automation, networks, and image processing. Reduction in marketing and service expenses and paper-handling represent enormous potential savings.

SMI should elect Micro Channel architecture for all purchases immediately. Their strategic plans for LANs, OS/2, image processing, and multimedia will be best served by Micro Channel systems. An economical choice for their workstation standard is a desktop 386SX system with an SCSI storage subsystem. The 386SX microprocessor provides the ability to run 32-bit OS/2 when it becomes available. The Micro Channel bus delivers high-performance image processing through the use of bus masters like IBM's Image Adapter/A. SMI's image strategy would be complemented by the SCSI bus master because almost all optical storage devices feature the SCSI interface. In addition, the systems are upgradeable by using bus masters like the Aox MicroMaster 486 previously described.

For their automated policy issuance program, a good choice would be a more powerful Micro Channel system with a multimedia marketing presentation using Micro Channel products. The Audio Visual Connection and a touch screen, and an image capture system with a removable SCSI read/write optical storage device for capturing and storing a photograph of the applicant, hand-written information, and the applicant's signature are indicated for this application. A policy and wallet card could be issued at the time of application and put in force pending verification of the applicant's motor vehicle or medical records and credit card information.

Micro Channel personal systems are a good choice for the personnel engaged in actuarial research at SMI because of the ability to accommodate compute-intensive and data base "engines" like the i860 Wizard adapter. Another excellent choice would be a Micro Channel technical workstation like one of the IBM RISC/System 6000 POWERstations.

A logical choice for the departmental LAN servers are 32-bit Micro Channel systems running OS/2. These I/O-intensive applications in a multitasking environment are a perfect fit for the performance and data integrity features of Micro Channel systems.

In the case of the existing inventory of AT-bus systems, there are a number of alternatives, including downgrading systems to less sophisticated applications. What this company should not do, however, is hold up implementation plans for their strategic applications because of their existing inventory of AT-bus systems. The cost savings and productivity increases for the image processing system and automated policy issuance program will quickly pay for the additional equipment costs.

BUS STRATEGIES

Let's look at three bus strategies and how they might fit in your organization. These are the choices for IBM-compatibles:

1. Continue to invest in AT-bus systems for the foreseeable future;
2. Maintain both AT and Micro Channel bus architectures; and
3. Transition as rapidly as possible to Micro Channel architecture systems.

The AT-Bus Strategy

Let's look at the first choice. The traditional PC/XT/AT bus does not allow the use of the full capabilities of 386 and 486 architecture and does not allow any 32-bit I/O devices. Under what conditions does this make sense? If your only use for now and the future are DOS personal productivity applications, this bus strategy makes a great deal of sense. This is especially true if you are willing to trade off a shorter equipment life for a lower initial price.

Standalone systems with limited performance requirements and single-tasking applications do not exploit the full potential of Micro Channel architecture. In addition, the inability to upgrade these systems with additional processing power dictates a strategy that is based on approximately a 2–3 year equipment life. This strategy may suit your requirements quite well in the near term.

In the longer term, however, this 16-bit strategy will necessarily give way to a 32-bit I/O bus just as the 8-bit PC bus yielded to the 16-bit AT bus when the price/performance ratio became attractive enough.

A Two-Bus Strategy

For many purposes, a two bus strategy utilizing both AT and Micro Channel systems is a viable approach for the near future. The AT bus is perfectly adequate for 286 and 386SX systems for DOS applications in a standalone environment or as DOS network requesters with moderate performance requirements. It is also a good choice for laptop systems because of their limited expandability, shorter equipment life, and rapidly changing display technology. If this two bus strategy is your choice, Micro Channel systems are appropriate selections for servers and for those users who require higher performance than the 386SX systems can deliver, especially for OS/2 or UNIX applications.

This two bus approach in a good interim strategy, but is not viable in the long term. Processor power will continue to come down the cost curve, and a 32-bit I/O bus will be required to effectively utilize it. It is only a matter of time, however, that this strategy will give way to either Micro Channel or EISA bus systems.

The Micro Channel Standard

There are benefits in having a single bus strategy in most environments. Even though few boards are moved from system to system, inventory management and purchasing power are important benefits of a single bus strategy. Another benefit lies in the reduction of support and software requirements. Multiple bus strategies can add unnecessary complexity in setup, service, and software requirements.

One of the advantages of Micro Channel architecture that adds value to managing the transition to the 32-bit environment is its 16-bit system and expansion board implementations. Because 16-bit systems and boards can be built that utilize almost all of the advanced features of this architecture, this brings value to a large number of end users.

A sensible transition plan, therefore, can be based on Micro Channel 386SX systems. This effectively positions you for the 32-bit future without paying the price for the higher function immediately. It also provides a good base on which to build future applications like image processing and multimedia. As you learned previously, many 16-bit Micro Channel boards offer throughput that approaches that of 32-bit boards in some applications. Many advanced function boards available today are 16-bit implementations.

You should plan on the 386SX microprocessors being around for awhile. Faster chips and integrated functions will prolong their lives. So, a near-term investment in 16-bit Micro Channel systems and boards is a good plan.

Micro Channel expansion boards are at the beginning of their useful life rather than near obsolescence. All Micro Channel boards have been designed and built since 1987 using modern electronics and VLSI circuitry. Many of the boards built for the AT bus were designed and built years ago with older, slower components that may reduce performance in newer systems.

TRANSITION PLANNING

At this point, you are probably convinced that Micro Channel architecture represents the best choice for the bus architecture for microcomputers for the future. However, what is a sensible transition plan? Many companies have large inventories of AT boards and AT bus machines. Introducing a different bus architecture into this environment complicates inventory management and end-user support. Standardizing on Micro Channel systems with a strategy of migration over time requires some careful planning.

Some appropriate steps are listed below:

1. New purchases should be limited to Micro Channel systems. If this isn't feasible, a good place to start is with those users with high-performance requirements, as well as for server applications. Establish Micro Channel systems as the workstation standard as soon as possible, using economical 386SX systems initially.
2. Identify key applications that conclusively demonstrate the value of Micro Channel architecture solutions. Image processing, multimedia, compute-intensive, and server applications are excellent showcases for Micro Channel systems because of their dramatic cost savings and productivity improvements.
3. Develop a used-equipment plan for older systems. The time-honored method is to downgrade these systems to other users. This is still the best plan if it doesn't interfere with implementing key applications in your organization. Other alternatives are trading for new systems, selling the inventory, or donating to nonprofit organizations. Get with your "bean counter" to discuss these options in terms of accounting practices.

A NEW PARADIGM

Introducing Micro Channel systems to new users requires a new paradigm for performance. Most people think of performance in terms of raw CPU power: in order to get better performance, you need a new system with a faster CPU. For systems based on Micro Channel architecture with its multimaster capabilities, a paradigm of distributed processing is required: performance benefits are derived from expansion boards. In other words, high-performance application-specific bus masters can deliver additional power to existing systems.

While this may not be quite as exciting as a new system, it is far more cost effective and versatile (although it's hard to imagine people bragging about their new adapter). In years to come, entire computers will reside solely on expansion boards.

Where Is This Bus Going, Anyway?

Let's turn up the clock speed and move beyond the transition to the 32-bit environment and look at what the future holds. The next ten years of computing will repeat the last decade in terms of exponential technology growth. Micro Channel architecture's high-speed multimaster capabilities will play a key role in balancing performance as the capabilities of other subsystems increase dramatically.

As we learned in Chapter 5, many exciting applications are on the horizon that are enabled by these advances in technology and Micro Channel architecture (Figure 7.1). The following section focuses on the workstation environment for the 90s and how technology directions and emerging applications will exploit Micro Channel's potential.

Microprocessors

Processor clock speeds have been doubling about every two years. If this trend continues, we could see 250-MHz microprocessors capable of processing a billion instructions per second by the end of this decade.

Another important trend in microprocessors is increasing integration of associated functions. Expect to see all kinds of devices like memory and DMA controllers rolled up with microprocessors in the same packaging. Several microprocessors will be integrated in the same chip. Some possibilities include RISC and CISC integration and multiple 80X86 microprocessors. Multiple processors will become a normal upgrade path for desktop systems, as well as playing a key role in server applications. Micro Channel's multimaster capabilities, 64-bit data transfers, and data integrity features will contribute directly to the efficient use of these advances.

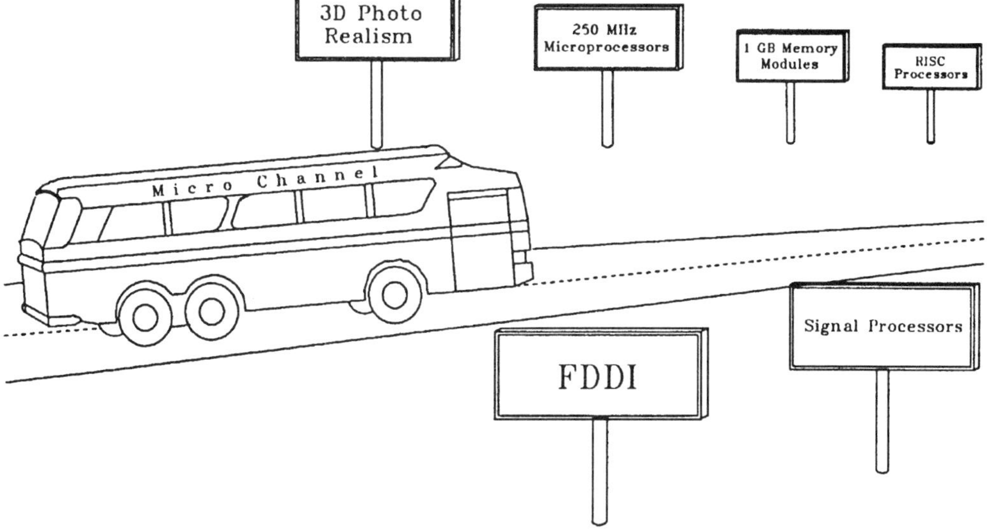

Figure 7.1 Where's this bus going, anyway?

Memory

Based on past history, memory prices will drop at a rate of approximately 30 percent per year. Workstations will have 16 MB of memory as their standard configuration relatively quickly. Within the next five years, 16-MB memory modules will become relatively common, and, by the end of the decade, we may see 1 GB memory modules! Systems will be designed with highly flexible memory controllers that are designed to take advantage of the increasing density and speed in memory technology.

Another important trend will be the decrease in the price of SRAM. High-speed SRAM will replace DRAM in many implementations. Large high-speed caches for all sorts of functions are enabled by these advances in memory technology, functions that Micro Channel's streaming-data procedures can effectively exploit.

Storage

The obvious directions are faster, denser, and cheaper. We will see 3.5-inch gigabyte fixed disk drives within the next five years. High-performance read/write optical drives will play a key role in enabling multimedia and image applications. SCSI will become the dominant storage interface and will be enhanced to much faster speeds. SCSI bus master adapters will become very intelligent in their ability to prefetch information and to manage its distribution to other devices using Micro Channel's peer-to-peer capabilities.

Communications

Besides the obvious trends toward rapidly increasing speeds, FAX will become pervasive and an integral part of system design. Every workstation will have the ability to send and receive images by using their built-in FAX modems. OS/2 and bus masters will be used to manage FAX-mail concurrently with routine applications. Workstations will be in operation 24 hours a day in order to receive and organize electronic mail. Cellular telephone technology will become a standard feature in portable systems.

Digital network communications will be in place by the mid-90s, replacing today's analog telephone communications by the end of the decade. The days of video mail and video telephones are not very far away!

Communications controllers based on Micro Channel architecture will play a key role. Very high-speed LAN adapters (>200 Mbs) based on fiber technology will require high speed multimaster I/O buses in order to use their capabilities.

Graphics and Image

Relatively soon, 3D photo-realism applications will be supported at the workstation by using bus master graphics adapters. Powerful graphics bus masters will also be used to meet the performance requirements for high-speed graphical and animated user interfaces. The convergence of television with computers will occur within the next five years, with HDTV capabilities toward the end of the decade. Flat-panel display technology will advance at a rapid rate, with color capabilities in the near future.

Powerful image processors like IBM's Image Adapter/A will be used to compress and decompress images and to display them on very high-resolutions displays. Within the next few years, image processing will become the number one productivity enhancement in business. It has been estimated that only about 2 percent of the world's business information has been digitized.[1] In the next decade, we will migrate rapidly toward a paperless society, using workstations to capture, compress, display, store, and communicate images.

PC on a Board?

Not only will this decade see the function of personal computers on expansion boards, but it will also see multiple PCs on a board! The Micro Channel bus is ideal for sharing peripherals and allowing these "PCs" to communicate between themselves. These sons and daughters of PCs will become even more powerful than their parents.

Talk, Talk, Talk!

Voice recognition and synthesis will play a very important role in the workstation of the future. Powerful chips, called digital signal processors (DSP), will become pervasive in computers, allowing voice to play a key role in the end-user interface. The multitasking operating system of the future will support voice as well as graphics and video. In the future, having a conversation with your computer is very likely!

The technology that converts sound from analog to digital signals and processes it for specific applications will produce many other innovative devices. Bringing the real world, which is predominately analog, into digital computers opens the door to applications beyond imagination. Some imaginable applications are handwriting and gesture recognition, and neural networks to help you make decisions.

SUMMARY

Having a vision of the future is very important in today's confusing environment. Knowing where you want to go is the first step to getting there. The last chapter of this book was designed to give you a clear view of the important trends in technology and applications for the 90s.

Managing transition in a changing environment is, perhaps, the most challenging of all tasks. Making the right decisions now and planning for the future are the tasks at hand. One thing is for sure: there is no question that a high-perfor-

[1]From remarks taken from the keynote address given by Mr. G. H. Conrades, IBM senior vice president and general manager, at the COMMEX®/Fall '89 Conference and Exposition in Las Vegas, Nevada.

mance multitasking bus architecture is an absolute requirement for the workstations of the 90s.

QUESTIONS

Now that you have graduated from the Micro Channel University, surely you don't have any remaining questions!

Appendix A

Glossary

Active High. A signal whose voltage must go high (positive) in order to produce an effect. The opposite of Active Low (negative).

Adapter. A unit used to attach a device to an I/O bus and make it operable. For example, a display adapter is used to attach a display to a bus and to make it operable.

Address. A number that represents a location in the address space of a computer. Addresses are assigned to memory and I/O devices.

Address Bus. The path along which addresses are transmitted. The address path width determines the maximum number of memory addresses available in a computer. Mathematically, the number of addresses is 2^n, where n is the width of the address bus. For example, a 24-bit address path permits 16 million addresses.

Address Space. The range of memory addresses that are supported in a computer. Divided into I/O and memory address space in Micro Channel architecture.

Analog. A continuously varying physical quantity. The opposite of **digital,** in which values are integers.

ANSI. American National Standards Institute. An organization devoted to establishing voluntary standards in the computer industry. Sponsored by the Computer and Business Equipment Manufacturers Association.

Application. The specific use of a computer system. For example, word processing. An application program is the program used to perform the application.

Arbitration. The procedure used to establish bus ownership by competing devices.

Arbitration Bus. The path used to transmit information related to bus ownership. It consists of signals that request and grant ownership of the bus and signals that indicate the priority, or arbitration levels, of the requesting devices.

Architecture. A set of rules that defines the limits of the capabilities of a computer system and provides commonality in structure and design.

ASCII. American National Standard Code for Information Exchange. Code developed by ANSI for the exchange of information among computers, data communication systems, and associated equipment. The ASCII character set consists of 128 possible characters of which 34 are control codes and 94 are text characters. The text characters consist of upper and lower case members of the alphabet, 10 digits, and a number of special characters. Each character consists of 7 or 8 bits, including a parity bit. An ASCII terminal is capable of displaying only ASCII characters as opposed to graphics.

Asynchronous Bus. A bus in which sending and receiving information is based on the timing characteristics of the sending and receiving devices rather than being based on predetermined times controlled by the bus timing characteristics.

Asynchronous Transmission. An unscheduled transfer. Transmission in which the time of the start of an occurrence is arbitrary.

Bus Bandwidth. The data transfer capability of a bus, usually expressed in megabytes per second (MB/sec).

Binary. A system of numbers to the base two. The digits used are 0 (zero) and 1 (one). Having only two possible states or values.

BIOS. Basic input/output system. An interface between hardware and software, developed to provide compatibility.

Bit. Either zero or one in the binary number system.

Buffer. Storage that is used to temporarily hold data. Buffers provide a method of managing the different transfer rates of the various functional units of a computer system.

Bus. The electrical path used for the transmission of information in a computer. A collection of common conductors that connect the various elements of a computer system used for the transmission of signals or power.

Bus Master. One of the three types of masters defined by Micro Channel architecture. A function that an expansion board or a device that is directly attached to the bus can have that allows it to gain control of the bus, and drive the address, data, and control lines. Sometimes used interchangeably with master. Bus masters can transfer information to and from memory slaves or to and from I/O slaves.

Byte. The amount of storage required for one alphanumeric character. Alternately, eight adjacent bits comprising the smallest addressable unit in personal computers.

Cache. Literally, to store in a hiding place for future use. A **memory cache** consists of very fast memory, usually static RAM, that is used to speed up the time for instructions and data to be fed to the processor. Instructions and data are temporarily stored in the cache for fast access by the processor. The memory cache logically resides between the processor and system memory. A **DASD cache** is used as temporary storage for disk drive data, as well as to speed up the effective retrieval time from disk drives. It may be or may not be part of system memory, but is normally dynamic RAM rather than static RAM.

CAD. Computer-Aided Design.

CAM. Computer-Aided Manufacturing.

CISC. Complex Instruction Set Computing. See also RISC.

Client/Server. The relationship established between two parties where one (the client) requests the other (the server) to perform some operation or work on its behalf.

Compatibility. The ability of a functional unit to conform to the requirements of a given interface. Examples of functional units include devices, expansion boards, adapters, and software.

Configuration. The hardware devices and programs that comprise a computer system or subsystem.

Configure. The process of describing to a computer system the installed devices for the purpose of assigning system resources required for their operation.

Control Block. A storage area used by a computer program to hold control information.

Data Bus. The path along which general information is transmitted in a computer. The width of the data bus determines how much information can be transferred at a time. For example, the IBM Personal System/2 Model 80 has a 32-bit data path, permitting 32 bits of information to be transferred simultaneously.

Default Master. The master that owns the bus when no other master requires it. In Micro Channel architecture, the system master is usually, but not necessarily, the default master.

Device. A generic term used to describe a unit that provides a specific function in a computer. For example, a storage device.

Device Driver. Operating system-specific software that is used to handle the requirements of a particular hardware device.

Diagnostics. Microcode used to detect and identify the source of hardware malfunctions.

DIP Switch. A small switch mounted in a dual in-line package.

Direct Memory Access. The process of transferring data between system memory and I/O devices without using the system CPU or system master.

Distributed Processing. A philosophy of computer processing in which some or all of the processing and control functions are situated in different locations (as opposed to centralized processing) and connected by transmission facilities.

DMA Controller. A master that supports data transfer between DMA slaves and memory slaves.

DMA Slave. A type of slave that requires the DMA controller for data transfers. One of the three types of slaves defined as participants on the Micro Channel bus. It is the only slave that can initiate a request for the channel and can arbitrate for the channel.

Duty Cycle. The ratio of on time to idle time of a device. Usually expressed as a percentage or decimal fraction.

Enable. To empower a circuit or device.

Exception Condition. An error condition in a computer. For example, a parity error.

Expanded Memory. A DOS technique used to expand memory above 640 KB. The EMS (Expanded Memory Specification) was jointly developed by Lotus, Intel, and Microsoft.

Expansion Board. A printed circuit board connected to a computer's expansion bus in parallel with others. Sometimes referred to as a card or an add-in board.

Extended Memory. Memory above 1 MB on 286-, 386SX-, 386-, and 486-based systems.

Field. An area designated for a particular category of data.

Geographic Addressing. A method of identifying the physical location of expansion boards and assigning I/O addresses accordingly. Geographic addressing is a simple method that enables automatic setup of expansion boards. NuBus uses geographic addressing. Micro Channel architecture uses expansion board identification numbers and programmable registers for automatic configuration.

Gigabyte (GB). 2^{30} power or 1,073,741,824 bytes.

IEEE. Institute of Electronic and Electrical Engineers.

Information Transfer Bus. A type of bus that may have CPU, input and output, and memory devices attached to it as opposed to an **I/O bus,** which is limited to I/O bus attachment. The Micro Channel bus is a general information transfer bus architecture.

I/O Address Space. One of the two types of address spaces defined by Micro Channel architecture, the other being the memory address space. It consists of 64 KB of I/O addresses addressed by 16 bits of the address bus.

I/O Bus. A bus that has input and output devices attached to it as opposed to an **information transfer bus,** which may have I/O, CPU, and memory devices attached to it.

I/O Slave. A type of slave selected by its I/O address. One of the three types of slaves defined as participants in Micro Channel architecture. An I/O slave may be selected by the system master and by bus masters.

Instruction. The direction that specifies an operation to be performed by a computer and the memory location of the data involved in the operation.

Integrated Adapter. The combination of an adapter and device that allows direct connection of the device. For example, many of the disk drives used in the Personal System/2 have integrated disk controllers and may be attached directly to the Micro Channel bus.

Interface. A shared boundary. A hardware component used to link two devices or buses. For example, the boundary between the Micro Channel expansion boards and the Micro Channel bus is called an interface.

Interrupt. Request for service by an I/O device. Alternately, the suspension of a process caused by an external event, managed in such a way that the process can be resumed.

Language Compiler. A program that translates instructions written in high level-language (Fortran, for example) into a machine-executable program. Its input is source code and its output is object code.

Latch. A storage element used in a logic circuit to capture information or to maintain a state.

Master. One of the participants of the Micro Channel bus that can drive the address and data bus control signals, causing data to be transferred to or from a slave. The three types of masters defined by Micro Channel architecture are the system master, the DMA controller, and the bus master.

Kilobyte (KB). 1,024 bytes.

Local Area Network (LAN). A collection of computers and associated devices connected by communication lines and limited to a small area (for example, an office building).

Megabyte (MB). 1,048,576 bytes. (In some of IBM's marketing literature, **megabyte** is sometimes abbreviated **Mb.**)

Memory Address Space. One of the two types of address spaces defined by Micro Channel architecture. It consists of either 16 MB (24-bit addressing) or 4 GB (32-bit addressing) of memory addresses.

Memory Slave. A type of slave selected by its memory address. One of the three types of slaves defined by Micro Channel architecture. A memory slave is accessible by all three types of Micro Channel masters.

Nonsystem Memory. Memory in the Micro Channel address space that is not allocated or controlled by the primary operating system. It may be physically located on a feature adapter, in which case it is referred to as memory-mapped I/O. Another example is that portion of memory occupied by the system BIOS.

Operating System. The software that controls the execution of programs, schedules tasks, allocates resources, and can provide numerous other system services.

Parallel Port. A port used to attach devices that transmit one byte of data at a time. Most printers attach to systems via the parallel port.

Parity. A condition of being either odd- or even-numbered. A parity bit is a binary digit added to a group of binary digits to make the sum either odd (odd parity) or even (even parity). It is a simple method of checking for the presence of extra or missing bits.

PEL, PIXEL, Picture Element. The smallest element of a computer graphics display that can be assigned a discrete color and intensity.

Performance. The amount of useful work that can be performed by a computer system in a given time. A measure of system productivity. Performance is primarily determined by throughput, response time, and system availability.

Private Memory. Memory that is not in the Micro Channel address space. For example, memory on a feature card that is utilized for buffering or as a large cache that cannot be accessed by other devices or the system CPU.

Procedure. A method of performing a given function that generally consists of several steps in a specified order.

Processor. A term often used instead of CPU where there may be more than one processor in a system with no one being more central in function than another.

Program. A sequence of instructions for a computer to execute.

Protect Mode. One of the modes of the 80286 and higher Intel microprocessors used for multitasking and in addressing extended memory.

Protocol. A set of rules, requirements, and procedures used for information transfer or exchange in computer systems.

Real Mode. One of the modes of the Intel family of microprocessors used for addressing memory below 1 MB. Used by DOS for single-tasking applications.

Response Time. The length of time required to service a request.

RISC. An acronym for Reduced Instruction Set Computer. A term used to refer to a class of microprocessor architectures, pioneered by IBM's John Cocke, that minimizes the complexity and number of operations in the instruction set of the microprocessor. This characteristic increases the number of instructions that can be processed simultaneously, thereby increasing the degree of parallelism. Operations that are infrequently used, such as multiplication, are performed using advanced compiler technology. The accompanying reduction in the instruction set provides a substantial increase in the price/performance characteristics of microprocessors. Examples include microprocessors used in IBM's RISC System/6000 family and Intel's i860.

SAA. Systems Application Architecture. An IBM architecture that provides a consistent set of interfaces across OS/2, OS/400®, VM™, and MVS™ operating systems. Interface consistency for programming, interconnection, and user interfaces are included in the architecture.

Scheduler. That part of the operating system that divides processor time (or other critical system resources) among several concurrent tasks, based on program priorities.

SCSI. An acronym for Small Computer System Interface. An industry standard that provides a consistent method of connecting devices to a computer. A device-independent interface that allows the attachment of multiple devices to a computer system.

Serial Port. A port used to attach devices that transfer data one bit at a time.

Slave. A participant in Micro Channel architecture that requires a master to perform data transfers to or from it. The slave is selected as either the source or the target for the transfer by the controlling master. There are three types of slaves: an I/O slave, a memory slave, and a DMA slave.

Slot. The expansion bus connector into which an expansion board is inserted.

Subsystem. The part of a system that does a specific function (for example, the storage subsystem). Alternately, a subordinate system that is capable of independent operation with the controlling system.

Subsystem Control Block (SCB). A storage area used to communicate control information to a subsystem.

Synchronous Bus. A bus in which the sending and receiving of information is controlled by timing signals. Information is transferred at predetermined times, based on the timing characteristics of the bus.

System Master. The master that controls and allocates the system resources, manages the system configuration, and upon which the primary operating system is loaded. One of the three types of masters defined as participants by Micro Channel architecture. The system master may or may not be the default master.

System Memory. Memory that is allocated and controlled by the primary operating system. Its presence is detected during the startup of the system as opposed to nonsystem or private memory. Its contents can be accessed or modified by a Micro Channel master.

Throughput. The number of tasks that can be performed by a computer system in a given amount of time.

Virtual Memory. A technique used to support programs that are larger than the total memory available. Only those segments that are needed are loaded by the operating system into memory.

Workstation. A computer device used by an individual to perform a job that is connected to other computers. A workstation may be a nonintelligent device, a "dumb terminal," or a personal computer.

Appendix B

Micro Channel Timing Diagrams

Timing diagrams are used to illustrate the signals and the proper sequence of events used in the various procedures defined by the architecture. These diagrams illustrate only when the signals used in a given procedure are active or inactive and their relative duration. A timing diagram illustrates one complete cycle of that particular procedure. In data transfers, all the procedures have one thing in common: there must be time for the address to stabilize before data flows, and it must remain stable throughout the data transfer process.

The following timing diagrams illustrate only relative times. The exact duration and sequence are contained in the technical reference manual for the architecture. They are included here as a supplement to Chapter 3.

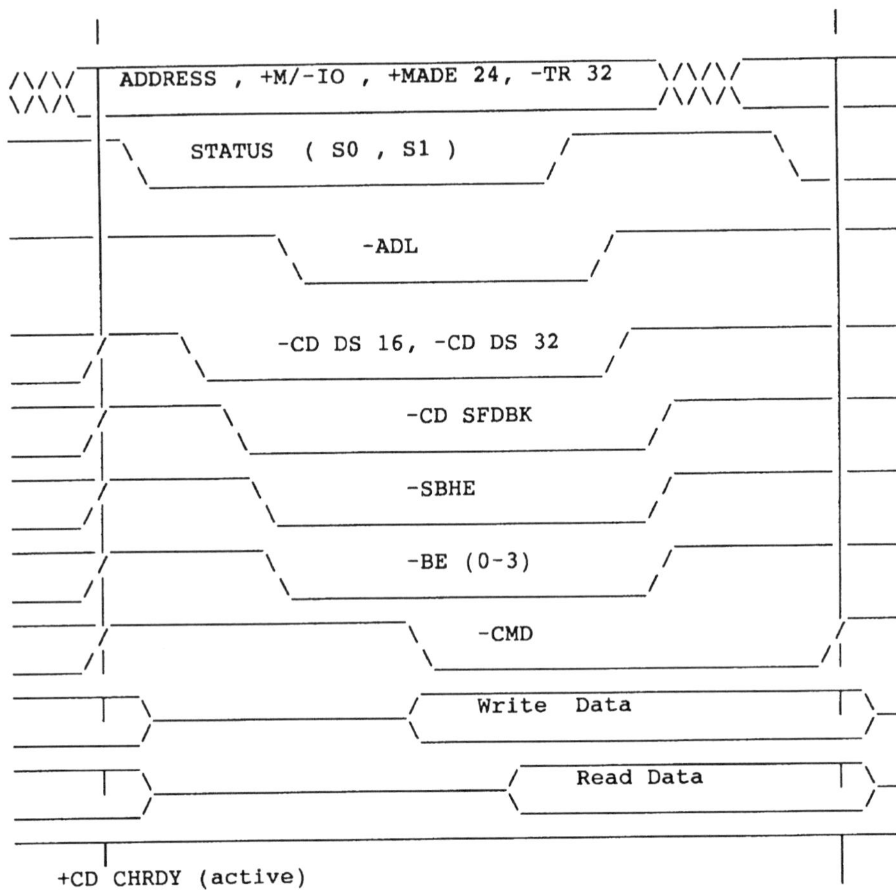

Figure B-1 Basic Transfer Cycle.

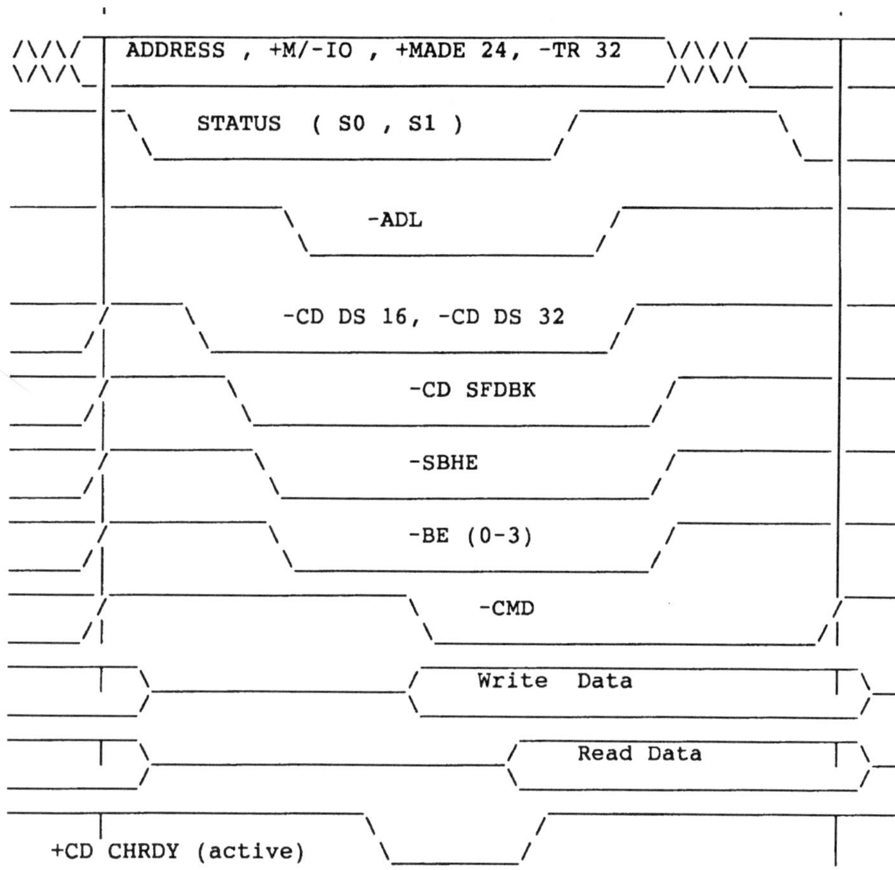

Figure B-2 Synchronous Extended Cycle.

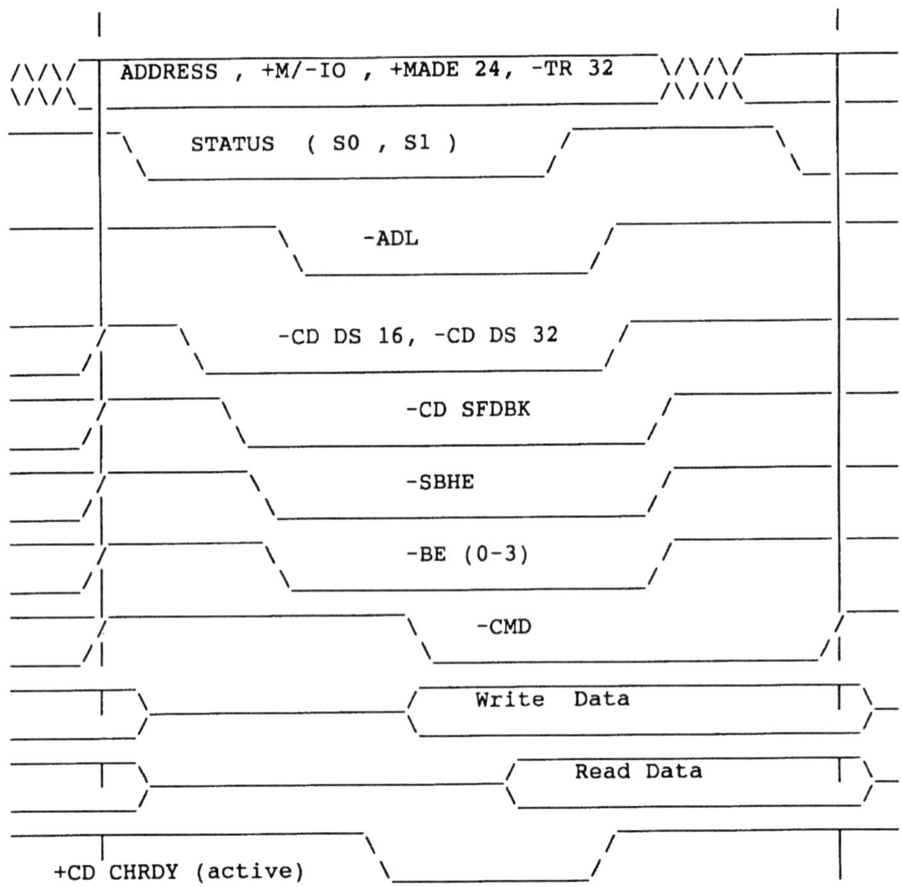

Figure B-3 Asynchronous Extended Cycle.

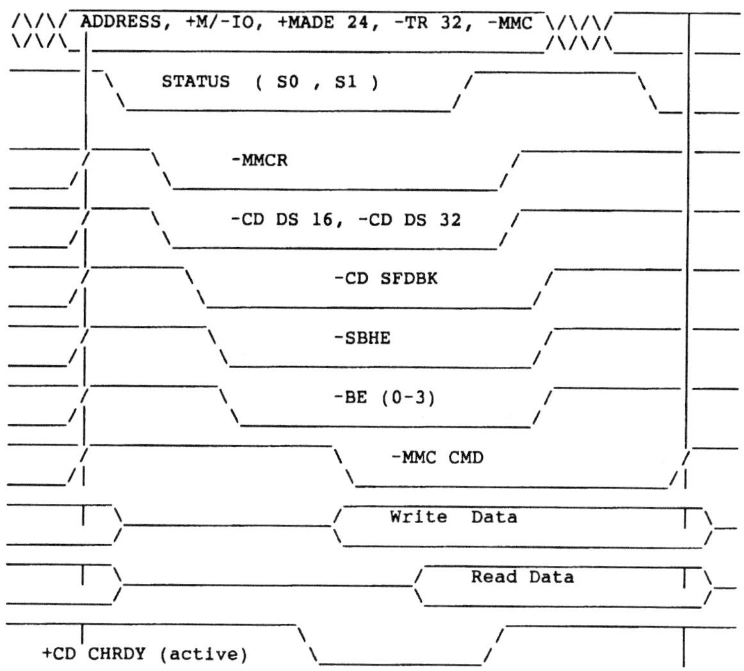

Figure B-4 Matched-Memory Transfer Cycle.

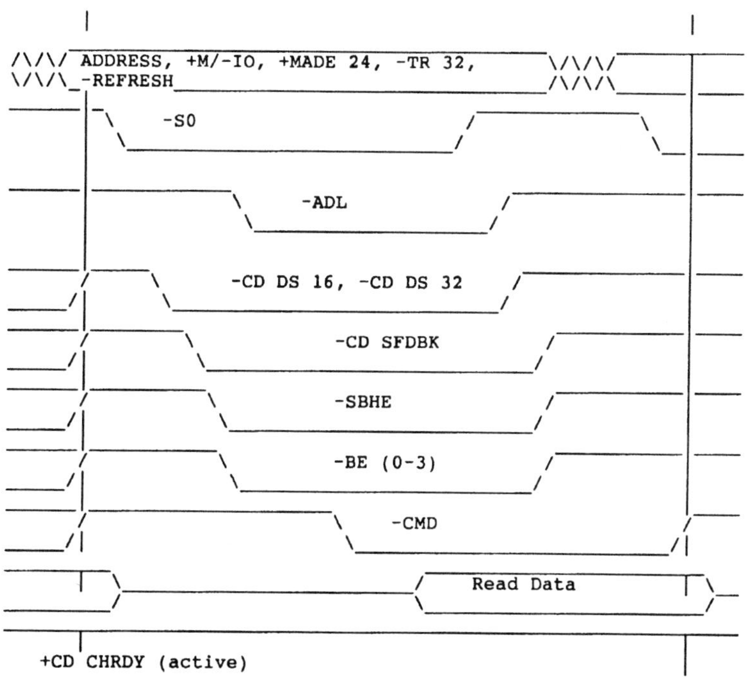

Figure B-5 Refresh Cycles.

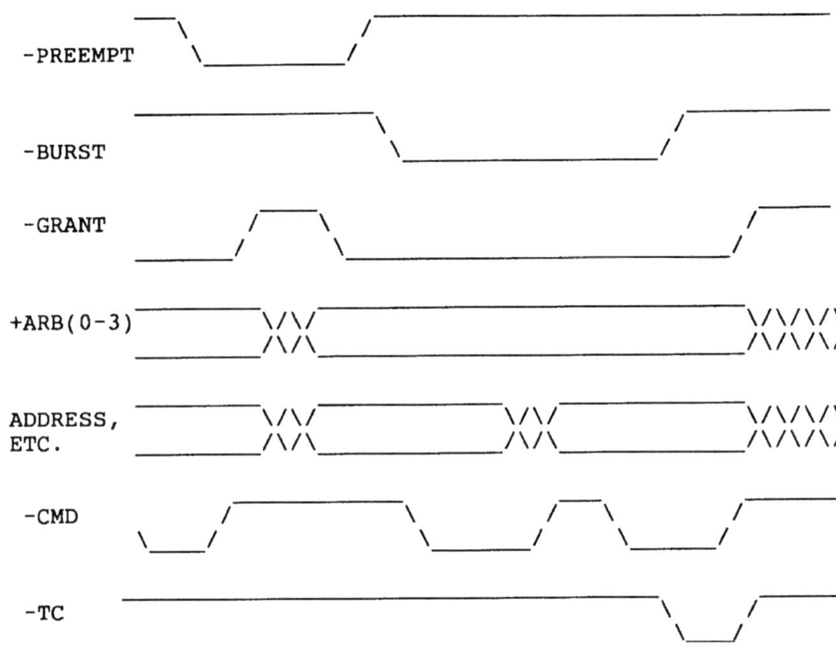

Figure B-6 Third Party DMA Read Transfer Cycle.

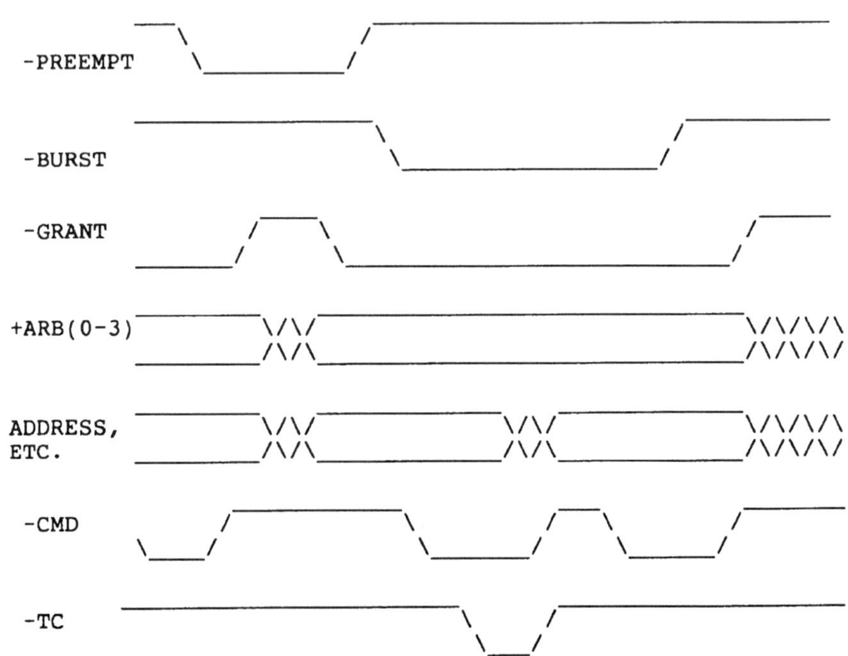

Figure B-7 Third-Party DMA Write Cycle.

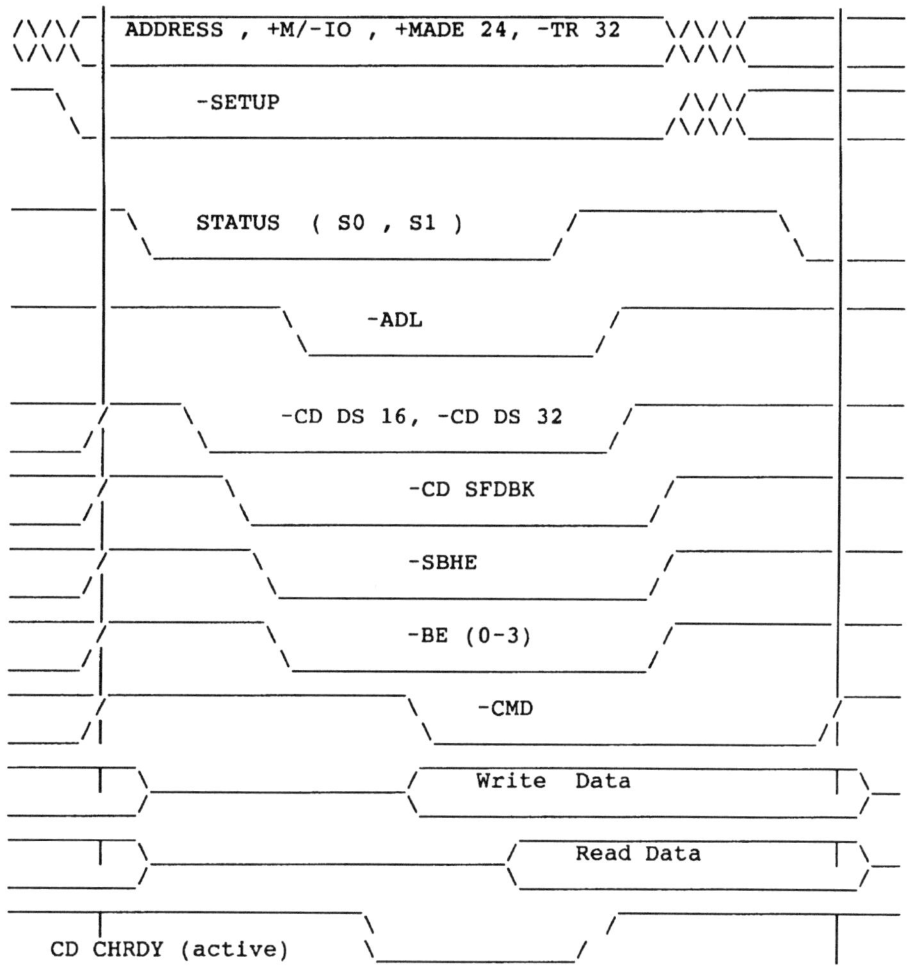

Figure B-8 Setup Cycle.

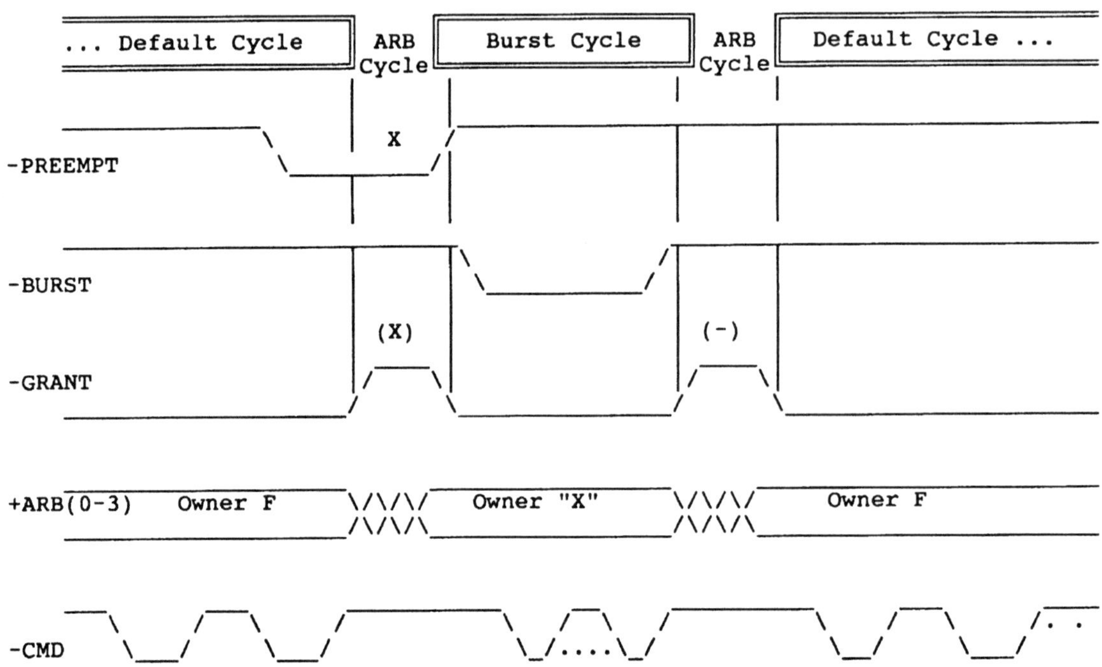

Figure B-9 Arbitration Cycles.

Appendix C

Micro Channel Chip Sets

Following is a list of companies offering Micro Channel chip sets.

IOV CHIP SETS

COMPANY: ACC Microelectronics Corporation
ADDRESS: 3295 Scott Boulevard
Suite 400
Santa Clara, CA 95054
PHONE: 1-408-980-0622
FAX: 1-408-980-0626

CHIP SET: ACC 5810 Interface Chip
AVAILABLE: 8/88
DESCRIPTION: The ACC 5810 allows designers to build Micro Channel* bus-compatible adapters in a short time and in a small real estate. It supports I/O slave, memory slave and DMA slave adapters with interrupt sharing. The flexible, predefined POS configuration simplifies the logic required for a Micro Channel bus adapter.

COMPANY: Advanced Microcomputer Systems, Inc.
ADDRESS: 1321 NW 65th Place
Fort Lauderdale, FL 33309
PHONE: 1-305-975-9515 / 1-800-972-3733
FAX: 1-305-975-9698

CHIP SET: MCPAL
AVAILABLE: 1/90
DESCRIPTION: Adaptor chip set for the Micro Channel* bus. It provides complete interface to the Micro Channel* bus. This chip set does not have a pre-assigned Programmable Option Select (POS) ID for inclusion in the user's Adapter Description File (ADF). The user must obtain a POS ID from IBM.

COMPANY: Capital Equipment Corp.
ADDRESS: 99 South Bedford Street
Burlington, MA 01803
PHONE: 1-617-273-1818 / 1-800-234-4232
FAX: 1-617-273-9057

CHIP SET: 88C01
AVAILABLE: 6/88
DESCRIPTION: A complete Micro Channel* bus interface on a chip. Includes over 20 user programmable features such as memory and I/O timing and decoding. Supports single and burst mode DMA, user defined POS bits, 8 POS registers and four independent chip selects. 84-pin CMOS PLCC package.

COMPANY: Chips & Technologies, Inc.
ADDRESS: 3050 Zanker Road
San Jose, CA 95134
PHONE: 1-408-434-0600

CHIP SET: 82C611 MicroCHIP**
AVAILABLE: 11/87
DESCRIPTION: The 82C611 MicroCHIP** (Micro Channel* bus Interface Part) is a general purpose interface component that contains most of the logic required to interface to the Micro Channel bus. It is suited for both memory and I/O applications. (See DK 611/612 MicroCHIPS** Development Kit under the development tool slave adapter listing.)

- - -

CHIP SET: 82C612 MicroCHIP**
AVAILABLE: 11/87
DESCRIPTION: The 82C612 MicroCHIP** (Micro Channel* bus Interface Part) is a general purpose interface component that contains most of the logic required to interface to the Micro Channel bus. It is suited for applications requiring DMA. (See DK 611/612 MicroCHIPS** Development Kit under the development tool slave adapter listing.)

- - -

CHIP SET: 82C614 Bus Master MicroCHIP**
AVAILABLE: 5/90
DESCRIPTION: The 82C614 provides a complete bus master interface on a single chip. The 82C614 was jointly developed with IBM and supports data streaming and parity. It is intended for bus master adapters that do not require local intelligence such as SCSI, LAN, high speed communications, and other adapters. (See DK614 Bus Master Development Kit under the development tool bus master adapters listing.)

COMPANY: Intel Corporation
ADDRESS: 1900 Prairie City Road
Folsom, CA 95630
PHONE: 1-916-351-8080 / 1-800-548-4725
FAX: 1-916-351-6710

CHIP SET: 82326 Slave Controller for the IBM* Micro Channel* Bus
AVAILABLE: 5/90
DESCRIPTION: High integration slave interface controller (I/O and DMA), 8-and 16-bit. Integrated 24 mA drivers. Features parity check, burst, arbitration and boot ROM. 124 1d PFP package. Designed by IBM.

- - -

CHIP SET: Intel** 82325 (MC/MD) Bus Master Interface Chip Set
AVAILABLE: 6/90
DESCRIPTION: Highest performance bus master chip set for 32-bit intelligent host adapters. Integrated 24mA drivers; needs just one ttl device for Micro Channel* interface. Supports data streaming (40 Mbyte/second transfer rates). Subsystem control block (SCB) architecture. Designed by IBM.

COMPANY: NCR Corporation
ADDRESS: 1635 Aeroplaza Drive
Colorado Springs, CO 80916
PHONE: 1-719-596-5612 / 1-800-525-2252
FAX: 1-719-597-8225

CHIP SET: 86C71
AVAILABLE: 7/90
DESCRIPTION: The 86C71 is a bus interface chip to connect the NCR53C700 to the Micro Channel* bus. It can perform both 16- and 32-bit transfers at rates up to 29 MBytes per second.

CHIP SET: MC Bus Interface Chip 86C01
AVAILABLE: 6/88
DESCRIPTION: VLSI chip implementing Micro Channel* bus POS registers and support logic to connect most peripheral chips.

CHIP SET: MC Bus Master DMA Chip 86C05
AVAILABLE: 9/89
DESCRIPTION: The NCR** 86C05 bus master VLSI chip is a high performance (20MB/second) buffered 32-bit wide DMA chip which supports a BIOS, a local microprocessor, and DMA operations with most peripheral chips.

COMPANY: PLX Technology
ADDRESS: 625 Clyde Avenue
Mountain View, CA 94043
PHONE: 1-415-960-0448 / 1-800-759-3735
FAX: 1-415-960-0479

CHIP SET: 3200 Bus Master Chip Set
AVAILABLE: 11/89
DESCRIPTION: Bus master interface chip set for the Micro Channel* bus. Performs local arbitration, command strobes and byte enables for 20MB/second bus masters.

CHIP SET: 40 Meg Streaming Data Bus Master Interface Chip Set
AVAILABLE: 3/90
DESCRIPTION: Bus master chip set for 40MB/second streaming data applications. Performs arbitration, generates streaming data and command strobe signals as well as byte enables and exception generation.

Appendix D

Micro Channel Bus Masters

Following is a description of the bus master adapters available for Micro Channel systems from non-IBM sources.

Reprinted courtesy of International Business Machines Corporation from the *Catalog of Micro Channel Expansion Adapters,* IBM Form number G360-2824-05.

IOV BUS MASTER ADAPTERS AND ADAPTER SUBSYSTEM PRODUCTS BY CATEGORY

Alternate General Purpose Bus Master Adapters

COMPANY: Aox Incorporated
ADDRESS: 486 Totten Pond Road
Waltham, MA 02154
PHONE: 1-617-890-4402 / 1-800-232-1269
FAX: 1-617-890-8445

ADAPTER NAME: MicroMASTER™ 386
SUPPORTS: PS/2 - YES RISC System/6000 - NO 9371 Model 14 - NO
AVAILABLE: 7/89
DESCRIPTION: 80386-based processor upgrade bus master for IBM* PS/2* Model 50, 50Z, 55 SX, 60, 70 and 80 computers. Available in 20, 25 and 33 MHz versions. Supports 80387 numeric co-processor and up to 8MB of 32-bit memory on card. Provides processor & memory upgrade capability for all Micro Channel* bus based PS/2 computer models.

ADAPTER NAME: MicroMASTER™ 486
SUPPORTS: PS/2 - YES RISC System/6000 - NO 9371 Model 14 - NO
AVAILABLE: 7/90
DESCRIPTION: 486-25MHz-based bus master processor upgrade board for IBM* PS/2* computers. Supports up to 8MB of 32-bit memory on board. Provides processor and memory upgradability for all Micro Channel* bus based PS/2 computers.

COMPANY: ARCO Electronic Control Ltd.
ADDRESS: Seven Hazerem Street
P.O. Box 8600
Tel-Aviv/Jaffa 61084
ISRAEL
PHONE: 972-3-512-3077
FAX: 972-3-822-228

ADAPTER NAME: AC-20600
SUPPORTS: PS/2 - YES RISC System/6000 - NO 9371 Model 14 - NO
AVAILABLE: 6/90
DESCRIPTION: The AC-2060D is a high speed, intelligent ESDI Winchester disk drive adapter. The AC-2060D may be installed with four ESDI hard disk drives for duplexing, mirroring and fault-tolerant operation. The AC-2060D is designed to easily connect an external disk drive to the Micro Channel* bus system.

COMPANY: National Instruments Corp.
ADDRESS: 6504 Bridge Point Parkway
Austin, TX 78730-5039
PHONE: 1-512-794-0100 / 1-800-433-3488
FAX: 1-512-794-8411

ADAPTER NAME: VME-MC2000
SUPPORTS: PS/2 - YES RISC System/6000 - NO 9371 Model 14 - NO
AVAILABLE: 12/90
DESCRIPTION: Interface kit for transparently linking PS/2 computers to the VMEbus with DOS software platform for high-performance operation. Kit includes MC-MXI and VME-MXI boards, cable and complete DOS software.*

ADAPTER NAME: VME-MC2030
SUPPORTS: PS/2 - YES RISC System/6000 - NO 9371 Model 14 - NO
AVAILABLE: 12/90
DESCRIPTION: Interface kit for transparently linking PS/2 computers to the VMEbus with OS/2* computer software platform for high-performance operation. Kit includes MC-MXI and VME-MXI boards, cable and complete OS/2* software.*

ADAPTER NAME: VME-MC6000
SUPPORTS: PS/2 - NO RISC System/6000 - YES 9371 Model 14 - NO
AVAILABLE: 12/90
DESCRIPTION: Interface kit for IBM RISC System/6000* POWERstations and POWERservers with a full-size board for the Micro Channel* bus, a VME board, MXIbus cable, and AIX* software tools for VME control. Benefits include highest cost to performance ratio, multiple mainframe control, and local or distant control.*

ADAPTER NAME: VXI-MC2000
SUPPORTS: PS/2 - YES RISC System/6000 - NO 9371 Model 14 - NO
AVAILABLE: 6/90
DESCRIPTION: Interface kit for transparently linking PS/2* computers directly to the VXIbus with DOS software platform for high-operation. Kit includes MC-MXI and VXI-MXI boards, cable and complete OS/2 computer software. Compatible with imbedded VXI PC controllers.

ADAPTER NAME: VXI-MC2030
SUPPORTS: PS/2 - YES RISC System/6000 - NO 9371 Model 14 - NO
AVAILABLE: 6/90
DESCRIPTION: Interface kit for transparently linking PS/2* computers directly to the VXIbus with OS/2* computer software platform for high- operation. Kit includes MC-MXI and VXI-MXI boards, cable and complete OS/2 computer software. Compatible with imbedded VXI PC controllers.

Alternate General Purpose Bus Master Adapters (Continued)

COMPANY: National Instruments Corp.
ADDRESS: 6504 Bridge Point Parkway
Austin, TX 78730-5039
PHONE: 1-512-794-0100 / 1-800-433-3488
FAX: 1-512-794-8411

ADAPTER NAME: VXI-MC6000
SUPPORTS: PS/2 - NO RISC System/6000 - YES 9371 Model 14 - NO
AVAILABLE: 12/90
DESCRIPTION: Interface kit for transparently linking RISC System/6000 POWERstations and POWERservers directly to the VXIbus with AIX* computer software for high-performance operation. Kit includes MC-MXI and VXI-MXI boards, cable and complete AIX software. Compatible with imbedded VXI PC controllers.*

COMPANY: PROMETA AB
ADDRESS: Box 4049
S-18204 Enebyberg
SWEDEN
PHONE: 46-8-661-0454 / 1-800-283-6382
FAX: 46-8-792-5220

ADAPTER NAME: WS/88K Bus Master
SUPPORTS: PS/2 - YES RISC System/6000 - NO 9371 Model 14 - NO
AVAILABLE: 6/90
DESCRIPTION: Based on the Motorola 88000 RISC architecture. The WS/88K Bus Master provides a complete UNIX** System V workstation. It runs all 88Open BCS UNIX applications in parallel with OS/2* or DOS computer software. Integrated Windows** software user interface. 4-8MB RAM, 17 MIPS 7 MFLOPS (one processor). 1-4 processors.

COMPANY: YARC Systems Corporation
ADDRESS: 27489 West Agoura Road
Agoura Hills, CA 91301
PHONE: 1-818-889-4388
FAX: 1-818-889-2658

ADAPTER NAME: micro785+**
SUPPORTS: PS/2 - YES RISC System/6000 - NO 9371 Model 14 - NO
AVAILABLE: 8/89
DESCRIPTION: The YARC Systems Micro 785+ is an advanced architecture coprocessor featuring a Motorola MC68020. It operates at 25MHz, 30MHz, 33MHz and 40MHz and offers up to 5 VAX** MIPS of power to the professional user. The system supports FORTRAN, C and Pascal compilers and applications, e.g., MIRA from Oklahoma Seismic.

Audio/Voice/Phone Bus Master Adapter

COMPANY: Advanced Microcomputer Systems, Inc.
ADDRESS: 1321 NW 65th Place
Fort Lauderdale, FL 33309
PHONE: 1-305-975-9515 / 1-800-972-3733
FAX: 1-305-975-9698

ADAPTER NAME: INFOFAX
SUPPORTS: PS/2 - YES RISC System/6000 - NO 9371 Model 14 - NO
AVAILABLE: 1/90
DESCRIPTION: Voice, modem and FAX capability. The card can record, store and play voice messages.

Integrated Services Digital Network (ISDN) Bus Master Adapter

COMPANY: ICL, Inc.
ADDRESS: 777 Long Ridge Road
Stamford, CT 06902
PHONE: 1-203-968-7222 / 1-800-446-4736
FAX: 1-203-968-0472

ADAPTER NAME: I3-ISDN Information Integrator
SUPPORTS: PS/2 - YES RISC System/6000 - NO 9371 Model 14 - NO
AVAILABLE: 7/90
DESCRIPTION: I3 is an ISDN upgrade package. It comprises an adapter for the Micro Channel* bus, ISDN telephone and application software including ISDN Telephone Manager, Phonebook, Switch Interfaces, V.120 and Voice/Data API. Supports X.25, SNA, 3270 and async data on D and B channels up to 64Kbps.

Modem Bus Master Adapters

COMPANY: Advanced Microcomputer Systems, Inc.
ADDRESS: 1321 NW 65th Place
Fort Lauderdale, FL 33309
PHONE: 1-305-975-9515 / 1-800-972-3733
FAX: 1-305-975-9698

ADAPTER NAME: XPress 96
SUPPORTS: PS/2 - YES RISC System/6000 - NO 9371 Model 14 - NO
AVAILABLE: 1/90
DESCRIPTION: V32 compatible 9600 baud modem with MNP** 5 error correction and compression combined with 9600 baud FAX.

COMPANY: Universal Communication A/S
ADDRESS: 1140, N-3001 Drammen
N-3001 Drammen
NORWAY
PHONE: 47-3-89-16-90
FAX: 47-3-88-07-89

ADAPTER NAME: UCOM 22 MC
SUPPORTS: PS/2 - YES RISC System/6000 - NO 9371 Model 14 - NO
AVAILABLE: 10/90
DESCRIPTION: Modem, asynchronous, V.21, v.22, v.22bis, Bell** 212A, Bell 103, V.27ter protocols supported. MNP** 2-5 error correction. SENDFAX automatic call and answer.

Multiprotocol Bus Master Adapters

COMPANY: ComTech International, Inc.
ADDRESS: P.O. Box 722
Bloomfield, CT 06002
PHONE: 1-203-286-8440
FAX: 1-203-286-8218

ADAPTER NAME: Channel/2**
SUPPORTS: PS/2 - YES RISC System/6000 - NO 9371 Model 14 - NO
AVAILABLE: 9/89
DESCRIPTION: An intelligent gateway for NetBIOS LANs with 2 channels. Supports up to 384 concurrent sessions over SDLC and/or X.25 communication line speeds of up to 64K bps on separate channels. LIM EMS 4.0 support for workstations.

ADAPTER NAME: Channel/2 Plus**
SUPPORTS: PS/2 - YES RISC System/6000 - NO 9371 Model 14 - NO
AVAILABLE: 6/90
DESCRIPTION: 80286-based advanced gateway multiplexer for NetBIOS LANs with 2 independent communication channels — High-speed channel with RS-422 interface supports up to 2MB/second; Low-speed channel with RS-232 interface supports up to 64KB/second. The hardware conducts all the SSCP-PU sessions with the host and appears as a multiple PU Cluster Controller. Supports up to 16 PU addresses and multiple host communication concurrently.

COMPANY: Informatique Aquia Systeme (I.A.S.)
ADDRESS: ZI - Route de Castets
40990 Saint Paul les Dax
FRANCE
PHONE: 33-58-91-99-94
FAX: 33-58-91-74-69

ADAPTER NAME: SC-MM
SUPPORTS: PS/2 - YES RISC System/6000 - YES 9371 Model 14 - NO
AVAILABLE: 6/90
DESCRIPTION: A high-performance full-duplex multiprotocol serial port adapter, dynamically software configurable between any of asynchronous (up to 38400 Bps), COP or BOP (up to 64 KBps). On- board bus master is a high-speed full-duplex DMA with special logic to avoid any frame loss with mono-flag between frames.

COMPANY: Siemens AG
ADDRESS: ZN Frankfurt, DI V4
Roedelheimer-Landstrasse 5-9
Frankfurt 6000
WEST GERMANY
PHONE: 49-(0)69-797-3741
FAX: 49-(0)69-797-3584

ADAPTER NAME: START-Board
SUPPORTS: PS/2 - YES RISC System/6000 - NO 9371 Model 14 - NO
AVAILABLE: 10/90
DESCRIPTION: An intelligent communication controller with an 80188 16MHz CPU and 1MB DRAM. Supports multiple protocols including async, sync, HDLC/SDLC and X.25. The adapter provides 6 ports (RS232C, SS81, a Centronics** port, 2 V.24 and X.21). Siemens provides software for X.25, RS232C and MSV1, which is downloaded to the adapter by OS/2* or SCO** XENIX** computer software.

Ethernet** Network Bus Master Adapters

COMPANY: BICC Data Networks, Inc.
ADDRESS: 1800 West Park Drive
Westborough, MA 01581
PHONE: 1-508-898-2422 / 1-800-447-6526
FAX: 1-508-898-3739

ADAPTER NAME: ISOLAN** 4110-3 Controller Card
SUPPORTS: PS/2 - YES RISC System/6000 - NO 9371 Model 14 - NO
AVAILABLE: 4/89
DESCRIPTION: A fully integrated, high-speed, IBM* PS/2* computer, bus master controller providing Ethernet** IEEE 80.23 local area networking. Innovative design maximizes overall performance by utilizing the total capacity of an Ethernet local area network and PS/2 computer bus master capability.

COMPANY: IMC Networks Corp.
ADDRESS: 1342 Bell Avenue
Suite 3E
Tustin, CA 92680
PHONE: 1-714-259-1020 / 1-800-624-1070
FAX: 1-714-259-1080

ADAPTER NAME: PCnic** MCAbus
SUPPORTS: PS/2 - YES RISC System/6000 - NO 9371 Model 14 - NO
AVAILABLE: 4/90
DESCRIPTION: 32-bit bus master Ethernet** LAN card for use with PS/2* Model 70 and 80 computers. Works as a fileserver or workstation under Novell** NetWare** 286 and NetWare 386 software, has full POS registers for I/O address and IRQ level selection, adheres to IEEE 802.3 Ethernet standard plus optionally supports 50, 75 and 93 Ohm coaxial cable.

Token Ring Network Bus Master Adapters

COMPANY: ACCTON Technology Corp.
ADDRESS: 2F., No. 56, Park Ave. II
Science-Based Industrial Park
Hsinchu 330077
TAIWAN, R.O.C.
PHONE: 886-35-770270
FAX: 886-35-770267

ADAPTER NAME: Ring Pair - MCM
SUPPORTS: PS/2 - YES RISC System/6000 - NO 9371 Model 14 - NO
AVAILABLE: 4/90
DESCRIPTION: A high performance 16-bit Micro Channel* bus master token ring LAN adapter. The adapter conforms to IEEE 802.5 standard and is compatible to IBM* Token Ring Network.

COMPANY: Lantana Technology Inc.
ADDRESS: 4393 Viewridge Avenue
Suite A
San Diego, CA 92123
PHONE: 1-619-565-6400
FAX: 1-619-565-0798

ADAPTER NAME: Cypress/2-16
SUPPORTS: PS/2 - YES RISC System/6000 - NO 9371 Model 14 - NO
AVAILABLE: 3/90
DESCRIPTION: Token Ring local area network bus master controller, 16 Mbps, 802.5 compatible. Support for NetWare**, PC LAN, LAN Server and LAN Manager software. Includes ASIC technology for low component count and increased reliability, remote boot option, 128K buffer memory and ring diagnostic LEDs. All options are programmable via software.

ADAPTER NAME: Cypress/2-4
SUPPORTS: PS/2 - YES RISC System/6000 - NO 9371 Model 14 - NO
AVAILABLE: 2/89
DESCRIPTION: Token Ring local area network bus master controller, 4MBps, 802.5 compatible. Support for NetWare**, PC LAN, LAN Server, and LAN Manager software. Includes 2K or 16K buffer memory, ring diagnostic LEDs, LLC 802.2 optional plug-in module.

ADAPTER NAME: Cypress / 2-4 + LLC
SUPPORTS: PS/2 - YES RISC System/6000 - NO 9371 Model 14 - NO
AVAILABLE: 2/89
DESCRIPTION: Token Ring compatible local area network controller. Utilizes bus master technology for increased performance. Includes LLC module for IBM 802.2 compatibility. Operates at 4M bits per second.

COMPANY: Madge Networks
ADDRESS: 1580 Oakland Road
Suite C-206
San Jose, CA 95131
PHONE: 1-408-441-1300 / 1-800-876-2343
FAX: 1-408-441-1335

ADAPTER NAME: MC Ringnode
SUPPORTS: PS/2 - YES RISC System/6000 - NO 9371 Model 14 - NO
AVAILABLE: 11/88
DESCRIPTION: High performance, bus master token ring network interface adapter including software support for PC LAN, LAN Server, LAN Manager, Banyan VINES**, NetWare**, and other NetBIOS-compatible LANs and installation diagnostics.

ADAPTER NAME: Smart 1614 MC Ringnode
SUPPORTS: PS/2 - YES RISC System/6000 - NO 9371 Model 14 - NO
AVAILABLE: 9/90
DESCRIPTION: Bus master token ring network interface adapter with 128K RAM permitting LAN protocol software to run on the card freeing DOS memory. Adapter speed is software selectable for 16Mbits or 4 Mbits. Software for PC Lan, LAN Server, LAN Manager, Banyan VINES** NetWare** and other NetBIOS-compatible LANs and installation diagnostics.

ADAPTER NAME: SMART MC Ringnode
SUPPORTS: PS/2 - YES RISC System/6000 - NO 9371 Model 14 - NO
AVAILABLE: 11/88
DESCRIPTION: Bus master token ring network interface adapter with 128KB RAM permitting LAN protocol software to run on the card freeing DOS memory. Software for PC LAN, LAN Server, LAN Manager, NetWare** Banyan VINES**, and other NetBIOS compatible LAN operating systems and installation diagnostics.

Token Ring Network Bus Master Adapters (Continued)

COMPANY: Olicom A/S
ADDRESS: Oeveroedvej 5
DK-2840 Holte
DENMARK
PHONE: 45-42-42-33-88
FAX: 45-42-42-56-65

ADAPTER NAME: OC-3126 PC/MC Adapter
SUPPORTS: PS/2 - YES RISC System/6000 - NO 9371 Model 14 - NO
AVAILABLE: 2/89
DESCRIPTION: High-performance, bus master Token Ring adapter for 4Mbps with 128KB RAM. Supports IBM* OS/2* EE, PC LAN, LAN Server, Personal Comm. 3270, AS/400* PC Support, APPC/PC, 3270 Emulation, Novell™ NetWare™ 286 and 386 server and DOS and OS/2* WS, 3Com™ 3+Open LAN Manager software.

ADAPTER NAME: OC-3128 MC 16/4 Adapter
SUPPORTS: PS/2 - YES RISC System/6000 - NO 9371 Model 14 - NO
AVAILABLE: 4/90
DESCRIPTION: High-performance bus master Token-Ring adapter for 16 and 4 Mbps with 128KB RAM. Supports IBM* OS/2* EE, PC LAN, LAN Server, Personal Comm. 3270, AS/400* PC Support, APPC/PC, 3270 Emulation, Novell™ NetWare™ 286 and 386 server and DOS and OS/2* WS, 3Com™ 3+Open LAN Manager software.

COMPANY: Proteon, Inc.
ADDRESS: Two Technology Drive
Westborough, MA 01581-5008
PHONE: 1-508-898-2800 / 1-800-545-7464
FAX: 1-508-366-8901

ADAPTER NAME: p1840 ProNET™-4 Bus Master Interface for IBM* Micro Channel* Bus
SUPPORTS: PS/2 - YES RISC System/6000 - NO 9371 Model 14 - NO
AVAILABLE: 1/89
DESCRIPTION: Connects IBM* PS/2* computers with Micro Channel* bus to high performance, 4MB/second ProNET™-4 Token Ring network. Compatible with IEEE 802.5 specification and IBM Token Ring. Uses 16-bit Micro Channel bus data path and POS feature for high speed and versatility. Compatible with Novell™ NetWare™ and IBM networking software.

ADAPTER NAME: p1890 ProNET™-4/16 Interface for IBM* Micro Channel* Bus
SUPPORTS: PS/2 - YES RISC System/6000 - NO 9371 Model 14 - NO
AVAILABLE: 9/90
DESCRIPTION: The p1890, Proteon's newest addition to the ProNET™-4/16 adapter family is designed for personal computers with the Micro Channel* bus. The p1890 features Proteon's bus master technology and supports popular networking software.

COMPANY: PureData
ADDRESS: 1740 South I-35
Carrollton, TX 75006
PHONE: 1-214-242-2040
FAX: 1-214-242-9487

ADAPTER NAME: PDuC8025
SUPPORTS: PS/2 - YES RISC System/6000 - NO 9371 Model 14 - NO
AVAILABLE: 1/90
DESCRIPTION: Software configurable, 16-bit, bus master adapter for Micro Channel* bus fileservers and workstations. This "2-in-1" card supports both shielded and unshielded twisted pair wiring — no external media filters are required. Software selectable 4 or 16MBps operation.

COMPANY: Racore Computer Products, Inc.
ADDRESS: 170 Knowles Drive
Los Gatos, CA 95030
PHONE: 1-408-374-8290 / 1-800-635-1274
FAX: 1-408-374-6653

ADAPTER NAME: Racore 4X16Mbit/sec 802.5 Token-Ring
SUPPORTS: PS/2 - YES RISC System/6000 - NO 9371 Model 14 - NO
AVAILABLE: 3/90
DESCRIPTION: Compatible with IEEE 802.5, IBM* Token-Ring Adapter and Micro Channel* bus. (Optional 802.2 capability offered). 128K DRAM standard, 512K DRAM option for server. 64K EPROM. Boot PROM option. Twisted pair or phone wire.

COMPANY: Western Digital Corporation
ADDRESS: 8105 Irvine Center Drive
Irvine, CA 92718
PHONE: 1-714-932-5000 / 1-800-832-4778
FAX: 1-714-932-6496

ADAPTER NAME: TokenCard MASTER/A™
SUPPORTS: PS/2 - YES RISC System/6000 - NO 9371 Model 14 - NO
AVAILABLE: 6/90
DESCRIPTION: High performance bus master Token Ring network adapter with on-board support for unshielded (IBM* Type 3) and shielded twisted pair cable (IBM Types 1 and 2). Includes diagnostics and drivers for IBM, LAN Manager, NetWare™, UNIX™ and other network software.

Other Network Bus Master Adapter

COMPANY: Northern Telecom Inc.
ADDRESS: 2305 Mission College Boulevard
Santa Clara, CA 95054
PHONE: 1-408-988-5550
FAX: 1-408-764-2545

ADAPTER NAME: LANSTAR/mc
SUPPORTS: PS/2 - YES RISC System/6000 - NO 9371 Model 14 - NO
AVAILABLE: 3/89
DESCRIPTION: A bus master LANSTAR network interface adapter, 2.56Mbps over unshielded twisted pair up to 2,000 feet to a hub. LANSTAR hub supports up to 1,134 nodes on a 40Mbps backplane without collision.

3270 Terminal Emulation Bus Master Adapter

COMPANY: AST Research, Inc.
ADDRESS: 16215 Alton Parkway
Irvine, CA 92718
PHONE: 1-714-727-9292
FAX: 1-714-727-9355

ADAPTER NAME: 3270/COAX II A - CUT TP
SUPPORTS: PS/2 - YES RISC System/6000 - NO 9371 Model 14 - NO
AVAILABLE: 10/87
DESCRIPTION: Local 3270/COAX connection to mainframe supports one 3278/79 host session; compatible with both IBM and IRMA hardware and software; supports IBM* OS/2* Extended Edition computer software.

X.25 Bus Master Adapters

COMPANY: METACOMP, Inc.
ADDRESS: 10635 Scripps Ranch Boulevard
Building F
San Diego, CA 92131
PHONE: 1-619-578-1800
FAX: 1-619-578-7965

ADAPTER NAME: PS-X.25 SERVER
SUPPORTS: PS/2 - YES RISC System/6000 - YES 9371 Model 14 - YES
AVAILABLE: 11/90
DESCRIPTION: This plug-and-play solution offers connectivity to worldwide public and private X.25 packet switching data networks. Fully CCITT-1988 compliant; supports Multi-Link feature. Simple programming interface. Four programmable channels of serial input/output. Bus master interface.

COMPANY: T.D.T. (Transfer Data Test GmbH)
ADDRESS: Piflaser Weg 10
D-8300 Landshut
WEST GERMANY
PHONE: 49-0871-801-0
FAX: 49-0871-801-10

ADAPTER NAME: T.D.T. Single Pad Karte Asynchron MC
SUPPORTS: PS/2 - YES RISC System/6000 - NO 9371 Model 14 - NO
AVAILABLE: 4/90
DESCRIPTION: The Single Pad Karte Asynchron is a special board for the IBM* PS/2* computers with the Micro Channel* architecture for X.25 networks. It runs with all asynchronous communication software (terminal emulation).

- - - - - - - - - - - - - - - - - - - -

ADAPTER NAME: T.D.T. Single Pad Karte Synchron MC
SUPPORTS: PS/2 - YES RISC System/6000 - NO 9371 Model 14 - NO
AVAILABLE: 5/90
DESCRIPTION: The Single Pad Karte Synchron is a special board for the IBM* PS/2* computers with the Micro Channel* architecture for X.25 networks. It runs with all IBM SNA emulation, 3270, 5250.

Digital I/O Bus Master Adapters

COMPANY: Bit 3 Computer Corporation
ADDRESS: 8120 Penn Avenue, South
Bloomington, MN 55431-1393
PHONE: 1-612-881-6955
FAX: 1-612-881-9674

ADAPTER NAME: MAC—A32/D16 VME
SUPPORTS: PS/2 - YES RISC System/6000 - YES 9371 Model 14 - NO
AVAILABLE: 4/90
DESCRIPTION: The Model 446 Adaptor makes IBM* PS/2* computers or RISC System/6000* POWERstations and POWERservers compatible with A32/D16 VMEbus. The memory mapped interface permits the PS/2 computer or RISC System/6000 POWERstation or POWERserver to directly access memory and I/O devices on the VMEbus. AIX* computer software driver support if available for the RISC System/6000 POWERstation or POWERserver.

COMPANY: Brain Boxes
ADDRESS: Unit 3G, Wavertree Technology Park
Wavertree Boulevard South
Liverpool L7 9PF
UNITED KINGDOM
PHONE: 44-051-220-2500/7190
FAX: 44-051-228-8828

ADAPTER NAME: PS DIO192/2
SUPPORTS: PS/2 - YES RISC System/6000 - NO 9371 Model 14 - NO
AVAILABLE: 8/90
DESCRIPTION: PS DIO192/2 gives 192 DIO lines by eight 8255 IC, in 4 pairs each having its own set of IRQ selection circuitry. Choice of 50 way IOC or 50 way D connector for 481/9 lines, others accessible via 50 pin headers. Flexible interrupt allocation. Compatible with Asyst and other software. Debugged and explained sample programs included.

Digital I/O Bus Master Adapters (Continued)

COMPANY: Brain Boxes
ADDRESS: Unit 3G, Wavertree Technology Park
Wavertree Boulevard South
Liverpool L7 9PF
UNITED KINGDOM
PHONE: 44-051-220-2500/7190
FAX: 44-051-228-8828

ADAPTER NAME: PS DIO 48/2
SUPPORTS: PS/2 - YES RISC System/6000 - NO 9371 Model 14 - NO
AVAILABLE: 8/90
DESCRIPTION: Half size DIO card gives 6 x 8 bit ports by two 8255 chips. The 48 I/O lines with 1 ground and 1 power/ground selectable line are accessible from either 50 way IDC or 50 way D connector. Flexible interrupt allocation. Compatible with Asyst, Labtech Notebook software. Complete with debugged and explained sample programs.

ADAPTER NAME: PS Timer DIO/2
SUPPORTS: PS/2 - YES RISC System/6000 - NO 9371 Model 14 - NO
AVAILABLE: 8/90
DESCRIPTION: Half size timer DIO adds 24 DIO lines and seven 5 channel 16-bit timer to PS/2* computers. All 45 I/O lines with 4 grounds and 1 + 5V/GND selectable line are accessible from either 50 way IDC or 50 way D connector. Compatible with Asyst, Labtech Notebook software. Debugged and explained sample programs included, e.g. 16 + 32-bit counting gated counting, etc.

IEEE 488 Bus Master Adapters

COMPANY: Brain Boxes
ADDRESS: Unit 3G, Wavertree Technology Park
Wavertree Boulevard South
Liverpool L7 9PF
UNITED KINGDOM
PHONE: 44-051-220-2500/7190
FAX: 44-051-228-8828

ADAPTER NAME: PS Elite/2
SUPPORTS: PS/2 - YES RISC System/6000 - NO 9371 Model 14 - NO
AVAILABLE: 8/89
DESCRIPTION: PS Elite/2 is half size card fitting any slot on the Micro Channel* bus. Has complete controller, listener, talker ability. Choice of 15 DMA arbitration levels, burst mode, 4 interrupt lines and 7 I/O addresses. Compatible with Lotus** Measure Asyst and all software that supports IBM* GPIB and NI PC2/2a cards.

COMPANY: National Instruments Corp.
ADDRESS: 6504 Bridge Point Parkway
Austin, TX 78730-5039
PHONE: 1-512-794-0100 / 1-800-433-3488
FAX: 1-512-794-8411

ADAPTER NAME: GPIB for the IBM* RISC System/6000* POWERstations and POWERservers
SUPPORTS: PS/2 - NO RISC System/6000 - YES 9371 Model 14 - NO
AVAILABLE: 9/90
DESCRIPTION: IEEE-488 interface kit for the RISC System/6000* POWERstations and POWERservers with complete software support for the AIX* operating system. Has FIFO buffers for high-speed DMA transfers. POS circuitry for selecting I/O address, interrupt level, and DMA channel (no hardware jumpers or switches).

Development Tool Bus Master Adapters

COMPANY: Brain Boxes
ADDRESS: Unit 3G, Wavertree Technology Park
Wavertree Boulevard South
Liverpool L7 9PF
UNITED KINGDOM
PHONE: 44-051-220-2500/7190
FAX: 44-051-228-8828

ADAPTER NAME: PS Proto/2
SUPPORTS: PS/2 - YES RISC System/6000 - NO 9371 Model 14 - NO
AVAILABLE: 5/89
DESCRIPTION: PS Proto/2 fits any Micro Channel* bus slot for PS/2* Model 50, 60 and 80 computers. The 132 Micro Channel bus fingers are gold-plated and each line taken to a through-plated hole. The 16-bit channel comprises 58 double-sided fingers allocated to 77 signal lines. Comes complete with 50 way D or 50 way IDC connector and matching bracket.

COMPANY: Chips & Technologies, Inc.
ADDRESS: 3050 Zanker Road
San Jose, CA 95134
PHONE: 1-408-434-0600

ADAPTER NAME: DK614 Bus Master Development Kit
SUPPORTS: PS/2 - YES RISC System/6000 - YES 9371 Model 14 - YES
AVAILABLE: 5/90
DESCRIPTION: The DK614 is a development tool allowing a board designer to evaluate the 82C614 Bus Master MicroCHIP** from Chips & Technologies, Inc. It is implemented as a full SCSI bus master adapter, but the 82C614 is useful for a wide variety of bus master applications.

COMPANY: Levco Sales
ADDRESS: 6181 Cornerstone Court East
Suite 101
San Diego, CA 92121
PHONE: 1-619-457-2011
FAX: 1-619-457-2325

ADAPTER NAME: RISClink
SUPPORTS: PS/2 - YES RISC System/6000 - NO 9371 Model 14 - NO
AVAILABLE: 6/89
DESCRIPTION: RISClink is a co-processor enhancement board featuring the inmos** transputer. RISKlink is a 32-bits wide RISC-based processor that can be used for parallel processing. RISClink features compilers such as C, Fortran and Pascal. RISClink provides 10 mips per chip and 2 MFLOP's.

Facsimile Bus Master Adapter

COMPANY: Pacific Image Communications, Inc.
ADDRESS: 1111 South Arroyo Parkway
Suite 430
Pasadena, CA 91105
PHONE: 1-818-441-0104
FAX: 1-818-441-2370

PRODUCT NAME: SuperFax MC
SUPPORTS: PS/2 - YES RISC System/6000 - NO 9371 Model 14 - NO
AVAILABLE: 4/89
DESCRIPTION: One of the first true bus master solutions running under Windows** software. Up to seven FAX boards can run concurrently in a true background mode with no degradation to the foreground task.

Fixed Disk Bus Master Adapters

COMPANY: ARCO Electronic Control Ltd.
ADDRESS: Seven Hazerem Street
P.O. Box 8600
Tel-Aviv/Jaffa 61084
ISRAEL
PHONE: 972-3-512-3077
FAX: 972-3-822-228

ADAPTER NAME: AC-2060 ESDI Controller
SUPPORTS: PS/2 - YES RISC System/6000 - NO 9371 Model 14 - NO
AVAILABLE: 2/90
DESCRIPTION: The ARCO AC-2060 ESDI Controller is a high-speed, intelligent ESDI Winchester drive controller. It operates as a bus master and transfers data between disk drives and system memory by using one bus cycle per word transfer.

COMPANY: CORE International
ADDRESS: 7171 North Federal Highway
Boca Raton, FL 33487
PHONE: 1-407-997-6055
FAX: 1-407-997-6009

ADAPTER NAME: CNT-IMC
SUPPORTS: PS/2 - YES RISC System/6000 - NO 9371 Model 14 - NO
AVAILABLE: 1/90
DESCRIPTION: 32-bit bus master ESDI fixed disk adaptor. Supports 2 drives with 1MB cache on board. 80C186 processor controlled with DMA on board. Supports all industry standard ESDI drives. DOS, Novell**, OS/2* computer software compatible.

ADAPTER NAME: CNT-MCA**
SUPPORTS: PS/2 - YES RISC System/6000 - NO 9371 Model 14 - NO
AVAILABLE: 12/88
DESCRIPTION: 15MHz ESDI hard disk controller, supports 2 drives. 2 controllers support duplexing under Novell** NetWare** 2.15 or 386 software. Can co-exist with IBM* controllers. DMA on board. 1500KB/second data transfer rate for 15MHz drives or 10MHz drives at 1100KB/second.

ADAPTER NAME: CNT-MCK
SUPPORTS: PS/2 - YES RISC System/6000 - NO 9371 Model 14 - NO
AVAILABLE: 12/89
DESCRIPTION: 20MHz ESDI hard disk controller supporting 2 hard disk drives and 2 floppy drives. Compatible with OS/2* and Novell** computer software. DMA on board. Can co-exist with IBM* controllers for duplexing. Supports IBM drives.

Graphics Bus Master Adapters

COMPANY: CalComp, Inc.
ADDRESS: 2411 West La Palma Avenue
Anaheim, California 92801
PHONE: 1-714-821-2800 / 1-800-225-2667
FAX: 1-603-885-8125

ADAPTER NAME: DrawingCard** Graphics Controller for Micro Channel* Architecture
SUPPORTS: PS/2 - YES RISC System/6000 - NO 9371 Model 14 - NO
AVAILABLE: 6/90
DESCRIPTION: High-resolution / performance, color graphics bus master controller for PS/2* computers. 1024 x 768 resolution refreshed at a rate of 60Hz and is available with either 4- or 8-bit planes to provide either 16 or 256 colors simultaneously from a standard palette of 16.7 million. The onboard TMS320C30 graphics engine, display list processor and custom gate arrays quickly perform the time-consuming and complex graphics processing tasks.

COMPANY: Graphic Software Systems, Inc. (GSS)
ADDRESS: 9590 Southwest Gemini Drive
Beaverton, OR 97005
PHONE: 1-503-641-2200
FAX: 1-503-543-8642

ADAPTER NAME: GSS** MC1000 Controller
SUPPORTS: PS/2 - YES RISC System/6000 - NO 9371 Model 14 - NO
AVAILABLE: 8/89
DESCRIPTION: The GSS** MC1000 is the Micro Channel* bus accelerator for graphics-based computing environments. Its custom hardware, bus master I/O, programmable graphics processor and optimized firmware interfaces accelerate graphics user interfaces and applications in DOS, OS/2* and UNIX** computer software.

Graphics Bus Master Adapters (Continued)

COMPANY: NEC Technologies, Inc.
ADDRESS: 1255 Michael Drive
Wood Dale, IL 60191
PHONE: 1-708-860-0335
FAX: 1-708-860-5618

ADAPTER NAME: MultiSync Graphics Engine
SUPPORTS: PS/2 - YES RISC System/6000 - NO 9371 Model 14 - NO
AVAILABLE: 11/89
DESCRIPTION: Speeds processing at high resolutions with the 50MHz TI34010 processor. Designed to optimize Presentation Manager* and Windows** software. Offers comprehensive compatibility in 1024 × 768 non-interlaced, 8514A, 800 × 600, and VGA. 1,000 + software packages supported. "PC MAGAZINE" Editor's Choice.

COMPANY: Pixelworks, Incorporated
ADDRESS: Seven Park Avenue
Hudson, NH 03051
PHONE: 1-603-880-1322 / 1-800-247-2476
FAX: 1-603-880-6558

ADAPTER NAME: Ultra Clipper/AX** Graphics
SUPPORTS: PS/2 - YES RISC System/6000 - NO 9371 Model 14 - NO
AVAILABLE: 11/89
DESCRIPTION: The Ultra Clipper/AX** Graphics controller is an extremely high-performance, high-resolution, true bus mastering graphics adapter for PS/2* computers with the Micro Channel* bus. The Ultra Clipper/AX is an AutoCAD** 10-specific graphics accelerator, incorporating algorithms specific to and optimized for all versions of AutoCAD 10 software.

ADAPTER NAME: Ultra Clipper** Graphics
SUPPORTS: PS/2 - YES RISC System/6000 - NO 9371 Model 14 - NO
AVAILABLE: 1/89
DESCRIPTION: High performance, 1280 × 1024 or 1024 × 768 graphics co- processor. Provides instant redraws, pans, and zooms through Display List Processing for AutoCAD** 9 and 10, VersaCAD and other CAD software packages. Support also for MicroCADAM Plus, Cornerstone, IBMCAD, Microsoft** Windows**, GEM**, Ventura Publisher** and many other applications. C processing libraries for DOS, OS/2*, AIX*, XENIX** and UNIX** computer software for the developer.

COMPANY: Univision Technologies, Inc.
ADDRESS: Three Burlington Woods
Burlington, MA 01803
PHONE: 1-617-221-6700
FAX: 1-617-221-6777

ADAPTER NAME: UDS-7000-TI Graphics Display Controller
SUPPORTS: PS/2 - NO RISC System/6000 - YES 9371 Model 14 - NO
AVAILABLE: 6/90
DESCRIPTION: TI34020 based graphics display card. From 640 × 480 up to 1600 × 1200 resolution. From 8 bit planes up to 32 bit planes. Fully supports TIGA software interface, and X-Windows** software.

Memory Bus Master Adapter — 32-Bit

COMPANY: AST Research, Inc.
ADDRESS: 16215 Alton Parkway
Irvine, CA 92718
PHONE: 1-714-727-9292
FAX: 1-714-727-9355

ADAPTER NAME: Rampage Plus/MC 386
SUPPORTS: PS/2 - YES RISC System/6000 - NO 9371 Model 14 - NO
AVAILABLE: 8/90
DESCRIPTION: AST Rampage Plus/MC 386 multifunction board takes full advantage of the IBM* Personal System/2* Model 70/80 computer's high performance 32-bit data bus. It provides expanded and/or extended memory capability with up to 8MB of memory and optional input/output functions in a single expansion slot.

Optical Disk Bus Master Adapter

COMPANY: XYXIS Corporation
ADDRESS: 14631 Martin Drive
Eden Prairie, MN 55344
PHONE: 1-612-949-2388
FAX: 1-612-949-2488

ADAPTER NAME: XY600RW Optical Drive
SUPPORTS: PS/2 - YES RISC System/6000 - NO 9371 Model 14 - NO
AVAILABLE: 10/89
DESCRIPTION: 600MB read-write-erase ISO standard magneto-optical drive. Each removable, cartridge capable of storing 600MB of information. 61 ms access time. Complete end user product. SCSI interface.

Performance Bus Master Adapter

COMPANY: Polywell Computers
ADDRESS: 61-C Airport Boulevard
South San Francisco, CA 94080
PHONE: 1-415-583-7222 / 1-800-999-1278
FAX: 1-415-583-1974

ADAPTER NAME: Accelerator 50/60
SUPPORTS: PS/2 - YES RISC System/6000 - NO 9371 Model 14 - NO
AVAILABLE: 1/89
DESCRIPTION: Accelerator board for PS/2* Models 50, 50Z and 60 computers that increases speed over 200% and maintains full hardware and software compatibility. Boosting Norton SI from 10 to 23, it uses 20MHz, 0-wait 80C286 CPU complement with 32K cache RAM. Easily installed.

Scanner Bus Master Adapters

COMPANY: Kun Ying Enterprise Co., Ltd.
ADDRESS: 11Fl., No. 116, Sec. 2, Nan King East Road
Taipei
TAIWAN, R.O.C.
PHONE: 886-(0)2-565-2817
FAX: 886-(0)2-551-0873

ADAPTER NAME: Scanner
SUPPORTS: PS/2 - YES RISC System/6000 - NO 9371 Model 14 - NO
AVAILABLE: 3/91
DESCRIPTION: An adapter subsystem consisting of an adapter and a handy scanner (black and white or color scanner) with the application software.

COMPANY: Panasonic Communications & Systems Company
ADDRESS: Two Panasonic Way
Mail Stop 7D-2
Secaucus, NJ 07094
PHONE: 1-201-348-7000 / 1-800-742-8086
FAX: 1-201-392-4792

ADAPTER NAME: FX-BS182
SUPPORTS: PS/2 - YES RISC System/6000 - NO 9371 Model 14 - NO
AVAILABLE: 5/89
DESCRIPTION: Gives connection to FX-RS505U/506U scanner. FX-RS505U is targeted for price conscious users, while FX-RS506U provides cost effective OCR solutions. FX-RS506U features 400 dpi, 16 grayscale and free OCR package. ScanDo utility program is included for both scanners.

SCSI Bus Master Adapters

COMPANY: Adaptec, Inc.
ADDRESS: 691 South Milpitas Boulevard
Milpitas, CA 95035
PHONE: 1-408-945-8600
FAX: 1-408-262-2533

ADAPTER NAME: AHA-1640
SUPPORTS: PS/2 - YES RISC System/6000 - NO 9371 Model 14 - NO
AVAILABLE: 12/88
DESCRIPTION: SCSI I/O channel supports CDROM, WORM, and magnetic disk and and tape devices. High performance multi-tasking mailbox architecture. Up to 256 active SCSI I/O processes with command queueing and command linking. Bus master data transfer up to 8MB. 5MB synchronous, and 2MB asynchronous continuous SCSI data transfer. SCSI-2 external connector. Much more.

COMPANY: CMS Enhancements, Inc.
ADDRESS: 1372 Valencia Avenue
Tustin, CA 92680
PHONE: 1-714-259-9555
FAX: 1-714-549-4004

ADAPTER NAME: Prevail HBA-MSPRV
SUPPORTS: PS/2 - YES RISC System/6000 - NO 9371 Model 14 - NO
AVAILABLE: 3/90
DESCRIPTION: Very high speed SCSI host adapter. Supports UNIX**, XENIX**, DOS and Novell** NetWare** computer software. Burst rate data transfers up to 80Mbit/second. Two-year warranty.

COMPANY: Future Domain Corporation
ADDRESS: 2801 McGaw Avenue
Irvine, CA 92714
PHONE: 1-714-253-0400
FAX: 1-714-253-0913

ADAPTER NAME: MCS-350
SUPPORTS: PS/2 - YES RISC System/6000 - NO 9371 Model 14 - NO
AVAILABLE: 10/87
DESCRIPTION: MCS-350 hose adapter interfaces IBM* PS/2* computers with the Micro Channel* bus with a wide variety of high-performance peripherals: disk, tape, optical disk and laser printers. Offers full Micro Channel bus compatibility with IBM-assigned ID numbers.

COMPANY: Our Business Machines, Inc.
ADDRESS: 12901 Ramona Boulevard
Suite J
Irwindale, CA 91706
PHONE: 1-818-337-9614 / 1-800-433-1435
FAX: 1-818-960-1766

ADAPTER NAME: ProScan** Professional Grayscale Scanner for IBM* PS/2* Computers
SUPPORTS: PS/2 - YES RISC System/6000 - NO 9371 Model 14 - NO
AVAILABLE: 10/90
DESCRIPTION: Micro Channel* bus adapter for the ProScan** professional grayscale scanner. The ProScan is a full page, roll feed, 300 dpi scanner with 256 levels of gray for desk top publishing and optical character recognition.

Security/Encryption Bus Master Adapter

COMPANY: Okiok Data Ltd.
ADDRESS: 3945 St. Martin West
Laval (Montreal), Quebec H7T 1B7
CANADA
PHONE: 1-514-681-1681
FAX: 1-514-681-1682

ADAPTER NAME: RAC/M IX
SUPPORTS: PS/2 - YES RISC System/6000 - NO 9371 Model 14 - NO
AVAILABLE: 10/90
DESCRIPTION: Intelligent cryptographic adapter designed for zero maintenance RAM based architecture no EPROMs, high speed DES encryption, user authentication, transparent disk encryption, access control, API, secure key storage and audit trail, key and password management, financial application services x9.9, x9.17, x9.23, x9.26, EDI, support to FBSS, LAN, centralized management.

Serial Port Bus Master Adapters

COMPANY: Advanced Microcomputer Systems, Inc.
ADDRESS: 1321 NW 65th Place
Fort Lauderdale, FL 33309
PHONE: 1-305-975-9515 / 1-800-972-3733
FAX: 1-305-975-9698

ADAPTER NAME: Extended Serial Port
SUPPORTS: PS/2 - YES RISC System/6000 - NO 9371 Model 14 - NO
AVAILABLE: 1/90
DESCRIPTION: Intelligent extended serial port conforms to ESP specifications proposed by Hayes.

COMPANY: Brain Boxes
ADDRESS: Unit 3G, Wavertree Technology Park
Wavertree Boulevard South
Liverpool L7 9PF
UNITED KINGDOM
PHONE: 44-051-220-2500/7190
FAX: 44-051-228-8828

ADAPTER NAME: PS 8 Port Serial
SUPPORTS: PS/2 - YES RISC System/6000 - NO 9371 Model 14 - NO
AVAILABLE: 8/90
DESCRIPTION: Full size 8-port serial card fitting any Micro Channel* bus slot. Providing 8 industrial standard RS232 asynchronous serial communication using + - 12 volt logic levels, distances up to 50 or 100 feet at speeds up to 20,000 bits per second. Compatible with all communication packages.

COMPANY: METACOMP, Inc.
ADDRESS: 10635 Scripps Ranch Boulevard
Building F
San Diego, CA 92131
PHONE: 1-619-578-1800
FAX: 1-619-578-7965

ADAPTER NAME: PScomm2/4**
SUPPORTS: PS/2 - YES RISC System/6000 - YES 9371 Model 14 - YES
AVAILABLE: 2/89
DESCRIPTION: High-performance bus master serial I/O controller provides 2 or 4 programmable channels. Built around an 80C186 16MHz CPU, relieves host processor of overhead associated with complex communications protocols. Supports most electrical/mechanical interface standards. OS/2* computer software driver available.

ADAPTER NAME: PSconnect**
SUPPORTS: PS/2 - YES RISC System/6000 - YES 9371 Model 14 - YES
AVAILABLE: 10/89
DESCRIPTION: Intelligent serial I/O communications subsystem supports async devices. One system card slot supports 127 eight- or sixteen- port Remote Async Concentrators (RACs). Twisted pair RJ-45 connectivity. Hub controller with fiber optic ports. Bus master interface. Drivers for IBM* AIX*, OS/2* and Microsoft** DOS 3.3 computer software are available.

COMPANY: The Clusterlink Corporation
ADDRESS: 8601 Georgia Avenue
Silver Spring, MD 20910
PHONE: 1-301-495-2020
FAX: 1-301-495-2029

ADAPTER NAME: Smart Eight/2**
SUPPORTS: PS/2 - YES RISC System/6000 - NO 9371 Model 14 - NO
AVAILABLE: 6/88
DESCRIPTION: Intelligent eight-port serial board with: C188 processor, 256K dual ported RAM, clock and boot. RJ11, RJ12, or RJ45. Multi- boards may be chained. Realtime OS & MS DOS compiler available to develop on-board applications.

Tape Drive Bus Master Adapter

COMPANY: Irwin Magnetic Systems, Inc.
ADDRESS: 2101 Commonwealth Boulevard
Ann Arbor, MI 48105-1561
PHONE: 1-313-930-9000
FAX: 1-313-995-8287

ADAPTER NAME: HA-200S Host Adapter for the IBM* Micro Channel* Architecture
SUPPORTS: PS/2 - YES RISC System/6000 - NO 9371 Model 14 - NO
AVAILABLE: 9/90
DESCRIPTION: SCSI host adapter for the Micro Channel* bus used to connect all Irwin** SCSI drives to Micro Channel bus-based CPUs including Irwin 1.3GB and 2.3GB tape backup series.

Uncategorized Bus Master Adapters

COMPANY: Al Alamiah Electronics Company
ADDRESS: Arabic Software Division
P.O. Box 8196
Salmiah
KUWAIT
PHONE: 965-531-9781
FAX: 965-533-1886

ADAPTER NAME: *SAKHR*** *Arabic ROM Card (Model AX35MC)*
SUPPORTS: *PS/2 - YES RISC System/6000 - NO 9371 Model 14 - NO*
AVAILABLE: *12/90*
DESCRIPTION: *The SAKHR** adapter integrates on ROM an Arabic operating system and following bilingual programs: presentation program, word processor, Arabic and English spelling checkers, English/Arabic dictionary, Arabic morphological processor, mail merge and Hijri calendar.*

COMPANY: Bus Tech, Inc.
ADDRESS: 131 Middlesex Turnpike
Burlington, MA 01803
PHONE: 1-215-540-2212
FAX: 1-617-272-0342

ADAPTER NAME: *MCCA*
SUPPORTS: *PS/2 - YES RISC System/6000 - YES 9371 Model 14 - YES*
AVAILABLE: *1/91*
DESCRIPTION: *Channel adapter for the Micro Channel* bus. MCCA is a single board controller that attaches the I/O channel of an IBM* System/370* or compatible mainframe to the Micro Channel bus interface. Channel speeds are 2.6MB per second - DC interlock and 3.0MB and 4.5MB per second streaming.*

Appendix E

IBM Micro Channel Adapters

Following is a description of the Micro Channel adapters available from IBM.

Reprinted courtesy of International Business Machines Corporation from the *Catalog of Micro Channel Expansion Adapters,* IBM Form number G360-2824-05.

IBM SLAVE ADAPTERS BY CATEGORY FOR PERSONAL SYSTEM/2 COMPUTERS

Audio/Voice/Phone Slave Adapter

ADAPTER NAME: Audio Capture and Playback Adapter/A for the IBM* Personal System/2*
FEATURE CODE: 2784
PART NUMBER: 34F2784
AVAILABLE: 9/89
DESCRIPTION: Adapter providing the capability to record and playback high quality sound for use with the PS/2* Model 50, 55 SX, 60, 65 SX, 70 and 80 computers. Sound can be recorded or played in either channel A or B or in stereo mode. Intended for use with the Audio Visual Connection, (AVC) licensed program. Accepts audio input signals from a microphone or line input cord through a standard mini-jack on the card. Converts the analog signal to a digital format, which is compressed and stored for later use. Sophisticated studio-like sound processing techniques employed in the AVC Audio Editor Components enable the user to alter the characteristics of the digitized sound. The adapter converts the compressed, digitized sound back to an analog signal for playback through headphones/speakers or an amplifier (line out). Technical information is provided with the adapter to allow independent application development directly to the adapter.

Modem Slave Adapters

ADAPTER NAME: IBM* Personal System/2* 300/1200/2400 Internal Modem/A
FEATURE CODE: 1755
PART NUMBER: 94X1755
AVAILABLE: 5/89
DESCRIPTION: Offers high-function, internal modem support for PS/2* Model 50, 55 SX, 60, 65 SX, 70, 80 and P70 computers. It is compatible with Hayes™ modems, although some unique functions are not supported, and it provides standards compatibility via CCITT V.22 bis, Bell™ 212A, and Bell 103 full duplex operation. Most functions are also compatible with the IBM* 5853 External Modem. Functions include automatic dial and answer and the ability to direct-connect into U.S. and Canadian public or private switched network telephone lines.

ADAPTER NAME: IBM* PS/2* Leased Line Modem
FEATURE CODE: 1862
PART NUMBER: 26F1862
AVAILABLE: 12/89
DESCRIPTION: Provides high performance FDX or HDX synchronous transmission on four-wire leased telephone lines with Communication Network Management (CNM) for PS/2* Model 50, 60, 70 and 80 computers. It is certified for operation in the U.S. and Canada, in a commercial environment. Compatible with the IBM* 786x series of modems and can transmit at data rates up to 14.4 kbps over leased telephone lines. It provides two-wire Switched Network Back Up with auto-answer, and LPDA-2 functions of IBM CNM modems operating with NetView* software. This modem is a full length feature card powered by the Micro Channel* bus interface. It requires a PS/2 communication adapter for data and control signals, connected via its external EIA RS-232 interface.

Multiprotocol Slave Adapter

ADAPTER NAME: IBM* Personal System/2* Multi-Protocol Adapter/A
FEATURE CODE: 3043
PART NUMBER: 6451003
AVAILABLE: 1/88
DESCRIPTION: Provides a full- or half-duplex multi-protocol serial data transmission channel. Supports asynchronous, bisynchronous, HDLC, or SDLC protocols. Will support modems or direct attachment at speeds of up to 19,200 bps and supports automatic protocol switching via software at setup. Supports all PS/2* Model 50, 55 SX, 60, 70, P70 and 80 computers.

Network Slave Adapters

ADAPTER NAME: IBM* PC Network Adapter II/A-Frequency 2
FEATURE CODE: 5647
PART NUMBER: 96X5647
AVAILABLE: 2/88
DESCRIPTION: Provides additional RF channels for connecting to the broadband IBM* PC Network. The broadband channels used by the Frequency 2 adapter are 2′ and O.

ADAPTER NAME: IBM* PC Network Adapter II/A-Frequency 3
FEATURE CODE: 5648
PART NUMBER: 96X5648
AVAILABLE: 2/88
DESCRIPTION: Provides additional RF channels for connecting to the broadband IBM* PC Network. The broadband channels used by the Frequency 3 adapter are 3′ and P.

Network Slave Adapters (Continued)

ADAPTER NAME: IBM* PC Network Baseband Adapter/A
FEATURE CODE: 1223
PART NUMBER: 1501223
AVAILABLE: 4/87
DESCRIPTION: The card includes a modular baseband modem for connecting to the baseband IBM* PC Network. The adapter features a 2 megabit/second transmission speed with a CSMA/CD access protocol and supports the IEEE 802.2 protocols via the IBM Local Area Network Support Program.

ADAPTER NAME: IBM* PC Network Broadband Adapter II/A
FEATURE CODE: 1222
PART NUMBER: 1501222
AVAILABLE: 4/87
DESCRIPTION: The adapter includes a modular broadband modem for connecting to the broadband IBM* PC Network. The adapter features a 2 megabit/second transmission speed with a CSMA/CD access protocol and supports the IEEE 802.2 protocols via the IBM Local Area Network Support Program. The broadband channels used by this adapter are T14 and J.

ADAPTER NAME: IBM* Token-Ring Network 16/4 Adapter/A
FEATURE CODE: 1133
PART NUMBER: 16F1133
AVAILABLE: 11/88
DESCRIPTION: Provides attachment of PS/2* computers with the Micro Channel* bus to the IBM* Token-Ring Network. It transmits and receives data at a rate either of 4 million or 16 million bits/second, and it has 64KB of RAM. The Remote Program Load feature has been upgraded to provide support as an optional feature for this adapter.

ADAPTER NAME: IBM* Token-Ring Network Adapter/A
FEATURE CODE: 4790
PART NUMBER: 69X8138
AVAILABLE: 4/87
DESCRIPTION: Provides for connection to the IBM* Token-Ring Network. It contains a microprocessor operating under control of adapter resident microcode. The adapter transmits and receives at a speed of 4 million bits/second using protocols conforming to IEEE 802.5 and ECMA 89 standards.

ADAPTER NAME: IBM* Token-Ring Network PS/2* Model P70 386 Adapter/A
FEATURE CODE: 1598
PART NUMBER: 39F9598
AVAILABLE: 1/90
DESCRIPTION: Permits attachment of the IBM* PS/2* Model P70 386 computer (8573-031, 8573-061 and 8573-121) to the IBM Token-Ring Network. This adapter is half-length and designed to fit in the short slot. It transmits and receives at four million bits/second using protocols conforming to IEEE 802.5 and ECMA 89 standards. It provides 16KB or RAM and all of the function of the IBM Token-Ring Network Adapter/A. A special L-angle connector/cable is provided to facilitate attachment to the IBM PS/2 Model P70 386 computer.

ADAPTER NAME: Token-Ring Network 16/4 Trace and Performance Adapter/A
FEATURE CODE: 5130
PART NUMBER: 74F5130
AVAILABLE: 6/90
DESCRIPTION: This multi-function feature card for the PS/2* computers with the Micro Channel* bus works with the Token-Ring Network 16/4 Trace and Performance Program to provide a real time view of the traffic on Token-Ring networks operating at 4 million bits per second (bps) or 16 million bps. This combination of hardware and software has facilities to analyze trace data, measure media usage and collect ring station traffic statistics. Using this data the customer can get valuable information for use in debugging application software, capacity planning and network reconfiguration. When this adapter is not being used for 16/4 TRN Trace and Performance activities, it will function the same as described for the IBM Token-Ring Network 16/4 Adapter/A (feature Code 1133, PN 16F1133); thus not requiring the total dedication of the PS/2 computer to network management functions.

SNA/SDLC/BSC Slave Adapter

ADAPTER NAME: IBM* Personal System/2* Dual Async Adapter/A
FEATURE CODE: 1014
PART NUMBER: 6451013
AVAILABLE: 12/88
DESCRIPTION: Provides asynchronous communications on two independent RS-232C ports. The feature is programmable and supports communications speeds from 50 to 19,200 bps. This adapter supports signal transmission across 50 feet of cable.

Terminal Emulation Slave Adapters

ADAPTER NAME: IBM* 3270 Connection
FEATURE CODE: 2000
PART NUMBER: 74F3465
AVAILABLE: 5/87
DESCRIPTION: Provides 3270 coaxial cable attachment to the IBM* 3174, 3274 and 3276 Control Units, 4321, 4331 or 4361 Processor Display/Printer Adapter, 4361 Workstation Adapter, and 9370 Workstation Subsystem Controller.

ADAPTER NAME: IBM* Display Station Emulation Adapter/A
FEATURE CODE: 7743
PART NUMBER: 92X0743
AVAILABLE: 7/88
DESCRIPTION: Provides emulation capability for twinaxial attachment of the PS/2* Model 50, 55 SX, 60, 65 SX, 70, P70 and 80 computers as a workstation to the IBM* 5520.

ADAPTER NAME: IBM* System 36/38 Workstation Emulation Adapter/A
FEATURE CODE: 6279
PART NUMBER: 69X6279
AVAILABLE: 12/87
DESCRIPTION: Provides emulation capability for twinaxial attachment of an PS/2* Model 50, 55 SX, 60, 65 SX, 70, P70 or 80 computer as a workstation to the IBM* AS/400*, IBM System/36 and IBM System/38.

Diskette Drive Slave Adapters

ADAPTER NAME: IBM* Personal System/2* 5.25-Inch Diskette Adapter/A
FEATURE CODE: 1007
PART NUMBER: 6451007
AVAILABLE: 11/88
DESCRIPTION: An adapter card that attaches either of the external 5.25″ diskette drives (48690001 for 360KB or 4869-002 for 1.2MB) to the PS/2* Model 50, 50Z, 55 SX, 60, 65 SX, 70, P70 or 80 computers, or the internal diskette drive feature (6451006) to the PS/2* Model 60, 65 SX, or 80 computers.

ADAPTER NAME: IBM* Personal System/2* 5.25-Inch External Diskette Drive Adapter/A
FEATURE CODE: 8760
PART NUMBER: 6450245
AVAILABLE: 5/87
DESCRIPTION: This feature allows the IBM* 4869001 5.25-inch External Diskette Drive (360KB) to be connected to the PS/2* Model 50, 50Z, 60, 70, or 80 (Model 041, 071, 111, 311 only) computers. The feature consists of an adapter card, an internal cable assemble, and a feature card.

Facsimile Slave Adapter

ADAPTER NAME: IBM Personal System/2* FaxConcentrator* Adapter/A*
FEATURE CODE: 2530
PART NUMBER: 94X2530
AVAILABLE: 1/91
DESCRIPTION: High function microprocessor based fax adapter that can provide voice prompting, telephone tone detection, and optical mark recognition functions when used with a suitable application program. Features include real-time processing of tasks such as compression (Image to Group 3), decompression, and format conversions (Group 3 to Group 4) within the adapter, as opposed to doing these tasks with software in the PS/2 computer's main processor. Can communicate with Group 3 facsimile devices over the public switched telephone network for the purpose of routing FAX data. Supports the IBM* Facsimile Support/400 program offering for the PS/2* computers, although it can be used with suitably developed programs for other PS/2 computer applications.*

Graphics Slave Adapters

ADAPTER NAME: IBM* 4055 InfoWindow* Display Attachment Kit
FEATURE CODE: 4239
PART NUMBER: 16F0481
AVAILABLE: 1/88
DESCRIPTION: Provides connection between the InfoWindow* Display and the PS/2* Model 50, 55 SX, 60, 70-E61 and 80 computers. The InfoWindow Attachment Kit includes two new attachment cards that provide the text, graphics, and interface controls.

Graphics Slave Adapters (Continued)

ADAPTER NAME: IBM* Personal System/2* Display Adapter 8514/A
FEATURE CODE: 4054
PART NUMBER: 1887972
AVAILABLE: 6/87
DESCRIPTION: An advanced function display adapter. When configured with the IBM* 8514 or 8515 Color Display, this adapter is suited for applications that require advanced function, high performance and large screen content (1024 x 768 format).

ADAPTER NAME: IBM* PS/2* Image Adapter/A 1MB
FEATURE CODE: 0072
PART NUMBER: 44F9914
AVAILABLE: 8/90
DESCRIPTION: This is the entry offering in a family of upgradable display adapters designed for image processing and general purpose applications requiring high resolution screen support. Supports all PS/2* computers with Micro Channel* architecture except the PS/2* Model P/70 386 computer. Upgrade path to 2MB and 3MB provided for applications requiring additional memory for improved performance or increased grayscale capability. All monochrome and color monitors for PS/2 computers are supported including the 8506 at resolutions up to 864 x 1200 with 256 levels of grayscale, the 8508 at up to 1600 x 1200 with 16 levels of grayscale, and the 6091-019 at up to 1280 x 1024 with 256 colors. Drivers are available for OS/2* Presentation Manager* 1.2, DOS Adapter Interface, Microsoft** Windows/286 Version 2.1, AIX* PS/2 Operating System Version 1.2, AIX PS/2 X- Windows Version 1.2, AIXwindows* Environment for PS/2 and AutoCAD** software.

ADAPTER NAME: IBM* PS/2* Image Adapter/A 3MB
FEATURE CODE: 0073
PART NUMBER: 44F9919
AVAILABLE: 8/90
DESCRIPTION: This image processing adapter has all the attributes of the IBM* PS/2* Image Adapter/A 1MB plus 2MB of additional memory. It can be upgraded to the IBM* PS/2* Image Adapter/A 3MB 6091 by adding the attachment cable for the IBM 6091-019 Color Display.

ADAPTER NAME: IBM* PS/2* Image Adapter/A 3MB 6091
FEATURE CODE: 0074
PART NUMBER: 44F9921
AVAILABLE: 8/90
DESCRIPTION: This adapter provides, in addition to the IBM* PS/2* Image Adapter/A 3MB, an attachment cable for the IBM 6091-019 Color Display.

Image Capture Slave Adapter

ADAPTER NAME: Video Capture Adapter/A for the IBM* Personal System/2*
FEATURE CODE: 2785
PART NUMBER: 34F2785
AVAILABLE: 9/89
DESCRIPTION: Provides the capability to capture, display and digitize high quality video images for use in presentations and applications with the PS/2* Model 50, 55SX, 60, 65 SX, 70 and 80 computers. Supported video signals for input and output are NTSC, Y/C (S-video), and RGB. Intended for use with the Audio Visual Connection (AVC) licensed program. Accepts video input signals through a multi-pin connection on the adapter. The on-board processor converts analog signals to digital format that can be manipulated, compressed and stored by software for later use. Sophisticated, detailed image processing techniques employed in the AVC Image Editor Components enable users to alter the characteristics of the digitized image. Output connectors, for attachment to a monitor, allow viewing of live or captured images. Technical information is provided with the adapter to allow independent application development directly to the adapter.

Memory Slave Adapter — 16-Bit

ADAPTER NAME: IBM* Personal System/2* 2-8MB 80286 Memory Expansion Option
FEATURE CODE: 8286
PART NUMBER: 6450609
AVAILABLE: 4/89
DESCRIPTION: A new memory adapter expandable up to 8MB for all models of the PS/2* computer Models 50, 50Z, 55 SX, 60 and 65 SX. This adapter provides memory expansion up to 8MB by using existing memory kits: 1MB Memory Module Kit — 85ns (PN 6450603) and 2MB Memory Module Kit — 85ns (6450604). This memory expansion option can be used with OS/2* computer software as extended memory, or as expanded memory. An expanded memory device driver compatible with LIM EMS Version 4.0 is included.

Memory Slave Adapters — 32-Bit

ADAPTER NAME: IBM* Personal System/2* 2-8MB 80386 Memory Expansion Option
FEATURE CODE: 5211
PART NUMBER: 6450605
AVAILABLE: 6/88
DESCRIPTION: A 2-8MB 32-bit Micro Channel* architecture extended memory expansion card containing 2MB of 85ns memory as standard. Up to three 1MB or 2MB memory module kits can be added to the card to provide 8MB of memory to the PS/2* Model 70, P70 and 80 computers.

ADAPTER NAME: IBM* PS/2* Enhanced 80386 Memory Expansion Option 2MB Kit
FEATURE CODE: 3077
PART NUMBER: 34F3077
AVAILABLE: 7/89
DESCRIPTION: This 2MB Kit contains a 32-bit full length adapter card available with 2MB of memory. It can be installed in any open 32-bit expansion slot of the PS/2* Model 70 or 80 computer and in the full sized expansion slot of the PS/2 Model P70 computer. This option kit combines the Enhanced 80386 Memory Expansion Option with an IBM* 2MB Memory Module Kit-85ns. This combination contains 2MB of memory, expandable up to 14MB with the installation of up to three additional 1MB, 2MB or 4MB Memory Module Kits.

ADAPTER NAME: IBM* PS/2* Enhanced 80386 Memory Expansion Option 4MB Kit
FEATURE CODE: 3011
PART NUMBER: 34F3011
AVAILABLE: 3/90
DESCRIPTION: This 4MB Kit contains a 32-bit full length adapter card available with 4MB of memory. It can be installed in any open 32-bit expansion slot of the IBM* PS/2* Model 70 or 80 computer and in the full sized expansion slot of the PS/2 Model P70 computer. This kit uses IBM 4MB memory technology to provide 4MB of high speed 80ns memory. Up to three additional 4MB Memory Module Kits may be installed on the adapter card increasing adapter memory up to 16MB. For installation in PS/2 Model 70, P70 and 80 computers, where a maximum of 16MB of memory is required, no more than three 4MB Kits should be installed on the adapter with a 2MB Kit installed in the fourth socket.

Multimedia Slave Adapter

ADAPTER NAME: M-Motion Video Adapter/A
FEATURE CODE: 3487
PART NUMBER: 34F3087
AVAILABLE: 3/90
DESCRIPTION: An adapter that allows PS/2* computers with Micro Channel* bus to display full motion, interactive color video on standard color PS/2 computer monitors. This adapter also provides full line audio and limited digital audio capabilities. It receives analog signals from an audio-video source, processes the signals and sends them to the PS/2 computer monitor and speaker.

Scanner Slave Adapters

ADAPTER NAME: IBM* 3117 Adapter/A
FEATURE CODE: 1029
PART NUMBER: 65X1925
AVAILABLE: 5/87
DESCRIPTION: Provides a unique interface for attaching the 3117 Scanner to the PS/2* Model 50, 60, 65 SX, 70, P70 and 80 computers via the 3117 PC Cable. The 3117 Adapter/A has the function of Digital halftone, Partial page scanning and Darkness control.

ADAPTER NAME: IBM* 3119 PageScanner* Adapter/A
FEATURE CODE: 5442
PART NUMBER: 94X2415
AVAILABLE: 8/88
DESCRIPTION: Provides a unique interface for attaching the 3119 PageScanner* to the PS/2* Model 50, 55 SX, 60, 65 SX, 70, P70 and 80 computers. The 3119 Adapter/A has the function of Digital halftone, Partial page scanning, Gray darkness control, Gray contrast control and Resolution conversion (1 x 1 to 600 x 600 pels per inch by 1 pel).

ADAPTER NAME: IBM* Personal System/2* High Speed Adapter/A
FEATURE CODE: 1028
PART NUMBER: 65X1905
AVAILABLE: 5/87
DESCRIPTION: Provides an RS-422A industry standard interface for attaching the 3118 Scanner or 3117 Scanner with 3117 Extension Unit to the PS/2* Model 50, 55 SX, 60, 70, P70 and 80 computers via a Serial Adapter Cable (PN: 6450217).

Serial Port Slave Adapters

ADAPTER NAME: IBM* Realtime Interface Co-Processor Multiport/2 and Related Features
FEATURE CODE: 6263
PART NUMBER: 09F1897
AVAILABLE: 3/88
DESCRIPTION: A versatile, programmable, intelligent, 80186-based co-processor that provides up to 8 serial input/output ports through various interface boards. Asynchronous protocol hardware support is provided on all ports with bit synchronous and character synchronous protocol support available on up to 6 ports. Communication data rates up to 64,000 bps full duplex can be achieved on one port or all 8 ports may be operated concurrently at up to 9,600 bps full duplex. The Co-Processor provides a realtime multitasking environment for supporting user applications and is supplied with 512KB of dual-ported memory.

ADAPTER NAME: IBM* Realtime Interface Co-Processor Multiport/2 with 1MB Memory and Related Features
FEATURE CODE: 6247
PART NUMBER: 16F1820
AVAILABLE: 10/88
DESCRIPTION: Provides the same function as the IBM* Realtime Interface Co- Processor Multiport/2 plus increased memory capacity of 1MB.

ADAPTER NAME: IBM* Realtime Interface Co-Processor Portmaster Adapter/A and Related Features
FEATURE CODE: 6360
PART NUMBER: 53F2601
AVAILABLE: 12/89
DESCRIPTION: A Micro Channel* bus master co-processor that complements and extends the capabilities of the current family of IBM* Realtime Interface Co-Processor adapters. Bus master extensions include capabilities and services to address adapter-to-system and adapter-to-adapter data transfers using the bus master capability of the Micro Channel architecture. Performance enhancements supporting full-duplex data rates of up to 64K bps for each of eight ports running concurrently or up to 2.048M bps for a single port can be achieved with the adapter. The one-slot adapter features a 12.5MHz Intel** 80C186 microprocessor and 512KB of on-board storage.

Tape Drive Slave Adapter

ADAPTER NAME: IBM* Personal System/2* 6157 Tape Drive Adapter
FEATURE CODE: 4160
PART NUMBER: 92X1458
AVAILABLE: 9/87
DESCRIPTION: Provides QIC-02 attachment (5MB/min burst data rate) of the IBM* 6157 Streaming Tape Drives, both Model 001 and 002, to PS/2* computers with the Micro Channel* bus. When used with the SYTOS PLUS**/IBM FILE BACKUP UTILITIES, DOS and OS/2* computer software files can be compressed up to 70% (50% average) effectively doubling the drive's capabilities. The full Presentation Manager* programs support unattended backup requirements for IBM OS/2 Local Area Network (LAN) Server Version 1.2 and the IBM Personal Computer LAN Program Version 1.3, including some OS/2 files that are always open, such as OS2SYS.INI and OS2.INI configuration files.

Uncategorized Slave Adapters

ADAPTER NAME: IBM* S/370 Channel Emulator/A
FEATURE CODE: 3205
PART NUMBER: 1674899
AVAILABLE: 11/89
DESCRIPTION: This card for the PS/2* Model 50, 55 SX, 60, 65 SX, 70, 80 and P70 computers, which emulates the operation of a System/370* channel, coupled with the Remote PrintManager software, may be used to channel attach IBM 3820, 3825, 3827, or 3835 Page Printers. The new S/370 Channel Emulator Technical Reference provides information about the programming interface which is needed to develop appropriate software to channel attach other System/370 devices.

ADAPTER NAME: IBM* Second Store Loop Adapter/A
FEATURE CODE: 6701
PART NUMBER: 83X7575
AVAILABLE: 3/90
DESCRIPTION: The Second Store Loop Adapter/A is physically the same as the adapter provided as part of the IBM* Store Controller Kit. This option monitors another store loop's activity and, with the 4680 Operating System, takes control of the monitored loop if it detects a lack of store controller activity.

Uncategorized Slave Adapters (Continued)

ADAPTER NAME: IBM* Store Controller Kit
FEATURE CODE: 6500
PART NUMBER: 83X8187
AVAILABLE: 3/90
DESCRIPTION: The IBM* Store Controller Kit allows the PS/2* Model 55 SX computer, with the IBM 4680 Operating System Version 2 (5601- 192) to become a store controller for the IBM 4680 Store System. The kit consists of a Store Loop Adapter/A and a Store Systems Shipment Group. The Store Loop Adapter/A in conjunction with the 4680 Operating System Version 2 will control a store loop to which can be attached up to 64 IBM 4683 Model 001 or A01 Point of Sale Terminals. Each 4683 Model 001 or A01 may have a 4683 Model 002 attached for a total of 128 terminals per store loop. The operational speed of the loop is 38,400 bits per second. The adapter contains two 2,000 character battery protected buffers to insure that data is correctly written to the disk before the buffer is released for the next operation. This same kit goes on the 8560, 8570 (selected Models) and 8580.

IBM BUS MASTER ADAPTERS BY CATEGORY FOR PERSONAL SYSTEM/2 COMPUTERS

General Purpose Bus Master Adapter

ADAPTER NAME: IBM* PS/2* Wizard Adapter
FEATURE CODE: 3462
PART NUMBER: 34F3062
AVAILABLE: 4/90
DESCRIPTION: An application accelerator that can significantly increase the performance of advanced, numeric-intensive applications on the PS/2* Model 70 and 80 computers. This bus master adapter uses the Intel** i860** microprocessor which features a RISC integer core, an advanced floating point processing unit, a graphics unit, internal instruction cache and internal data cache in a single 1-million transistor chip. The adapter also contains 2MB of random access memory (RAM), which is expandable to a total of 8MB using the IBM* PS/2 Wizard Memory Expansion Option (PN 34F3061). The adapter uses a set of application device drivers, shipped with the product, that enable operation with IBM Operating System/2* computer software. Software toolkits are available that enable developers to port C and FORTRAN applications to execute on the PS/2 Wizard Adapters.

SCSI Bus Master Adatpers

ADAPTER NAME: IBM* Personal System/2* Micro Channel* SCSI Adapter
FEATURE CODE: 1005
PART NUMBER: 6451005
AVAILABLE: 3/90
DESCRIPTION: A 16-bit bus master adapter that provides expandability for all PS/2* computers with the Micro Channel* bus. The adapter provides connection for multiple internal and/or external SCSI devices and has a 8.3MB per second Micro Channel bus burst transfer rate. The adapter card may be installed in a 16- or 32-bit card slot and provides the ability to connect SCSI high performance fixed disk drives, scanners, printers, CD-ROM drives, and other SCSI peripherals.

ADAPTER NAME: IBM* Personal System/2* Micro Channel* SCSI Adapter with Cache
FEATURE CODE: 1018
PART NUMBER: 6451018
AVAILABLE: 3/90
DESCRIPTION: A 32-bit bus master adapter that provides expandability for all PS/2* computers with the Micro Channel* bus. This adapter can be installed in either a 16- or 32-bit card slot, has a 16.6MB burst transfer rate, 512KB Cache buffer, and adheres to the Small Computer System Interface (SCSI) that supports connection for multiple internal and/or external SCSI devices. These devices include SCSI high performance fixed disk drives, scanners, CD-ROM drives, and other SCSI peripherals.

Serial Port Bus Master Adapters

ADAPTER NAME: IBM* Realtime Interface Co-Processor Portmaster Adapter/A and Related Features
FEATURE CODE: 6360
PART NUMBER: 53F2601
AVAILABLE: 12/89
DESCRIPTION: A Micro Channel* bus master co-processor that complements and extends the capabilities of the current family of IBM* Realtime Interface Co-Processor adapters. Bus master extensions include capabilities and services to address adapter-to-system and adapter-to-adapter data transfers using the bus master capability of the Micro Channel architecture. Performance enhancements supporting full-duplex data rates of up to 64K bps for each of eight ports running concurrently or up to 2.048M bps for a single port can be achieved with the adapter. The one-slot adapter features a 12.5MHz Intel** 80C186 microprocessor and 512KB of on-board storage.

ADAPTER NAME: IBM* Realtime Interface Co-Processor Portmaster Adapter/A with 1MB Memory and Related Features
FEATURE CODE: 6364
PART NUMBER: 53F2604
AVAILABLE: 12/89
DESCRIPTION: Provides the same function as the IBM* Realtime Interface Co-Processor Portmaster Adapter/A plus increased memory capacity of 1MB.

ADAPTER NAME: IBM* Realtime Interface Co-Processor Portmaster Adapter/A with 2MB Memory and Related Features
FEATURE CODE: 6368
PART NUMBER: 53F2607
AVAILABLE: 12/89
DESCRIPTION: Provides the same function as the IBM* Realtime Interface Co-Processor Portmaster Adapter/A plus increased memory capacity of 2MB.

IBM SLAVE ADAPTERS BY CATEGORY FOR RISC SYSTEM/6000* POWERSTATIONS AND POWERSERVERS

Terminal Emulation Slave Adapter

ADAPTER NAME: IBM* 3270 Connection
FEATURE CODE: 2990
AVAILABLE: 6/90
DESCRIPTION: Provides the support to attach a RISC System/6000* system unit to a mainframe and allows the system unit to respond like an IBM* 3278 or 3279 Display Terminal. This adapter supports coaxial cable attachment between the RISC System/6000 system unit and any of the following: IBM 3174 and 3274 Display Control Units, IBM 4331 and 4361 Integrated Display/Printer Adapter, IBM 4331 and 4361 Integrated Work/Station Adapter, and IBM 9370 Workstation Subsystem Controller.

X.25 Slave Adapter

ADAPTER NAME: IBM* X.25 Interface Co-Processor/2
FEATURE CODE: 2960
AVAILABLE: 6/90
DESCRIPTION: The X.25 Interface Co-Processor/2 attaches a RISC System/6000* system unit to an X.25 packet switched network. This adapter provides a single port that will accommodate one of three selectable interfaces: X.21, EIA-322-D/V.24, and V.35. The adapter's on-board software is capable of processing inbound and outbound data streams to off-load communications tasks from the system processor. The adapter supports full duplex synchronous or asynchronous protocols and is supplied with 512KB of memory.

Graphics Slave Adapter

ADAPTER NAME: IBM* RISC System/6000* Graphics Input Device Adapter
FEATURE CODE: 2810
AVAILABLE: 6/90
DESCRIPTION: Provides attachment of the IBM* 6094 Model 010 Dials and the IBM 6094 Model 020 Lighted Program Function Keyboard to the IBM RISC System/6000. This two-port card provides control lines as well as DC power to the attached devices. The Micro Channel* bus interface is an 8-bit I/O slave with data and address parity.

Serial Port Slave Adapters

ADAPTER NAME: IBM* RISC System/6000* 16-Port Async Adapter - EIA-232
FEATURE CODE: 2955
AVAILABLE: 6/90
DESCRIPTION: Provides support for attaching up to 16 EIA-232-D asynchronous serial devices, such as terminals, or printers, to a RISC System/6000* system unit. Data rates up to 38.4K bps are supported on each port. It supports cabling up to 61m (200 feet). Sixteen-byte buffering is provided on transmit and receive. The Micro Channel* bus interface is an 8/16-bit I/O slave which supports data and address parity.

ADAPTER NAME: IBM* RISC System/6000* 16-Port Async Adapter - EIA-422A
FEATURE CODE: 2957
AVAILABLE: 6/90
DESCRIPTION: Provides support for attaching up to 16 EIA-422A asynchronous serial devices, such as terminals, or printers, to a RISC System/6000* system unit. Data rates up to 38.4K bps are supported on each port. It supports cabling up to 1200m (4,000 feet). Sixteen-byte buffering is provided on transmit and receive. The Micro Channel* bus interface is an 8/16-bit I/O slave which supports data and address parity.

ADAPTER NAME: IBM* RISC System/6000* 64-Port Async Controller
FEATURE CODE: 6400
AVAILABLE: 6/90
DESCRIPTION: Provides support for attaching up to 64 EIA-232-D asynchronous serial devices, such as terminals, or printers, from a single I/O slot in a RISC System/6000* system unit. The controller has connectors to attach up to 4 external 16-Port Async Concentrators (RISC System/6000 Feature Code #6401). A concentrator provides 16 connections for EIA-232 asynchronous devices. Although application dependent, data rates up to 38.4K bps are supported on each port. Cabling distances of up to 762m (2,500 feet) between controller and concentrator are supported. EIA-232 cabling of up to 61m (200 feet) between concentrator and device is supported. The Micro Channel* bus interface is an 8/16-bit memory slave.

ADAPTER NAME: IBM* RISC System/6000* 8-Port Async Adapter - EIA-232
FEATURE CODE: 2930
AVAILABLE: 6/90
DESCRIPTION: Provides support for attaching up to 8 EIA-232-D asynchronous serial devices, such as terminals, modems or printers, to a RISC System/6000* system unit. Data rates up to 38.4K bps are supported on each port. Sixteen byte buffering is provided on transmit and receive. Full modem control lines are provided. The Micro Channel* bus interface is an 8/16-bit I/O slave which supports data and address parity.

Serial Port Slave Adapters (Continued)

ADAPTER NAME: IBM* RISC System/6000* 8-Port Async Adapter - EIA-422A
FEATURE CODE: 2940
AVAILABLE: 6/90
DESCRIPTION: Provides support for attaching up to 8 EIA-422A asynchronous serial devices, such as terminals, or printers, to a RISC System/6000* system unit. Data rates up to 38.4K bps are supported on each port. This adapter supports cabling up to 1220m (4,000 feet). Sixteen-byte buffering is provided on transmit and receive. The Micro Channel* bus interface is an 8/16-bit I/O slave which supports data and address parity.

ADAPTER NAME: IBM* RISC System/6000* 8-Port Async Adapter - MIL-STD-188
FEATURE CODE: 2950
AVAILABLE: 6/90
DESCRIPTION: Provides support for attaching up to 8 MIL-STD-188 asynchronous serial devices, such as terminals, or printers, to a RISC System/6000* system unit. It meets the requirements of MIL-STD 188-114 for unbalanced voltage digital interface. It supports cabling up to 30M (100 feet) at 38K bps and 61m (200 feet) at 19.2K bps. Sixteen-byte buffering is provided on transmit and receive. The Micro Channel* bus interface is an 8/16-bit I/O slave which supports data and address parity.

IBM BUS MASTER ADAPTERS BY CATGORY FOR RISC SYSTEM/6000* POWERSTATIONS AND POWERSERVERS

Multiprotocol Bus Master Adapter

ADAPTER NAME: IBM* RISC System/6000* 4-Port Multiprotocol Communications Controller
FEATURE CODE: 2700
AVAILABLE: 6/90
DESCRIPTION: Attaches a RISC System/6000* system unit to synchronous communications networks using EIA-422A, V.35 and X.21 physical specifications. The controller supports SDLC and BSC protocols, prepares all inbound and outbound data, performs address searches and in general relieves the system processor of many communications tasks. It is designed to support 4 ports concurrently at data rates up to 64K bps per port with appropriate user provided software. This adapter is supplied with 512KB of RAM for data buffering. The Micro Channel* bus interface is a 16-bit data and 32-bit address bus master.

Network Bus Master Adapters

ADAPTER NAME: IBM* RISC System/6000* Ethernet** High-Performance LAN Adapter
FEATURE CODE: 2980
AVAILABLE: 6/90
DESCRIPTION: This is a high performance bus master adapter which attaches the RISC System/6000* system unit to Ethernet** networks. It is designed to provide connection to a 10 Megabit Carrier Sense Multiple Access/Collision Detection Ethernet network and is compatible with IEEE 802.3 and Ethernet external interfaces. The Micro Channel* bus interface is a 32-bit bus master which supports data and address parity.

ADAPTER NAME: IBM* RISC System/6000* Token-Ring High-Performance Network Adapter
FEATURE CODE: 2970
AVAILABLE: 6/90
DESCRIPTION: This adapter is designed to allow an IBM* RISC System/6000* system unit to attach to 4M bps or 16M bps Token-Ring local area networks. It is cable and network compatible with all IBM Token-Ring adapters and those for PS/2* computers. No new cables or network components are required. The Micro Channel* bus interface is a 2-byte bus master which supports streaming data mode and address and data parity.

Graphics Bus Master Adapters

ADAPTER NAME: IBM* RISC System/6000* 5085 Attachment Adapter
FEATURE CODE: 2802
AVAILABLE: 6/90
DESCRIPTION: Provides two functions for the IBM* RISC System/6000* system unit. This adapter provides a direct connection to the IBM 5085 Graphics Processor so that the 5085 can utilize the RISC System/6000 based applications. The adapter also provides a switching capability that allows the 5085 to bypass the RISC System/6000 and utilize the applications that reside on the System/370* mainframe. The Micro Channel* bus interface is a 16-bit data 24-bit address bus master which supports data and address parity.

ADAPTER NAME: IBM* RISC System/6000* 5086 Attachment Adapter
FEATURE CODE: 2801
AVAILABLE: 6/90
DESCRIPTION: Provides two functions for the IBM* RISC System/6000* system unit. This adapter provides a direct connection to the IBM 5086 Graphics Processor so that the 5086 can utilize the RISC System/6000 based applications. The adapter also provides a switching capability that allows the 5086 to bypass the RISC System/6000 and utilize the applications that reside on the System/370* mainframe. The Micro Channel* bus interface is a 16-bit data 24-bit address bus master which supports data and address parity.

ADAPTER NAME: IBM* RISC System/6000* Color Graphics Display Adapter
FEATURE CODE: 2770
AVAILABLE: 6/90
DESCRIPTION: Provides support for 16-inch, 19-inch, and 23-inch analog non- interlaced, 1280 x 1024 60Hz color graphic displays on the IBM* RISC System/6000* system unit. Two hundred and fifty-six concurrent colors may be displayed from a palette of 16.7 million. This adapter occupies one slot on the Micro Channel* bus and is the larger (type 5) form factor card. The Micro Channel bus interface is a 32-bit bus master which supports streaming data and address parity.

ADAPTER NAME: IBM* RISC System/6000* Grayscale Graphics Display Adapter
FEATURE CODE: 2760
AVAILABLE: 6/90
DESCRIPTION: Provides support for the IBM* 8508 19-inch monochrome, analog non-interlaced 1280 x 1024 67Hz graphic display on the IBM* RISC System/6000* system unit. Sixteen concurrent shades of gray may be displayed from a palette of 256 shades of gray. This adapter occupies one card slot on the Micro Channel* bus and is the larger (type 5) form factor card. The Micro Channel bus interface is a 32-bit bus master which supports streaming data and address parity.

Graphics Bus Master Adapters (Continued)

ADAPTER NAME: IBM* RISC System/6000* High Performance 24-bit 3D Color Graphics Processor
FEATURE CODE: 2781
AVAILABLE: 6/90
DESCRIPTION: This processor has the same features as the IBM* RISC System/6000* High Performance 8-bit Color Graphics Processor (Feature Code 2780) with the addition of the 24-bit Color Graphics Frame Buffer Upgrade (RISC System/6000 Feature Code #2783) as a standard feature. The 24-bit Frame Buffer card is the larger (type 5) form factor. One optional feature is available. The 24-bit Z-Buffer Solid Rendering Option (RISC System/6000 Feature Code #2782) provides for hidden line and hidden surface removal and enables smooth surface rendering. The Micro Channel* bus interface is a 32-bit bus master which supports data and address parity and streaming data mode.

ADAPTER NAME: IBM* RISC System/6000* High Performance 8-Bit 3D Color Graphics Processor
FEATURE CODE: 2780
AVAILABLE: 6/90
DESCRIPTION: Provides support for 16", 19" and 23" analog non-interlaced, 1280 x 1024 60Hz color graphic displays. May display 256 concurrent colors from a palette of 16.7 million. Characteristics include: 8-bit pixels, 2 overlay planes, 2 window control planes, support of a variety of graphics functions: lighting, shading, clipping, pan, zoom, anti-aliased lines, arbitrary shaped windows, and so on. Requires 2 adjacent slots on the Micro Channel* bus. Optional features: the 24-bit Z-Buffer Solid Rendering Option (RISC System/6000* Feature Code #2782) for hidden line/surface removal and smooth surface rendering, and the 24-Bit Color Graphics Frame Buffer (RISC System/6000 Feature Code #2783) for additional 16-bit buffer, 16 sets of 256 concurrent colors, 2 additional overlay planes, 2 additional window control planes, and 24-bit "true color". These options plug onto the Graphics Processor.

ADAPTER NAME: IBM* RISC System/6000* System/370* Host Interface Adapter
FEATURE CODE: 2800
AVAILABLE: 6/90
DESCRIPTION: This adapter is designed to work as either a high speed connection to the System/370* mainframe for high speed file transfer or in conjunction with either the 5086 or the 5085 Attachment Adapter. It provides high speed file transfer between the RISC System/6000* system unit and the System/370 through an IBM* 5088 Graphics Control Unit. The Micro Channel* bus interface is a 16-bit data 24-bit address bus master which supports data and address parity.

SCSI Bus Master Adapter

ADAPTER NAME: IBM* RISC System/6000* SCSI High-Performance Internal/External I/O Controller
FEATURE CODE: 2828
AVAILABLE: 6/90
DESCRIPTION: Provides high performance attachment of single-ended internal or external SCSI disk drives, CD-ROM, and tape drives for the IBM* RISC System/6000* system unit. The controller supports SCSI parity, acts as a SCSI initiator, and accepts multiple commands per device. The Micro Channel* bus interface is a 4-byte (32- bit) bus master which supports data and address parity and streaming data mode.

IBM SLAVE ADAPTERS BY CATGORY FOR ENTERPRISE SYSTEM/9371 MODEL 10 AND MODEL 12 AND S/370 SIDE OF THE MODEL 14

Network Slave Adapters

ADAPTER NAME: IBM* Token-Ring Adapter
FEATURE CODE: 6034
AVAILABLE: 3/90
DESCRIPTION: Provides access to a high-speed 4 or 16 Mbps IBM* Token-Ring network compatible with the IEEE 802.5 standard for interconnecting information processing equipment. Ring Error Monitor support will be provided for Model 10 and 12. Maximum: one per Model 10, 2 per Model 12, one per Model 14. Field installation. Only one adapter can be installed per System Board. May have an impact on quantity of attached devices. The Token-Ring allows the software to configure a maximum number of 64 logical connections between the 9371 and other ring stations. Since the overall throughput capability is shared between the logical connections the number of links doing actual data transfer simultaneously is limited by the required data rate per individual link.

ADAPTER NAME: IEEE 802.3 Local Area Network Adapter
FEATURE CODE: 6035
AVAILABLE: 3/90
DESCRIPTION: Compatible with IEEE 802.3 standard or the Ethernet** local area network. The adapter provides communication with the IBM* ES/9370 Information Systems, other vendors' systems, and work stations compatible with IEEE 802.3 local area networks. It supports a network with a transmission speed of 10 Mbps using Carrier Sense Multiple Access with Collision Detection (CSMA/CD). Maximum: one per Model 10, two per Model 12, one per Model 14. Field installation. Only one adapter can be installed per System Board. May have an impact on quantity of attached devices.

SNA/SDLC/BSC Slave Adapters

ADAPTER NAME: Dual Async Adapter
FEATURE CODE: 6011
AVAILABLE: 3/90
DESCRIPTION: Provides two serial asynchronous communication ports for attachment of modems and other peripheral devices, such as the IBM* 3151 Model 310 and 410. Maximum: one per Model 10, two per Model 12, one per Model 14. Field installation. Only one adapter can be installed per System Board. The maximum line speed is 9600 bps for each port.

ADAPTER NAME: High Performance SDLC Adapter
FEATURE CODE: 6027
AVAILABLE: 3/90
DESCRIPTION: Provides one interface port for the attachment of modems or direct connection to SDLC/SNA device such as the 3174 Controller at speeds up to 64,000 bps. Physical interfaces supported by this adapter are RS-232-C/V.24, V.35, and X.21 leased and circuit switched lines. Maximum: three per Model 10, eight per Model 12, three per Model 14. Field installation. No more than five adapters can be installed on System Board B on the Model 12. The maximum line speed per adapter is 64,000 bps.

Terminal Emulation Slave Adapter

ADAPTER NAME: 3270 Adapter
FEATURE CODE: 6120
AVAILABLE: 6/90
DESCRIPTION: Provides three coax ports for the attachment of 3270 terminals and printers and the IBM* 3299 Multiplexor. Using IBM 3299 multiplexors expands the number of attachments to 24. SNA and non-SNA capability is provided. Maximum: one per Model 10, two per Model 12, one per Model 14. Field installation. Only one adapter can be installed per System Board.

X.25 Slave Adapter

ADAPTER NAME: X.25/HDLC Packet Network Adapter
FEATURE CODE: 6029
AVAILABLE: 3/90
DESCRIPTION: This adapter provides one interface port that is capable of supporting X.25/HDLC communication at line speeds ranging from 2,400 to 64,000 bps. Physical interfaces supported by this adapter are X.21BIS/V.24/RS-232-C, X.21BIS/V.35 and X.21. This feature provides the physical and data link layers for connecting to X.25 packet switched networks. However, the packet layer must be provided by appropriate System/370* software such as VTAM X.25 Communications Adapter Support. Maximum: one per Model 10, two per Model 12, one per Model 14. Field installation. Only one adapter can be installed per System Board. Maximum line speed on Model 10 and 12 is 64,000 bps. Maximum line speed on Model 14 is 19,200 bps.

Graphics Slave Adapter

ADAPTER NAME: 5080 Graphics Adapter
FEATURE CODE: 7010
AVAILABLE: 3/90
DESCRIPTION: Used to attach 5080 Graphics System Workstations. Up to four 5085 Model 2A or 5086 Graphics Processors may be attached. Maximum: one per Model 10, two per Model 12, one per Model 14. Field installation. Only one adapter can be installed per System Board.

Printer Slave Adapter

ADAPTER NAME: High Speed Printer Adapter
FEATURE CODE: 7040
AVAILABLE: 6/90
DESCRIPTION: Provides for the attachment of the IBM* 3825, 3827 and 3835 page printers and the IBM 6262 Model 14 and 22 Impact Line Printers. The feature includes an adapter card, a 3 meter (10 feet) attachment cable, and Bus and Tag channel terminators. Maximum: one per Model 10, two per Model 12, one per Model 14. Only one adapter can be installed per System Board and one printer can be attached per adapter.

SCSI Slave Adapter

ADAPTER NAME: DASD Adapter
SUPPORTS: 9371 Model 12
FEATURE CODE: 4050
AVAILABLE: 3/90
DESCRIPTION: Provides the capability on a Model 12 to attach some or all of the optional drives to System Board B. The additional adapter is used to balance DASD activity across 2 system boards and contains a second 512KB file cache, both of which can reduce service time. The maximum of six DASD drives is the same with or without this adapter. This feature uses one I/O slot on the second system board. Maximum: one for the Model 12. Field installation.

Serial Port Slave Adapters

ADAPTER NAME: 8 Port RS-232-C (1MB) Adapter
FEATURE CODE: 7022
AVAILABLE: 3/90
DESCRIPTION: Provides eight EIA RS-232-C (CCITT V.24) serial I/O ports. An 8-port cable and connector is included. The adapter has a 1MB memory. Maximum: three per Model 10, ten per Model 12, three per Model 14. Field installation. Depends on customer programming.

ADAPTER NAME: 8-Port RS-232-C Adapter (512KB)
FEATURE CODE: 6022
AVAILABLE: 3/90
DESCRIPTION: Provides eight EIA RS-232-C (CCITT V.24) serial I/O ports. An 8-port cable and connector is included. All eight ports may be used for asynchronous communications. The first two ports may also be used for synchronous communications. Devices may be up to 15.2 meters (50 feet) away without a modem. For greater distances, a modem may be used. Each port is capable of line speeds of up to 19,200 bps. The maximum number of lines and maximum data rates supported by one adapter are dependent upon line speeds selected and the mix of protocols. This adapter may be used with System/370* communications. It can also be programmed to support special protocols or applications. Maximum: three per Model 10, ten per Model 12, three per Model 14. Field installation. Maximum line speed for all ports per adapter varies by usage. Ports 0 and 1, if used for synchronous communication, can both be SDLC or both be BSC but not one of each.

ADAPTER NAME: 8 Port RS-232-C/RS-422-A (1MB) Adapter
FEATURE CODE: 7024
AVAILABLE: 3/90
DESCRIPTION: Provides four EIA RS-232-C (CCITT V.24) serial I/O ports and four RS-422-A (CCITT V.11) serial I/O ports. An 8-port cable and connector is included. The adapter has a 1MB memory. Maximum: three per Model 10, ten per Model 12, three per Model 14. Field installation. Depends on customer programming.

ADAPTER NAME: 8-Port RS-232-C/RS-422-A Adapter (512KB)
FEATURE CODE: 6024
AVAILABLE: 3/90
DESCRIPTION: Provides four EIA RS-232-C (CCITT V.24) serial I/O ports and four RS-422-A (CCITT V.11) serial I/O ports. An 8-port cable and connector is included. All eight ports may be used for asynchronous communications. The first two RS-232-C ports may also be used for synchronous (SDLC, BSC) communications. Each port is capable of line speeds of up to 19,200 bps. The maximum number of lines and maximum data rates supported by one adapter are dependent upon line speeds selected and the mix of protocols. This adapter may be used with S/370 communications. It can also be programmed to support special protocols or applications. Maximum: three per Model 10, ten per Model 12, three per Model 14. Field installation. The maximum line speed for all ports per adapter varies by usage. Ports 0 and 1, if used for synchronous communication, must operated with either SDLC or BSC but not both.

ADAPTER NAME: 8 Port RS-422-A (1MB) Adapter
FEATURE CODE: 7026
AVAILABLE: 3/90
DESCRIPTION: Provides eight RS-422-A serial I/O ports. An 8 port cable and connector is included. The adapter has a 1MB memory. Maximum: three per Model 10, ten per Model 12, three per Model 14. Field installation. Depends on customer programming.

Serial Port Slave Adapters (Continued)

ADAPTER NAME: 8-Port RS-422-A Adapter (512KB)
FEATURE CODE: 6026
AVAILABLE: 3/90
DESCRIPTION: Provides eight RS-422-A serial I/O ports. An 8-port cable and connector is included. All eight ports in each adapter are capable of asynchronous communications. Devices can be attached up to 1,219 meters (4000 feet) away. No modem is required. Each port is capable of line speeds of up to 19,200 bps. The maximum number of lines and maximum data rates supported by the adapter are dependent upon line speeds selected and the mix of protocols. This adapter may be used with S/370 communications. It can also be programmed to support special protocols or applications. Maximum: three per Model 10, ten per Model 12, three per Model 14. Field installation. The maximum line speed for all ports per adapter varies by usage.

Tape Drive Slave Adapter

ADAPTER NAME: Half-Inch Tape Unit Adapter
FEATURE CODE: 4051
AVAILABLE: 3/90
DESCRIPTION: Provides attach of one IBM* 9348 Model 12 Magnetic Tape Unit. This feature includes the System Unit adapter and a 5 meter (16.4 feet) attachment cable and is used to attach the IBM 9348 Model 12 reel type magnetic tape unit mounted in a stand alone enclosure. It has a data storage capacity of up to 40 million bytes of data at 1600 bpi and up to 140 million bytes of data at 6250 bpi. It autoloads and autothreads reels of industry standard one half-inch magnetic tape and can be used for data interchange with other systems with one half-inch reel type magnetic tape units. This feature uses one I/O slot. No prerequisite. Maximum: one per Model 10, two per Model 12, one per Model 14. Field installation. Only one adapter can be installed per system board.

Uncategorized Slave Adapter

ADAPTER NAME: Data Exchange Adapter
SUPPORTS: 9371 370 side of Model 14
FEATURE CODE: 4014
AVAILABLE: 6/90
DESCRIPTION: Provides a direct, hardware connection between the System/370* processor and the PS/2* processor in a Model 14. This high speed connection is logically divided into two concurrent communication paths. East path is a full duplex path that may be used independently. Using this feature, customers may develop applications which benefit from the ability to directly exchange data between PS/2 and System/370 programs. The Data Exchange Adapter uses a shared storage buffer (RAM memory) to provide a memory-mapped window for communications between the adapter and application programs. The first 32-bit slot must be available on the PS/2 side. Maximum: one. Field installation. Support is not available for all operating systems.

IBM SLAVE ADAPTERS BY CATEGORY FOR ENTERPRISE SYSTEM/9371 MODEL 14 (PS/2* COMPUTER SIDE OF THE MODEL 14)

Network Slave Adapters

ADAPTER NAME: IBM* Token-Ring Network 16/4 Adapter A
FEATURE CODE: 6044
AVAILABLE: 3/90
DESCRIPTION: Provides for attachment to IBM* Token-Ring Networks operating at either 4 or 16 Mbps. Maximum: one. Field installation.

ADAPTER NAME: IEEE 802.3 Local Area Network Adapter Feature
FEATURE CODE: 6045
AVAILABLE: 3/90
DESCRIPTION: This is the Ungermann-Bass NIC PS/2* Adapter 1542 for use with Ethernet** local area networks. This feature provides a connection to a 10M Carrier Sense Multiple Access/Collision Detection (CSMA/CD) Ethernet network. The adapter attaches to the network via IEEE 802.3 AUI cable that is connected to a CSMA/CD transceiver. The cable and transceiver are not included with the adapter. Maximum: one. Field installation.

SNA/SDLC/BSC Slave Adapter

ADAPTER NAME: IBM* Personal System/2* Dual Async Adapter
FEATURE CODE: 6010
AVAILABLE: 3/90
DESCRIPTION: Provides asynchronous communication on two RS-232-C ports. Supports speeds from 50 to 19,200 bps. Signal transmission is supported across 50 feet of cable. Maximum: three. Field installation. Total system load will limit the practical number of ports and the speed of each port.

X.25 Slave Adapter

ADAPTER NAME: IBM* X.25 Interface Co-Processor/2
FEATURE CODE: 6049
AVAILABLE: 3/90
DESCRIPTION: A high speed intelligent communications adapter that can provide a full duplex, synchronous or asynchronous X.21, X.21 bis V.24 (RS-232) or X.21 bis V.35 interface by means of a selectable cable option.

Memory Slave Adapter — 32-Bit

ADAPTER NAME: IBM* PS/2* Enhanced 80386 Memory Expansion Option without Memory
FEATURE CODE: 8004
AVAILABLE: 3/90
DESCRIPTION: This card is required for greater than 4MB of PS/2* computer memory on the Model 14. The card contains no memory. 2MB and 4MB modules may be installed on the card. Up to four modules may be installed. Both 2MB and 4MB modules may be used but no more than three 4MB modules should be installed. Requires an available 32-bit slot. Maximum: one. Field installation.

SCSI Slave Adapter

ADAPTER NAME: SCSI Adapter (DASD Adapter)
FEATURE CODE: 4050
AVAILABLE: 3/90
DESCRIPTION: The DASD Adapter allows some or all of the four optional DASD drives to be attached to the PS/2* computer side. Requires an available 32-bit slot. Maximum: one. Field installation. Only DASD Drives (#4045) should be installed in the Model 14 for this adapter.

Serial Port Slave Adapters

ADAPTER NAME: Eight Port RS-232-C Interface Board (1MB)
FEATURE CODE: 7021
AVAILABLE: 3/90
DESCRIPTION: Provides eight EIA RS-232-C/CCITT V.24 serial I/O ports. The first two ports can support asynchronous, bit synchronous, and character synchronous protocol hardware. Either of the first two ports can support 19.2K bps full duplex ASYNC protocols and 38.4K bps full duplex HDLC/SDLC protocols. Asynchronous protocol hardware is supported on the remaining six ports. Included in this feature are both the interface board and the IBM* Realtime Interface Co-Processor Multiport/2 adapter with 1MB of memory. Maximum: four. Field installation. Synchronous protocols are only supported on the first tow ports.

ADAPTER NAME: Eight Port RS-232-C Interface Board (512KB)
FEATURE CODE: 6021
AVAILABLE: 3/90
DESCRIPTION: Provides eight EIA RS-232-C/CCITT V.24 serial I/O ports. The first two ports can support asynchronous, bit synchronous, and character synchronous protocol hardware. Either of the first two ports can support 19.2K bps full duplex ASYNC protocols and 38.4K bps full duplex HDLC/SDLC protocols. Asynchronous protocol hardware is supported on the remaining 6 ports. Included in this feature are both the interface board and the IBM* Real-Time Interface Co-Processor Multiport/2 adapter with 512KB of memory. Maximum: four. Field installation. Synchronous protocols are only supported on the first two ports.

Serial Port Slave Adapters (Continued)

ADAPTER NAME: Eight Port RS-422-A Interface Board
FEATURE CODE: 7025
AVAILABLE: 3/90
DESCRIPTION: Provides eight EIA RS-422-A serial ports. Asynchronous hardware support is provided on all eight ports. The first port can also support bit synchronous and character synchronous protocols. The first port can operate at 64K bps full duplex. Line speeds in excess of 64K bps can be achieved with appropriate adapter resident communications programs. Included in this feature are both the interface board and the IBM* Realtime Interface Co- Processor Multiport/2 adapter with 1MB of memory. Maximum: four. Field installation. Synchronous protocols are supported by only one port.

ADAPTER NAME: Eight Port RS-422-A Interface Board (512KB)
FEATURE CODE: 6025
AVAILABLE: 3/90
DESCRIPTION: Provides eight EIA RS-422-A serial ports. Asynchronous hardware support is provided on all eight ports. The first port can also support bit synchronous and character synchronous protocols. The first port can operate at 64K bps full duplex. Line speeds in excess of 64K bps can be achieved with appropriate adapter resident communications programs. Included in this feature are both the interface board and the IBM* Realtime Interface Co-Processor Multiport/2 adapter with 512KB of memory. Synchronous protocols are supported by only one port. Maximum: four. Field installation.

ADAPTER NAME: RS-232-C/RS-422-A Interface Board (1MB)
FEATURE CODE: 7023
AVAILABLE: 3/90
DESCRIPTION: Provides four EIA RS-232-C/CCITT V.24 serial I/O ports (ports 0 through 3) and four EIA RS-422-A serial I/O ports (ports 4 through 7). Asynchronous protocol hardware is supported on all eight ports. Bit synchronous and character synchronous protocol hardware can be supported on the first two ports. Either of the first two ports can support 19.2K bps full duplex ASYNC protocols and 38.4K bps full duplex HDLC/SDLC protocols. Included in this feature are both the interface board and the IBM* Realtime Interface Co-Processor Multiport/2 adapter with 1MB of memory. Maximum: four. Field installation. Synchronous protocols are only supported on the first two ports.

ADAPTER NAME: RS-232-C/RS-422-A Interface Board (512KB)
FEATURE CODE: 6023
AVAILABLE: 3/90
DESCRIPTION: Provides four EIA RS-232-C/CCITT V.24 serial I/O ports (ports 0 through 3) and four EIA RS-422-A serial I/O ports (ports 4 through 7). Asynchronous protocol hardware is supported on all eight ports. Bit synchronous and character synchronous protocol hardware can be supported on the first two ports. Either of the first two ports can support 19.2K bps full duplex async protocols and 38.4 K bps full duplex HDLC/SDLC protocols. Included in this feature are both the interface board and the IBM* Realtime Interface Co-Processor Multiport/2 adapter with 512KB of memory. Maximum: four. Field installation. Synchronous protocols are only supported on the first two ports.

Uncategorized Slave Adapters

ADAPTER NAME: Data Exchange Adapter
FEATURE CODE: 4014
AVAILABLE: 6/90
DESCRIPTION: Provides a direct, hardware connection between the system/370* processor and the PS/2* processor in a Model 14. This high speed connection is logically divided into two concurrent communication paths. East path is a full duplex path that may be used independently. Using this feature, customers may develop applications which benefit from the ability to directly exchange data between PS/2 and System/370 programs. The Data Exchange Adapter uses a shared storage buffer (RAM memory) to provide a memory-mapped window for communications between the adapter and application programs. The first 32-bit slot must be available on the PS/2 side. Maximum: one. Field installation. Support is not available for all operating systems.

ADAPTER NAME: IBM* PS/2* S/370 Channel Emulator/A Adapter
FEATURE CODE: 7041
AVAILABLE: 3/90
DESCRIPTION: This adapter card and cable for the PS/2* computer emulate the operation of an IBM* System/370* channel. S/370 channel Bus (P/N 2282675) and Tag (P/N 2282676) are included. When coupled with the appropriate software, the adapter supports attachment of channel devices. Diagnostics are provided with the adapter. The "IBM S/370 Channel Emulator Technical Reference" (S544-3499) provides the programming interface. Remote PrintManager Version 3.0 provides software support for supported printers for DOS 3.3 or later release. Field installation. The feature may not work with devices with stringent turnaround timing requirements.

Appendix F

Micro Channel Developers Information

PROGRAMMABLE OPTION SELECT ID

If you are developing a Micro Channel adapter, you should obtain a Micro Channel POS ID from IBM. IDs can be obtained by calling one of the following numbers:

1-800-426-7763 in the United States

1-404-835-6647 in Canada

1-404-835-6647 in Latin America

44-256-475050, Ext 8030, in Europe

03-808-4912 in Japan

61-2-481-1205 in Asia

61-2-634-8369 in Australia and New Zealand

DEVELOPER ASSISTANCE

To enroll in the IBM Developer Assistance Program, call 1-407-982-6408 for an application form.

Developer assistance outside the United States can be obtained by calling:

1-416-443-4212 in Canada

1-407-443-3358 in Latin America

44-256-475050, Ext. 8053, in Europe

03-808-4912 in Japan

81-(0)462-73-3206 in Asia, Australia, and New Zealand

MICRO CHANNEL DEVELOPERS ASSOCIATION

The Micro Channel Developers Association was announced in late 1990, with the following founder members:

Aox Corporation

Apricot Computers®, Ltd.

Chips & Technologies, Inc.

Core International®

Cumulus Corporation®

IBM Corporation

NCR Corporation

NEC Corporation

NSTL

Olivetti Corporation

Reply Corporation

Siemens® Corporation

Western Digital®

The following is an excerpt from the announcement information:

The Micro Channel Developers Association was formed by 14 computer industry leaders in order to capitalize on the capabilities of Micro Channel architecture and facilitate its evolution as an industry-wide open architecture with the fast release of a broad range of innovative, compatible products.

Currently, more than 800 companies worldwide are developing Micro Channel products, including add-on boards, chip sets, computer systems and software enhancements. The architecture is incorporated widely across the IBM product line—from the PS/2 and RS/6000 families through its 9370 systems.

Increasingly, developers and users are seeking an architecture with the power and bandwidth of the Micro Channel to handle smarter peripherals, build more intelligent controller subsystems, and connect numbers of users over local area networks.

The association will also serve as an information resource. It will gather and disseminate data about Micro Channel architecture, provide industry requirements to IBM, and develop education and training programs.

The idea for the Micro Channel Developers Association originated from companies developing Micro Channel products who wanted a formal way to disseminate ideas and information. The association complements the support IBM currently provides Micro Channel developers, which includes worldwide seminars, technical documentation, and assistance via a toll-free telephone number.

For additional information, contact:

Micro Channel Developers Association

Suite 293

15 East Putnam Avenue

Greenwich, CT 06830

For information regarding the NSTL Micro Channel bus compatibility testing program, contact:

National Software Testing Laboratories, Inc.

Plymouth Corporate Center

Box 1000

Plymouth Meeting, PA 19462

(215) 941-9600

Appendix G

IBM PS/2 Fixed Disk Drive Characteristics

Following is a summary of the characteristics of the fixed disk drive used in IBM Personal System/2 systems.

A SUMMARY OF PERSONAL SYSTEM/2 FIXED DISKS AND DISKETTE DRIVES

Direct Access Storage Devices (DASD) are distinguished by a number of characteristics relating to capacity and performance. These characteristics do not always apply to different drives and devices. For example, the number of cylinders is more relevant to fixed disks than it is to diskettes, while the converse is true of tracks per inch. Use caution before making conclusions based on comparisons.

Some of the characteristics that determine capacity include the number of sectors per track, tracks per inch, the number of cylinders, bytes per sector, (usually 512), and the number of heads and platters. Factors contributing to performance include data transfer rate, average access (seek) time, average track-to-track access time, interleave factor, caching (if any), and controller/drive interface type. The best known of these factors, average access time, is not the best indicator of drive performance but rather a common bottleneck.

Because PS/2 DASD devices represent departures from previous technologies, exercise particular caution before making comparisons. For example, on ESDI PS/2 drives, actual physical sectors are mapped to logical sectors via Relative Block Addressing to maintain compatibility with DOS applications. This indirection causes most benchmark programs to incorrectly report many PS/2 drive specifications. In other words, the benchmark may think it is measuring a sequential read based on physically contiguous sectors when in reality the sectors are only logically contiguous and are physically far apart. The converse is also possible. In any event, few benchmarks accurately reflect PS/2 DASD performance. Again, nothing can replace hands-on experience in comparing systems.

Reprinted courtesy of International Business Machines Corporation from *Personal System/2 Reference Tables,* IBM Form number G325-5008.

TABLE G-1 IBM PS/2 ST-506 FIXED DISK DRIVES

Drive that is standard on: or available as Feature # or Part #:	#4107 78X8958	#4110 27F4130	8530–E21 8530–021 #4115 6451031	8530–E31	8550–021†	#1030 6451030	855x–031 #3046 6450354	85xx–041
Capacity:	20MB	20MB	20MB	30MB	20MB	30MB	30MB	44MB
Integrated Controller?	Yes	No	Yes	Yes	No	No	Yes	No
Size	3.5"	3.5"	3.5"	3.5"	3.5"	3.5"	3.5"	5.25"
Drive Type:	26	N/A	26	33	30		33	31
Sectors/Track:	17	26	17	25	17	25	25	17
Heads:	4	4	4	4	4	4	4	7
Autopark Heads?	No	Yes	Yes	Yes	No	No	No	Yes
Cylinders:	610	400	610	615	610	615	615	733
Data Transfer Rate:	5.0Mbps	7.5Mbps	7.5Mbps	7.5Mbps	5.0Mbps	7.5Mbps	7.5Mbps	5.0Mbps
Access (Seek) Time								
Average:	80ms	38ms	27ms	27ms	80ms	39ms	39ms	40ms
Track-to-Track:	15ms	15ms	15ms	15ms	15ms	15ms	15ms	15ms
Interleave:	2:1	3:1	3:1	3:1	1:1	3:1	1:1	1:1
Power Draw (Watts)								
Idle:	15.5	15.5	15.5		15.5	12	12	31
Max:	17	17	17		17	14	14	39
Also supported on:	8525-xxx	8525-xxx	8530-001 8530-E01			8530-001 8530-E01	8550-061	

TABLE G-2 IBM PS/2 ESDI FIXED DISK DRIVES

Drive that is standard on: or available as Feature #: or Part #:	**8573–031**	**8550–061 8555–061 857x–x61 #666 6450606**	**8570–B61**	**857x–x21**	**85xx–071 #3051 6450355**	**18580–111 #8730 6450377**	**8580–311 #6023 6450381**
Capacity:	30MB	60MB	60MB	120MB	70MB	115MB	314MB
Integrated Controller?	Yes	Yes	Yes	Yes	No	No	No
Size:	3.5"	3.5"	3.5"	3.5"	5.25"	5.25"	5.25"
Sectors/track:	32	26	32	32	36	36	34
Heads:	2	6	4	4	7	7	15
Autopark Heads?	Yes	Yes	Yes	Yes	Yes	Yes	Yes
Cylinders:		762	928	920	583	915	1225
Data Transfer Rate:	10Mbps	8.4Mbps	10.2Mbps	10Mbps	10Mbps	10Mbps	10Mbps
Access (Seek) Time							
Average:	19ms	27ms	23ms	23ms	30ms	28ms	23ms
Track-to-Track:	5ms	15ms	5ms	5ms	5ms	5ms	5ms
Interleave: 1:1	1:1	1:1	1:1	1:1	1:1	1:1	1:1
Power Draw (Watts)							
Idle:	12	13	13	13	31	31	35
Max	17	19	19	19	139	39	42
Also supported on:		8550–021 8550–031			8580–011 8580–311	8560–071 8580–071 8580–0311	8580–071 8580–111

Appendix H

Micro Channel Configuration Reference Guide for IBM PS/2 Systems

The following is a Micro Channel configuration reference guide to IBM PS/2 systems.

Reprinted courtesy of International Business Machines Corporation from *Personal System/2 Reference Tables,* IBM Form number G325-5008.

TABLE H-1 MICRO CHANNEL CONFIGURATION REFERENCE

Feature Name	ID File Name (.ADF)	Feature Number	Part Number	Diagnosis File Name (.DGS)	Files Included with Reference Diskette? 50/60 1.06	55/65 1.03	70/80 1.10	P70 1.04	70/486 1.04
Wizard i860 Attached Processor	@0FC7	#3462	34F3062						
Audio Capture and Playback Adapter/A	@6E6C	#2784	34F2784						
Micro Channel Compatible Key Card	@6147								
Video Capture Adapter/A	@704E	#2785	34F2785						
IBM PS/2 SCSI Adapter	@8EFE	#1005	6451005		X	X	X	X	X
IBM PS/2 SCSI Adapter w/Cache	@8EFF	#1018	6451018		X	X	X	X	X
IBM 5080 Serial Link Adapter	@8484								
Realtime Interface Co-Processor Portmaster Adapter (512KB)	@8F70	#6360	53F2601	DEV141					
Realtime Interface Co-Processor Portmaster Adapter (1MB)	@8F70	#6364	53F2604	DEV141					
Realtime Interface Co-Processor Portmaster Adapter (2MB)	@8F70	#6368	53F2608	DEV141					
ESDI Fixed Disk Controller	@DDFF			ESDI	X	X	X	X	
Multi-Protocol Adapter/A	@DEFF	#3042	6450348	MPCA	X	X	X	X	X
Multi-Protocol Adapter/A	@DEFF	#3043	6451003	MPCA	X	X	X	X	X
6157 Streaming Tape Drive Adapter	@DFBF	#4160	92X1458	TAPEADAP					
5.25-inch Diskette Drive Adapter/A	@DFFA	#1007	6451007	DSKT5					
InfoWindow GPIB2 Card	@DFFC	#4239	83X9239	DFFC					
IBM 3363 Optical Disk Controller	@DF7F		63X4166	USOPDIAG					
Integrated Fixed Disk Controller	@DF9F			HARDFILE	X	X	X	X	X
Token-Ring Network Adapter/A	@E000	#4790	69X8138	E000					
Token-Ring Network 16/4 Adapter/A	@E001	#1133	16F1133	E000					
S/370 Channel Emulator/A	@E014	#3205	1674899	S370CHAN					
300/1200/2400 Internal Modem/A	@E016	#1755	94X1755	MODEM24				X	
High Speed Adapter/A	@E04E	#1028	65X1905	HSAR					

TABLE H-1 MICRO CHANNEL CONFIGURATION REFERENCE (continued)

Feature Name	ID File Name (.ADF)	Feature Number	Part Number	Diagnosis File Name (.DGS)	Files Included with Reference Diskette? 50/60 1.06	55/65 1.03	70/80 1.10	P70 1.04	70/486 1.04
3119 Adapter/A	@E04F	#5442	94X2415	GFGR					
3270 Connection, Version A	@E7FF	#2000	25F8060	IBMCONN	X	X	X		
3270 Connection, Version B	@E1FF	#2000	25F8448	IBMCONN	X	X	X		
300/1200 Internal Modem/A	@EDFF	#0349	6450349	MODEM	X	X	X	X	X
IBM 4684 Device Channel	@EECE			US4684					
Dual Async Adapter/A	@EEFF	#1014	6451013	ASYNC	X	X	X	X	X
Display Adapter 8514/A	@EF7F	#4054	1887972	EF7F	X	X	X		X
InfoWindow VGA Control Card	@EFBF	#4239	83X9239	EFBF					
IBM Store Loop Controller	@EFCF	#6500	83X8187	USSLOOP					
IBM ISDN Interface Co-Processor/2	@EFE0								
PC Network Adapter II/A	@EFEF	#1222	1501222	NETWORK	X	X	X	X	X
Real-Time Interface Co-Processor Multiport/2	@EFF0	#6247	16F1820	MPORT		X			
Real-Time Interface Co-Processor Multiport/2	@EFF0	#6263	09F1897	MPORT		X			
X.25 Interface Co-Processor/2	@EFF0	#6401	16F1858	MPORT		X			
Personal PagePrinter Adapter/A	@EFF6	#7002	75X8267	EFF6					
3117 Adapter/A	@F04F	#1029	65X1925	GFDR					
2–8MB 80286 Memory Expansion Option	@F7F7	#8286	6450609	XEXPMEM		X			
80286 Expanded Memory Adapter/A	@F7FE	#3920	1497252	XMA					
0–8MB Expanded Memory Option	@F7FE	#7259	1497259	XMA					
80386 Memory Expansion Option	@FAFF	#3019	6450367	MEMORY		X	X	X	X
2–8MB 80386 Memory Expansion Option	@FCFF	#5211	645065	MEMORY		X	X	X	X
Enhanced 80386 Memory Expansion Option 4MB Kit	@FDDF	#3011	34F3011	FDDF					

TABLE H-1 MICRO CHANNEL CONFIGURATION REFERENCE (continued)

Feature Name	ID File Name (.ADF)	Feature Number	Part Number	Diagnosis File Name (.DGS)	Files Included with Reference Diskette?				
					50/60 1.06	55/65 1.03	70/80 1.10	P70 1.04	70/486 1.04
Enhanced 80386 Memory Expansion Option 2MB Kit	@FDDF	#3077	34F3077	FDDF					
80286 Memory Expansion Option	@FEFE	#3006	6450344	XEXPMEM	X	X			
System 36/38 Work Station Emulation Adapter/A	@FFF8	#6279	69X6279	FFF8					

Appendix I

IBM Patent Licensing Practices

The following is a summary statement regarding IBM's licensing of Micro Channel architecture in personal systems:

> *Under IBM's current patent license agreement, personal systems conforming to IBM's Micro Channel architecture accrue royalties, in practice, at the same rate as systems conforming to IBM's AT architecture, such as EISA. The royalty rates are effectively capped at 3% and IBM has no current plans to change those rates. An initial $25,000 is payable at signing, but that advance is fully creditable towards future patent royalties under the agreement.*

A summary of IBM's patent licensing practices obtained from IBM Commercial Relations, 2000 Purchase St., Purchase, N.Y. 10577 follows:

> *IBM is generally willing to grant nonexclusive licenses in the field of information handling systems under its patents, except those directed to ornamental designs, upon reasonable and non-discriminatory terms and conditions to those who respect IBM's intellectual property rights. The principal provisions of such a license are outlined below.*
>
> *The royalty for use of IBM's patents may be based on the licensee's selling price of each product covered by one or more licensed patents or on the royalty portion selling price of such product, the choice being left to the licensee.*
>
> *If the royalty is based on the selling price, the royalty rates are as follows. For royalty calculation purposes IBM has divided its patents into two groups called Category I and Category II. The royalty rates are 1% of the selling price if the product is covered by one Category I patent, and 2% of the selling price if the product is covered by two or more*

Category I patents. If the product is covered by one, two, or three or more Category II patents, the royalty will be respectively 1%, 2%, or 3% of selling price, added to any royalty incurred for Category I patents. A listing of the Category II patents will be furnished upon written request.

The royalty portion selling price of a product is the licensee's selling price multiplied by the ratio of the sum of the manufacturing cost of its patented portions to its total manufacturing cost. If the royalty is based on the royalty portion selling price, then the rate is 8% of the royalty portion selling price.

Included in the agreement is an option for IBM to obtain a nonexclusive royalty bearing license under patents of the licensee on terms similar to those described above.

Each licensee must make an initial payment of $25,000 upon entering an agreement with IBM unless only a single patent is licensed, in which case a $5,000 initial payment shall apply. The payment may be fully credited against future royalties, but is not refundable.

A license under IBM's patents does not include any rights to know-how or other technical information, or licenses under other intellectual property rights such as trademarks or copyrights. Also, it does not include any assurance that a license under the patents of others is not needed; a licensee must make its own determination on that matter.

This highlights IBM's present patent licensing practices and is subject to change at any time, as well as to variation to conform to local laws and regulations.

Index

A

B

N

O

P

R

S

T

U

V

W

X

Y